THE SOCRATIC WRITINGS

MEMORABILIA, ECONOMIST,
SYMPOSIUM, APOLOGY, AND HIERO

By XENOPHON

Translated by H. G. DAKYNS

The Socratic Writings
By Xenophon
Translated by H. G. Dakyns

Print ISBN 13: 978-1-4209-7933-6
eBook ISBN 13: 978-1-4209-8068-4

This edition copyright © 2021. Digireads.com Publishing.

All rights reserved. No part of this publication may be reproduced, distributed, or transmitted in any form or by any means, including photocopying, recording, or other electronic or mechanical methods, without the prior written permission of the publisher, except in the case of brief quotations embodied in critical reviews and certain other noncommercial uses permitted by copyright law.

Cover Image: a detail of "The Death of Socrates", by Charles Alphonse Dufresnoy, c. 1650 / Bridgeman Images.

Please visit *www.digireads.com*

CONTENTS

THE MEMORABILIA 5

    BOOK I 5
    BOOK II 33
    BOOK III 66
    BOOK IV 105

THE ECONOMIST 147

THE SYMPOSIUM 221

THE APOLOGY 267

HIERO 275

The Memorabilia

OR

RECOLLECTIONS OF SOCRATES

BOOK I

I

I have often wondered by what arguments those who indicted[1] Socrates could have persuaded the Athenians that his life was justly forfeit to the state. The indictment was to this effect: "Socrates is guilty of crime in refusing to recognise the gods acknowledged by the state, and importing strange divinities of his own; he is further guilty of corrupting the young."

In the first place, what evidence did they produce that Socrates refused to recognise the gods acknowledged by the state? Was it that he did not sacrifice? or that he dispensed with divination? On the contrary, he was often to be seen engaged in sacrifice, at home or at the common altars of the state. Nor was his dependence on divination less manifest. Indeed that saying of his, "A divinity[2] gives me a sign," was on everybody's lips. So much so that, if I am not mistaken, it lay at the root of the imputation that he imported novel divinities; though there was no greater novelty in his case than in that of other believers in oracular help, who commonly rely on omens of all sorts: the flight or cry of birds, the utterances of man, chance meetings,[3] or a victim's entrails. Even according to the popular conception, it is not the mere fowl, it is not the chance individual one meets, who knows what things are profitable for a man, but it is the gods who vouchsafe by such instruments to signify the same. This was also the tenet of Socrates. Only, whereas men ordinarily speak of being turned aside, or urged onwards by birds, or other creatures encountered on the path, Socrates suited his language to his conviction. "The divinity," said he, "gives me a sign." Further, he would constantly advise his associates to do this, or beware of doing that, upon the authority of this same divine voice; and,

---

[1] (oi grapsamenoi) = Melêtus (below, IV. iv. 4, viii. 4; *Apol.* 11, 19), Anytus (*Apol.* 29), and Lycon. See Plat. *Apol.* II. v. 18; Diog. Laert. II. v. (*Socr.*); M. Schanz, "*Plat. Apol. mit deutschen Kemmentar, Einleitung*," S. 5 foll.

[2] Or, "A divine something." See "*Encyc. Brit.*" "Socrates." Dr. H. Jackson; "*The Daemon of Socrates*," F. W. H. Myers; K. Joel, "*Der echte und der Xenophontische Sokrates*," i. p. 70 foll.; cf. Aristot. "*M. M.*" 1182 a 10.

[3] See Aesch. "*P. V.*" 487, (enodious te sombolous), "and pathway tokens," L. Campbell; Arist. "*Birds*," 721, (sombolon ornin): "*Frogs*," 196, (to sometukhon exion); "*Eccl.*" 792; Hor. *Od.* iii. 27, 1-7.

as a matter of fact, those who listened to his warnings prospered, whilst he who turned a deaf ear to them repented afterwards.[4] Yet, it will be readily conceded, he would hardly desire to present himself to his everyday companions in the character of either knave or fool. Whereas he would have appeared to be both, supposing[5] the God-given revelations had but revealed his own proneness to deception. It is plain he would not have ventured on forecast at all, but for his belief that the words he spoke would in fact be verified. Then on whom, or what, was the assurance rooted, if not upon God? And if he had faith in the gods, how could he fail to recognise them?

But his mode of dealing with his intimates has another aspect. As regards the ordinary necessities of life,[6] his advice was, "Act as you believe[7] these things may best be done." But in the case of those darker problems, the issues of which are incalculable, he directed his friends to consult the oracle, whether the business should be undertaken or not. "No one," he would say, "who wishes to manage a house or city with success: no one aspiring to guide the helm of state aright, can afford to dispense with aid from above. Doubtless, skill in carpentering, building, smithying, farming, of the art of governing men, together with the theory of these processes, and the sciences of arithmetic, economy, strategy, are affairs of study, and within the grasp of human intelligence. Yet there is a side even of these, and that not the least important, which the gods reserve to themselves, the bearing of which is hidden from mortal vision. Thus, let a man sow a field or plant a farm never so well, yet he cannot foretell who will gather in the fruits: another may build him a house of fairest proportion, yet he knows not who will inhabit it. Neither can a general foresee whether it will profit him to conduct a campaign, nor a politician be certain whether his leadership will turn to evil or good. Nor can the man who weds a fair wife, looking forward to joy, know whether through her he shall not reap sorrow. Neither can he who has built up a powerful connection in the state know whether he shall not by means of it be cast out of his city. To suppose that all these matters lay within the scope of human judgment, to the exclusion of the preternatural, was preternatural folly. Nor was it less extravagant to go and consult the will of Heaven on any questions which it is given to us to decide by dint of learning. As

---

[4] See "*Anab.*" III. i. 4; *Symp.* iv. 48.

[5] Or, "if his vaunted manifestations from heaven had but manifested the falsity of his judgment."

[6] Or, "in the sphere of the determined," (ta anagkaia) = certa, quorum eventus est necessarius; "things positive, the law-ordained department of life," as we might say. See Grote, *H. G.* i. ch. xvi. 500 and *passim.*

[7] Reading (os nomizoien), or if (os enomizen), translate "As to things with certain results, he advised them to do them in the way in which he believed they would be done best"; *i.e.* he did not say, "follow your conscience," but, "this course seems best to me under the circumstances."

though a man should inquire, "Am I to choose an expert driver as my coachman, or one who has never handled the reins?" "Shall I appoint a mariner to be skipper of my vessel, or a landsman?" And so with respect to all we may know by numbering, weighing, and measuring. To seek advice from Heaven on such points was a sort of profanity. "Our duty is plain," he would observe; "where we are permitted to work through our natural faculties, there let us by all means apply them. But in things which are hidden, let us seek to gain knowledge from above, by divination; for the gods," he added, "grant signs to those to whom they will be gracious."

Again, Socrates ever lived in the public eye; at early morning he was to be seen betaking himself to one of the promenades, or wrestling-grounds; at noon he would appear with the gathering crowds in the market-place; and as day declined, wherever the largest throng might be encountered, there was he to be found, talking for the most part, while any one who chose might stop and listen. Yet no one ever heard him say, or saw him do anything impious or irreverent. Indeed, in contrast to others he set his face against all discussion of such high matters as the nature of the Universe; how the "kosmos," as the *savants*[8] phrase it, came into being;[9] or by what forces the celestial phenomena arise. To trouble one's brain about such matters was, he argued, to play the fool. He would ask first: Did these investigators feel their knowledge of things human so complete that they betook themselves to these lofty speculations? Or did they maintain that they were playing their proper parts in thus neglecting the affairs of man to speculate on the concerns of God? He was astonished they did not see how far these problems lay beyond mortal ken; since even those who pride themselves most on their discussion of these points differ from each other, as madmen do. For just as some madmen, he said, have no apprehension of what is truly terrible, others fear where no fear is; some are ready to say and do anything in public without the slightest symptom of shame;[10] others think they ought not so much as to set foot among their fellow-men; some honour neither temple, nor altar, nor aught else sacred to the name of God; others bow down to stocks and stones and worship the very beasts:—so is it with those thinkers whose minds are cumbered with cares[11] concerning the Universal Nature. One sect[12] has discovered that Being is one and indivisible. Another[13] that it

---

[8] Lit. "the sophists." See H. Sidgwick, "*J. of Philol.*" iv. 1872; v. 1874.

[9] Reading (ephu). Cf. Lucian, "*Icaromenip.*" xlvi. 4, in imitation of this passage apparently; or if (ekhei), translate "is arranged." See Grote, *H. G.* viii. 573.

[10] See "*Anab.*" V. iv. 30.

[11] See Arist. "*Clouds*," 101, (merimnophrontistai kaloi te kagathoi).

[12] *e.g.* Xenophanes and Parmenides, see Grote, *Plato*, I. i. 16 foll.

[13] *e.g.* Leucippus and Democritus, *ib.* 63 foll.

is infinite in number. If one[14] proclaims that all things are in a continual flux, another[15] replies that nothing can possibly be moved at any time. The theory of the universe as a process of birth and death is met by the counter theory, that nothing ever could be born or ever will die. But the questioning of Socrates on the merits of these speculators sometimes took another form. The student of human learning expects, he said, to make something of his studies for the benefit of himself or others, as he likes. Do these explorers into the divine operations hope that when they have discovered by what forces the various phenomena occur, they will create winds and waters at will and fruitful seasons? Will they manipulate these and the like to suit their needs? or has no such notion perhaps ever entered their heads, and will they be content simply to know how such things come into existence? But if this was his mode of describing those who meddle with such matters as these, he himself never wearied of discussing human topics. What is piety? what is impiety? What is the beautiful? what the ugly? What the noble? what the base? What are meant by just and unjust? what by sobriety and madness? what by courage and cowardice? What is a state? what is a statesman? what is a ruler over men? what is a ruling character? and other like problems, the knowledge of which, as he put it, conferred a patent of nobility on the possessor,[16] whereas those who lacked the knowledge might deservedly be stigmatised as slaves.

Now, in so far as the opinions of Socrates were unknown to the world at large, it is not surprising that the court should draw false conclusions respecting them; but that facts patent to all should have been ignored is indeed astonishing.

At one time Socrates was a member of the Council,[17] he had taken the senatorial oath, and sworn "as a member of that house to act in conformity with the laws." It was thus he chanced to be President of the Popular Assembly,[18] when that body was seized with a desire to put the nine[19] generals, Thrasyllus, Erasinides, and the rest, to death by a single inclusive vote. Whereupon, in spite of the bitter resentment of the people, and the menaces of several influential citizens, he refused to put the question, esteeming it of greater importance faithfully to abide by the oath which he had taken, than to gratify the people wrongfully, or to screen himself from the menaces of the mighty. The fact being, that with regard to the care bestowed by the gods upon men, his belief

---

[14] *e.g.* Heraclitus, *ib.* 27 foll.

[15] *e.g.* Zeno, *ib.* ii. 96.

[16] Or, "was distinctive of the 'beautiful and good.'" For the phrase see below, ii. 2 *et passim*.

[17] Or "Senate." Lit. "*the Boulê.*"

[18] Lit. "*Epistates of the Ecclesia.*" See Grote, *H. G.* viii. 271; Plat. *Apol.* 32 B.

[19] (ennea) would seem to be a slip of the pen for (okto), eight. See *Hell.* I. v. 16; vi. 16; vi. 29; vii. 1 foll.

differed widely from that of the multitude. Whereas most people seem to imagine that the gods know in part, and are ignorant in part, Socrates believed firmly that the gods know all things—both the things that are said and the things that are done, and the things that are counselled in the silent chambers of the heart. Moreover, they are present everywhere, and bestow signs upon man concerning all the things of man.

I can, therefore, but repeat my former words. It is a marvel to me how the Athenians came to be persuaded that Socrates fell short of sober-mindedness as touching the gods. A man who never ventured one impious word or deed against the gods we worship, but whose whole language concerning them, and his every act, closely coincided, word for word, and deed for deed, with all we deem distinctive of devoutest piety.

II

No less surprising to my mind is the belief that Socrates corrupted the young. This man, who, beyond what has been already stated, kept his appetites and passions under strict control, who was pre-eminently capable of enduring winter's cold and summer's heat and every kind of toil, who was so schooled to curtail his needs that with the scantiest of means he never lacked sufficiency—is it credible that such a man could have made others irreverent or lawless, or licentious, or effeminate in face of toil? Was he not rather the saving of many through the passion for virtue which he roused in them, and the hope he infused that through careful management of themselves they might grow to be truly beautiful and good—not indeed that he ever undertook to be a teacher of virtue, but being evidently virtuous himself he made those who associated with him hope that by imitating they might at last resemble him.

But let it not be inferred that he was negligent of his own body or approved of those who neglected theirs. If excess of eating, counteracted by excess of toil, was a dietary of which he disapproved,[20] to gratify the natural claim of appetite in conjunction with moderate exercise was a system he favoured, as tending to a healthy condition of the body without trammelling the cultivation of the spirit. On the other hand, there was nothing dandified or pretentious about him; he indulged in no foppery of shawl or shoes, or other effeminacy of living.

Least of all did he tend to make his companions greedy of money. He would not, while restraining passion generally, make capital out of the one passion which attached others to himself; and by this abstinence, he believed, he was best consulting his own freedom; in so

---

[20] See (Plat.) "*Erast.*" 132 C.

much that he stigmatised those who condescended to take wages for their society as vendors of their own persons, because they were compelled to discuss for the benefits of their paymasters. What surprised him was that any one possessing virtue should deign to ask money as its price instead of simply finding his reward in the acquisition of an honest friend, as if the new-fledged soul of honour could forget her debt of gratitude to her greatest benefactor.

For himself, without making any such profession, he was content to believe that those who accepted his views would play their parts as good and true friends to himself and one another their lives long. Once more then: how should a man of this character corrupt the young? unless the careful cultivation of virtue be corruption.

But, says the accuser,[21] by all that's sacred! did not Socrates cause his associates to despise the established laws when he dwelt on the folly of appointing state officers by ballot?[22] a principle which, he said, no one would care to apply in selecting a pilot or a flute-player or in any similar case, where a mistake would be far less disastrous than in matters political. Words like these, according to the accuser, tended to incite the young to contemn the established constitution, rendering them violent and headstrong. But for myself I think that those who cultivate wisdom and believe themselves able to instruct their fellow-citizens as to their interests are least likely to become partisans of violence. They are too well aware that to violence attach enmities and dangers, whereas results as good may be obtained by persuasion safely and amicably. For the victim of violence hates with vindictiveness as one from whom something precious has been stolen, while the willing subject of persuasion is ready to kiss the hand which has done him a service. Hence compulsion is not the method of him who makes wisdom his study, but of him who wields power untempered by reflection. Once more: the man who ventures on violence needs the support of many to fight his battles, while he whose strength lies in persuasiveness triumphs single-handed, for he is conscious of a cunning to compel consent unaided. And what has such a one to do with the spilling of blood? since how ridiculous it were to do men to death rather than turn to account the trusty service of the living.

But, the accuser answers, the two men[23] who wrought the greatest evils to the state at any time—to wit, Critias and Alcibiades—were both companions of Socrates—Critias the oligarch, and Alcibiades the democrat. Where would you find a more arrant thief, savage, and

---

[21] (o kategoros) = Polycrates possibly. See M. Schantz, *op. cit.*, "*Einleitung,*" S. 6: "*Die Anklagerede des Polykrates*"; Introduction, p. xxxii. foll.

[22] *i.e.* staking the election of a magistrate on the colour of a bean. See Aristot. "*Ath. Pol.*" viii. 2, and Dr. Sandys *ad loc.*

[23] See *Hell.* I. and II. *passim.*

murderer[24] than the one? where such a portent of insolence, incontinence, and high-handedness as the other? For my part, in so far as these two wrought evil to the state, I have no desire to appear as the apologist of either. I confine myself to explaining what this intimacy of theirs with Socrates really was.

Never were two more ambitious citizens seen at Athens. Ambition was in their blood. If they were to have their will, all power was to be in their hands; their fame was to eclipse all other. Of Socrates they knew—first that he lived an absolutely independent life on the scantiest means; next that he was self-disciplined to the last degree in respect of pleasures; lastly that he was so formidable in debate that there was no antagonist he could not twist round his little finger. Such being their views, and such the character of the pair, which is the more probable: that they sought the society of Socrates because they felt the fascination of his life, and were attracted by the bearing of the man? or because they thought, if only we are leagued with him we shall become adepts in statecraft and unrivalled in the arts of speech and action? For my part I believe that if the choice from Heaven had been given them to live such a life as they saw Socrates living to its close, or to die, they would both have chosen death.

Their acts are a conclusive witness to their characters. They no sooner felt themselves to be the masters of those they came in contact with than they sprang aside from Socrates and plunged into that whirl of politics but for which they might never have sought his society.

It may be objected: before giving his companions lessons in politics Socrates had better have taught them sobriety.[25] Without disputing the principle, I would point out that a teacher cannot fail to discover to his pupils his method of carrying out his own precepts, and this along with argumentative encouragement. Now I know that Socrates disclosed himself to his companions as a beautiful and noble being, who would reason and debate with them concerning virtue and other human interests in the noblest manner. And of these two I know that as long as they were companions of Socrates even they were temperate, not assuredly from fear of being fined or beaten by Socrates, but because they were persuaded for the nonce of the excellence of such conduct.

Perhaps some self-styled philosophers[26] may here answer: "Nay, the man truly just can never become unjust, the temperate man can

---

[24] Reading (kleptistatos te kai biaiotatos kai phonikotatos), or if (pleonektistatos te kai biaiotatis), translate "such a manner of greed and violence as the one, of insolence, etc., as the other?" See Grote, *H. G.* viii. 337.

[25] (sophrosune) = "sound-mindedness," "temperance." See below, IV. iii. 1.

[26] In reference to some such tenet as that of Antisthenes ap. Diog. Laert. VI. ix. 30, (areskei d' autois kai ten areten didakten einai, katha phesin 'Antisthenes en to 'Rraklei kai anapobleton uparkhein). Cf. Plat. *"Protag."* 340 D, 344 D.

never become intemperate, the man who has learnt any subject of knowledge can never be as though he had learnt it not." That, however, is not my own conclusion. It is with the workings of the soul as with those of the body; want of exercise of the organ leads to inability of function, here bodily, there spiritual, so that we can neither do the things that we should nor abstain from the things we should not. And that is why fathers keep their sons, however temperate they may be, out of the reach of wicked men, considering that if the society of the good is a training in virtue so also is the society of the bad its dissolution.

To this the poet[27] is a witness, who says:

"From the noble thou shalt be instructed in nobleness; but, and if thou minglest with the base thou wilt destroy what wisdom thou hast now";

And he[28] who says:

"But the good man has his hour of baseness as well as his hour of virtue"—

to whose testimony I would add my own. For I see that it is impossible to remember a long poem without practice and repetition; so is forgetfulness of the words of instruction engendered in the heart that has ceased to value them. With the words of warning fades the recollection of the very condition of mind in which the soul yearned after holiness; and once forgetting this, what wonder that the man should let slip also the memory of virtue itself! Again I see that a man who falls into habits of drunkenness or plunges headlong into licentious love, loses his old power of practising the right and abstaining from the wrong. Many a man who has found frugality easy whilst passion was cold, no sooner falls in love than he loses the faculty at once, and in his prodigal expenditure of riches he will no longer withhold his hand from gains which in former days were too base to invite his touch. Where then is the difficulty of supposing that a man may be temperate to-day, and to-morrow the reverse; or that he who once has had it in his power to act virtuously may not quite lose that power?[29] To myself, at all events, it seems that all beautiful and noble things are the result of constant practice and training; and pre-eminently the virtue of temperance, seeing that in one and the same bodily frame pleasures are planted and spring up side by side with the soul and keep whispering in her ear, "Have done with self-restraint, make haste to gratify us and the

---

[27] Theognis, 35, 36. See *Symp.* ii. 4; Plat. "Men." 95 D.
[28] The author is unknown. See Plat. "*Protag.*" l.c.
[29] Cf. *Cyrop.* V. i. 9 foll.; VI. i. 41.

body."[30]

But to return to Critias and Alcibiades, I repeat that as long as they lived with Socrates they were able by his support to dominate their ignoble appetites;[31] but being separated from him, Critias had to fly to Thessaly,[32] where he consorted with fellows better versed in lawlessness than justice. And Alcibiades fared no better. His personal beauty on the one hand incited bevies of fine ladies[33] to hunt him down as fair spoil, while on the other hand his influence in the state and among the allies exposed him to the corruption of many an adept in the arts of flattery; honoured by the democracy and stepping easily to the front rank he behaved like an athlete who in the games of the Palaestra is so assured of victory that he neglects his training; thus he presently forgot the duty which he owed himself.

Such were the misadventures of these two. Is the sequel extraordinary? Inflated with the pride of ancestry,[34] exalted by their wealth, puffed up by power, sapped to the soul's core by a host of human tempters, separate moreover for many a long day from Socrates—what wonder that they reached the full stature of arrogancy! And for the offences of these two Socrates is to be held responsible! The accuser will have it so. But for the fact that in early days, when they were both young and of an age when dereliction from good feeling and self-restraint might have been expected, this same Socrates kept them modest and well-behaved, not one word of praise is uttered by the accuser for all this. That is not the measure of justice elsewhere meted. Would a master of the harp or flute, would a teacher of any sort who has turned out proficient pupils, be held to account because one of them goes away to another teacher and turns out to be a failure? Or what father, if he have a son who in the society of a certain friend remains an honest lad, but falling into the company of some other becomes a good-for-nothing, will that father straightway accuse the earlier instructor? Will not he rather, in proportion as the boy deteriorates in the company of the latter, bestow more heartfelt praise upon the former? What father, himself sharing the society of his own children, is held to blame for their transgressions, if only his own goodness be established? Here would have been a fair test to apply to Socrates: Was he guilty of any base conduct himself? If so let him be set down as a knave, but if, on the contrary, he never faltered in sobriety from beginning to end, how in the name of justice is he to be held to account for a baseness which was not in him?

---

[30] See my remarks, "*Hellenica Essays*," p. 371 foll.
[31] Cf. (Plat.) "*Theag.*" 130 A.
[32] See *Hell.* II. iii. 36.
[33] Cf. Plut. "*Ages.*," "*Alcib.*"
[34] Or, "became overweening in arrogance." Cf. "*Henry VIII.* II. iv. 110": "But your heart is crammed with arrogancy, spleen, and pride."

I go further: if, short of being guilty of any wrong himself, he saw the evil doings of others with approval, reason were he should be held blameworthy. Listen then: Socrates was well aware that Critias was attached to Euthydemus,[35] aware too that he was endeavouring to deal by him after the manner of those wantons whose love is carnal of the body. From this endeavour he tried to deter him, pointing out how illiberal a thing it was, how ill befitting a man of honour to appear as a beggar before him whom he loved, in whose eyes he would fain be precious, ever petitioning for something base to give and base to get.

But when this reasoning fell on deaf ears and Critias refused to be turned aside, Socrates, as the story goes, took occasion of the presence of a whole company and of Euthydemus to remark that Critias appeared to be suffering from a swinish affection, or else why this desire to rub himself against Euthydemus like a herd of piglings scraping against stones.

The hatred of Critias to Socrates doubtless dates from this incident. He treasured it up against him, and afterwards, when he was one of the Thirty and associated with Charicles as their official lawgiver,[36] he framed the law against teaching the art of words[37] merely from a desire to vilify Socrates. He was at a loss to know how else to lay hold of him except by levelling against him the vulgar charge[38] against philosophers, by which he hoped to prejudice him with the public. It was a charge quite unfounded as regards Socrates, if I may judge from anything I ever heard fall from his lips myself or have learnt about him from others. But the animus of Critias was clear. At the time when the Thirty were putting citizens, highly respectable citizens, to death wholesale, and when they were egging on one man after another to the commission of crime, Socrates let fall an observation: "It would be sufficiently extraordinary if the keeper of a herd of cattle[39] who was continually thinning and impoverishing his cattle did not admit himself to be a sorry sort of herdsman, but that a ruler of the state who was continually thinning and impoverishing the citizens should neither be ashamed nor admit himself to be a sorry sort of ruler was more extraordinary still." The remark being reported to the government, Socrates was summoned by Critias and Charicles, who proceeded to point out the law and forbade him to converse with the young. "Was it open to him," Socrates inquired of the speaker, "in case he failed to understand their commands in any point, to ask for an explanation?"

---

[35] See below, IV. ii. 1 (if the same person).
[36] Lit. *Nomothetes*. See *Hell.* II. iii. 2; Dem. 706. For Charicles see Lys. "c. Eratosth." S. 56; Aristot. "*Pol.*" v. 6. 6.
[37] See Diog. Laert. II. v. (*Socr.*)
[38] *i.e.* (to ton etto logon kreitto poiein), "of making the worse appear the better cause." Cf. Arist. *Clouds.*
[39] See Dio Chrys. *Or.* 43.

"Certainly," the two assented.

Then Socrates: I am prepared to obey the laws, but to avoid transgression of the law through ignorance I need instruction: is it on the supposition that the art of words tends to correctness of statement or to incorrectness that you bid us abstain from it? for if the former, it is clear we must abstain from speaking correctly, but if the latter, our endeavour should be to amend our speech.

To which Charicles, in a fit of temper, retorted: In consideration of your ignorance,[40] Socrates, we will frame the prohibition in language better suited to your intelligence: we forbid you to hold any conversation whatsoever with the young.

Then Socrates: To avoid all ambiguity then, or the possibility of my doing anything else than what you are pleased to command, may I ask you to define up to what age a human being is to be considered young?

For just so long a time (Charicles answered) as he is debarred from sitting as a member of the Council,[41] as not having attained to the maturity of wisdom; accordingly you will not hold converse with any one under the age of thirty.

Soc. In making a purchase even, I am not to ask, what is the price of this? if the vendor is under the age of thirty?

Cha. Tut, things of that sort: but you know, Socrates, that you have a way of asking questions, when all the while you know how the matter stands. Let us have no questions of that sort.

Soc. Nor answers either, I suppose, if the inquiry concerns what I know, as, for instance, where does Charicles live? or where is Critias to be found?

Oh yes, of course, things of that kind (replied Charicles), while Critias added: But at the same time you had better have done with your shoemakers, carpenters, and coppersmiths.[42] These must be pretty well trodden out at heel by this time, considering the circulation you have given them.

Soc. And am I to hold away from their attendant topics also—the just, the holy, and the like?

Most assuredly (answered Charicles), and from cowherds in particular; or else see that you do not lessen the number of the herd yourself.

Thus the secret was out. The remark of Socrates about the cattle had come to their ears, and they could not forgive the author of it.

Perhaps enough has been said to explain the kind of intimacy which had subsisted between Critias and Socrates, and their relation to

---

[40] See Aristot. "de Soph. El." 183 b7.
[41] The Boulê or Senate. See W. L. Newman, *Pol. Aristot.* i. 326.
[42] Cf. Plat. *Gorg.* 491 A; *Symp.* 221 E; Dio Chrys. *Or.* 55, 560 D, 564 A.

one another. But I will venture to maintain that where the teacher is not pleasing to the pupil there is no education. Now it cannot be said of Critias and Alcibiades that they associated with Socrates because they found him pleasing to them. And this is true of the whole period. From the first their eyes were fixed on the headship of the state as their final goal. During the time of their intimacy with Socrates there were no disputants whom they were more eager to encounter than professed politicians.

Thus the story is told of Alcibiades—how before the age of twenty he engaged his own guardian, Pericles, at that time prime minister of the state, in a discussion concerning laws.

Alc. Please, Pericles, can you teach me what a law is?

Per. To be sure I can.

Alc. I should be so much obliged if you would do so. One so often hears the epithet "law-abiding" applied in a complimentary sense; yet, it strikes me, one hardly deserves the compliment, if one does not know what a law is.

Per. Fortunately there is a ready answer to your difficulty. You wish to know what a law is? Well, those are laws which the majority, being met together in conclave, approve and enact as to what it is right to do, and what it is right to abstain from doing.

Alc. Enact on the hypothesis that it is right to do what is good? or to do what is bad?

Per. What is good, to be sure, young sir, not what is bad.

Alc. Supposing it is not the majority, but, as in the case of an oligarchy, the minority, who meet and enact the rules of conduct, what are these?

Per. Whatever the ruling power of the state after deliberation enacts as our duty to do, goes by the name of laws.

Alc. Then if a tyrant, holding the chief power in the state, enacts rules of conduct for the citizens, are these enactments law?

Per. Yes, anything which a tyrant as head of the state enacts, also goes by the name of law.

Alc. But, Pericles, violence and lawlessness—how do we define them? Is it not when a stronger man forces a weaker to do what seems right to him—not by persuasion but by compulsion?

Per. I should say so.

Alc. It would seem to follow that if a tyrant, without persuading the citizens, drives them by enactment to do certain things—that is lawlessness?

Per. You are right; and I retract the statement that measures passed by a tyrant without persuasion of the citizens are law.

Alc. And what of measures passed by a minority, not by persuasion of the majority, but in the exercise of its power only? Are we, or are we not, to apply the term violence to these?

Per. I think that anything which any one forces another to do without persuasion, whether by enactment or not, is violence rather than law.

Alc. It would seem that everything which the majority, in the exercise of its power over the possessors of wealth, and without persuading them, chooses to enact, is of the nature of violence rather than of law?

To be sure (answered Pericles), adding: At your age we were clever hands at such quibbles ourselves. It was just such subtleties which we used to practise our wits upon; as you do now, if I mistake not.

To which Alcibiades replied: Ah, Pericles, I do wish we could have met in those days when you were at your cleverest in such matters.

Well, then, as soon as the desired superiority over the politicians of the day seemed to be attained, Critias and Alcibiades turned their backs on Socrates. They found his society unattractive, not to speak of the annoyance of being cross-questioned on their own shortcomings. Forthwith they devoted themselves to those affairs of state but for which they would never have come near him at all.

No; if one would seek to see true companions of Socrates, one must look to Crito,[43] and Chaerephon, and Chaerecrates, to Hermogenes, to Simmias and Cebes, to Phaedondes and others, who clung to him not to excel in the rhetoric of the Assembly or the law-courts, but with the nobler ambition of attaining to such beauty and goodliness of soul as would enable them to discharge the various duties of life to house and family, to relatives and friends, to fellow-citizens, and to the state at large. Of these true followers not one in youth or old age was ever guilty, or thought guilty, of committing any evil deed.

"But for all that," the accuser insists, "Socrates taught sons to pour contumely upon their fathers[44] by persuading his young friends that he could make them wiser than their sires, or by pointing out that the law allowed a son to sue his father for aberration of mind, and to imprison him, which legal ordinance he put in evidence to prove that it might be well for the wiser to imprison the more ignorant."

Now what Socrates held was, that if a man may with justice incarcerate another for no better cause than a form of folly or ignorance, this same person could not justly complain if he in his turn were kept in bonds by his superiors in knowledge; and to come to the bottom of such questions, to discover the difference between madness and ignorance was a problem which he was perpetually working at. His

---

[43] For these true followers, familiar to us in the pages of Plato, (*Crito, Apol., Phaedo,* etc) see Cobet, *Pros. Xen.*

[44] See *Apol.* 20; Arist. *Clouds,* 1407, where Pheidippides "drags his father Strepsiades through the mire."

opinion came to this: If a madman may, as a matter of expediency to himself and his friends, be kept in prison, surely, as a matter of justice, the man who knows not what he ought to know should be content to sit at the feet of those who know, and be taught.

But it was the rest of their kith and kin, not fathers only (according to the accuser), whom Socrates dishonoured in the eyes of his circle of followers, when he said that "the sick man or the litigant does not derive assistance from his relatives,[45] but from his doctor in the one case, and his legal adviser in the other." "Listen further to his language about friends," says the accuser: "'What is the good of their being kindly disposed, unless they can be of some practical use to you? Mere goodness of disposition is nothing; those only are worthy of honour who combine with the knowledge of what is right the faculty of expounding it;'[46] and so by bringing the young to look upon himself as a superlatively wise person gifted with an extraordinary capacity for making others wise also, he so worked on the dispositions of those who consorted with him that in their esteem the rest of the world counted for nothing by comparison with Socrates."

Now I admit the language about fathers and the rest of a man's relations. I can go further, and add some other sayings of his, that "when the soul (which is alone the indwelling centre of intelligence) is gone out of a man, be he our nearest and dearest friend, we carry the body forth and bury it out of sight." "Even in life," he used to say, "each of us is ready to part with any portion of his best possession—to wit, his own body—if it be useless and unprofitable. He will remove it himself, or suffer another to do so in his stead. Thus men cut off their own nails, hair, or corns; they allow surgeons to cut and cauterise them, not without pains and aches, and are so grateful to the doctor for his services that they further give him a fee. Or again, a man ejects the spittle from his mouth as far as possible.[47] Why? Because it is of no use while it stays within the system, but is detrimental rather."

Now by these instances his object was not to inculcate the duty of burying one's father alive or of cutting oneself to bits, but to show that lack of intelligence means lack of worth;[48] and so he called upon his hearers to be as sensible and useful as they could be, so that, be it father or brother or any one else whose esteem he would deserve, a man should not hug himself in careless self-interest, trusting to mere relationship, but strive to be useful to those whose esteem he coveted.

But (pursues the accuser) by carefully culling the most immoral

---

[45] See Grote, *H. G.* v. 535.

[46] Cf. Thuc. ii. 60. Pericles says, "Yet I with whom you are so angry venture to say of myself, that I am as capable as any one of devising and explaining a sound policy."—Jowett.

[47] See Aristot. *Eth. Eud.* vii. 1.

[48] *i.e.* "*witless* and *worthless* are synonymous."

passages of the famous poets, and using them as evidences, he taught his associates to be evildoers and tyrranical: the line of Hesiod[49] for instance—

No work is a disgrace; slackness of work is the disgrace—

"interpreted," says the accuser, "by Socrates as if the poet enjoined us to abstain from no work wicked or ignoble; do everything for the sake of gain."

Now while Socrates would have entirely admitted the propositions that "it is a blessing and a benefit to a man to be a worker," and that "a lazy do-nothing is a pestilent evil," that "work is good and idleness a curse," the question arises, whom did he mean by workers? In his vocabulary only those were good workmen[50] who were engaged on good work; dicers and gamblers and others engaged on any other base and ruinous business he stigmatised as the "idle drones"; and from this point of view the quotation from Hesiod is unimpeachable—

No work is a disgrace; only idlesse is disgrace.

But there was a passage from Homer[51] for ever on his lips, as the accuser tells us—the passage which says concerning Odysseus,

> What prince, or man of name,
> He found flight-giv'n, he would restrain with words of gentlest blame:
> "Good sir, it fits you not to fly, or fare as one afraid,
> You should not only stay yourself, but see the people stayed."

> Thus he the best sort us'd; the worst, whose spirits brake out in noise,[52]
> He cudgell'd with his sceptre, chid, and said, "Stay, wretch, be still,
> And hear thy betters; thou art base, and both in power and skill
> Poor and unworthy, without name in counsel or in war."
> We must not all be kings.

The accuser informs us that Socrates interpreted these lines as though the poet approved the giving of blows to commoners and poor folk. Now no such remark was ever made by Socrates; which indeed

---

[49] *Works and Days*, 309 ('Ergon d' ouden oneidos). Cf. Plat. *Charm.* 163 C.
[50] See below, III. ix. 9.
[51] *Il.* ii. 188 foll., 199 foll. (so Chapman).
[52] Lit. "But whatever man of the people he saw and found him shouting."—W. Leaf.

would have been tantamount to maintaining that he ought to be beaten himself. What he did say was, that those who were useful neither in word nor deed, who were incapable of rendering assistance in time of need to the army or the state or the people itself, be they never so wealthy, ought to be restrained, and especially if to incapacity they added effrontery.

As to Socrates, he was the very opposite of all this—he was plainly a lover of the people, and indeed of all mankind. Though he had many ardent admirers among citizens and strangers alike, he never demanded any fee for his society from any one,[53] but bestowed abundantly upon all alike of the riches of his soul—good things, indeed, of which fragments accepted gratis at his hands were taken and sold at high prices to the rest of the community by some,[54] who were not, as he was, lovers of the people, since with those who had not money to give in return they refused to discourse. But of Socrates be it said that in the eyes of the whole world he reflected more honour on the state and a richer lustre than ever Lichas,[55] whose fame is proverbial, shed on Lacedaemon. Lichas feasted and entertained the foreign residents in Lacedaemon at the Gymnopaediae most handsomely. Socrates gave a lifetime to the outpouring of his substance in the shape of the greatest benefits bestowed on all who cared to receive them. In other words, he made those who lived in his society better men, and sent them on their way rejoicing.

To no other conclusion, therefore, can I come but that, being so good a man, Socrates was worthier to have received honour from the state than death. And this I take to be the strictly legal view of the case, for what does the law require?[56] "If a man be proved to be a thief, a filcher of clothes, a cut-purse, a housebreaker, a man-stealer, a robber of temples, the penalty is death." Even so; and of all men Socrates stood most aloof from such crimes.

To the state he was never the cause of any evil—neither disaster in war, nor faction, nor treason, nor any other mischief whatsoever. And if his public life was free from all offence, so was his private. He never hurt a single soul either by deprivation of good or infliction of evil, nor did he ever lie under the imputation of any of those misdoings. Where then is his liability to the indictment to be found? Who, so far from disbelieving in the gods, as set forth in the indictment, was conspicuous beyond all men for service to heaven; so far from corrupting the young—a charge alleged with insistence by the prosecutor—was notorious for the zeal with which he strove not only to stay his

---

[53] See *Symp.* iv. 43; Plat. *Hipp. maj.* 300 D; *Apol.* 19 E.
[54] See Diog. Laert. II. viii. 1.
[55] See *Hell.* III. ii. 21; Thuc. v. 50; Plut. *Cim.* 284 C. For the Gymnopaediae, see Paus. III. xi. 9; Athen. xiv. p. 631.
[56] See *Symp.* iv. 36; Plat. *Rep.* 575 B; *Gorg.* 508 E.

associates from evil desires, but to foster in them a passionate desire for that loveliest and queenliest of virtues without which states and families crumble to decay.[57] Such being his conduct, was he not worthy of high honour from the state of Athens?

III

It may serve to illustrate the assertion that he benefited his associates partly by the display of his own virtue and partly by verbal discourse and argument, if I set down my various recollections[58] on these heads. And first with regard to religion and the concerns of heaven. In conduct and language his behaviour conformed to the rule laid down by the Pythia[59] in reply to the question, "How shall we act?" as touching a sacrifice or the worship of ancestors, or any similar point. Her answer is: "*Act according to the law and custom of your state, and you will act piously.*" After this pattern Socrates behaved himself, and so he exhorted others to behave, holding them to be but busybodies and vain fellows who acted on any different principle.

His formula or prayer was simple: "Give me that which is best for me," for, said he, the gods know best what good things are—to pray for gold or silver or despotic power were no better than to make some particular throw at dice or stake in battle or any such thing the subject of prayer, of which the future consequences are manifestly uncertain.[60]

If with scant means he offered but small sacrifices he believed that he was in no wise inferior to those who make frequent and large sacrifices from an ampler store. It were ill surely for the very gods themselves, could they take delight in large sacrifices rather than in small, else oftentimes must the offerings of bad men be found acceptable rather than of good; nor from the point of view of men themselves would life be worth living if the offerings of a villain rather than of a righteous man found favour in the sight of Heaven. His belief was that the joy of the gods is greater in proportion to the holiness of the giver, and he was ever an admirer of that line of Hesiod which says,

According to thine ability do sacrifice to the immortal gods.[61]

"Yes," he would say, "in our dealings with friends and strangers alike, and in reference to the demands of life in general, there is no better motto for a man than that: '*let a man do according to his ability.*'"

---

[57] Or, "the noblest and proudest virtue by means of which states and families are prosperously directed."

[58] Hence the title of the work, ('Apomenmoneumata), *Recollections, Memoirs, Memorabilia.* See Diog. Laert. *Xen.* II. vi. 48.

[59] The Pythia at Delphi.

[60] See (Plat.) *Alcib. II.* 142 foll.; Valerius Max. vii. 2; "Spectator," No. 207.

[61] Hesiod, *Works and Days*, 336. See *Anab.* III. ii. 9.

Or to take another point. If it appeared to him that a sign from heaven had been given him, nothing would have induced him to go against heavenly warning: he would as soon have been persuaded to accept the guidance of a blind man ignorant of the path to lead him on a journey in place of one who knew the road and could see; and so he denounced the folly of others who do things contrary to the warnings of God in order to avoid some disrepute among men. For himself he despised all human aids by comparison with counsel from above.

The habit and style of living to which he subjected his soul and body was one which under ordinary circumstances[62] would enable any one adopting it to look existence cheerily in the face and to pass his days serenely: it would certainly entail no difficulties as regards expense. So frugal was it that a man must work little indeed who could not earn the quantum which contented Socrates. Of food he took just enough to make eating a pleasure—the appetite he brought to it was sauce sufficient; while as to drinks, seeing that he only drank when thirsty, any draught refreshed.[63] If he accepted an invitation to dinner, he had no difficulty in avoiding the common snare of over-indulgence, and his advice to people who could not equally control their appetite was to avoid taking what would allure them to eat if not hungry or to drink if not thirsty.[64] Such things are ruinous to the constitution, he said, bad for stomachs, brains, and soul alike; or as he used to put it, with a touch of sarcasm,[65] "It must have been by feasting men on so many dainty dishes that Circe produced her pigs; only Odysseus through his continency and the 'promptings[66] of Hermes' abstained from touching them immoderately, and by the same token did not turn into a swine." So much for this topic, which he touched thus lightly and yet seriously.

But as to the concerns of Aphrodite, his advice was to hold strongly aloof from the fascination of fair forms: once lay finger on these and it is not easy to keep a sound head and a sober mind. To take a particular case. It was a mere kiss which, as he had heard, Critobulus[67] had some time given to a fair youth, the son of Alcibiades.[68] Accordingly Critobulus being present, Socrates propounded the question.

Soc. Tell me, Xenophon, have you not always believed Critobulus to be a man of sound sense, not wild and self-willed? Should you not

---

[62] (ei me ti daimonion eie), "save under some divinely-ordained calamity." Cf. *Cyrop.* I. vi. 18; *Symp.* viii. 43.
[63] See *Ages.* ix; Cic. *Tusc.* v. 34, 97; *de Fin.* ii. 28, 90.
[64] Cf. Plut. *Mor.* 128 D; Clement, *Paedag.* 2. 173, 33; *Strom.* 2, 492, 24; Aelian, *N. A.* 8, 9.
[65] "Half in gibe and half in jest," in ref. to *Od.* x. 233 foll.: "So she let them in..."
[66] (upothemosune), "inspiration." Cf. *Il.* xv. 412; *Od.* xvi. 233.
[67] For Critobulus (the son of Crito) see "Econ." i. 1 foll.; *Symp.* i. 3 foll.
[68] See Isocr. *Or.* xvi. Cobet conj. (ton tou 'Axiokhou uion), *i.e.* Clinias.

have said that he was remarkable for his prudence rather than thoughtless or foolhardy?

Xen. Certainly that is what I should have said of him.

Soc. Then you are now to regard him as quite the reverse—a hot-blooded, reckless libertine: this is the sort of man to throw somersaults into knives,[69] or to leap into the jaws of fire.

Xen. And what have you seen him doing, that you give him so bad a character?

Soc. Doing? Why, has not the fellow dared to steal a kiss from the son of Alcibiades, most fair of youths and in the golden prime?

Xen. Nay, then, if that is the foolhardy adventure, it is a danger which I could well encounter myself.

Soc. Pour soul! and what do you expect your fate to be after that kiss? Let me tell you. On the instant you will lose your freedom, the indenture of your bondage will be signed; it will be yours on compulsion to spend large sums on hurtful pleasures; you will have scarcely a moment's leisure left for any noble study; you will be driven to concern yourself most zealously with things which no man, not even a madman, would choose to make an object of concern.

Xen. O Heracles! how fell a power to reside in a kiss!

Soc. Does it surprise you? Do you not know that the tarantula, which is no bigger than a threepenny bit,[70] has only to touch the mouth and it will afflict its victim with pains and drive him out of his senses.

Xen. Yes, but then the creature injects something with its bite.

Soc. Ah, fool! and do you imagine that these lovely creatures infuse nothing with their kiss, simply because you do not see the poison? Do you not know that this wild beast which men call beauty in its bloom is all the more terrible than the tarantula in that the insect must first touch its victim, but this at a mere glance of the beholder, without even contact, will inject something into him—yards away—which will make him man. And may be that is why the Loves are called "archers," because these beauties wound so far off.[71] But my advice to you, Xenophon, is, whenever you catch sight of one of these fair forms, to run helter-skelter for bare life without a glance behind; and to you, Critobulus, I would say, "Go abroad for a year: so long time will it take to heal you of this wound."

Such (he said), in the affairs of Aphrodite, as in meats and drinks, should be the circumspection of all whose footing is insecure. At least they should confine themselves to such diet as the soul would dispense with, save for some necessity of the body; and which even so ought to

---

[69] Cf. *Symp.* ii. 10, iv. 16. See Schneider *ad loc.*

[70] Lit. "a half-obol piece." For the (phalaggion) see Aristot. "H. A." ix. 39, 1.

[71] L. Dindorf, etc. regard the sentence as a gloss. Cf. *Symp.* iv. 26 ((isos de kai... entimoteron estin)).

set up no disturbance.⁷² But for himself, it was clear, he was prepared at all points and invulnerable. He found less difficulty in abstaining from beauty's fairest and fullest bloom than many others from weeds and garbage. To sum up:⁷³ with regard to eating and drinking and these other temptations of the sense, the equipment of his soul made him independent; he could boast honestly that in his moderate fashion⁷⁴ his pleasures were no less than theirs who take such trouble to procure them, and his pains far fewer.

IV

A belief is current, in accordance with views maintained concerning Socrates in speech and writing, and in either case conjecturally, that, however powerful he may have been in stimulating men to virtue as a theorist, he was incapable of acting as their guide himself.⁷⁵ It would be well for those who adopt this view to weigh carefully not only what Socrates effected "by way of castigation" in cross-questioning whose who conceived themselves to be possessed of all knowledge, but also his everyday conversation with those who spent their time in close intercourse with himself. Having done this, let them decide whether he was incapable of making his companions better.

I will first state what I once heard fall from his lips in a discussion with Aristodemus, ⁷⁶ "the little," as he was called, on the topic of divinity.⁷⁷ Socrates had observed that Aristodemus neither sacrificed nor gave heed to divination, but on the contrary was disposed to ridicule those who did.

So tell me, Aristodemus (he began), are there any human beings who have won your admiration for their wisdom?

Ar. There are.

Soc. Would you mention to us their names?

Ar. In the writings of epic poetry I have the greatest admiration for Homer.... And as a dithyrambic poet for Melanippides.⁷⁸ I admire also Sophocles as a tragedian, Polycleitus as a sculptor, and Zeuxis as a

---

⁷² Cf. *Symp.* iv. 38.

⁷³ L. Dindorf (brackets) this passage as spurious.

⁷⁴ On the principle "enough is as good as a feast," (arkountos).

⁷⁵ *Al.* "If any one believes that Socrates, as represented in certain dialogues (*e.g.* of Plato, Antisthenes, etc.) of an imaginary character, was an adept ((protrepsasthai)) in the art of stimulating people to virtue negatively but scarcely the man to guide ((proagein)) his hearers on the true path himself." Cf. (Plat.) *Clitophon*, 410 B; Cic. *de Or*. I. xlvii. 204; Plut. *Mor.* 798 B. See Grote, *Plato*, iii. 21; K. Joel, *op. cit.* p. 51 foll.; Cf. below, IV. iii. 2.

⁷⁶ See Plat. *Symp.* 173 B: "He was a little fellow who never wore any shoes, Aristodemus, of the deme of Cydathenaeum."—Jowett.

⁷⁷ Or, "the divine element."

⁷⁸ Melanippides, 430 B.C. See Cobet, *Pros. Xen.* s.n.

painter.

Soc. Which would you consider the more worthy of admiration, a fashioner of senseless images devoid of motion or one who could fashion living creatures endowed with understanding and activity?

Ar. Decidedly the latter, provided his living creatures owed their birth to design and were not the offspring of some chance.

Soc. But now if you had two sorts of things, the one of which presents no clue as to what it is for, and the other is obviously for some useful purpose—which would you judge to be the result of chance, which of design?

Ar. Clearly that which is produced for some useful end is the work of design.

Soc. Does it not strike you then that he who made man from the beginning[79] did for some useful end furnish him with his several senses—giving him eyes to behold the visible word, and ears to catch the intonations of sound? Or again, what good would there be in odours if nostrils had not been bestowed upon us? what perception of sweet things and pungent, and of all the pleasures of the palate, had not a tongue been fashioned in us as an interpreter of the same? And besides all this, do you not think this looks like a matter of foresight, this closing of the delicate orbs of sight with eyelids as with folding doors, which, when there is need to use them for any purpose, can be thrown wide open and firmly closed again in sleep? and, that even the winds of heaven may not visit them too roughly, this planting of the eyelashes as a protecting screen?[80] this coping of the region above the eyes with cornice-work of eyebrow so that no drop of sweat fall from the head and injure them? again this readiness of the ear to catch all sounds and yet not to be surcharged? this capacity of the front teeth of all animals to cut and of the "grinders" to receive the food and reduce it to pulp? the position of the mouth again, close to the eyes and nostrils as a portal of ingress for all the creature's supplies? and lastly, seeing that matter passing out[81] of the body is unpleasant, this hindward direction of the passages, and their removal to a distance from the avenues of sense? I ask you, when you see all these things constructed with such show of foresight can you doubt whether they are products of chance or intelligence?

Ar. To be sure not! Viewed in this light they would seem to be the handiwork of some wise artificer,[82] full of love for all things living.[83]

Soc. What shall we say of this passion implanted in man to beget offspring, this passion in the mother to rear her babe, and in the

---

[79] Cf. Aristot. *de Part. Animal.* 1. For the "teleological" views see IV. iii. 2 foll.
[80] "Like a sieve" or "colander."
[81] "That which goeth out of a man."
[82] "Demiurge."
[83] Passage referred to by Epictetus ap. Stob. *Flor.* 121, 29.

creature itself, once born, this deep desire of life and fear of death?

Ar. No doubt these do look like the contrivances of some one deliberately planning the existence of living creatures.

Soc. Well, and doubtless you feel to have a spark of wisdom yourself?

Ar. Put your questions, and I will answer.

Soc. And yet you imagine that elsewhere no spark of wisdom is to be found? And that, too, when you know that you have in your body a tiny fragment only of the mighty earth, a little drop of the great waters, and of the other elements, vast in their extent, you got, I presume, a particle of each towards the compacting of your bodily frame? Mind alone, it would seem, which is nowhere to be found,[84] you had the lucky chance to snatch up and make off with, you cannot tell how. And these things around and about us, enormous in size, infinite in number, owe their orderly arrangement, as you suppose, to some vacuity of wit?

Ar. It may be, for my eyes fail to see the master agents of these, as one sees the fabricators of things produced on earth.

Soc. No more do you see your own soul, which is the master agent of your body; so that, as far as that goes, you may maintain, if you like, that you do nothing with intelligence,[85] but everything by chance.

At this point Aristodemus: I assure you, Socrates, that I do not disdain the Divine power. On the contrary, my belief is that the Divinity is too grand to need any service which I could render.

Soc. But the grander that power is, which deigns to tend and wait upon you, the more you are called upon to honour it.

Ar. Be well assured, if I could believe the gods take thought for all men, I would not neglect them.

Soc. How can you suppose that they do not so take thought? Who, in the first place, gave to man alone of living creatures his erect posture, enabling him to see farther in front of him and to contemplate more freely the height above, and to be less subject to distress than other creatures (endowed like himself with eyes and ears and mouth).[86] Consider next how they gave to the beast of the field[87] feet as a means of progression only, but to man they gave in addition hands—those hands which have achieved so much to raise us in the scale of happiness above all animals. Did they not make the tongue also? which belongs indeed alike to man and beast, but in man they fashioned it so as to play on different parts of the mouth at different times, whereby we

---

[84] Cf. Plat. *Phileb.* 30 B: "*Soc.* May our body be said to have a soul? Pro. Clearly. *Soc.* And whence comes that soul, my dear Protarchus, unless the body of the universe, which contains elements similar to our bodies but finer, has also a soul? Can there be any other source?"—Jowett. Cic. *de N. D.* ii. 6; iii. 11.

[85] Or, "by your wit," (gnome).

[86] See Kühner for an attempt to cure the text.

[87] (erpetois), a "poetical" word. Cf. *Od.* iv. 418; Herod. i. 140.

can produce articulate speech, and have a code of signals to express our every want to one another. Or consider the pleasures of the sexual appetite; limited in the rest of the animal kingdom to certain seasons, but in the case of man a series prolonged unbroken to old age. Nor did it content the Godhead merely to watch over the interests of man's body. What is of far higher import, he implanted in man the noblest and most excellent type of soul. For what other creature, to begin with, has a soul to appreciate the existence of the gods who have arranged this grand and beauteous universe? What other tribe of animals save man can render service to the gods? How apt is the spirit of man to take precautions against hunger and thirst, cold and heat, to alleviate disease and foster strength! how suited to labour with a view to learning! how capable of garnering in the storehouse of his memory all that he has heard or seen or understood! Is it not most evident to you that by the side of other animals men live and move a race of gods—by nature excellent, in beauty of body and of soul supreme? For, mark you, had a creature of man's wit been encased in the body of an ox,[88] he would have been powerless to carry out his wishes, just as the possession of hands divorced from human wit is profitless. And then you come, you who have obtained these two most precious attributes, and give it as your opinion, that the gods take no thought or care for you. Why, what will you have them to do, that you may believe and be persuaded that you too are in their thoughts?

Ar. When they treat me as you tell us they treat you, and send me counsellors to warn me what I am to do and what abstain from doing,[89] I will believe.

Soc. Send you counsellors! Come now, what when the people of Athens make inquiry by oracle, and the gods' answer comes? Are you not an Athenian? Think you not that to you also the answer is given? What when they send portents to forewarn the states of Hellas? or to all mankind? Are you not a man? a Hellene? Are not these intended for you also? Can it be that you alone are excepted as a signal instance of Divine neglect? Again, do you suppose that the gods could have implanted in the heart of man the belief in their capacity to work him weal or woe had they not the power? Would not men have discovered the imposture in all this lapse of time? Do you not perceive that the wisest and most perdurable of human institutions—be they cities or tribes of men—are ever the most God-fearing; and in the individual man the riper his age and judgment, the deeper his religiousness? Ay, my good sir (he broke forth), lay to heart and understand that even as your own mind within you can turn and dispose of your body as it lists, so ought we to think that the wisdom which abides within the universal

---

[88] See Aristot. *de Part. Animal.* iv. 10.
[89] See IV. iii. 12.

frame does so dispose of all things as it finds agreeable to itself; for hardly may it be that your eye is able to range over many a league, but that the eye of God is powerless to embrace all things at a glance; or that to your soul it is given to dwell in thought on matters here or far away in Egypt or in Sicily, but that the wisdom and thought of God is not sufficient to include all things at one instant under His care. If only you would copy your own behaviour[90] where human beings are concerned. It is by acts of service and of kindness that you discover which of your fellows are willing to requite you in kind. It is by taking another into your counsel that you arrive at the secret of his wisdom. If, on like principle, you will but make trial of the gods by acts of service, whether they will choose to give you counsel in matters obscure to mortal vision, you shall discover the nature and the greatness of Godhead to be such that they are able at once to see all things and to hear all things and to be present everywhere, nor does the least thing escape their watchful care.

To my mind the effect of words like these was to cause those about him to hold aloof from unholiness, baseness, and injustice, not only whilst they were seen of men, but even in the solitary place, since they must believe that no part of their conduct could escape the eye of Heaven.

V

I suppose it may be taken as admitted that self-control is a noble acquirement for a man.[91] If so, let us turn and consider whether by language like the following he was likely to lead his listeners onwards[92] to the attainment of this virtue. "Sirs," he would say, "if a war came upon us and we wished to choose a man who would best help us to save ourselves and to subdue our enemy, I suppose we should scarcely select one whom we knew to be a slave to his belly, to wine, or lust, and prone to succumb to toil or sleep. Could we expect such an one to save us or to master our foes? Or if one of us were nearing the end of his days, and he wished to discover some one to whom he might entrust his sons for education, his maiden daughters for protection, and his property in general for preservation, would he deem a libertine worthy of such offices? Why, no one would dream of entrusting his flocks and herds, his storehouses and barns, or the superintendence of his works to the tender mercies of an intemperate slave. If a butler or an errand boy with such a character were offered to us we would not take him as a free gift. And if he would not accept an intemperate slave, what pains

---

[90] Or, "reason as you are wont to do."
[91] Lit. "a beautiful and brave possession."
[92] (proubibaze).

should the master himself take to avoid that imputation.[93] For with the incontinent man it is not as with the self-seeker and the covetous. These may at any rate be held to enrich themselves in depriving others. But the intemperate man cannot claim in like fashion to be a blessing to himself if a curse to his neighbours; nay, the mischief which he may cause to others is nothing by comparison with that which redounds against himself, since it is the height of mischief to ruin—I do not say one's own house and property—but one's own body and one's own soul. Or to take an example from social intercourse, no one cares for a guest who evidently takes more pleasure in the wine and the viands than in the friends beside him—who stints his comrades of the affection due to them to dote upon a mistress. Does it not come to this, that every honest man is bound to look upon self-restraint as the very corner-stone of virtue:[94] which he should seek to lay down as the basis and foundation of his soul? Without self-restraint who can lay any good lesson to heart or practise it when learnt in any degree worth speaking of? Or, to put it conversely, what slave of pleasure will not suffer degeneracy of soul and body? By Hera,[95] well may every free man pray to be saved from the service of such a slave; and well too may he who is in bondage to such pleasures supplicate Heaven to send him good masters, seeing that is the one hope of salvation left him."

Well-tempered words: yet his self-restraint shone forth even more in his acts than in his language. Not only was he master over the pleasures which flow from the body, but of those also which are fed by riches, his belief being that he who receives money from this or that chance donor sets up over himself a master, and binds himself to an abominable slavery.

VI

In this context some discussions with Antiphon the sophist[96] deserve record. Antiphon approaches Socrates in hope of drawing away his associates, and in their presence thus accosts him.

Antiphon. Why, Socrates, I always thought it was expected of students of philosophy to grow in happiness daily; but you seem to have reaped other fruits from your philosophy. At any rate, you exist, I do not say live, in a style such as no slave serving under a master would put up with. Your meat and your drink are of the cheapest sort, and as to clothes, you cling to one wretched cloak which serves you for

---

[93] Or, "how should the master himself beware lest he fall into that category."
[94] (krepida). See Pind. *Pyth.* iv. 138; *ib.* vii. 3; *ib.* fr. 93.
[95] See below, III. x. 9, xi. 5; IV. ii. 9, iv. 8; *Econ.* x. 1; *Cyrop.* I. iv. 12; Plat. *Phaedr.* 230 B. Cf. Shakesp. "by'r Lakin."
[96] (o teratoskopos), "jealous of Socrates," according to Aristotle ap. Diog. Laert. II. v. 25. See Cobet, *Pros. Xen.*

summer and winter alike; and so you go the whole year round, without shoes to your feet or a shirt to your back. Then again, you are not for taking or making money, the mere seeking of which is a pleasure, even as the possession of it adds to the sweetness and independence of existence. I do not know whether you follow the common rule of teachers, who try to fashion their pupils in imitation of themselves,[97] and propose to mould the characters of your companions; but if you do you ought to dub yourself professor of the art of wretchedness.[98]

Thus challenged, Socrates replied: One thing to me is certain, Antiphon; you have conceived so vivid an idea of my life of misery that for yourself you would choose death sooner than live as I do. Suppose now we turn and consider what it is you find so hard in my life. Is it that he who takes payment must as a matter of contract finish the work for which he is paid, whereas I, who do not take it, lie under no constraint to discourse except with whom I choose? Do you despise my dietary on the ground that the food which I eat is less wholesome and less stengthening than yours, or that the articles of my consumption are so scarce and so much costlier to procure than yours? Or have the fruits of your marketing a flavour denied to mine? Do you not know the sharper the appetite the less the need of sauces, the keener the thirst the less the desire for out-of-the-way drinks? And as to raiment, clothes, you know, are changed on account of cold or else of heat. People only wear boots and shoes in order not to gall their feet and be prevented walking. Now I ask you, have you ever noticed that I keep more within doors than others on account of the cold? Have you ever seen me battling with any one for shade on account of the heat? Do you not know that even a weakling by nature may, by dint of exercise and practice, come to outdo a giant who neglects his body? He will beat him in the particular point of training, and bear the strain more easily. But you apparently will not have it that I, who am for ever training myself to endure this, that, and the other thing which may befall the body, can brave all hardships more easily than yourself for instance, who perhaps are not so practised. And to escape slavery to the belly or to sleep or lechery, can you suggest more effective means than the possession of some powerful attraction, some counter-charm which shall gladden not only in the using, but by the hope enkindled of its lasting usefulness? And yet this you do know; joy is not to him who feels that he is doing well in nothing—it belongs to one who is persuaded that things are progressing with him, be it tillage or the working of a vessel,[99] or any of the thousand and one things on which a man may chance to be employed. To him it is given to rejoice as he

---

[97] Or, "try to turn out their pupils as copies of themselves."
[98] See Arist. *Clouds*, (on o kakodaimon Sokrates kai Khairephon).
[99] "The business of a shipowner or skipper."

reflects, "I am doing well." But is the pleasured derived from all these put together half as joyous as the consciousness of becoming better oneself, of acquiring better and better friends? That, for my part, is the belief I continue to cherish.

Again, if it be a question of helping one's friends or country, which of the two will have the larger leisure to devote to these objects—he who leads the life which I lead to-day, or he who lives in the style which you deem so fortunate? Which of the two will adopt a soldier's life more easily—the man who cannot get on without expensive living, or he to whom whatever comes to hand suffices? Which will be the readier to capitulate and cry "mercy" in a siege—the man of elaborate wants, or he who can get along happily with the readiest things to hand? You, Antiphon, would seem to suggest that happiness consists of luxury and extravagance; I hold a different creed. To have no wants at all is, to my mind, an attribute of Godhead;[100] to have as few wants as possible the nearest approach to Godhead; and as that which is divine is mightiest, so that is next mightiest which comes closest to the divine.

Returning to the charge at another time, this same Antiphon engaged Socrates in conversation thus.

Ant. Socrates, for my part, I believe you to be a good and upright man; but for your wisdom I cannot say much. I fancy you would hardly dispute the verdict yourself, since, as I remark, you do not ask a money payment for your society; and yet if it were your cloak now, or your house, or any other of your possessions, you would set some value upon it, and never dream, I will not say of parting with it gratis, but of exchanging it for less than its worth. A plain proof, to my mind, that if you thought your society worth anything, you would ask for it not less than its equivalent in gold.[101] Hence the conclusion to which I have come, as already stated: good and upright you may be, since you do not cheat people from pure selfishness; but wise you cannot be, since your knowledge is not worth a cent.

To this onslaught Socrates: Antiphon, it is a tenet which we cling to that beauty and wisdom have this in common, that there is a fair way and a foul way in which to dispose of them. The vendor of beauty purchases an evil name, but supposing the same person have discerned a soul of beauty in his lover and makes that man his friend, we regard his choice as sensible.[102] So is it with wisdom; he who sells it for money to the first bidder we name a sophist,[103] as though one should say a man who prostitutes his wisdom; but if the same man, discerning the noble nature of another, shall teach that other every good thing, and make him his friend, of such a one we say he does that which it is the

---

[100] Cf. Aristot. *Eth. N.* x. viii. 1.
[101] Or rather "money," lit. "silver."
[102] Add "and a sign of modesty," (sophrona nomizomen).
[103] (sophistas). See Grote, *H. G.* viii. 482 foll.; *Hunting*, xi. foll.

duty of every good citizen of gentle soul to do. In accordance with this theory, I too, Antiphon, having my tastes, even as another finds pleasure in his horse and his hounds,[104] and another in his fighting cocks, so I too take my pleasure in good friends; and if I have any good thing myself I teach it them, or I commend them to others by whom I think they will be helped forwards on the path of virtue. The treasures also of the wise of old, written and bequeathed in their books,[105] I unfold and peruse in common with my friends. If our eye light upon any good thing we cull it eagerly, and regard it as great gain if we may but grow in friendship with one another.

As I listened to this talk I could not but reflect that he, the master, was a person to be envied, and that we, his hearers, were being led by him to beauty and nobility of soul.

Again on some occasion the same Antiphon asked Socrates how he expected to make politicians of others when, even if he had the knowledge, he did not engage in politics himself.

Socrates replied: I will put to you a question, Antiphon: Which were the more statesmanlike proceeding, to practise politics myself single-handed, or to devote myself to making as many others as possible fit to engage in that pursuit?

VII

Let us here turn and consider whether by deterring his associates from quackery and false seeming he did not directly stimulate them to the pursuit of virtue.[106] He used often to say there was no better road to renown than the one by which a man became good at that wherein he desired to be reputed good.[107] The truth of the concept he enforced as follows: "Let us reflect on what a man would be driven to do who wanted to be thought a good flute player, without really being so. He would be forced to imitate the good flute player in the externals of his art, would he not? and first or all, seeing that these artists always have a splendid equipment,[108] and travel about with a long train of attendants, he must have the same; in the next place, they can command the plaudits of a multitude, he therefore must pack a conclave of clackers. But one thing is clear: nothing must induce him to give a performance, or he will be exposed at once, and find himself a laughing-stock not only as a sorry sort of flute player, but as a wretched imposter. And now he has a host of expenses to meet; and not one advantage to be

---

[104] Cf. Plat. *Lys.* 211 E.
[105] Cf. *Symp.* iv. 27.
[106] (apotrepon proutrepen). See K. Joel, *op. cit.* p. 450 foll.
[107] Cf. *Cyrop.* I. vi. 22.
[108] Or, "furniture of the finest," like Arion's in Herod. i. 24. Schneid. cf. Demosth. 565. 6.

reaped; and worse than all his evil reputation. What is left him but to lead a life stale and unprofitable, the scorn and mockery of men? Let us try another case. Suppose a man wished to be thought a good general or a good pilot, though he were really nothing of the sort, let us picture to our minds how it will fare with him. Of two misfortunes one: either with a strong desire to be thought proficient in these matters, he will fail to get others to agree with him, which will be bad enough; or he will succeed, with worse result; since it stands to reason that anyone appointed to work a vessel or lead an army without the requisite knowledge will speedily ruin a number of people whom he least desires to hurt, and will make but a sorry exit from the stage himself." Thus first by one instance and then another would he demonstrate the unprofitableness of trying to appear rich, or courageous, or strong, without really being the thing pretended. "You are sure sooner or later to have commands laid upon you beyond your power to execute, and failing just where you are credited with capacity, the world will give you no commiseration." "I call that man a cheat, and a great cheat too," he would say, "who gets money or goods out of some one by persuasion, and defrauds him; but of all imposters he surely is the biggest who can delude people into thinking that he is fit to lead the state, when all the while he is a worthless creature."[109]

BOOK II

I

Now, if the effect of such discourses was, as I imagine, to deter his hearers from the paths of quackery and false-seeming,[110] so I am sure that language like the following was calculated to stimulate his followers to practise self-control and endurance: self-control in the matters of eating, drinking, sleeping, and the cravings of lust; endurance of cold and heat and toil and pain. He had noticed the undue licence which one of his acquaintances allowed himself in all such matters.[111] Accordingly he thus addressed him:

Tell me, Aristippus (Socrates said), supposing you had two children entrusted to you to educate, one of them must be brought up with an aptitude for government, and the other without the faintest

---

[109] Here follows the sentence [emoi men oun edokei kai tou alazoneuesthai apotrepein tous sunontas toiade dialegomenos], which, for the sake of convenience, I have attached to the first sentence of Bk. II. ch. i. [edokei de moi... ponou.] I believe that the commentators are right in bracketing both one and the other as editorial interpolations.

[110] This sentence in the Greek concludes Bk. I. There is something wrong or very awkward in the text here.

[111] Cf. Grote, *Plato*, III. xxxviii. p. 530.

propensity to rule—how would you educate them? What do you say? Shall we begin our inquiry from the beginning, as it were, with the bare elements of food and nutriment?

Ar. Yes, food to begin with, by all means, being a first principle,[112] without which there is no man living but would perish.

Soc. Well, then, we may expect, may we not, that a desire to grasp food at certain seasons will exhibit itself in both the children?

Ar. It is to be expected.

Soc. Which, then, of the two must be trained, of his own free will,[113] to prosecute a pressing business rather than gratify the belly?

Ar. No doubt the one who is being trained to govern, if we would not have affairs of state neglected during[114] his government.

Soc. And the same pupil must be furnished with a power of holding out against thirst also when the craving to quench it comes upon him?

Ar. Certainly he must.

Soc. And on which of the two shall we confer such self-control in regard to sleep as shall enable him to rest late and rise early, or keep vigil, if the need arise?

Ar. To the same one of the two must be given that endurance also.

Soc. Well, and a continence in regard to matters sexual so great that nothing of the sort shall prevent him from doing his duty? Which of them claims that?

Ar. The same one of the pair again.

Soc. Well, and on which of the two shall be bestowed, as a further gift, the voluntary resolution to face toils rather than turn and flee from them?

Ar. This, too, belongs of right to him who is being trained for government.

Soc. Well, and to which of them will it better accord to be taught all knowledge necessary towards the mastery of antagonists?

Ar. To our future ruler certainly, for without these parts of learning all his other capacities will be merely waste.

Soc.[115] Will not a man so educated be less liable to be entrapped by rival powers, and so escape a common fate of living creatures, some of which (as we all know) are hooked through their own greediness, and often even in spite of a native shyness; but through appetite for food they are drawn towards the bait, and are caught; while others are similarly ensnared by drink?

Ar. Undoubtedly.

Soc. And others again are victims of amorous heat, as quails, for

---

[112] Aristippus plays upon the word (arkhe).
[113] (proairesis).
[114] Lit. "along of."
[115] (§§. 4, 5, L. Dind. ed Lips.)

instance, or partridges, which, at the cry of the hen-bird, with lust and expectation of such joys grow wild, and lose their power of computing dangers: on they rush, and fall into the snare of the hunter?

Aristippus assented.

Soc. And would it not seem to be a base thing for a man to be affected like the silliest bird or beast? as when the adulterer invades the innermost sanctum[116] of the house, though he is well aware of the risks which his crime involves,[117] the formidable penalties of the law, the danger of being caught in the toils, and then suffering the direst contumely. Considering all the hideous penalties which hang over the adulterer's head, considering also the many means at hand to release him from the thraldom of his passion, that a man should so drive headlong on to the quicksands of perdition[118]—what are we to say of such frenzy? The wretch who can so behave must surely be tormented by an evil spirit?[119]

Ar. So it strikes me.

Soc. And does it not strike you as a sign of strange indifference that, whereas the greater number of the indispensable affairs of men, as for instance, those of war and agriculture, and more than half the rest, need to be conducted under the broad canopy of heaven,[120] yet the majority of men are quite untrained to wrestle with cold and heat?

Aristippus again assented.

Soc. And do you not agree that he who is destined to rule must train himself to bear these things lightly?

Ar. Most certainly.

Soc. And whilst we rank those who are self-disciplined in all these matters among persons fit to rule, we are bound to place those incapable of such conduct in the category of persons without any pretension whatsoever to be rulers?

Ar. I assent.

Soc. Well, then, since you know the rank peculiar to either section of mankind, did it ever strike you to consider to which of the two you are best entitled to belong?

Yes I have (replied Aristippus). I do not dream for a moment of ranking myself in the class of those who wish to rule. In fact, considering how serious a business it is to cater for one's own private needs, I look upon it as the mark of a fool not to be content with that, but to further saddle oneself with the duty of providing the rest of the community with whatever they may be pleased to want. That, at the

---

[116] (eis as eirktas). The *penetralia*.

[117] Or, "he knows the risks he runs of suffering those penalties with which the law threatens his crime should he fall into the snare, and being caught, be mutilated."

[118] Or, "leap headlong into the jaws of danger."

[119] (kakodaimonontos).

[120] Or, "in the open air."

cost of much personal enjoyment, a man should put himself at the head of a state, and then, if he fail to carry through every jot and tittle of that state's desire, be held to criminal account, does seem to me the very extravagance of folly. Why, bless me! states claim to treat their rulers precisely as I treat my domestic slaves. I expect my attendants to furnish me with an abundance of necessaries, but not to lay a finger on one of them themselves. So these states regard it as the duty of a ruler to provide them with all the good things imaginable, but to keep his own hands off them all the while.[121] So then, for my part, if anybody desires to have a heap of pother himself,[122] and be a nuisance to the rest of the world, I will educate him in the manner suggested, and he shall take his place among those who are fit to rule; but for myself, I beg to be enrolled amongst those who wish to spend their days as easily and pleasantly as possible.

Soc. Shall we then at this point turn and inquire which of the two are likely to lead the pleasanter life, the rulers or the ruled?

Ar. By all means let us do so.

Soc. To begin then with the nations and races known to ourselves.[123] In Asia the Persians are the rulers, while the Syrians, Phrygians, Lydians are ruled; and in Europe we find the Scythians ruling, and the Maeotians being ruled. In Africa[124] the Carthaginians are rulers, the Libyans ruled. Which of these two sets respectively leads the happier life, in your opinion? Or, to come nearer home—you are yourself a Hellene—which among Hellenes enjoy the happier existence, think you, the dominant or the subject states?

Nay,[125] I would have you to understand (exclaimed Aristippus) that I am just as far from placing myself in the ranks of slavery; there is, I take it, a middle path between the two which it is my ambition to tread, avoiding rule and slavery alike; it lies through freedom—the high road which leads to happiness.

Soc. True, if only your path could avoid human beings, as it avoids rule and slavery, there would be something in what you say. But being placed as you are amidst human beings, if you purpose neither to rule nor to be ruled, and do not mean to dance attendance, if you can help it, on those who rule, you must surely see that the stronger have an art to seat the weaker on the stool of repentance[126] both in public and in private, and to treat them as slaves. I daresay you have not failed to

---

[121] Or, "but he must have no finger in the pie himself."

[122] See Kühner *ad loc.*

[123] Or, "the outer world, the non-Hellenic races and nationalities of which we have any knowledge."

[124] Lit. "Libya."

[125] Or, "Pardon me interrupting you, Socrates; but I have not the slightest intention of placing myself." See W. L. Newman, *op. cit.* i. 306.

[126] See *Symp.* iii. 11; *Cyrop.* II. ii. 14; Plat. *Ion*, 535 E; L. Dindorf *ad loc.*

note this common case: a set of people has sown and planted, whereupon in comes another set and cuts their corn and fells their fruit-trees, and in every way lays siege to them because, though weaker, they refuse to pay them proper court, till at length they are persuaded to accept slavery rather than war against their betters. And in private life also, you will bear me out, the brave and powerful are known to reduce the helpless and cowardly to bondage, and to make no small profit out of their victims.

Ar. Yes, but I must tell you I have a simple remedy against all such misadventures. I do not confine myself to any single civil community. I roam the wide world a foreigner.

Soc. Well, now, that is a masterly stroke, upon my word![127] Of course, ever since the decease of Sinis, and Sciron, and Procrustes,[128] foreign travellers have had an easy time of it. But still, if I bethink me, even in these modern days the members of free communities do pass laws in their respective countries for self-protection against wrong-doing. Over and above their personal connections, they provide themselves with a host of friends; they gird their cities about with walls and battlements; they collect armaments to ward off evil-doers; and to make security doubly sure, they furnish themselves with allies from foreign states. In spite of all which defensive machinery these same free citizens do occasionally fall victims to injustice. But you, who are without any of these aids; you, who pass half your days on the high roads where iniquity is rife;[129] you, who, into whatever city you enter, are less than the least of its free members, and moreover are just the sort of person whom any one bent on mischief would single out for attack—yet you, with your foreigner's passport, are to be exempt from injury? So you flatter yourself. And why? Will the state authorities cause proclamation to be made on your behalf: "*The person of this man Aristippus is secure; let his going out and his coming in be free from danger*"? Is that the ground of your confidence? or do you rather rest secure in the consciousness that you would prove such a slave as no master would care to keep? For who would care to have in his house a fellow with so slight a disposition to work and so strong a propensity to extravagance? Suppose we stop and consider that very point: how do masters deal with that sort of domestic? If I am not mistaken, they chastise his wantonness by starvation; they balk his thieving tendencies by bars and bolts where there is anything to steal; they hinder him from running away by bonds and imprisonment; they drive the sluggishness out of him with the lash. Is it not so? Or how do you proceed when you discover the like tendency in one of your domestics?

---

[127] Or, "Well foiled!" "A masterly fall! my prince of wrestlers."
[128] For these mythical highway robbers, see Diod. iv. 59; and for Sciron in particular, Plut. *Theseus*, 10.
[129] Or, "where so many suffer wrong."

Ar. I correct them with all the plagues, till I force them to serve me properly. But, Socrates, to return to your pupil educated in the royal art,[130] which, if I mistake not, you hold to be happiness: how, may I ask, will he be better off than others who lie in evil case, in spite of themselves, simply because they suffer perforce, but in his case the hunger and the thirst, the cold shivers and the lying awake at nights, with all the changes he will ring on pain, are of his own choosing? For my part I cannot see what difference it makes, provided it is one and the same bare back which receives the stripes, whether the whipping be self-appointed or unasked for; nor indeed does it concern my body in general, provided it be my body, whether I am beleaguered by a whole armament of such evils[131] of my own will or against my will—except only for the folly which attaches to self-appointed suffering.

Soc. What, Aristippus, does it not seem to you that, as regards such matters, there is all the difference between voluntary and involuntary suffering, in that he who starves of his own accord can eat when he chooses, and he who thirsts of his own free will can drink, and so for the rest; but he who suffers in these ways perforce cannot desist from the suffering when the humour takes him? Again, he who suffers hardship voluntarily, gaily confronts his troubles, being buoyed on hope[132]—just as a hunter in pursuit of wild beasts, through hope of capturing his quarry, finds toil a pleasure—and these are but prizes of little worth in return for their labours; but what shall we say of their reward who toil to obtain to themselves good friends, or to subdue their enemies, or that through strength of body and soul they may administer their households well, befriend their friends, and benefit the land which gave them birth? Must we not suppose that these too will take their sorrows lightly, looking to these high ends? Must we not suppose that they too will gaily confront existence, who have to support them not only their conscious virtue, but the praise and admiration of the world?[133] And once more, habits of indolence, along with the fleeting pleasures of the moment, are incapable, as gymnastic trainers say, of setting up[134] a good habit of body, or of implanting in the soul any knowledge worthy of account; whereas by painstaking endeavour in the pursuit of high and noble deeds, as good men tell us, through endurance we shall in the end attain the goal. So Hesiod somewhere says:[135]

Wickedness may a man take wholesale with ease, smooth is the

---

[130] Cf. below, IV. ii. 11; Plat. *Statesm.* 259 B; *Euthyd.* 291 C; K. Joel, *op. cit.* p. 387 foll. "Aristippus anticipates Adeimantus" (*Rep.* 419), W. L. Newman, *op. cit.* i. 395.

[131] Cf. "suffers the slings and arrows of outrageous fortune."

[132] Cf. above, I. vi. 8.

[133] Or, "in admiration of themselves, the praise and envy of the world at large."

[134] See Hippocrates, *V. Med.* 18.

[135] Hesiod, *Works and Days*, 285. See Plat. *Prot.* 340 C; *Rep.* ii. 364 D; *Laws,* iv. 718 E.

Xenophon 39

way and her dwelling-place is very nigh; but in front of virtue the immortal gods have placed toil and sweat, long is the path and steep that leads to her, and rugged at the first, but when the summit of the pass is reached, then for all its roughness the path grows easy.

And Epicharmus[136] bears his testimony when he says:
The gods sell us all good things in return for our labours.

And again in another passage he exclaims:
Set not thine heart on soft things, thou knave, lest thou light upon the hard.

And that wise man Prodicus[137] delivers himself in a like strain concerning virtue in that composition of his about Heracles, which crowds have listened to.[138] This, as far as I can recollect it, is the substance at least of what he says:

"When Heracles was emerging from boyhood into the bloom of youth, having reached that season in which the young man, now standing upon the verge of independence, shows plainly whether he will enter upon the path of virtue or of vice, he went forth into a quiet place, and sat debating with himself which of those two paths he should pursue; and as he there sat musing, there appeared to him two women of great stature which drew nigh to him. The one was fair to look upon, frank and free by gift of nature,[139] her limbs adorned with purity and her eyes with bashfulness; sobriety set the rhythm of her gait, and she was clad in white apparel. The other was of a different type; the fleshy softness of her limbs betrayed her nurture, while the complexion of her skin was embellished that she might appear whiter and rosier than she really was, and her figure that she might seem taller than nature made her; she stared with wide-open eyes, and the raiment wherewith she was clad served but to reveal the ripeness of her bloom. With frequent glances she surveyed her person, or looked to see if others noticed her; while ever and anon she fixed her gaze upon the shadow of herself intently.

"Now when these two had drawn near to Heracles, she who was first named advanced at an even pace[140] towards him, but the other, in her eagerness to outstrip her, ran forward to the youth, exclaiming, 'I see you, Heracles, in doubt and difficulty what path of life to choose; make me your friend, and I will lead you to the pleasantest road and easiest. This I promise you: you shall taste all of life's sweets and

---

[136] Epicharmus of Cos, the chief comic poet among the Dorians, fl. 500 B.C. Cf. Plat. *Theaet.* 152 E, "the prince of comedy"; *Gorg.* 505 D.

[137] Prodicus of Ceos. See Plat. *Men.* 24; *Cratyl.* 1; Philostr. *Vit. Soph.* i. 12.

[138] Or, "which he is fond of reciting as a specimen of style." The title of the (epideixis) was ('Orai) according to Suidas, (Prodikos).

[139] Reading (eleutherion phusei,...) or if (eleutherion, phusei...) translate "nature had adorned her limbs..."

[140] Or, "without change in her demeanour."

escape all bitters. In the first place, you shall not trouble your brain with war or business; other topics shall engage your mind;[141] your only speculation, what meat or drink you shall find agreeable to your palate; what delight[142] of ear or eye; what pleasure of smell or touch; what darling lover's intercourse shall most enrapture you; how you shall pillow your limbs in softest slumber; how cull each individual pleasure without alloy of pain; and if ever the suspicion steal upon you that the stream of joys will one day dwindle, trust me I will not lead you where you shall replenish the store by toil of body and trouble of soul. No! others shall labour, but you shall reap the fruit of their labours; you shall withhold your hand from nought which shall bring you gain. For to all my followers I give authority and power to help themselves freely from every side.'

"Heracles hearing these words made answer: 'What, O lady, is the name you bear?' To which she: 'Know that my friends call be Happiness, but they that hate me have their own nicknames[143] for me, Vice and Naughtiness.'

"But just then the other of those fair women approached and spoke: 'Heracles, I too am come to you, seeing that your parents are well known to me, and in your nurture I have gauged your nature; wherefore I entertain good hope that if you choose the path which leads to me, you shall greatly bestir yourself to be the doer of many a doughty deed of noble emprise; and that I too shall be held in even higher honour for your sake, lit with the lustre shed by valorous deeds.[144] I will not cheat you with preludings of pleasure,[145] but I will relate to you the things that are according to the ordinances of God in very truth. Know then that among things that are lovely and of good report, not one have the gods bestowed upon mortal men apart from toil and pains. Would you obtain the favour of the gods, then must you pay these same gods service; would you be loved by your friends, you must benefit these friends; do you desire to be honoured by the state, you must give the state your aid; do you claim admiration for your virtue from all Hellas, you must strive to do some good to Hellas; do you wish earth to yield her fruits to you abundantly, to earth must you pay your court; do you seek to amass riches from your flocks and herds, on them must you bestow your labour; or is it your ambition to be potent as a warrior, able to save your friends and to subdue your foes, then

---

[141] Reading (diese), or (dioisei), "you shall continue speculating solely."

[142] It will be recollected that Prodicus prided himself on (orthotes onomaton). Possibly Xenophon is imitating (caricaturing?) his style. (terphtheies, estheies, euphrantheies).

[143] So the vulg. (upokorizomenoi) is interpreted. Cobet (*Pros. Xen.* p. 36) suggests (upoknizomenoi) = "quippe qui desiderio pungantur."

[144] Or, "bathed in the splendour of thy virtues."

[145] Or, "honeyed overtures of pleasure."

must you learn the arts of war from those who have the knowledge, and practise their application in the field when learned; or would you e'en be powerful of limb and body, then must you habituate limbs and body to obey the mind, and exercise yourself with toil and sweat.'

"At this point, (as Prodicus relates) Vice broke in exclaiming: 'See you, Heracles, how hard and long the road is by which yonder woman would escort you to her festal joys.[146] But I will guide you by a short and easy road to happiness.'

"Then spoke Virtue: 'Nay, wretched one, what good thing hast thou? or what sweet thing art thou acquainted with—that wilt stir neither hand nor foot to gain it? Thou, that mayest not even await the desire of pleasure, but, or ever that desire springs up, art already satiated; eating before thou hungerest, and drinking before thou thirsteth; who to eke out an appetite must invent an army of cooks and confectioners; and to whet thy thirst must lay down costliest wines, and run up and down in search of ice in summer-time; to help thy slumbers soft coverlets suffice not, but couches and feather-beds must be prepared thee and rockers to rock thee to rest; since desire for sleep in thy case springs not from toil but from vacuity and nothing in the world to do. Even the natural appetite of love thou forcest prematurely by every means thou mayest devise, confounding the sexes in thy service. Thus thou educatest thy friends: with insult in the night season and drowse of slumber during the precious hours of the day. Immortal, thou art cast forth from the company of gods, and by good men art dishonoured: that sweetest sound of all, the voice of praise, has never thrilled thine ears; and the fairest of all fair visions is hidden from thine eyes that have never beheld one bounteous deed wrought by thine own hand. If thou openest thy lips in speech, who will believe thy word? If thou hast need of aught, none shall satisfy thee. What sane man will venture to join thy rabble rout? Ill indeed are thy revellers to look upon, young men impotent of body, and old men witless in mind: in the heyday of life they batten in sleek idleness, and wearily do they drag through an age of wrinkled wretchedness: and why? they blush with shame at the thought of deeds done in the past, and groan for weariness at what is left to do. During their youth they ran riot through their sweet things, and laid up for themselves large store of bitterness against the time of eld. But my companionship is with the gods; and with the good among men my conversation; no bounteous deed, divine or human, is wrought without my aid. Therefore am I honoured in Heaven pre-eminently, and upon earth among men whose right it is to honour me;[147] as a beloved fellow-worker of all craftsmen; a faithful guardian of house and lands, whom the owners bless; a kindly helpmeet of

---

[146] Hesiod, *Theog.* 909; Milton, *L'Allegro*, 12.
[147] Reading (ois prosekei), or if (proseko), translate "to whom I am attached."

servants;[148] a brave assistant in the labours of peace; an unflinching ally in the deeds of war; a sharer in all friendships indispensable. To my friends is given an enjoyment of meats and drinks, which is sweet in itself and devoid of trouble, in that they can endure until desire ripens, and sleep more delicious visits them than those who toil not. Yet they are not pained to part with it; nor for the sake of slumber do they let slip the performance of their duties. Among my followers the youth delights in the praises of his elders, and the old man glories in the honour of the young; with joy they call to memory their deeds of old, and in to-day's well-doing are well pleased. For my sake they are dear in the sight of God, beloved of their friends and honoured by the country of their birth. When the appointed goal is reached they lie not down in oblivion with dishonour, but bloom afresh—their praise resounded on the lips of men for ever.[149] Toils like these, O son of noble parents, Heracles, it is yours to meet with, and having endured, to enter into the heritage assured you of transcendent happiness.'"

This, Aristippus, in rough sketch is the theme which Prodicus pursues[150] in his "Education of Heracles by Virtue," only he decked out his sentiments, I admit, in far more magnificent phrases than I have ventured on. Were it not well, Aristippus, to lay to heart these sayings, and to strive to bethink you somewhat of that which touches the future of our life?

II

At another time, he had noticed the angry temper shown by Lamprocles, the elder of his sons, towards their mother, and thus addressed himself to the lad.

Soc. Pray, my son, did you ever hear of certain people being called ungrateful?

That I have (replied the young man).

Soc. And have you understood what it is they do to get that bad name?

Lamp. Yes, I have: when any one has been kindly treated, and has it in his power to requite the kindness but neglects to do so, men call him ungrateful.

Soc. And you admit that people reckon the ungrateful among wrongdoers?

Lamp. I do.

Soc. And has it ever struck you to inquire whether, as regards the right or wrong of it, ingratitude may not perhaps resemble some such

---

[148] Cf. "Econ." v. 8.
[149] Or, "so true is it, a branch is left them; undying honour to their name!"
[150] Reading (diokei), al. (diokei) = "so Prodicus arranged the parts of his discourse."

conduct as the enslavement, say, of prisoners, which is accounted wrong towards friends but justifiable towards enemies?

Lamp. Yes, I have put that question to myself. In my opinion, no matter who confers the kindness, friend or foe, the recipient should endeavour to requite it, failing which he is a wrongdoer.

Soc. Then if that is how the matter stands, ingratitude would be an instance of pure unadulterate wrongdoing?

Lamprocles assented to the proposition.

Soc. It follows, then, that in proportion to the greatness of the benefit conferred, the greater his misdoing who fails to requite the kindness?

Lamprocles again assented.

Socrates continued: And where can we hope to find greater benefits than those which children derive from their parents—their father and mother who brought them out of nothingness into being, who granted them to look upon all these fair sights, and to partake of all those blessings which the gods bestow on man, things so priceless in our eyes that one and all we shudder at the thought of leaving them, and states have made death the penalty for the greatest crimes, because there is no greater evil through fear of which to stay iniquity.

You do not suppose that human beings produce children for the sake of carnal pleasure[151] merely; were this the motive, street and bordell are full of means to quit them of that thrall; whereas nothing is plainer than the pains we take to seek out wives who shall bear us the finest children.[152] With these we wed, and carry on the race. The man has a twofold duty to perform: partly in cherishing her who is to raise up children along with him, and partly towards the children yet unborn in providing them with things that he thinks will contribute to their well-being—and of these as large a store as possible. The woman, conceiving, bears her precious burthen with travail and pain, and at the risk of life itself—sharing with that within her womb the food on which she herself is fed. And when with much labour she has borne to the end and brought forth her offspring, she feeds it and watches over it with tender care—not in return for any good thing previously received, for indeed the babe itself is little conscious of its benefactor and cannot even signify its wants; only she, the mother, making conjecture of what is good for it, and what will please it, essays to satisfy it;[153] and for many months she feeds it night and day, enduring the toil nor recking what return she shall receive for all her trouble. Nor does the care and kindness of parents end with nurture; but when the children seem of an age to learn, they teach them themselves whatever cunning they

---

[151] Lit. "the joys of Aphrodite."
[152] "For the procreation of children." See below, IV. iv. 22; *Pol. Lac.* i.
[153] Lit. "to leave nought lacking."

possess, as a guide to life, or where they feel that another is more competent, to him they send them to be taught at their expense. Thus they watch over their children, doing all in their power to enable them to grow up to be as good as possible.

So be it (the youth answered); but even if she have done all that, and twenty times as much, no soul on earth could endure my mother's cross-grained temper.

Then Socrates: Which, think you, would be harder to bear—a wild beast's savagery or a mother's?

Lamp. To my mind, a mother's—at least if she be such as mine.

Soc. Dear me! And has this mother ever done you any injury—such as people frequently receive from beasts, by bite or kick?

Lamp. If she has not done quite that, she uses words which any one would sooner sell his life than listen to.

Soc. And how many annoyances have you caused your mother, do you suppose, by fretfulness and peevishness in word and deed, night and day, since you were a little boy? How much sorrow and pain, when you were ill?

Lamp. Well, I never said or did anything to bring a blush to her cheeks.

Soc. No, come now! Do you suppose it is harder for you to listen to your mother's speeches than for actor to listen to actor on the tragic stage,[154] when the floodgates of abuse are opened?

Lamp. Yes; for the simple reason that they know it is all talk on their parts. The inquisitor may cross-question, but he will not inflict a fine; the threatener may hurl his menaces, but he will do no mischief—that is why they take it all so easily.

Soc. Then ought you to fly into a passion, who know well enough that, whatever your mother says, she is so far from meaning you mischief that she is actually wishing blessings to descend upon you beyond all others? Or do you believe that your mother is really ill disposed towards you?

Lamp. No, I do not think that.

Soc. Then this mother, who is kindly disposed to you, and takes such tender care of you when you are ill to make you well again, and to see that you want for nothing which may help you; and, more than all, who is perpetually pleading for blessings in your behalf and offering her vows to Heaven[155]—can you say of her that she is cross-grained and harsh? For my part, I think, if you cannot away with such a mother, you cannot away with such blessings either.

But tell me (he proceeded), do you owe service to any living being, think you? or are you prepared to stand alone? Prepared not to please or

---

[154] See Grote, *H. G.* viii. 457; Plut. *Solon*, xxix.
[155] Or, "paying vows."

try to please a single soul? to follow none? To obey neither general nor ruler of any sort? Is that your attitude, or do you admit that you owe allegiance to somebody?

Lamp. Yes; certainly I owe allegiance.

Soc. May I take it that you are willing to please at any rate your neighbour, so that he may kindle a fire for you in your need, may prove himself a ready helpmate in good fortune, or if you chance on evil and are stumbling, may friendlily stand by your side to aid?

Lamp. I am willing.

Soc. Well, and what of that other chance companion—your fellow-traveller by land or sea? what of any others, you may light upon? is it indifferent to you whether these be friends or not, or do you admit that the goodwill of these is worth securing by some pains on your part?

Lamp. I do.

Soc. It stands thus then: you are prepared to pay attention to this, that, and the other stranger, but to your mother who loves you more than all else, you are bound to render no service, no allegiance? Do you not know that whilst the state does not concern itself with ordinary ingratitude or pass judicial sentence on it; whilst it overlooks the thanklessness of those who fail to make return for kindly treatment, it reserves its pains and penalties for the special case? If a man render not the service and allegiance due to his parents, on him the finger of the law is laid; his name is struck off the roll; he is forbidden to hold the archonship—which is as much as to say, "Sacrifices in behalf of the state offered by such a man would be no offerings, being tainted with impiety; nor could aught else be 'well and justly' performed of which he is the doer." Heaven help us! If a man fail to adorn the sepulchre of his dead parents the state takes cognisance of the matter, and inquisition is made in the scrutiny of the magistrates.[156] And as for you, my son, if you are in your sober senses, you will earnestly entreat your mother, lest the very gods take you to be an ungrateful being, and on their side also refuse to do you good; and you will beware of men also, lest they should perceive your neglect of your parents, and with one consent hold you in dishonour;[157] and so you find yourself in a desert devoid of friends. For if once the notion be entertained that here is a man ungrateful to his parents, no one will believe that any kindness shown you would be other than thrown away.

---

[156] Lit. "the *docimasia.*" See Gow, *Companion,* xiv.
[157] "Visit with *atimia.*"

III

At another time the differences between two brothers named Chaerephon and Chaerecrates, both well known to him, had drawn his attention; and on seeing the younger of the two he thus addressed him.

Soc. Tell me, Chaerecrates, you are not, I take it, one of those strange people who believe that goods are better and more precious than a brother;[158] and that too although the former are but senseless chattels which need protection, the latter a sensitive and sensible being who can afford it; and what is more, he is himself alone, whilst as for them their name is legion. And here again is a marvellous thing: that a man should count his brother a loss, because the goods of his brother are not his; but he does not count his fellow-citizens loss, and yet their possessions are not his; only it seems in their case he has wits to see that to dwell securely with many and have enough is better than to own the whole wealth of a community and to live in dangerous isolation; but this same doctrine as applied to brothers they ignore. Again, if a man have the means, he will purchase domestic slaves, because he wants assistants in his work; he will acquire friends, because he needs their support; but this brother of his—who cares about brothers? It seems a friend may be discovered in an ordinary citizen, but not in a blood relation who is also a brother. And yet it is a great vantage-ground towards friendship to have sprung from the same loins and to have been suckled at the same breasts, since even among beasts a certain natural craving, and sympathy springs up between creatures reared together.[159] Added to which, a man who has brothers commands more respect from the rest of the world than the man who has none, and who must fight his own battles.[160]

Chaer. I daresay, Socrates, where the differences are not profound, reason would a man should bear with his brother, and not avoid him for some mere trifle's sake, for a brother of the right sort is, as you say, a blessing; but if he be the very antithesis of that, why should a man lay his hand to achieve the impossible?

Soc. Well now, tell me, is there nobody whom Chaerephon can please any more than he can please yourself; or do some people find him agreeable enough?

Chaer. Nay, there you hit it. That is just why I have a right to detest him. He can be pleasing enough to others, but to me, whenever he appears on the scene, he is not a blessing—no! but by every manner

---

[158] Cf. *Merchant of Venice*, II. viii. 17: "Justice! the law! my ducats, and my daughter!"

[159] Or, "a yearning after their foster-brothers manifests itself in animals." See *Cyrop.* VIII. vii. 14 foll. for a parallel to this discussion.

[160] Lit. "and is less liable to hostility."

of means the reverse.

Soc. May it not happen that just as a horse is no gain to the inexpert rider who essays to handle him, so in like manner, if a man tries to deal with his brother after an ignorant fashion, this same brother will kick?

Chaer. But is it likely now? How should I be ignorant of the art of dealing with my brother if I know the art of repaying kind words and good deeds in kind? But a man who tries all he can to annoy me by word and deed, I can neither bless nor benefit, and, what is more, I will not try.

Soc. Well now, that is a marvellous statement, Chaerecrates. Your dog, the serviceable guardian of your flocks, who will fawn and lick the hand of your shepherd, when you come near him can only growl and show his teeth. Well; you take no notice of the dog's ill-temper, you try to propitiate him by kindness; but your brother? If your brother were what he ought to be, he would be a great blessing to you—that you admit; and, as you further confess, you know the secret of kind acts and words, yet you will not set yourself to apply means to make him your best of friends.

Chaer. I am afraid, Socrates, that I have no wisdom or cunning to make Chaerephon bear himself towards me as he should.

Soc. Yet there is no need to apply any recondite or novel machinery. Only bait your hook in the way best known to yourself, and you will capture him; whereupon he will become your devoted friend.

Chaer. If you are aware that I know some love-charm, Socrates, of which I am the happy but unconscious possessor, pray make haste and enlighten me.

Soc. Answer me then. Suppose you wanted to get some acquaintance to invite you to dinner when he next keeps holy day,[161] what steps would you take?

Chaer. No doubt I should set him a good example by inviting him myself on a like occasion.

Soc. And if you wanted to induce some friend to look after your affairs during your absence abroad, how would you achieve your purpose?

Chaer. No doubt I should present a precedent in undertaking to look after his in like circumstances.

Soc. And if you wished to get some foreign friend to take you under his roof while visiting his country, what would you do?

Chaer. No doubt I should begin by offering him the shelter of my own roof when he came to Athens, in order to enlist his zeal in furthering the objects of my visit; it is plain I should first show my

---

[161] "When he next does sacrifice"; see *Hiero*, viii. 3. Cf. Theophr. *Char.* xv. 2, and Prof. Jebb's note *ad loc.*

readiness to do as much for him in a like case.

Soc. Why, it seems you are an adept after all in all the philtres known to man, only you chose to conceal your knowledge all the while; or is it that you shrink from taking the first step because of the scandal you will cause by kindly advances to your brother? And yet it is commonly held to redound to a man's praise to have outstripped an enemy in mischief or a friend in kindness. Now if it seemed to me that Chaerephon were better fitted to lead the way towards this friendship,[162] I should have tried to persuade him to take the first step in winning your affection, but now I am persuaded the first move belongs to you, and to you the final victory.

Chaer. A startling announcement, Socrates, from your lips, and most unlike you, to bid me the younger take precedence of my elder brother. Why, it is contrary to the universal custom of mankind, who look to the elder to take the lead in everything, whether as a speaker or an actor.

Soc. How so? Is it not the custom everywhere for the younger to step aside when he meets his elder in the street and to give him place? Is he not expected to get up and offer him his seat, to pay him the honour of a soft couch,[163] to yield him precedence in argument?

My good fellow, do not stand shilly-shallying,[164] but put out your hand caressingly, and you will see the worthy soul will respond at once with alacrity. Do you not note your brother's character, proud and frank and sensitive to honour? He is not a mean and sorry rascal to be caught by a bribe—no better way indeed for such riff-raff. No! gentle natures need a finer treatment. You can best hope to work on them by affection.

Chaer. But suppose I do, and suppose that, for all my attempts, he shows no change for the better?

Soc. At the worst you will have shown yourself to be a good, honest, brotherly man, and he will appear as a sorry creature on whom kindness is wasted. But nothing of the sort is going to happen, as I conjecture. My belief is that as soon as he hears your challenge, he will embrace the contest; pricked on by emulous pride, he will insist upon getting the better of you in kindness of word and deed.

At present you two are in the condition of two hands formed by God to help each other, but which have let go their business and have turned to hindering one another all they can. You are a pair of feet fashioned on the Divine plan to work together, but which have neglected this in order to trammel each other's gait. Now is it not insensate stupidity[165] to use for injury what was meant for advantage? And yet in fashioning two brothers God intends them, methinks, to be

---

[162] Reading (pros ten philian), or if (phusin), transl. "natural disposition."

[163] Lit. "with a soft bed," or, as we say, "the best bedroom."

[164] Or, "have no fears, essay a soothing treatment."

[165] "Boorishness verging upon monomania."

of more benefit to one another than either two hands, or two feet, or two eyes, or any other of those pairs which belong to man from his birth.[166] Consider how powerless these hands of ours if called upon to combine their action at two points more than a single fathom's length apart;[167] and these feet could not stretch asunder[168] even a bare fathom; and these eyes, for all the wide-reaching range we claim for them, are incapable of seeing simultaneously the back and front of an object at even closer quarters. But a pair of brothers, linked in bonds of amity, can work each for the other's good, though seas divide them.[169]

IV

I have at another time heard him discourse on the kindred theme of friendship in language well calculated, as it seemed to me, to help a man to choose and also to use his friends aright.

He (Socrates) had often heard the remark made that of all possessions there is none equal to that of a good and sincere friend; but, in spite of this assertion, the mass of people, as far as he could see, concerned themselves about nothing so little as the acquisition of friends. Houses, and fields, and slaves, and cattle, and furniture of all sorts (he said) they were at pains to acquire, and they strove hard to keep what they had got; but to procure for themselves this greatest of all blessings, as they admitted a friend to be, or to keep the friends whom they already possessed, not one man in a hundred ever gave himself a thought. It was noticeable, in the case of a sickness befalling a man's friend and one of his own household simultaneously, the promptness with which the master would fetch the doctor to his domestic, and take every precaution necessary for his recovery, with much expenditure of pains; but meanwhile little account would be taken of the friend in like condition, and if both should die, he will show signs of deep annoyance at the death of his domestic, which, as he reflects, is a positive loss to him; but as regards his friend his position is in no wise materially affected, and thus, though he would never dream of leaving his other possessions disregarded and ill cared for, friendship's mute appeal is met with flat indifference.[170]

Or to take (said he) a crowning instance:[171] with regard to ordinary possessions, however multifarious these may be, most people are at least acquainted with their number, but if you ask a man to enumerate

---

[166] "With which man is endowed at birth."
[167] "More than an 'arms'-stretch' asunder."
[168] Lit. "reach at one stretch two objects, even over that small distance."
[169] "Though leagues separate them."
[170] Or, "the cry of a friend for careful tending falls on deaf ears."
[171] Or, "Nor had he failed to observe another striking contrast." Cf. Cic. *Lael.* 17; Diog. Laert. ii. 30.

his friends, who are not so very many after all perhaps, he cannot; or if, to oblige the inquirer, he essays to make a list, he will presently retract the names of some whom he had previously included.[172] Such is the amount of thought which people bestow upon their friends.

And yet what thing else may a man call his own is comparable to this one best possession! what rather will not serve by contrast to enhance the value of an honest friend! Think of a horse or a yoke of oxen; they have their worth; but who shall gauge the worth of a worthy friend? Kindlier and more constant than the faithfullest of slaves—this is that possession best named all-serviceable.[173] Consider what the post is that he assigns himself! to meet and supplement what is lacking to the welfare of his friends, to promote their private and their public interests, is his concern. Is there need of kindly action in any quarter? he will throw in the full weight of his support. Does some terror confound? he is at hand to help and defend by expenditure of money and of energy,[174] by appeals to reason or resort to force. His the privilege alike to gladden the prosperous in the hour of success and to sustain their footing who have well-nigh slipped. All that the hands of a man may minister, all that the eyes of each are swift to see, the ears to hear, and the feet to compass, he with his helpful arts will not fall short of. Nay, not seldom that which a man has failed to accomplish for himself, has missed seeing or hearing or attaining, a friend acting in behalf of friend will achieve vicariously. And yet, albeit to try and tend a tree for the sake of its fruit is not uncommon, this copious mine of wealth—this friend—attracts only a lazy and listless attention on the part of more than half the world.

V

I remember listening to another argument of his, the effect of which would be to promote self-examination. The listener must needs be brought to ask himself, "Of what worth am I to my friends?" It happened thus. One of those who were with him was neglectful, as he noted, of a friend who was at the pinch of poverty (Antisthenes).[175] Accordingly, in the presence of the negligent person and of several others, he proceeded to question the sufferer.

Soc. What say you, Antisthenes?—have friends their values like domestic slaves? One of these latter may be worth perhaps two

---

[172] *i.e.* "like a chess-player recalling a move."
[173] "A vessel fit for all work indeed is this friend." Cf. *Ar. Ach.* 936, (pagkhreston aggos estai), like the "leather bottel."
[174] Or, "by dint of his diplomacy."
[175] Antisthenes, "cynicorum et stoicorum parens." Cic. *de Or.* iii. 17; *ad Att.* xii. 38. See below, *Mem.* III. iii. 17; *Symp.* passim; Diog. Laert. II. v.; VI. i.

minae,[176] another only half a mina, a third five, and a fourth as much as ten; while they do say that Nicias,[177] the son of Niceratus, paid a whole talent for a superintendent of his silver mines. And so I propound the question to myself as follows: "Have friends, like slaves, their market values?"

Not a doubt of it (replied Antisthenes). At any rate, I know that I would rather have such a one as my friend than be paid two minae, and there is such another whose worth I would not estimate at half a mina, and a third with whom I would not part for ten, and then again a fourth whose friendship would be cheap if it cost me all the wealth and pains in the world to purchase it.

Well then (continued Socrates), if that be so, would it not be well if every one were to examine himself: "What after all may I chance to be worth to my friends?" Should he not try to become as dear as possible, so that his friends will not care to give him up? How often do I hear the complaint: "My friend So-and-so has given me up"; or "Such an one, whom I looked upon as a friend, has sacrificed me for a mina." And every time I hear these remarks, the question arises in my mind: If the vendor of a worthless slave is ready to part with him to a purchaser for what he will fetch—is there not at least a strong temptation to part with a base friend when you have a chance of making something on the exchange? Good slaves, as far as I can see, are not so knocked down to the hammer; no, nor good friends so lightly parted with.

VI

Again, in reference to the test to be applied, if we would gauge the qualifications of a friend worth the winning, the following remarks of Socrates could not fail, I think, to prove instructive.[178]

Tell me (said Socrates, addressing Critobulus), supposing we stood in need of a good friend, how should we set about his discovery? We must, in the first place, I suppose, seek out one who is master of his appetites, not under the dominion, that is, of his belly, not addicted to the wine-cup or to lechery or sleep or idleness, since no one enslaved to such tyrants could hope to do his duty either by himself or by his friends, could he?

Certainly not (Critobulus answered).

Soc. Do you agree, then, that we must hold aloof from every one so dominated?

---

[176] A mina = £4 *circ.*

[177] For Nicias see Thuc. vii. 77 foll.; *Revenues*, iv. 14; Plut. *Nic.* IV. v.; Lys. *de bon. Aristoph.* 648.

[178] Or, "Again, as to establishing a test of character, since a friend worth having must be of a particular type, I cannot but think that the following remarks would prove instructive."

Cri. Most assuredly.

Well then (proceeded Socrates), what shall we say of the spendthrift who has lost his independence and is for ever begging of his neighbours; if he gets anything out of them he cannot repay, but if he fails to get anything, he hates you for not giving—do you not think that this man too would prove but a disagreeable friend?

Cri. Certainly.

Soc. Then we must keep away from him too?

Cri. That we must.

Soc. Well! and what of the man whose strength lies in monetary transactions?[179] His one craving is to amass money; and for that reason he is an adept at driving a hard bargain[180]—glad enough to take in, but loath to pay out.

Cri. In my opinion he will prove even a worse fellow than the last.

Soc. Well! and what of that other whose passion for money-making is so absorbing that he has no leisure for anything else, save how he may add to his gains?

Cri. Hold aloof from him, say I, since there is no good to be got out of him or his society.

Soc. Well! what of the quarrelsome and factious person[181] whose main object is to saddle his friends with a host of enemies?

Cri. For God's sake let us avoid him also.

Soc. But now we will imagine a man exempt indeed from all the above defects—a man who has no objection to receive kindnesses, but it never enters into his head to do a kindness in return.

Cri. There will be no good in him either. But, Socrates, what kind of man shall we endeavour to make our friend? what is he like?

Soc. I should say he must be just the converse of the above: he has control over the pleasures of the body, he is kindly disposed,[182] upright in all his dealings,[183] very zealous is he not to be outdone in kindness by his benefactors, if only his friends may derive some profit from his acquaintance.

Cri. But how are we to test these qualities, Socrates, before acquaintance?

Soc. How do we test the merits of a sculptor?—not by inferences drawn from the talk of the artist merely. No, we look to what he has already achieved. These former statues of his were nobly executed, and we trust he will do equally well with the rest.

Cri. You mean that if we find a man whose kindness to older friends is established, we may take it as proved that he will treat his

---

[179] Or, "the money-lender? He has a passion for big money-bags."
[180] Or, "hard in all his dealings."
[181] "The partisan."
[182] Reading (eunous), or if (euorkos), transl. "a man of his word."
[183] Or, "easy to deal with."

newer friends as amiably?

Soc. Why, certainly, if I see a man who has shown skill in the handling of horses previously, I argue that he will handle others no less skilfully again.

Cri. Good! and when we have discovered a man whose friendship is worth having, how ought we to make him our friend?

Soc. First we ought to ascertain the will of Heaven whether it be advisable to make him our friend.

Cri. Well! and how are we to effect the capture of this friend of our choice, whom the gods approve? will you tell me that?

Not, in good sooth (replied Socrates), by running him down like a hare, nor by decoying him like a bird, or by force like a wild boar.[184] To capture a friend against his will is a toilsome business, and to bind him in fetters like a slave by no means easy. Those who are so treated are apt to become foes instead of friends.[185]

Cri. But how convert them into friends?

Soc. There are certain incantations, we are told, which those who know them have only to utter, and they can make friends of whom they list; and there are certain philtres also which those who have the secret of them may administer to whom they like and win their love.

Cri. From what source shall we learn them?

Soc. You need not go farther than Homer to learn that which the Sirens sang to Odysseus,[186] the first words of which run, I think, as follows:

Hither, come hither, thou famous man, Odysseus, great glory of the Achaeans!

Cri. And did the magic words of this spell serve for all men alike? Had the Sirens only to utter this one incantation, and was every listener constrained to stay?

Soc. No; this was the incantation reserved for souls athirst for fame, of virtue emulous.

Cri. Which is as much as to say, we must suit the incantation to the listener, so that when he hears the words he shall not think that the enchanter is laughing at him in his sleeve. I cannot certainly conceive a method better calculated to excite hatred and repulsion than to go to some one who knows that he is small and ugly and a weakling, and to breathe in his ears the flattering tale that he is beautiful and tall and stalwart. But do you know any other love-charms, Socrates?

Soc. I cannot say that I do; but I have heard that Pericles[187] was skilled in not a few, which he poured into the ear of our city and won her love.

---

[184] Reading (kaproi), al. (ekhthroi), "an enemy."
[185] Or, "Hate rather than friendship is the outcome of these methods."
[186] *Od.* xii. 184.
[187] See above, I. ii. 40; *Symp.* viii. 39.

Cri. And how did Themistocles[188] win our city's love?

Soc. Ah, that was not by incantation at all. What he did was to encircle our city with an amulet of saving virtue.[189]

Cri. You would imply, Socrates, would you not, that if we want to win the love of any good man we need to be good ourselves in speech and action?

And did you imagine (replied Socrates) that it was possible for a bad man to make good friends?

Cri. Why, I could fancy I had seen some sorry speech-monger who was fast friends with a great and noble statesman; or again, some born commander and general who was boon companion with fellows quite incapable of generalship.[190]

Soc. But in reference to the point we were discussing, may I ask whether you know of any one who can attach a useful friend to himself without being of use in return?[191] Can service ally in friendship with disservice?

Cri. In good sooth no. But now, granted it is impossible for a base man to be friends with the beautiful and noble,[192] I am concerned at once to discover if one who is himself of a beautiful and noble character can, with a wave of the hand, as it were, attach himself in friendship to every other beautiful and noble nature.

Soc. What perplexes and confounds you, Critobulus, is the fact that so often men of noble conduct, with souls aloof from baseness, are not friends but rather at strife and discord with one another, and deal more harshly by one another than they would by the most good-for-nothing of mankind.

Cri. Yes, and this holds true not of private persons only, but states, the most eager to pursue a noble policy and to repudiate a base one, are frequently in hostile relation to one another. As I reason on these things my heart fails me, and the question, how friends are to be acquired, fills me with despondency. The bad, as I see, cannot be friends with one another. For how can such people, the ungrateful, or reckless, or covetous, or faithless, or incontinent, adhere together as friends? Without hesitation I set down the bad as born to be foes not friends, and as bearing the birthmark of internecine hate. But then again, as you suggest, no more can these same people harmonise in friendship with the good. For how should they who do evil be friends with those who

---

[188] See below, III. vi. 2; IV. ii. 2.

[189] See Herod. vii. 143, "the wooden wall"; Thuc. i. 93, "'the walls' of Athens."

[190] Or, "Why, yes, when I see some base orator fast friends with a great leader of the people; or, again, some fellow incapable of generalship a comrade to the greatest captains of his age."

[191] Add, "Can service ally in friendship with disservice? Must there not be a reciprocity of service to make friendship lasting?"

[192] (kalous kagathous).

hate all evil-doing? And if, last of all, they that cultivate virtue are torn by party strife in their struggle for the headship of the states, envying one another, hating one another, who are left to be friends? where shall goodwill and faithfulness be found among men?

Soc. The fact is there is some subtlety in the texture of these things.[193] Seeds of love are implanted in man by nature. Men have need of one another, feel pity, help each other by united efforts, and in recognition of the fact show mutual gratitude. But there are seeds of war implanted also. The same objects being regarded as beautiful or agreeable by all alike, they do battle for their possession; a spirit of disunion[194] enters, and the parties range themselves in adverse camps. Discord and anger sound a note of war: the passion of more-having, staunchless avarice, threatens hostility; and envy is a hateful fiend.[195]

But nevertheless, through all opposing barriers friendship steals her way and binds together the beautiful and good among mankind.[196] Such is their virtue that they would rather possess scant means painlessly than wield an empire won by war. In spite of hunger and thirst they will share their meat and drink without a pang. Not bloom of lusty youth, nor love's delights can warp their self-control; nor will they be tempted to cause pain where pain should be unknown. It is theirs not merely to eschew all greed of riches, not merely to make a just and lawful distribution of wealth, but to supply what is lacking to the needs of one another. Theirs it is to compose strife and discord not in painless oblivion simply, but to the general advantage. Theirs also to hinder such extravagance of anger as shall entail remorse hereafter. And as to envy they will make a clean sweep and clearance of it: the good things which a man possesses shall be also the property of his friends, and the goods which they possess are to be looked upon as his. Where then is the improbability that the beautiful and noble should be sharers in the honours[197] of the state not only without injury, but even to their mutual advantage?

They indeed who covet and desire the honours and offices in a state for the sake of the liberty thereby given them to embezzle the public moneys, to deal violently by their fellow-creatures, and to batten in luxury themselves, may well be regarded as unjust and villainous persons incapable of harmony with one another. But if a man desire to obtain these selfsame honours in order that, being himself secure against wrong-doing, he may be able to assist his friends in what is right, and, raised to a high position,[198] may essay to confer some

---

[193] *i.e.* a cunning intertwining of the threads of warp and woof.
[194] Cf. Shelley, "The devil of disunion in their souls."
[195] The diction is poetical.
[196] Or, as we say, "the elite of human kind."
[197] "And the offices."
[198] "As archon," or "raised to rule."

blessing on the land of his fathers, what is there to hinder him from working in harmony with some other of a like spirit? Will he, with the "beautiful and noble" at his side, be less able to aid his friends? or will his power to benefit the community be shortened because the flower of that community are fellow-workers in that work? Why, even in the contests of the games it is obvious that if it were possible for the stoutest combatants to combine against the weakest, the chosen band would come off victors in every bout, and would carry off all the prizes. This indeed is against the rules of the actual arena; but in the field of politics, where the beautiful and good hold empery, and there is nought to hinder any from combining with whomsoever a man may choose to benefit the state, it will be a clear gain, will it not, for any one engaged in state affairs to make the best men his friends, whereby he will find partners and co-operators in his aims instead of rivals and antagonists? And this at least is obvious: in case of foreign war a man will need allies, but all the more if in the ranks opposed to him should stand the flower of the enemy.[199] Moreover, those who are willing to fight your battles must be kindly dealt with, that goodwill may quicken to enthusiasm; and one good man[200] is better worth your benefiting that a dozen knaves, since a little kindness goes a long way with the good, but with the base the more you give them the more they ask for.

So keep a good heart, Critobulus; only try to become good yourself, and when you have attained, set to your hand to capture the beautiful and good. Perhaps I may be able to give you some help in this quest, being myself an adept in Love's lore.[201] No matter who it is for whom my heart is aflame; in an instant my whole soul is eager to leap forth. With vehemence I speed to the mark. I, who love, demand to be loved again; this desire in me must be met by counter desire in him; this thirst for his society by thirst reciprocal for mine. And these will be your needs also, I foresee, whenever you are seized with longing to contract a friendship. Do not hide from me, therefore, whom you would choose as a friend, since, owing to the pains I take to please him who pleases me, I am not altogether unversed, I fancy, in the art of catching men.[202]

Critobulus replied: Why, these are the very lessons of instruction, Socrates, for which I have been long athirst, and the more particularly if this same love's lore will enable me to capture those who are good of soul and those who are beautiful of person.

Soc. Nay, now I warn you, Critobulus, it is not within the province of my science to make the beautiful endure him who would lay hands upon them. And that is why men fled from Scylla, I am persuaded,

---

[199] Lit. "the beautiful and good."
[200] Or, "the best, though few, are better worth your benefiting than the many base."
[201] "An authority in matters of love." Cf. Plat. *Symp.* 177 D; Xen. *Symp.* viii. 2.
[202] See below, III. xi. 7; cf. Plat. *Soph.* 222; N. T. Matt. iv. 19, (alieis anthropon).

because she laid hands upon them; but the Sirens were different—they laid hands on nobody, but sat afar off and chanted their spells in the ears of all; and therefore, it is said, all men endured to listen, and were charmed.

Cri. I promise I will not lay violent hands on any; therefore, if you have any good device for winning friends, instruct your pupil.

Soc. And if there is to be no laying on of the hands, there must be no application either of the lips; is it agreed?

Cri. No, nor application of the lips to any one—not beautiful.

Soc. See now! you cannot open your mouth without some luckless utterance. Beauty suffers no such liberty, however eagerly the ugly may invite it, making believe some quality of soul must rank them with the beautiful.

Cri. Be of good cheer then; let the compact stand thus: "Kisses for the beautiful, and for the good a rain of kisses." So now teach us the art of catching friends.

Soc. Well then, when you wish to win some one's affection, you will allow me to lodge information against you to the effect that you admire him and desire to be his friend?

Cri. Lodge the indictment, with all my heart. I never heard of any one who hated his admirers.

Soc. And if I add to the indictment the further charge that through your admiration you are kindly disposed towards him, you will not feel I am taking away your character?

Cri. Why, no; for myself I know a kindly feeling springs up in my heart towards any one whom I conceive to be kindly disposed to me.

Soc. All this I shall feel empowered to say about you to those whose friendship you seek, and I can promise further help; only there is a comprehensive "if" to be considered: if you will further authorise me to say that you are devoted to your friends; that nothing gives you so much joy as a good friend; that you pride yourself no less on the fine deeds of those you love than on your own; and on their good things equally with your own; that you never weary of plotting and planning to procure them a rich harvest of the same; and lastly, that you have discovered a man's virtue is to excel his friends in kindness and his foes in hostility. If I am authorised thus to report of you, I think you will find me a serviceable fellow-hunter in the quest of friends, which is the conquest of the good.

Cri. Why this appeal to me?—as if you had not free permission to say exactly what you like about me.

Soc. No; that I deny, on the authority of Aspasia.[203] I have it from

---

[203] Aspasia, daughter of Axiochus, of Miletus. See *Econ.* iii. 14; Plat. *Menex.* 235 E; Aesch. Socrat. ap. Cic. *de Invent.* I. xxxi. 51. See Grote, *H. G.* vi. 132 foll.; Cobet, *Pros. Xen.*

her own lips. "Good matchmakers," she said tome, "were clever hands at cementing alliances between people, provided the good qualities they vouched for were truthfully reported; but when it came to their telling lies, for her part she could not compliment them.[204] Their poor deluded dupes ended by hating each other and the go-betweens as well." Now I myself am so fully persuaded of the truth of this that I feel it is not in my power to say aught in your praise which I cannot say with truth.

Cri. Really, Socrates, you are a wonderfully good friend to me—in so far as I have any merit which will entitle me to win a friend, you will lend me a helping hand, it seems; otherwise you would rather not forge any petty fiction for my benefit.

Soc. But tell me, how shall I assist you best, think you? By praising you falsely or by persuading you to try to be a good man? Or if it is not plain to you thus, look at the matter by the light of some examples. I wish to introduce you to a shipowner, or to make him your friend: I begin by singing your praises to him falsely thus, "You will find him a good pilot"; he catches at the phrase, and entrusts his ship to you, who have no notion of guiding a vessel. What can you expect but to make shipwreck of the craft and yourself together? or suppose by similar false assertions I can persuade the state at large to entrust her destinies to you—"a man with a fine genius for command," I say, "a practised lawyer," "a politician born," and so forth. The odds are, the state and you may come to grief through you. Or to take an instance from everyday life. By my falsehoods I persuade some private person to entrust his affairs to you as "a really careful and business-like person with a head for economy." When put to the test would not your administration prove ruinous, and the figure you cut ridiculous? No, my dear friend, there is but one road, the shortest, safest, best, and it is simply this: *In whatsoever you desire to be deemed good, endeavour to be good.* For of all the virtues namable among men, consider, and you will find there is not one but may be increased by learning and practice. For my part then, Critobulus, these are the principles on which we ought to go a-hunting; but if you take a different view, I am all attention, please instruct me.

Then Critobulus: Nay, Socrates, I should be ashamed to gainsay what you have said; if I did, it would neither be a noble statement nor a true.[205]

---

[204] Reading (ouk ethelein epainein), or if (ouk ophelein epainousas) with Kühner transl. "Good matchmakers, she told me, have to consult truth when reporting favourably of any one: then indeed they are terribly clever at bringing people together: whereas false flatterers do no good; their dupes," etc.

[205] (kala... alethe).

VII

He had two ways of dealing with the difficulties of his friends: where ignorance was the cause, he tried to meet the trouble by a dose of common sense; or where want and poverty were to blame, by lessoning them that they should assist one another according to their ability; and here I may mention certain incidents which occurred within my own knowledge. How, for instance, he chanced upon Aristarchus wearing the look of one who suffered from a fit of the "sullens," and thus accosted him.

Soc. You seem to have some trouble on your mind, Aristarchus; if so, you should share it with your friends. Perhaps together we might lighten the weight of it a little.

Aristarchus answered: Yes, Socrates, I am in sore straits indeed. Ever since the party strife declared itself in the city,[206] what with the rush of people to Piraeus, and the wholesale banishments, I have been fairly at the mercy of my poor deserted female relatives. Sisters, nieces, cousins, they have all come flocking to me for protection. I have fourteen free-born souls, I tell you, under my single roof, and how are we to live? We can get nothing out of the soil—that is in the hands of the enemy; nothing from my house property, for there is scarcely a living soul left in the city; my furniture? no one will buy it; money? there is none to be borrowed—you would have a better chance to find it by looking for it on the road than to borrow it from a banker. Yes, Socrates, to stand by and see one's relatives die of hunger is hard indeed, and yet to feed so many at such a pinch impossible.

After he listened to the story, Socrates asked: How comes it that Ceramon,[207] with so many mouths to feed, not only contrives to furnish himself and them with the necessaries of life, but to realise a handsome surplus, whilst you being in like plight[208] are afraid you will one and all perish of starvation for want of the necessaries of life?

Ar. Why, bless your soul, do you not see he has only slaves and I have free-born souls to feed?

Soc. And which should you say were the better human beings, the free-born members of your household or Ceramon's slaves?

Ar. The free souls under my roof without a doubt.

Soc. Is it not a shame, then, that he with his baser folk to back him should be in easy circumstances, while you and your far superior household are in difficulties?

Ar. To be sure it is, when he has only a set of handicraftsmen to

---

[206] *i.e.* circa 404-403 B.C. See *Hell.* II. iv.

[207] An employer of labour, apparently, on a grand scale.

[208] Lit. "with *your* large family to feed." L. Dindorf would like to read (su de oligous), "you with your small family."

feed, and I my liberally-educated household.

Soc. What is a handicraftsman? Does not the term apply to all who can make any sort of useful product or commodity?

Ar. Certainly.

Soc. Barley meal is a useful product, is it not?

Ar. Pre-eminently so.

Soc. And loaves of bread?

Ar. No less.

Soc. Well, and what do you say to cloaks for men and for women—tunics, mantles, vests?[209]

Ar. Yes, they are all highly useful commodities.

Soc. Then your household do not know how to make any of these?

Ar. On the contrary, I believe they can make them all.

Soc. Then you are not aware that by means of the manufacture of one of these alone—his barley meal store—Nausicydes[210] not only maintains himself and his domestics, but many pigs and cattle besides, and realises such large profits that he frequently contributes to the state benevolences;[211] while there is Cyrêbus, again, who, out of a bread factory, more than maintains the whole of his establishment, and lives in the lap of luxury; and Dêmeas of Collytus gets a livelihood out of a cloak business, and Menon as a mantua-maker, and so, again, more than half the Megarians[212] by the making of vests.

Ar. Bless me, yes! They have got a set of barbarian fellows, whom they purchase and keep, to manufacture by forced labour whatever takes their fancy. My kinswomen, I need not tell you, are free-born ladies.

Soc. Then, on the ground that they are free-born and your kinswomen, you think that they ought to do nothing but eat and sleep? Or is it your opinion that people who live in this way—I speak of free-born people in general—lead happier lives, and are more to be congratulated, than those who give their time and attention to such useful arts of life as they are skilled in? Is this what you see in the world, that for the purpose of learning what it is well to know, and of recollecting the lessons taught, or with a view to health and strength of body, or for the sake of acquiring and preserving all that gives life its charm, idleness and inattention are found to be helpful, whilst work and study are simply a dead loss? Pray, when those relatives of yours were taught what you tell me they know, did they learn it as barren information which they would never turn to practical account, or, on

---

[209] For these articles of dress see Becker's *Charicles*, Exc. i. to Sc. xi. "Dress."

[210] Nausicydes. Cobet, *Pros. Xen.* cf. Aristoph. *Eccles.* 426.

[211] Lit. "state liturgies," or "to the burden of the public services." For these see Gow, *Companion*, xviii. "Athenian Finance."

[212] Cf. Arist. *Acharnians*, 519, (esukophantei Megareon ta khlaniskia). See Dr. Merry's note *ad loc.*

the contrary, as something with which they were to be seriously concerned some day, and from which they were to reap advantage? Do human beings in general attain to well-tempered manhood by a course of idling, or by carefully attending to what will be of use? Which will help a man the more to grow in justice and uprightness, to be up and doing, or to sit with folded hands revolving the ways and means of existence? As things now stand, if I am not mistaken, there is no love lost between you. You cannot help feeling that they are costly to you, and they must see that you find them a burthen? This is a perilous state of affairs, in which hatred and bitterness have every prospect of increasing, whilst the pre-existing bond of affection[213] is likely to be snapped.

But now, if only you allow them free scope for their energies, when you come to see how useful they can be, you will grow quite fond of them, and they, when they perceive that they can please you, will cling to their benefactor warmly. Thus, with the memory of former kindnesses made sweeter, you will increase the grace which flows from kindnesses tenfold; you will in consequence be knit in closer bonds of love and domesticity. If, indeed, they were called upon to do any shameful work, let them choose death rather than that; but now they know, it would seem, the very arts and accomplishments which are regarded as the loveliest and the most suitable for women; and the things which we know, any of us, are just those which we can best perform, that is to say, with ease and expedition; it is a joy to do them, and the result is beautiful.[214] Do not hesitate, then, to initiate your friends in what will bring advantage to them and you alike; probably they will gladly respond to your summons.

Well, upon my word (Aristarchus answered), I like so well what you say, Socrates, that though hitherto I have not been disposed to borrow, knowing that when I had spent what I got I should not be in a condition to repay, I think I can now bring myself to do so in order to raise a fund for these works.

Thereupon a capital was provided; wools were purchased; the good man's relatives set to work, and even whilst they breakfasted they worked, and on and on till work was ended and they supped. Smiles took the place of frowns; they no longer looked askance with suspicion, but full into each other's eyes with happiness. They loved their kinsman for his kindness to them. He became attached to them as helpmates; and the end of it all was, he came to Socrates and told him with delight how matters fared; "and now," he added, "they tax me with being the only drone in the house, who sit and eat the bread of idleness."

---

[213] Or, "the original stock of kindliness will be used up."
[214] Or, "with ease, rapidity, pleasure and effect."

To which Socrates: Why do not you tell them the fable of the dog?[215] Once on a time, so goes the story, when beasts could speak, the sheep said to her master, "What a marvel is this, master, that to us, your own sheep, who provide you with fleeces and lambs and cheese, you give nothing, save only what we may nibble off earth's bosom; but with this dog of yours, who provides you with nothing of the sort, you share the very meat out of your mouth." When the dog heard these words, he answered promptly, "Ay, in good sooth, for is it not I who keep you safe and sound, you sheep, so that you are not stolen by man nor harried by wolves; since, if I did not keep watch over you, you would not be able so much as to graze afield, fearing to be destroyed." And so, says the tale, the sheep had to admit that the dog was rightly preferred to themselves in honour. And so do you tell your flock yonder that like the dog in the fable you are their guardian and overseer, and it is thanks to you that they are protected from evil and evildoers, so that they work their work and live their lives in blissful security.

VIII

At another time chancing upon an old friend whom he had not seen for a long while, he greeted him thus.

Soc. What quarter of the world do you hail from, Euthêrus?

The other answered: From abroad, just before the close of the war; but at present from the city itself.[216] You see, since we have been denuded of our possessions across the frontier,[217] and my father left me nothing in Attica, I must needs bide at home, and provide myself with the necessaries of life by means of bodily toil, which seems preferable to begging from another, especially as I have no security on which to raise a loan.

Soc. And how long do you expect your body to be equal to providing the necessaries of life for hire?

Euth. Goodness knows, Socrates—not for long.

Soc. And when you find yourself an old man, expenses will not diminish, and yet no one will care to pay you for the labour of your hands.

Euth. That is true.

Soc. Would it not be better then to apply yourself at once to such work as will stand you in good stead when you are old—that is, address yourself to some large proprietor who needs an assistant in managing

---

[215] See Joseph Jacobs, *The Fables of Aesop*, vol. i. p. 26 foll., for "a complete list of the Fables given in Greek literature up to the fall of Greek independence." Cf. Hesiod, *Works and Days*, 202 foll.; Archilochus, 89 [60], Bergk; Herod. i. 141; Aesch. *Myrmid.* fr. 123; Aristot. *Rhet.* II. xx.

[216] Lit. "from here." The conversation perhaps takes place in Piraeus 404 B.C.

[217] Or, "colonial possession." Cf. *Symp.* iv. 31.

Xenophon

his estate?[218] By superintending his works, helping to get in his crops, and guarding his property in general, you will be a benefit to the estate and be benefited in return.

I could not endure the yoke of slavery, Socrates! (he exclaimed).

Soc. And yet the heads of departments in a state are not regarded as adopting the badge of slavery because they manage the public property, but as having attained a higher degree of freedom rather.

Euth. In a word, Socrates, the idea of being held to account to another is not at all to my taste.

Soc. And yet, Euthêrus, it would be hard to find a work which did not involve some liability to account; in fact it is difficult to do anything without some mistake or other, and no less difficult, if you should succeed in doing it immaculately, to escape all unfriendly criticism. I wonder now whether you find it easy to get through your present occupations entirely without reproach. No? Let me tell you what you should do. You should avoid censorious persons and attach yourself to the considerate and kind-hearted, and in all your affairs accept with a good grace what you can and decline what you feel you cannot do. Whatever it be, do it heart and soul, and make it your finest work.[219] There lies the method at once to silence fault-finders and to minister help to your own difficulties. Life will flow smoothly, risks will be diminished, provision against old age secured.

IX

At another time, as I am aware, he had heard a remark made by Crito[220] that life at Athens was no easy matter for a man who wished to mind his own affairs.

As, for instance, at this moment (Crito proceeded) there are a set of fellows threatening me with lawsuits, not because they have any misdemeanour to allege against me, but simply under the conviction that I will sooner pay a sum of money than be troubled further.

To which Socrates replied: Tell me, Crito, you keep dogs, do you not, to ward off wolves from your flocks?

Cr. Certainly; it pays to do so.

Soc. Then why do you not keep a watchman willing and competent to ward off this pack of people who seek to injure you?

I should not at all mind (he answered), if I were not afraid he might turn again and rend his keeper.

What! (rejoined Socrates), do you not see that to gratify a man like yourself is far pleasanter as a matter of self-interest than to quarrel with

---

[218] Cf. *Cyrop.* VIII. iii. 48.
[219] Or, "study to make it your finest work, the expression of a real enthusiasm."
[220] Crito. See above, I. ii. 48; Cobet, *P. X*"; cf. Plat. *Rep.* viii. 549 C.

you? You may be sure there are plenty of people here who will take the greatest pride in making you their friend.

Accordingly, they sought out Archedêmus,[221] a practical man with a clever tongue in his head[222] but poor; the fact being, he was not the sort to make gain by hook or by crook, but a lover of honesty and of too good a nature himself to make his living as a pettifogger.[223] Crito would then take the opportunity of times of harvesting and put aside small presents for Archedêmus of corn and oil, or wine, or wool, or any other of the farm produce forming the staple commodities of life, or he would invite him to a sacrificial feast, and otherwise pay him marked attention. Archedêmus, feeling that he had in Crito's house a harbour of refuge, could not make too much of his patron, and ere long he had hunted up a long list of iniquities which could be lodged against Crito's pettifogging persecutors themselves, and not only their numerous crimes but their numerous enemies; and presently he prosecuted one of them in a public suit, where sentence would be given against him "what to suffer or what to pay."[224] The accused, conscious as he was of many rascally deeds, did all he could to be quit of Archedêmus, but Archedêmus was not to be got rid of. He held on until he had made the informer not only loose his hold of Crito but pay himself a sum of money; and now that Archedêmus had achieved this and other similar victories, it is easy to guess what followed.[225] It was just as when some shepherd has got a very good dog, all the other shepherds wish to lodge their flocks in his neighbourhood that they too may reap the benefit of him. So a number of Crito's friends came begging him to allow Archedêmus to be their guardian also, and Archedêmus was overjoyed to do something to gratify Crito, and so it came about that not only Crito abode in peace, but his friends likewise. If any of those people with whom Archedêmus was not on the best of terms were disposed to throw it in his teeth that he accepted his patron's benefits and paid in flatteries, he had a ready retort: "Answer me this question—which is the more scandalous, to accept kindnesses from honest folk and to repay them, with the result that I make such people my friends but quarrel with knaves, or to make enemies of honourable gentlemen[226] by

---

[221] Archedêmus, possibly the demagogue, *Hell.* I. vii. 2. So Cobet, *P. X.*, but see Grote, *H. G.* viii. 245.

[222] Lit. "very capable of speech and action"—the writer's favourite formula for the well-trained Athenian who can speak fluently and reason clearly, and act energetically and opportunely.

[223] Reading (kai euphuesteros on) (or (e os))... (apo sukophanton) (or (sukophantion)), after Cobet, *P. X.* s.v. Archedêmus. The MSS. give (kai ephe raston einai)—"nothing is easier," he said, "than recovering from sycophants."

[224] For this formula cf. *Econ.* vi. 24. Cf. Plat. *Statesm.* 299 A.

[225] (ede tote). Cf. Plat. *Laws*, vi. 778 C.

[226] Lit. the (kaloi kagathoi), which like (khrestous) and (ponerous) has a political as well as an ethical meaning.

attempts to do them wrong, with the off-chance indeed of winning the friendship of some scamps in return for my co-operation, but the certainty of losing in the tone of my acquaintances?"[227]

The net result of the whole proceedings was that Archedêmus was now Crito's right hand,[228] and by the rest of Crito's friends he was held in honour.

X

Again I may cite, as known to myself,[229] the following discussion; the arguments were addressed to Diodôrus, one of his companions. The master said:

Tell me, Diodôrus, if one of your slaves runs away, are you at pains to recover him?

More than that (Diodôrus answered), I summon others to my aid and I have a reward cried for his recovery.

Soc. Well, if one of your domestics is sick, do you tend him and call in the doctors to save his life?

Diod. Decidedly I do.

Soc. And if an intimate acquaintance who is far more precious to you than any of your household slaves is about to perish of want, you would think it incumbent on you to take pains to save his life? Well! now you know without my telling you that Hermogenes[230] is not made of wood or stone. If you helped him he would be ashamed not to pay you in kind. And yet—the opportunity of possessing a willing, kindly, and trusty assistant well fitted to do your bidding, and not merely that, but capable of originating useful ideas himself, with a certain forecast of mind and judgment—I say such a man is worth dozens of slaves. Good economists tell us that when a precious article may be got at a low price we ought to buy. And nowadays when times are so bad it is possible to get good friends exceedingly cheap.

Diodôrus answered: You are quite right, Socrates; bid Hermogenes come to me.

Soc. Bid Hermogenes come to you!—not I indeed! since for aught I can understand you are no better entitled to summon him that to go to him yourself, nor is the advantage more on his side than your own.

Thus Diodôrus went off in a trice to seek Hermogenes, and at no great outlay won to himself a friend—a friend whose one concern it now was to discover how, by word or deed, he might help and gladden Diodôrus.

---

[227] Lit. "must associate with these (the (ponerois)) instead of those (the (kalois te kagathois)).
[228] He was No. 1—(eis).
[229] Or, "for which I can personally vouch."
[230] Hermogenes, presumably the son of Hipponicus. See I. ii. 48.

BOOK III

I

Aspirants to honour and distinction[231] derived similar help from Socrates, who in each case stimulated in them a persevering assiduity towards their several aims, as the following narratives tend to show. He had heard on one occasion of the arrival in Athens of Dionysodorus,[232] who professed to teach the whole duty of a general.[233] Accordingly he remarked to one of those who were with him—a young man whose anxiety to obtain the office of Strategos[234] was no secret to him:

Soc. It would be monstrous on the part of any one who sought to become a general[235] to throw away the slightest opportunity of learning the duties of the office. Such a person, I should say, would deserve to be fined and punished by the state far more than the charlatan who without having learnt the art of a sculptor undertakes a contract to carve a statue. Considering that the whole fortunes of the state are entrusted to the general during a war, with all its incidental peril, it is only reasonable to anticipate that great blessings or great misfortunes will result in proportion to the success or bungling of that officer. I appeal to you, young sir, do you not agree that a candidate who, while taking pains to be elected neglects to learn the duties of the office, would richly deserve to be fined?

With arguments like these he persuaded the young man to go and take lessons. After he had gone through the course he came back, and Socrates proceeded playfully to banter him.

Soc. Behold our young friend, sirs, as Homer says of Agamemnon, of mein majestical,[236] so he; does he not seem to move more majestically, like one who has studied to be a general? Of course, just as a man who has learned to play the harp is a harper, even if he never touch the instrument, or as one who has studied medicine is a physician, though he does not practise, so our friend here from this time forward is now and ever shall be a general, even though he does not receive a vote at the elections. But the dunce who has not the science is neither general nor doctor, no, not even if the whole world appointed him. But (he proceeded, turning to the youth), in case any of us should

---

[231] (ton kalon) = everything which the (kalos te kagathos) should aim at, but especially the honourable offices of state such as the *Archonship, Strategia, Hipparchia*, etc. See Plat. *Laches*.

[232] Dionysodorus of Chios, presumably. See Plat. *Euthyd.* 271 C foll.

[233] A professor of the science and art of strategy.

[234] Lit. "that honour," *sc.* the *Strategia*.

[235] *i.e.* "head of the war department, and commander-in-chief," etc.

[236] *Il.* iii. 169, 170.

ever find ourselves captain or colonel[237] under you, to give us some smattering of the science of war, what did the professor take as the starting-point of his instruction in generalship? Please inform us.

Then the young man: He began where he ended; he taught me tactics[238]—tactics and nothing else.

Yet surely (replied Socrates) that is only an infinitesimal part of generalship. A general[239] must be ready in furnishing the material of war: in providing the commissariat for his troops; quick in devices, he must be full of practical resource; nothing must escape his eye or tax his endurance; he must be shrewd, and ready of wit, a combination at once of clemency and fierceness, of simplicity and of insidious craft; he must play the part of watchman, of robber; now prodigal as a spendthrift, and again close-fisted as a miser, the bounty of his munificence must be equalled by the narrowness of his greed; impregnable in defence, a very dare-devil in attack—these and many other qualities must he possess who is to make a good general and minister of war; they must come to him by gift of nature or through science. No doubt it is a grand thing also to be a tactician, since there is all the difference in the world between an army properly handled in the field and the same in disorder; just as stones and bricks, woodwork and tiles, tumbled together in a heap are of no use at all, but arrange them in a certain order—at bottom and atop materials which will not crumble or rot, such as stones and earthen tiles, and in the middle between the two put bricks and woodwork, with an eye to architectural principle,[240] and finally you get a valuable possession—to wit, a dwelling-place.

The simile is very apt, Socrates[241] (replied the youth), for in battle, too, the rule is to draw up the best men in front and rear, with those of inferior quality between, where they may be led on by the former and pushed on by the hinder.

Soc. Very good, no doubt, if the professor taught you to distinguish good and bad; but if not, where is the use of your learning? It would scarcely help you, would it, to be told to arrange coins in piles, the best coins at top and bottom and the worst in the middle, unless you were first taught to distinguish real from counterfeit.

The Youth. Well no, upon my word, he did not teach us that, so that the task of distinguishing between good and bad must devolve on ourselves.

Soc. Well, shall we see, then, how we may best avoid making blunders between them?

---

[237] Or, "brigadier or captain," lit. *taxiarch* or *lochâgos*.
[238] Cf. *Cyrop.* I. vi. 12 foll.; VIII. v. 15.
[239] A *stratêgos*. For the duties and spheres of action of this officer, see Gow, *op. cit.* xiv. 58.
[240] "As in the building of a house." See Vitrivius, ii. 3; Plin. xxv. 14.
[241] Cf. *Il.* iv. 297 foll.; *Cyrop.* VI. iii. 25; Polyb. x. 22.

I am ready (replied the youth).

Soc. Well then! Let us suppose we are marauders, and the task imposed upon us is to carry off some bullion; it will be a right disposition of our forces if we place in the vanguard those who are the greediest of gain?[242]

The Youth. I should think so.

Soc. Then what if there is danger to be faced? Shall the vanguard consist of men who are greediest of honour?

The Youth. It is these, at any rate, who will face danger for the sake of praise and glory.[243] Fortunately such people are not hid away in a corner; they shine forth conspicuous everywhere, and are easy to be discovered.

Soc. But tell me, did he teach you how to draw up troops in general, or specifically where and how to apply each particular kind of tactical arrangement?

The Youth. Nothing of the sort.

Soc. And yet there are and must be innumerable circumstances in which the same ordering of march or battle will be out of place.

The Youth. I assure you he did not draw any of these fine distinctions.

He did not, did not he? (he answered). Bless me! Go back to him again, then, and ply him with questions; if he really has the science, and is not lost to all sense of shame, he will blush to have taken your money and then to have sent you away empty.

II

At another time he fell in with a man who had been chosen general and minister of war, and thus accosted him.

Soc. Why did Homer, think you, designate Agamemnon "shepherd of the peoples"?[244] Was it possibly to show that, even as a shepherd must care for his sheep and see that they are safe and have all things needful, and that the objects of their rearing be secured, so also must a general take care that his soldiers are safe and have their supplies, and attain the objects of their soldiering? Which last is that they may get the mastery of their enemies, and so add to their own good fortune and happiness; or tell me, what made him praise Agamemnon, saying—

He is both a good king and a warrior bold?[245]

---

[242] "Whose fingers itch for gold."
[243] Cf. Shakesp. "seeking the bubble reputation even in the cannon's mouth."
[244] *Il.* ii. 243. "The People's Pastor," Chapman.
[245] *Il.* iii. 179; cf. *Symp.* iv. 6. A favourite line of Alexander the Great's, it is said.

Did he mean, perhaps, to imply that he would be a 'warrior bold,' not merely in standing alone and bravely battling against the foe, but as inspiring the whole of his host with like prowess; and by a 'good king,' not merely one who should stand forth gallantly to protect his own life, but who should be the source of happiness to all over whom he reigns? Since a man is not chosen king in order to take heed to himself, albeit nobly, but that those who chose him may attain to happiness through him. And why do men go soldiering except to ameliorate existence?[246] and to this end they choose their generals that they may find in them guides to the goal in question. He, then, who undertakes that office is bound to procure for those who choose him the thing they seek for. And indeed it were not easy to find any nobler ambition than this, or aught ignobler than its opposite.

After such sort he handled the question, what is the virtue of a good leader? and by shredding off all superficial qualities, laid bare as the kernel of the matter that it is the function of every leader to make those happy whom he may be called upon to lead.[247]

III

The following conversation with a youth who had just been elected hipparch[248] (or commandant of cavalry), I can also vouch for.[249]

Soc. Can you tell us what set you wishing to be a general of cavalry, young sir? What was your object? I suppose it was not simply to ride at the head of the "knights," an honour not denied to the mounted archers,[250] who ride even in front of the generals themselves?

Hipp. You are right.

Soc. No more was it for the sake merely of public notoriety, since a madman might boast of that fatal distinction.[251]

Hipp. You are right again.

Soc. Is this possibly the explanation? you think to improve the cavalry—your aim would be to hand it over to the state in better condition than you find it; and, if the cavalry chanced to be called out, you at their head would be the cause of some good thing to Athens?

Hipp. Most certainly.

Soc. Well, and a noble ambition too, upon my word—if you can achieve your object. The command to which you are appointed concerns horses and riders, does it not?

Hipp. It does, no doubt.

---

[246] Of, "that life may reach some flower of happiness."
[247] Cf. Plat. *Rep.* 342.
[248] Cf. *Hipparch.*
[249] Lit. "I know he once held."
[250] Lit. "Hippotoxotai." See Boeckh, *P. E. A.* II. xxi. p. 264 (Eng. tr.)
[251] Or, "as we all know, 'Tom Fool' can boast," etc.

Soc. Come then, will you explain to us first how you propose to improve the horses.

Hipp. Ah, that will scarcely form part of my business, I fancy. Each trooper is personally responsible for the condition of his horse.

Soc. But suppose, when they present themselves and their horses,[252] you find that some have brought beasts with bad feet or legs or otherwise infirm, and others such ill-fed jades that they cannot keep up on the march; others, again, brutes so ill broken and unmanageable that they will not keep their place in the ranks, and others such desperate plungers that they cannot be got to any place in the ranks at all. What becomes of your cavalry force then? How will you charge at the head of such a troop, and win glory for the state?

Hipp. You are right. I will try to look after the horses to my utmost.

Soc. Well, and will you not lay your hand to improve the men themselves?

Hipp. I will.

Soc. The first thing will be to make them expert in mounting their chargers?

Hipp. That certainly, for if any of them were dismounted he would then have a better chance of saving himself.

Soc. Well, but when it comes to the hazard of engagement, what will you do then? Give orders to draw the enemy down to the sandy ground[253] where you are accustomed to manœuvre, or endeavour beforehand to put your men through their practice on ground resembling a real battlefield?

Hipp. That would be better, no doubt.

Soc. Well, shall you regard it as a part of your duty to see that as many of your men as possible can take aim and shoot on horseback?[254]

Hipp. It will be better, certainly.

Soc. And have you thought how to whet the courage of your troopers? to kindle in them rage to meet the enemy?—which things are but stimulants to make stout hearts stouter?

Hipp. If I have not done so hitherto, I will try to make up for lost time now.

Soc. And have you troubled your head at all to consider how you are to secure the obedience of your men? for without that not one particle of good will you get, for all your horses and troopers so brave and so stout.

Hipp. That is a true saying; but how, Socrates, should a man best bring them to this virtue?[255]

---

[252] For this phrase, see Schneider and Kühner *ad loc.*
[253] *e.g.* the hippodrome at Phaleron.
[254] Cf. *Hipparch*, i. 21.
[255] (protrepsasthai). See above, I. ii. 64; below, IV. v. 1.

Soc. I presume you know that in any business whatever, people are more apt to follow the lead of those whom they look upon as adepts; thus in case of sickness they are readiest to obey him whom they regard as the cleverest physician; and so on a voyage the most skilful pilot; in matters agricultural the best farmer, and so forth.

Hipp. Yes, certainly.

Soc. Then in this matter of cavalry also we may reasonably suppose that he who is looked upon as knowing his business best will command the readiest obedience.

Hipp. If, then, I can prove to my troopers that I am better than all of them, will that suffice to win their obedience?

Soc. Yes, if along with that you can teach them that obedience to you brings greater glory and surer safety to themselves.

Hipp. How am I to teach them that?

Soc. Upon my word! How are you to teach them that? Far more easily, I take it, than if you had to teach them that bad things are better than good, and more advantageous to boot.

Hipp. I suppose you mean that, besides his other qualifications a commandant of cavalry must have command of speech and argument?[256]

Soc. Were you under the impression that the commandant was not to open his mouth? Did it never occur to you that all the noblest things which custom[257] compels us to learn, and to which indeed we owe our knowledge of life, have all been learned by means of speech[258] and reason; and if there be any other noble learning which a man may learn, it is this same reason whereby he learns it; and the best teachers are those who have the freest command of thought and language, and those that have the best knowledge of the most serious things are the most brilliant masters of disputation. Again, have you not observed that whenever this city of ours fits out one of her choruses—such as that, for instance, which is sent to Delos[259]—there is nothing elsewhere from any quarter of the world which can compete with it; nor will you find in any other state collected so fair a flower of manhood as in Athens?[260]

Hipp. You say truly.

Soc. But for all that, it is not in sweetness of voice that the Athenians differ from the rest of the world so much, nor in stature of body or strength of limb, but in ambition and that love of honour[261] which most of all gives a keen edge to the spirit in the pursuit of things

---

[256] Or, "practise the art of oratory"; "express himself clearly and rationally." See Grote, *H. G.* VIII. lxvii. p. 463 *note; Hipparch,* i. 24; viii. 22.

[257] Cf. Arist. "Rhet." ii. 12, (oi neoi pepaideuntai upo tou nomou monon).

[258] (dia logou).

[259] See Thuc. iii. 104; and below, IV. viii. 2.

[260] See references ap. Schneider and Kühner; *Symp.* iv. 17.

[261] See below, v. 3; Dem. "de Cor." 28 foll.

lovely and of high esteem.

Hipp. That, too, is a true saying.

Soc. Do you not think, then, that if a man devoted himself to our cavalry also, here in Athens, we should far outstrip the rest of the world, whether in the furnishing of arms and horses, or in orderliness of battle-array, or in eager hazardous encounter with the foe, if only we could persuade ourselves that by so doing we should obtain honour and distinction?

Hipp. It is reasonable to think so.

Soc. Have no hesitation, therefore, but try to guide your men into this path,[262] whence you yourself, and through you your fellow-citizens, will reap advantage.

Yes, in good sooth, I will try (he answered).

IV

At another time, seeing Nicomachides on his way back from the elections (of magistrates),[263] he asked him: Who are elected generals, Nicomachides?

And he: Is it not just like them, these citizens of Athens—just like them, I say—to go and elect, not me, who ever since my name first appeared on the muster-roll have literally worn myself out with military service—now as a captain, now as a colonel—and have received all these wounds from the enemy, look you! (at the same time, and suiting the action to the word, he bared his arms and proceeded to show the scars of ancient wounds)—they elect not me (he went on), but, if you please, Antisthenes! who never served as a hoplite[264] in his life nor in the cavalry ever made a brilliant stroke, that I ever heard tell of; no! in fact, he has got no science at all, I take it, except to amass stores of wealth.

But still (returned Socrates), surely that is one point in his favour—he ought to be able to provide the troops with supplies.

Nic. Well, for the matter of that, merchants are good hands at collecting stores; but it does not follow that a merchant or trader will be able to command an army.

But (rejoined Socrates) Antisthenes is a man of great pertinacity, who insists on winning, and that is a very necessary quality in a general.[265] Do not you see how each time he has been choragos[266] he

---

[262] Or, "to conduct which will not certainly fail of profit to yourself or through you to..."

[263] Cf. *Pol. Ath.* i. 3; Aristot. *Ath. Pol.* 44. 4; and Dr. Sandys' note *ad loc.* p. 165 of his edition.

[264] Cf. Lys. xiv. 10.

[265] See Grote, *Plato*, i. 465 foll.

[266] Choir-master, or Director of the Chorus. It was his duty to provide and preside

has been successful with one chorus after another?

Nic. Bless me! yes; but there is a wide difference between standing at the head of a band of singers and dancers and a troop of soldiers.

Soc. Still, without any practical skill in singing or in the training of a chorus, Antisthenes somehow had the art to select the greatest proficients in both.

Nic. Yes, and by the same reasoning we are to infer that on a campaign he will find proficients, some to marshal the troops for him and others to fight his battles?

Soc. Just so. If in matters military he only exhibits the same skill in selecting the best hands as he has shown in matters of the chorus, it is highly probable he will here also bear away the palm of victory; and we may presume that if he expended so much to win a choric victory with a single tribe,[267] he will be ready to expend more to secure a victory in war with the whole state to back him.

Nic. Do you really mean, Socrates, that it is the function of the same man to provide efficient choruses and to act as commander-in-chief?

Soc. I mean this, that, given a man knows what he needs to provide, and has the skill to do so, no matter what the department of things may be—house or city or army—you will find him a good chief and director[268] of the same.

Then Nicomachides: Upon my word, Socrates, I should never have expected to hear you say that a good housekeeper[269] and steward of an estate would make a good general.

Soc. Come then, suppose we examine their respective duties, and so determine[270] whether they are the same or different.

Nic. Let us do so.

Soc. Well then, is it not a common duty of both to procure the ready obedience of those under them to their orders?

Nic. Certainly.

Soc. And also to assign to those best qualified to perform them their distinctive tasks?

That, too, belongs to both alike (he answered).

Soc. Again, to chastise the bad and reward the good belongs to both alike, methinks?

Nic. Decidedly.

Soc. And to win the kindly feeling of their subordinates must

---

over a chorus to sing, dance, or play at any of the public festivals, defraying the cost as a state service of (leitourgia). See *Pol. Ath.* iii. 4; *Hiero*, ix. 4; Aristot. *Pol. Ath.* 28. 3.

[267] See Dem. *against Lept.* 496. 26. Each tribe nominated such of its members as were qualified to undertake the burden.

[268] Or, "representative."

[269] Or, "economist"; cf. *Cyrop.* I. vi. 12.

[270] Lit. "get to know."

surely be the noble ambition of both?

That too (he answered).

Soc. And do you consider it to the interest of both alike to win the adherence of supporters and allies?[271]

Nic. Without a doubt.

Soc. And does it not closely concern them both to be good guardians of their respective charges?

Nic. Very much so.

Soc. Then it equally concerns them both to be painstaking and prodigal of toil in all their doings?

Nic. Yes, all these duties belong to both alike, but the parallel ends when you come to actual fighting.

Soc. Yet they are both sure to meet with enemies?

Nic. There is no doubt about that.

Soc. Then is it not to the interest of both to get the upper hand of these?

Nic. Certainly; but you omit to tell us what service organisation and the art of management will render when it comes to actual fighting.

Soc. Why, it is just then, I presume, it will be of most service, for the good economist knows that nothing is so advantageous or so lucrative as victory in battle, or to put it negatively, nothing so disastrous and expensive as defeat. He will enthusiastically seek out and provide everything conducive to victory, he will painstakingly discover and guard against all that tends to defeat, and when satisfied that all is ready and ripe for victory he will deliver battle energetically, and what is equally important, until the hour of final preparation has arrived,[272] he will be cautious to deliver battle. Do not despise men of economic genius, Nicomachides; the difference between the devotion requisite to private affairs and to affairs of state is merely one of quantity. For the rest the parallel holds strictly, and in this respect pre-eminently, that both are concerned with human instruments: which human beings, moreover, are of one type and temperament, whether we speak of devotion to public affairs or of the administration of private property. To fare well in either case is given to those who know the secret of dealing with humanity, whereas the absence of that knowledge will as certainly imply in either case a fatal note of discord.[273]

---

[271] In reference to the necessity of building up a family connection or political alliances cf. Arist. "Pol." iii. 9, 13.

[272] Lit. "as long as he is unprepared."

[273] L. Dindorf, *Index Graec.* Ox. ed.; cf. Hor. *Ep.* II. ii. 144, "sed verae numerosque modosque ediscere vitae," "the harmony of life," Conington.

V

A conversation held with Pericles the son of the great statesman may here be introduced.[274] Socrates began:

I am looking forward, I must tell you, Pericles, to a great improvement in our military affairs when you are minister of war.[275] The prestige of Athens, I hope, will rise; we shall gain the mastery over our enemies.

Pericles replied: I devoutly wish your words might be fulfilled, but how this happy result is to be obtained, I am at a loss to discover.

Shall we (Socrates continued), shall we balance the arguments for and against, and consider to what extent the possibility does exist?

Pray let us do so (he answered).

Soc. Well then, you know that in point of numbers the Athenians are not inferior to the Boeotians?

Per. Yes, I am aware of that.

Soc. And do you think the Boeotians could furnish a better pick of fine healthy men than the Athenians?

Per. I think we should very well hold our own in that respect.

Soc. And which of the two would you take to be the more united people—the friendlier among themselves?

Per. The Athenians, I should say, for so many sections of the Boeotians, resenting the selfish policy[276] of Thebes, are ill disposed to that power, but at Athens I see nothing of the sort.

Soc. But perhaps you will say that there is no people more jealous of honour or haughtier in spirit.[277] And these feelings are no weak spurs to quicken even a dull spirit to hazard all for glory's sake and fatherland.

Per. Nor is there much fault to find with Athenians in these respects.

Soc. And if we turn to consider the fair deeds of ancestry,[278] to no people besides ourselves belongs so rich a heritage of stimulating memories, whereby so many of us are stirred to pursue virtue with devotion and to show ourselves in our turn also men of valour like our sires.

Per. All that you say, Socrates, is most true, but do you observe

---

[274] Or, "On one occasion Pericles was the person addressed in conversation." For Pericles see *Hell.* I. v. 16; vii. 15; Plut. *Pericl.* 37 (Clough, i. 368).

[275] "Stratêgos."

[276] "The self-aggrandisement."

[277] Reading (megalophronestatoi), after Cobet. See *Hipparch*, vii. 3; or if as vulg. (philophronestatoi), transl. "more affable."

[278] See Wesley's anthem, Eccles. xliv. 1, "Let us now praise famous men and our fathers that begat us."

that ever since the disaster of the thousand under Tolmides at Lebadeia, coupled with that under Hippocrates at Delium,[279] the prestige of Athens by comparison with the Boeotians has been lowered, whilst the spirit of Thebes as against Athens had been correspondingly exalted, so that those Boeotians who in old days did not venture to give battle to the Athenians even in their own territory unless they had the Lacedaemonians and the rest of the Peloponnesians to help them, do nowadays threaten to make an incursion into Attica single-handed; and the Athenians, who formerly, if they had to deal with the Boeotians[280] only, made havoc of their territory, are now afraid the Boeotians may some day harry Attica.

To which Socrates: Yes, I perceive that this is so, but it seems to me that the state was never more tractably disposed, never so ripe for a really good leader, as to-day. For if boldness be the parent of carelessness, laxity, and insubordination, it is the part of fear to make people more disposed to application, obedience, and good order. A proof of which you may discover in the behaviour of people on shipboard. It is in seasons of calm weather when there is nothing to fear that disorder may be said to reign, but as soon as there is apprehension of a storm, or an enemy in sight, the scene changes; not only is each word of command obeyed, but there is a hush of silent expectation; the mariners wait to catch the next signal like an orchestra with eyes upon the leader.

Per. But indeed, given that now is the opportunity to take obedience at the flood, it is high time also to explain by what means we are to rekindle in the hearts of our countrymen[281] the old fires—the passionate longing for antique valour, for the glory and the wellbeing of the days of old.

Well (proceeded Socrates), supposing we wished them to lay claim to certain material wealth now held by others, we could not better stimulate them to lay hands on the objects coveted than by showing them that these were ancestral possessions[282] to which they had a natural right. But since our object is that they should set their hearts on virtuous pre-eminence, we must prove to them that such headship combined with virtue is an old time-honoured heritage which pertains to them beyond all others, and that if they strive earnestly after it they will soon out-top the world.

Por. How are we to inculcate this lesson?

Soc. I think by reminding them of a fact already registered in their

---

[279] Lebadeia, 447 B.C.; Delium, 424 B.C. For Tolmides and Hippocrates see Thuc. i. 113; iv. 100 foll.; Grote, *H. G.* v. 471; vi. 533.

[280] Reading (ote B. monoi), al. (ou monoi), "when the Boeotians were *not* unaided."

[281] Reading (anerasthenai), Schneider's emendation of the vulg. (aneristhenai).

[282] Cf. Solon in the matter of Salamis, Plut. *Sol.* 8; Bergk. *Poet. Lyr. Gr. Solon*, SALAMIS, i. 2, 3.

minds,[283] that the oldest of our ancestors whose names are known to us were also the bravest of heroes.

Per. I suppose you refer to that judgment of the gods which, for their virtue's sake, Cecrops and his followers were called on to decide?[284]

Soc. Yes, I refer to that and to the birth and rearing of Erectheus,[285] and also to the war[286] which in his days was waged to stay the tide of invasion from the whole adjoining continent; and that other war in the days of the Heraclidae[287] against the men of Peloponnese; and that series of battles fought in the days of Theseus[288]—in all which the virtuous pre-eminence of our ancestry above the men of their own times was made manifest. Or, if you please, we may come down to things of a later date, which their descendants and the heroes of days not so long anterior to our own wrought in the struggle with the lords of Asia,[289] nay of Europe also, as far as Macedonia: a people possessing a power and means of attack far exceeding any who had gone before—who, moreover, had accomplished the doughtiest deeds. These things the men of Athens wrought partly single-handed,[290] and partly as sharers with the Peloponnesians in laurels won by land and sea. Heroes were these men also, far outshining, as tradition tells us, the peoples of their time.

Per. Yes, so runs the story of their heroism.

Soc. Therefore it is that, amidst the many changes of inhabitants, and the migrations which have, wave after wave, swept over Hellas, these maintained themselves in their own land, unmoved; so that it was a common thing for others to turn to them as to a court of appeal on points of right, or to flee to Athens as a harbour of refuge from the hand of the oppressor.[291]

Then Pericles: And the wonder to me, Socrates, is how our city ever came to decline.

Soc. I think we are victims of our own success. Like some athlete,[292] whose facile preponderance in the arena has betrayed him into laxity until he eventually succumbs to punier antagonists, so we Athenians, in the plenitude of our superiority, have neglected ourselves and are become degenerate.

Per. What then ought we to do now to recover our former virtue?

---

[283] Or, "to which their ears are already opened."
[284] See Apollodorus, iii. 14.
[285] Cf. *Il.* ii. 547, ('Erekhtheos megaletoros k.t.l.)
[286] Cf. Isoc. *Paneg.* 19, who handles all the topics.
[287] Commonly spoken of as "the Return." See Grote, *H. G.* II. ch. xviii.
[288] Against the Amazons and Thracians; cf. Herod. ix. 27; Plut. *Thes.* 27.
[289] The "Persian" wars; cf. Thucyd. I. i.
[290] He omits the Plataeans.
[291] Cf. (Plat.) *Menex.*; Isocr. *Paneg.*
[292] Reading (athletai tines), or if (alloi tines), translate "any one else."

Soc. There need be no mystery about that, I think. We can rediscover the institutions of our forefathers—applying them to the regulation of our lives with something of their precision, and not improbably with like success; or we can imitate those who stand at the front of affairs to-day,[293] adapting to ourselves their rule of life, in which case, if we live up to the standard of our models, we may hope at least to rival their excellence, or, by a more conscientious adherence to what they aim at, rise superior.

You would seem to suggest (he answered) that the spirit of beautiful and brave manhood has taken wings and left our city;[294] as, for instance, when will Athenians, like the Lacedaemonians, reverence old age—the Athenian, who takes his own father as a starting-point for the contempt he pours upon grey hairs? When will he pay as strict an attention to the body, who is not content with neglecting a good habit,[295] but laughs to scorn those who are careful in this matter? When shall we Athenians so obey our magistrates—we who take a pride, as it were, in despising authority? When, once more, shall we be united as a people—we who, instead of combining to promote common interests, delight in blackening each other's characters,[296] envying one another more than we envy all the world besides; and—which is our worst failing—who, in private and public intercourse alike, are torn by dissension and are caught in a maze of litigation, and prefer to make capital out of our neighbour's difficulties rather than to render natural assistance? To make our conduct consistent, indeed, we treat our national interests no better than if they were the concerns of some foreign state; we make them bones of contention to wrangle over, and rejoice in nothing so much as in possessing means and ability to indulge these tastes. From this hotbed is engendered in the state a spirit of blind folly[297] and cowardice, and in the hearts of the citizens spreads a tangle of hatred and mutual hostility which, as I often shudder to think, will some day cause some disaster to befall the state greater than it can bear.[298]

Do not (replied Socrates), do not, I pray you, permit yourself to believe that Athenians are smitten with so incurable a depravity. Do you not observe their discipline in all naval matters? Look at their prompt and orderly obedience to the superintendents at the gymnastic contests,[299] their quite unrivalled subservience to their teachers in the

---

[293] Sc. the Lacedaemonians. See W. L. Newman, *op. cit.* i. 396.

[294] Or, "is far enough away from Athens."

[295] See below, III. xii. 5; *Pol. Ath.* i. 13; *Rev.* iv. 52.

[296] Or, "to deal despitefully with one another."

[297] Reading (ateria). See L. Dindorf *ad loc.*, Ox. ed. lxii. Al. (apeiria), a want of skill, or (ataxia), disorderliness. Cf. *Pol. Ath.* i. 5.

[298] Possibly the author is thinking of the events of 406, 405 B.C. (see *Hell.* I. vii. and II.), and history may repeat itself.

[299] *Epistatai, i.e.* stewards and training-masters.

Xenophon 79

training of our choruses.

Yes (he answered), there's the wonder of it; to think that all those good people should so obey their leaders, but that our hoplites and our cavalry, who may be supposed to rank before the rest of the citizens in excellence of manhood,[300] should be so entirely unamenable to discipline.

Then Socrates: Well, but the council which sits on Areopagos is composed of citizens of approved[301] character, is it not?

Certainly (he answered).

Soc. Then can you name any similar body, judicial or executive, trying cases or transacting other business with greater honour, stricter legality, higher dignity, or more impartial justice?

No, I have no fault to find on that score (he answered).

Soc. Then we ought not to despair as though all sense of orderliness and good discipline had died out of our countrymen.

Still (he answered), if it is not to harp upon one string, I maintain that in military service, where, if anywhere, sobriety and temperance, orderliness and good discipline are needed, none of these essentials receives any attention.

May it not perhaps be (asked Socrates) that in this department they are officered by those who have the least knowledge?[302] Do you not notice, to take the case of harp-players, choric performers, dancers, and the like, that no one would ever dream of leading if he lacked the requisite knowledge? and the same holds of wrestlers or pancratiasts.

Moreover, while in these cases any one in command can tell you where he got the elementary knowledge of what he presides over, most generals are amateurs and improvisers.[303] I do not at all suppose that you are one of that sort. I believe you could give as clear an account of your schooling in strategy as you could in the matter of wrestling. No doubt you have got at first hand many of your father's "rules for generalship," which you carefully preserve, besides having collected many others from every quarter whence it was possible to pick up any knowledge which would be of use to a future general. Again, I feel sure you are deeply concerned to escape even unconscious ignorance of anything which will be serviceable to you in so high an office; and if you detect in yourself any ignorance, you turn to those who have knowledge in these matters (sparing neither gifts nor gratitude) to supplement your ignorance by their knowledge and to secure their help.

To which Pericles: I am not so blind, Socrates, as to imagine you

---

[300] (kalokagathia).
[301] Technically, they must have passed the (dokimasia). And for the "Aeropagos" see Grote, *H. G.* v. 498; Aristot. *Pol.* ii. 12; *Ath. Pol.* 4. 4, where see Dr. Sandys' note, p. 18.
[302] (episteme). See below, III. ix. 10.
[303] Cf. *Pol. Lac.* xiii. 5.

say these words under the idea that I am truly so careful in these matters; but rather your object is to teach me that the would-be general must make such things his care. I admit in any case all you say.

Socrates proceeded: Has it ever caught your observation, Pericles, that a high mountain barrier stretches like a bulwark in front of our country down towards Boeotia—cleft, moreover, by narrow and precipitous passes, the only avenues into the heart of Attica, which lies engirdled by a ring of natural fortresses?[304]

Per. Certainly I have.

Soc. Well, and have you ever heard tell of the Mysians and Pisidians living within the territory of the great king,[305] who, inside their mountain fortresses, lightly armed, are able to rush down and inflict much injury on the king's territory by their raids, while preserving their own freedom?

Per. Yes, the circumstance is not new to me.

And do you not think (added Socrates) that a corps of young able-bodied Athenians, accoutred with lighter arms,[306] and holding our natural mountain rampart in possession, would prove at once a thorn in the enemy's side offensively, whilst defensively they would form a splendid bulwark to protect the country?

To which Pericles: I think, Socrates, these would be all useful measures, decidedly.

If, then (replied Socrates), these suggestions meet your approbation, try, O best of men, to realise them—if you can carry out a portion of them, it will be an honour to yourself and a blessing to the state; while, if you fail in any point, there will be no damage done to the city nor discredit to yourself.

VI

Glaucon,[307] the son of Ariston, had conceived such an ardour to gain the headship of the state that nothing could hinder him but he must deliver a course of public speeches,[308] though he had not yet reached the age of twenty. His friends and relatives tried in vain to stop him making himself ridiculous and being dragged down from the bema.[309]

---

[304] The mountains are Cithaeron and Parnes N., and Cerata N.W.

[305] For this illustration see *Anab.* III. ii. 23; cf. *Econ.* iv. 18, where Socrates (XS) refers to Cyrus's expedition and death.

[306] Cf. the reforms of Iphicrates.

[307] Glaucon, Plato's brother. Grote, *Plato*, i. 508.

[308] "Harangue the People."

[309] See Plat. *Protag.* 319 C: "And if some person offers to give them advice who is not supposed by them to have any skill in the art (sc. of politics), even though he be good-looking, and rich, and noble, they will not listen to him, but laugh at him, and hoot him, until he is either clamoured down and retires of himself; or if he persists, he is dragged away or put out by the constables at the command of the prytanes" (Jowett). Cf.

Socrates, who took a kindly interest in the youth for the sake of Charmides[310] the son of Glaucon, and of Plato, alone succeeded in restraining him. It happened thus. He fell in with him, and first of all, to get him to listen, detained him by some such remarks as the following:[311]

Ah, Glaucon (he exclaimed), so you have determined to become prime minister?[312]

Glauc. Yes, Socrates, I have.

Soc. And what a noble aim! if aught human ever deserved to be called noble; since if you succeed in your design, it follows, as the night the day, you will be able not only to gratify your every wish, but you will be in a position to benefit your friends, you will raise up your father's house, you will exalt your fatherland, you will become a name thrice famous in the city first, and next in Hellas, and lastly even among barbarians perhaps, like Themistocles; but be it here or be it there, wherever you be, you will be the observed of all beholders.[313]

The heart of Glaucon swelled with pride as he drank in the words, and gladly he stayed to listen.

Presently Socrates proceeded: Then this is clear, Glaucon, is it not? that you must needs benefit the city, since you desire to reap her honours?

Glauc. Undoubtedly.

Then, by all that is sacred (Socrates continued), do not keep us in the dark, but tell us in what way do you propose first to benefit the state? what is your starting-point?[314] When Glaucon remained with sealed lips, as if he were now for the first time debating what this starting-point should be, Socrates continued: I presume, if you wished to improve a friend's estate, you would endeavour to do so by adding to its wealth, would you not? So here, maybe, you will try to add to the wealth of the state?

Most decidedly (he answered).

Soc. And we may take it the state will grow wealthier in proportion as her revenues increase?

Glauc. That seems probable, at any rate.

Soc. Then would you kindly tell us from what sources the revenues of the state are at present derived, and what is their present magnitude? No doubt you have gone carefully into the question, so that if any of

---

Aristoph. *Knights*, 665, (kath eilkon auton oi prutaneis kai toxotai).

[310] For Charmides (maternal uncle of Plato and Glaucon, cousin of Critias) see ch. vii. below; Plato the philosopher, Glaucon's brother, see Cobet, *Pros. Xen.* p. 28.

[311] Or, "and in the first instance addressing him in such terms he could not choose but hear, detained him." See above, II. vi. 11. Socrates applies his own theory.

[312] (prostateuein).

[313] "The centre of attraction—the cynosure of neighbouring eyes."

[314] Or, "tell us what your starting-point will be in the path of benefaction."

these are failing you may make up the deficit, or if neglected for any reason, make some new provision.[315]

Glauc. Nay, to speak the truth, these are matters I have not thoroughly gone into.

Never mind (he said) if you have omitted the point; but you might oblige us by running through the items or heads of expenditure. Obviously you propose to remove all those which are superfluous?

Glauc. Well, no. Upon my word I have not had time to look into that side of the matter either as yet.

Soc. Then we will postpone for the present the problem of making the state wealthier; obviously without knowing the outgoings and the incomings it would be impossible to deal with the matter seriously.

But, Socrates (Glaucon remarked), it is possible to enrich the state out of the pockets of her enemies!

Yes, to be sure, considerably (answered Socrates), in the event of getting the better of them; but in the event of being worsted, it is also possible to lose what we have got.

A true observation (he replied).

And therefore (proceeded Socrates), before he makes up his mind with what enemy to go to war, a statesman should know the relative powers of his own city and the adversary's, so that, in case the superiority be on his own side, he may throw the weight of his advice into the scale of undertaking war; but if the opposite he may plead in favour of exercising caution.

You are right (he answered).

Soc. Then would you for our benefit enumerate the land and naval forces first of Athens and then of our opponents?

Glauc. Pardon me. I could not tell you them off-hand at a moment's notice.

Or (added Socrates), if you have got the figures on paper, you might produce them. I cannot tell how anxious I am to hear your statement.

Glauc. No, I assure you, I have not got them even on paper yet.

Soc. Well then, we will defer tending advice on the topic of peace or war, in a maiden speech at any rate.[316] I can understand that, owing to the magnitude of the questions, in these early days of your ministry you have not yet fully examined them. But come, I am sure that you have studied the defences of the country, at all events, and you know exactly how many forts and outposts are serviceable[317] and how many are not; you can tell us which garrisons are strong enough and which defective; and you are prepared to throw in the weight of your advice in

---

[315] Or, "or if others have dropped out or been negligently overlooked, you may replace them."

[316] See *Econ.* xi. 1.

[317] Or, "advantageously situated." See the author's own tract on *Revenues*.

favour of increasing the serviceable outposts and sweeping away those that are superfluous?

Glauc. Yes, sweep them all away, that's my advice; for any good that is likely to come of them! Defences indeed! so maintained that the property of the rural districts is simply pilfered.

But suppose you sweep away the outposts (he asked), may not something worse, think you, be the consequence? will not sheer plundering be free to any ruffian who likes?... But may I ask is this judgment the result of personal inspection? have you gone yourself and examined the defences? or how do you know that they are all maintained as you say?

Glauc. I conjecture that it is so.

Soc. Well then, until we have got beyond the region of conjecture shall we defer giving advice on the matter? (It will be time enough when we know the facts.)

Possibly it would be better to wait till then (replied Glaucon).

Soc. Then there are the mines,[318] but, of course, I am aware that you have not visited them in person, so as to be able to say why they are less productive than formerly.

Well, no; I have never been there myself (he answered).

Soc. No, Heaven help us! an unhealthy district by all accounts; so that, when the moment for advice on that topic arrives, you will have an excuse ready to hand.

I see you are making fun of me (Glaucon answered).

Soc. Well, but here is a point, I am sure, which you have not neglected. No, you will have thoroughly gone into it, and you can tell us. For how long a time could the corn supplies from the country districts support the city? how much is requisite for a single year, so that the city may not run short of this prime necessary, before you are well aware; but on the contrary you with your full knowledge will be in a position to give advice on so vital a question, to the aid or may be the salvation of your country?

It is a colossal business this (Glaucon answered), if I am to be obliged to give attention to all these details.

Soc. On the other hand, a man could not even manage his own house or his estate well, without, in the first place, knowing what he requires, and, in the second place, taking pains, item by item, to supply his wants. But since this city consists of more than ten thousand houses, and it is not easy to pay minute attention to so many all at once, how is it you did not practise yourself by trying to augment the resources of one at any rate of these—I mean your own uncle's? The service would not be thrown away. Then if your strength suffices in the single case you might take in hand a larger number; but if you fail to relieve one,

---

[318] Again the author's tract on *Revenues* is a comment on the matter.

how could you possibly hope to succeed with many? How absurd for a man, if he cannot carry half a hundredweight, to attempt to carry a whole![319]

Glauc. Nay, for my part, I am willing enough to assist my uncle's house, if my uncle would only be persuaded to listen to my advice.

Soc. Then, when you cannot persuade your uncle, do you imagine you will be able to make the whole Athenian people, uncle and all, obey you? Be careful, Glaucon (he added), lest in your thirst for glory and high repute you come to the opposite. Do you not see how dangerous it is for a man to speak or act beyond the range[320] of his knowledge? To take the cases known to you of people whose conversation or conduct clearly transcends these limits: should you say they gain more praise or more blame on that account? Are they admired the rather or despised? Or, again, consider those who do know what they say and what they do; and you will find, I venture to say, that in every sort of undertaking those who enjoy repute and admiration belong to the class of those endowed with the highest knowledge; whilst conversely the people of sinister reputation, the mean and the contemptible, emanate from some depth of ignorance and dulness. If therefore what you thirst for is repute and admiration as a statesman, try to make sure of one accomplishment: in other words, the knowledge as far as in you lies of what you wish to do.[321] If, indeed, with this to distinguish you from the rest of the world you venture to concern yourself with state affairs, it would not surprise me but that you might reach the goal of your ambition easily.

VII

Now Charmides,[322] the son of Glaucon, was, as Socrates observed, a man of mark and influence: a much more powerful person in fact than the mass of those devoted to politics at that date, but at the same time he was a man who shrank from approaching the people or busying himself with the concerns of the state. Accordingly Socrates addressed him thus:

Tell me, Charmides, supposing some one competent to win a victory in the arena and to receive a crown,[323] whereby he will gain honour himself and make the land of his fathers more glorious in

---

[319] Lit. "a single talent's weight... to carry two."

[320] Or, "to talk of things which he does not know, or to meddle with them."

[321] Or, "try as far as possible to achieve one thing, and that is to know the business which you propose to carry out."

[322] See last chapter for his relationship to Glaucon (the younger) and Plato; for a conception of his character, Plato's dialogue *Charmides*; "Theag." 128 E; *Hell.* II. iv. 19; *Symp.* iv. 31; Grote, *Plato*, i. 480.

[323] In some conquest (*e.g.* of the Olympic games) where the prize is a mere wreath.

Xenophon

Hellas,[324] were to refuse to enter the lists—what kind of person should you set him down to be?

Clearly an effeminate and cowardly fellow (he answered).

Soc. And what if another man, who had it in him, by devotion to affairs of state, to exalt his city and win honour himself thereby, were to shrink and hesitate and hang back—would he too not reasonably be regarded as a coward?

Possibly (he answered); but why do you address these questions to me?

Because (replied Socrates) I think that you, who have this power, do hesitate to devote yourself to matters which, as being a citizen, if for no other reason, you are bound to take part in.[325]

Charm. And wherein have you detected in me this power, that you pass so severe a sentence upon me?

Soc. I have detected it plainly enough in those gatherings[326] in which you meet the politicians of the day, when, as I observe, each time they consult you on any point you have always good advice to offer, and when they make a blunder you lay your finger on the weak point immediately.

Charm. To discuss and reason in private is one thing, Socrates, to battle in the throng of the assembly is another.

Soc. And yet a man who can count, counts every bit as well in a crowd as when seated alone by himself; and it is the best performer on the harp in private who carries off the palm of victory in public.

Charm. But do you not see that modesty and timidity are feelings implanted in man's nature? and these are much more powerfully present to us in a crowd than within the circle of our intimates.

Soc. Yes, but what I am bent on teaching you is that while you feel no such bashfulness and timidity before the wisest and strongest of men, you are ashamed of opening your lips in the midst of weaklings and dullards.[327] Is it the fullers among them of whom you stand in awe, or the cobblers, or the carpenters, or the coppersmiths, or the merchants, or the farmers, or the hucksters of the market-place exchanging their wares, and bethinking them how they are to buy this thing cheap, and to sell the other dear—is it before these you are ashamed, for these are the individual atoms out of which the Public Assembly is composed?[328] And what is the difference, pray, between your behaviour and that of a man who, being the superior of trained athletes, quails before a set of amateurs? Is it not the case that you who can argue so readily with the foremost statesmen in the city, some of

---

[324] Cf. Pindar passim.
[325] Or add, "and cannot escape from."
[326] See above, I. v. 4; here possibly of political club conversation.
[327] Cf. Cic. *Tusc.* v. 36, 104; Plat. *Gorg.* 452 E, 454 B.
[328] Cf. Plat. *Protag.* 319 C. See W. L. Newman, *op. cit.* i. 103.

whom affect to look down upon you—you, with your vast superiority over practised popular debaters—are no sooner confronted with a set of folk who never in their lives gave politics a thought, and into whose heads certainly it never entered to look down upon you—than you are afraid to open your lips in mortal terror of being laughed at?

Well, but you would admit (he answered) that sound argument does frequently bring down the ridicule of the Popular Assembly.

Soc. Which is equally true of the others.[329] And that is just what rouses my astonishment, that you who can cope so easily with these lordly people (when guilty of ridicule) should persuade yourself that you cannot stand up against a set of commoners.[330] My good fellow, do not be ignorant of yourself![331] do not fall into that commonest of errors—theirs who rush off to investigate the concerns of the rest of the world, and have no time to turn and examine themselves. Yet that is a duty which you must not in cowardly sort draw back from: rather must you brace ourself to give good heed to your own self; and as to public affairs, if by any manner of means they may be improved through you, do not neglect them. Success in the sphere of politics means that not only the mass of your fellow-citizens, but your personal friends and you yourself last but not least, will profit by your action.

VIII

Once when Aristippus[332] set himself to subject Socrates to a cross-examination, such as he had himself undergone at the hands of Socrates on a former occasion,[333] Socrates, being minded to benefit those who were with him, gave his answers less in the style of a debater guarding against perversions of his argument, than of a man persuaded of the supreme importance of right conduct.[334]

Aristippus asked him "if he knew of anything good,"[335] intending in case he assented and named any particular good thing, like food or drink, or wealth, or health, or strength, or courage, to point out that the thing named was sometimes bad. But he, knowing that if a thing troubles us, we immediately want that which will put an end to our

---

[329] (oi eteroi), *i.e.* "the foremost statesmen" mentioned before. *Al.* "the opposite party," the "Tories," if one may so say, of the political clubs.

[330] Lit. "those... these."

[331] Ernesti aptly cf. Cic. *ad Quint.* iii. 6. See below, III. ix. 6; IV. ii. 24.

[332] For Aristippus see above, p. 38; for the connection, (boulomenos tous sunontas ophelein), between this and the preceeding chapter, see above, Conspectus, p. xxvi.

[333] Possibly in reference to the conversation above. In reference to the present dialogue see Grote, *Plato*, I. xi. p. 380 foll.

[334] For (prattein ta deonta) cf. below, III. ix. 4, 11; Plat. *Charm.* 164 B; but see J. J. Hartman, *An. Xen.* p. 141.

[335] See Grote, *Plato*, ii. 585, on *Philebus.*

trouble, answered precisely as it was best to do.[336]
Soc. Do I understand you to ask me whether I know anything good for fever?
No (he replied), that is not my question.
Soc. Then for inflammation of the eyes?
Aristip. No, nor yet that.
Soc. Well then, for hunger?
Aristip. No, nor yet for hunger.
Well, but (answered Socrates) if you ask me whether I know of any good thing which is good for nothing, I neither know of it nor want to know.

And when Aristippus, returning to the charge, asked him "if he knew of any thing beautiful."
He answered: Yes, many things.
Aristip. Are they all like each other?
Soc. On the contrary, they are often as unlike as possible.
How then (he asked) can that be beautiful which is unlike the beautiful?
Soc. Bless me! for the simple reason that it is possible for a man who is a beautiful runner to be quite unlike another man who is a beautiful boxer,[337] or for a shield, which is a beautiful weapon for the purpose of defence, to be absolutely unlike a javelin, which is a beautiful weapon of swift and sure discharge.
Aristip. Your answers are no better now than[338] when I asked you whether you knew any good thing. They are both of a pattern.
Soc. And so they should be. Do you imagine that one thing is good and another beautiful? Do not you know that relatively to the same standard all things are at once beautiful and good?[339] In the first place, virtue is not a good thing relatively to one standard and a beautiful thing relatively to another standard; and in the next place, human beings, on the same principle[340] and relatively to the same standard, are called "beautiful and good"; and so the bodily frames of men relatively to the same standards are seen to be "beautiful and good," and in general all things capable of being used by man are regarded as at once beautiful and good relatively to the same standard—the standing being in each case what the thing happens to be useful for.[341]
Aristip. Then I presume even a basket for carrying dung[342] is a

---

[336] Or, "made the happiest answer."
[337] See Grote, *H. G.* x. 164, in reference to Epaminondas and his gymnastic training; below, III. x. 6.
[338] Or, "You answer precisely as you did when..."
[339] Or, "*good* and *beautiful* are convertible terms: whatever is *good* is *beautiful*, or whatever is *beautiful* is *good*."
[340] Or, "in the same breath." Cf. Plat. "*Hipp. maj.*" 295 D; *Gorg.* 474 D.
[341] Or, "and this standard is the serviceableness of the thing in question."
[342] Cf. Plat. "*Hipp. maj.*" 288 D, 290 D; and Grote's note, *loc. cit.* p. 381: "in regard

beautiful thing?
Soc. To be sure, and a spear of gold an ugly thing, if for their respective uses—the former is well and the latter ill adapted.
Aristip. Do you mean to assert that the same things may be beautiful and ugly?
Soc. Yes, to be sure; and by the same showing things may be good and bad: as, for instance, what is good for hunger may be bad for fever, and what is good for fever bad for hunger; or again, what is beautiful for wrestling is often ugly for running; and in general everything is good and beautiful when well adapted for the end in view, bad and ugly when ill adapted for the same.

Similarly when he spoke about houses,[343] and argued that "the same house must be at once beautiful and useful"—I could not help feeling that he was giving a good lesson on the problem: "how a house ought to be built." He investigated the matter thus:
Soc. "Do you admit that any one purposing to build a perfect house[344] will plan to make it at once as pleasant and as useful to live in as possible?" and that point being admitted,[345] the next question would be:
"It is pleasant to have one's house cool in summer and warm in winter, is it not?" and this proposition also having obtained assent, "Now, supposing a house to have a southern aspect, sunshine during winter will steal in under the verandah,[346] but in summer, when the sun traverses a path right over our heads, the roof will afford an agreeable shade, will it not? If, then, such an arrangement is desirable, the southern side of a house should be built higher to catch the rays of the winter sun, and the northern side lower to prevent the cold winds finding ingress; in a word, it is reasonable to suppose that the pleasantest and most beautiful dwelling place will be one in which the owner can at all seasons of the year find the pleasantest retreat, and stow away his goods with the greatest security."

Paintings[347] and ornamental mouldings are apt (he said) to deprive one of more joy[348] than they confer.

The fittest place for a temple or an altar (he maintained) was some site visible from afar, and untrodden by foot of man:[349] since it was a

---

to the question wherein consists (to kalon)?"
[343] See K. Joel, *op. cit.* p. 488; "Classical Review," vii. 262.
[344] Or, "the ideal house"; lit. "a house as it should be."
[345] See below, IV. vi. 15.
[346] Or, "porticoes" or "collonade."
[347] See *Econ.* ix. 2; Plat. *Hipp. maj.* 298 A; *Rep.* 529; Becker, *Charicles,* 268 (Engl. trans.)
[348] (euphrosunas), archaic or "poetical" = "joyance." See *Hiero,* vi. 1.
[349] *e.g.* the summit of Lycabettos, or the height on which stands the temple of Phygaleia. Cf. Eur. *Phoen.* 1372, (Pallados khrusaspidos blepsas pros oikon euxato) of

glad thing for the worshipper to lift up his eyes afar off and offer up his orison; glad also to wend his way peaceful to prayer unsullied.[350]

IX

Being again asked by some one: could *courage* be taught,[351] or did it come by nature? he answered: I imagine that just as one body is by nature stronger than another body to encounter toils, so one soul by nature grows more robust than another soul in face of dangers. Certainly I do note that people brought up under the same condition of laws and customs differ greatly in respect of daring. Still my belief is that by learning and practice the natural aptitude may always be strengthened towards courage. It is clear, for instance, that Scythians or Thracians would not venture to take shield and spear and contend with Lacedaemonians; and it is equally evident that Lacedaemonians would demur to entering the lists of battle against Thracians if limited to their light shields and javelins, or against Scythians without some weapon more familiar than their bows and arrows.[352] And as far as I can see, this principle holds generally: the natural differences of one man from another may be compensated by artificial progress, the result of care and attention. All which proves clearly that whether nature has endowed us with keener or blunter sensibilities, the duty of all alike is to learn and practise those things in which we would fain achieve distinction.

Between *wisdom* and *sobriety of soul* (which is *temperance*) he drew no distinction.[353] Was a man able on the one hand to recognise things beautiful and good sufficiently to live in them? Had he, on the other hand, knowledge of the "base and foul" so as to beware of them? If so, Socrates judged him to be wise at once and sound of soul (or temperate).[354]

And being further questioned whether "he considered those who

---

Eteocles.
[350] See Vitruvius, i. 7, iv. 5, ap. Schneid. *ad loc.*; W. L. Newman, *op. cit.* i. 338.
[351] Or, "When some one retorted upon him with the question: 'Can courage be taught?'" and for this problem see IV. vi. 10, 11; *Symp.* ii. 12; Plat. *Lach.*; *Protag.* 349; *Phaedr.* 269 D; K. Joel, *op. cit.* p. 325 foll.; Grote, *Plato*, i. 468 foll., ii. 60; Jowett, *Plato*, i. 77, 119; Newman, *op. cit.* i. 343.
[352] Or, "against Thracians with light shields and javelins, or against Scythians with bows and arrows"; and for the national arms of these peoples respectively see Arist. *Lysistr.* 563; *Anab.* III. iv. 15; VI. VII. *passim.*
[353] But cf. IV. vi. 7; K. Joel, *op. cit.* p. 363.
[354] Reading (alla to... kai to), or more lit. "he discovered the wise man and sound of soul in his power not only to recognise things 'beautiful and good,' but to live and move and have his being in them; as also in his gift of avoiding consciously things base." Or if (alla ton... kai ton...) transl. "The man who not only could recognise the beautiful and good, but lived, etc., in that world, and who moreover consciously avoided things base, in the judgment of Socrates was wise and sound of soul." Cf. Plat. *Charm.*

have the knowledge of right action, but do not apply it, to be wise and self-controlled?"—"Not a whit more," he answered, "than I consider them to be unwise and intemperate.[355] Every one, I conceive, deliberately chooses what, within the limits open to him, he considers most conducive to his interest, and acts accordingly. I must hold therefore that those who act against rule and crookedly[356] are neither wise nor self-controlled.

He said that *justice*, moreover, and all other *virtue* is *wisdom*. That is to say, things just, and all things else that are done with virtue, are "beautiful and good"; and neither will those who know these things deliberately choose aught else in their stead, nor will he who lacks the special knowledge of them be able to do them, but even if he makes the attempt he will miss the mark and fail. So the wise alone can perform the things which are "beautiful and good"; they that are unwise cannot, but even if they try they fail. Therefore, since all things just, and generally all things "beautiful and good," are wrought with virtue, it is clear that justice and all other virtue is wisdom.

On the other hand, *madness* (he maintained) was the opposite to wisdom; not that he regarded simple ignorance as madness,[357] but he put it thus: for a man to be ignorant of himself, to imagine and suppose that he knows what he knows not, was (he argued), if not madness itself, yet something very like it. The mass of men no doubt hold a different language: if a man is all abroad on some matter of which the mass of mankind are ignorant, they do not pronounce him "mad";[358] but a like aberration of mind, if only it be about matters within the scope of ordinary knowledge, they call madness. For instance, any one who imagined himself too tall to pass under a gateway of the Long Wall without stooping, or so strong as to try to lift a house, or to attempt any other obvious impossibility, is a madman according to them; but in the popular sense he is not mad, if his obliquity is confined to small matters. In fact, just as strong desire goes by the name of *passion* in popular parlance, so mental obliquity on a grand scale is entitled *madness*.

In answer to the question: what is *envy*? he discovered it to be a certain kind of pain; not certainly the sorrow felt at the misfortunes of a friend or the good fortune of an enemy—that is not envy; but, as he said, "envy is felt by those alone who are annoyed at the successes of their friends." And when some one or other expressed astonishment

---

[355] For the phrase "not a whit the more" see below, III. xii. 1; *Econ.* xii. 18. *Al.* "I should by no means choose to consider them wise and self-controlled rather than foolish and intemperate."

[356] "Who cannot draw a straight line, ethically speaking."

[357] See K. Joel, *op. cit.* p. 346; Grote, *Plato*, i. 400.

[358] Or, "they resent the term 'mad' being applied to people who are all abroad," etc. See Comte, *Pos. Pol.* i. 575; ii. 373 (Engl. trans.).

Xenophon

that any one friendlily disposed to another should be pained at his well-doing, he reminded him of a common tendency in people: when any one is faring ill their sympathies are touched, they rush to the aid of the unfortunate; but when fortune smiles on others, they are somehow pained. "I do not say," he added, "this could happen to a thoughtful person; but it is no uncommon condition of a silly mind."[359]

In answer to the question: what is *leisure*? I discover (he said) that most men do something:[360] for instance, the dice player,[361] the gambler, the buffoon, do something, but these have leisure; they can, if they like, turn and do something better; but nobody has leisure to turn from the better to the worse, and if he does so turn, when he has no leisure, he does but ill in that.

(To pass to another definition.) They are not *kings* or *rulers* (he said) who hold the sceptre merely, or are chosen by fellows out of the street,[362] or are appointed by lot, or have stepped into office by violence or by fraud; but those who have the special knowledge[363] how to rule. Thus having won the admission that it is the function of a ruler to enjoin what ought to be done, and of those who are ruled to obey, he proceeded to point out by instances that in a ship the ruler or captain is the man of special knowledge, to whom, as an expert, the shipowner himself and all the others on board obey. So likewise, in the matter of husbandry, the proprietor of an estate; in that of sickness, the patient; in that of physical training of the body, the youthful athlete going through a course; and, in general, every one directly concerned in any matter needing attention and care will either attend to this matter personally, if he thinks he has the special knowledge; or, if he mistrusts his own science, will be eager to obey any expert on the spot, or will even send and fetch one from a distance. The guidance of this expert he will follow, and do what he has to do at his dictation.

And thus, in the art of spinning wool, he liked to point out that women are the rulers of men—and why? because they have the knowledge of the art, and men have not.

And if any one raised the objection that a *tyrant* has it in his power not to obey good and correct advice, he would retort: "Pray, how has he the option not to obey, considering the penalty hanging over him who disobeys the words of wisdom? for whatever the matter be in which he disobeys the word of good advice, he will fall into error, I presume, and falling into error, be punished." And to the suggestion that the tyrant

---

[359] Or, "a man in his senses... a simpleton"; for the sentiment L. Dind. cf. Isocr. *ad Demonic.* 7 D.

[360] See above, I. ii. 57; and in ref. to these definitions, K. Joel, *op. cit.* p. 347 foll.

[361] For "dice-playing" see Becker, *Charicl.* 354 (Engl. trans.); for "buffoonery," ib. 98; *Symp.*

[362] Tom, Dick, and Harry (as we say).

[363] The (episteme). See above, III. v. 21; Newman, *op. cit.* i. 256.

could, if he liked, cut off the head of the man of wisdom, his answer was: "Do you think that he who destroys his best ally will go scot free, or suffer a mere slight and passing loss? Is he more likely to secure his salvation that way, think you, or to compass his own swift destruction?"[364]

When some one asked him: "What he regarded as the best pursuit or business[365] for a man?" he answered: "*Successful conduct*";[366] and to a second question: "Did he then regard good fortune as an end to be pursued?"—"On the contrary," he answered, "for myself, I consider fortune and conduct to be diametrically opposed. For instance, to succeed in some desirable course of action without seeking to do so, I hold to be good fortune; but to do a thing well by dint of learning and practice, that according to my creed is successful conduct,[367] and those who make this the serious business of their life seem to me to do well."

They are at once the best and the dearest in the sight of God[368] (he went on to say) who for instance in husbandry do well the things of farming, or in the art of healing all that belongs to healing, or in statecraft the affairs of state; whereas a man who does nothing well— nor well in anything—is (he added) neither good for anything nor dear to God.

X

But indeed,[369] if chance brought him into conversation with any one possessed of an art, and using it for daily purposes of business, he never failed to be useful to this kind of person. For instance, stepping one time into the studio of Parrhasius[370] the painter, and getting into conversation with him—

I suppose, Parrhasius (said he), painting may be defined as "a representation of visible objects," may it not?[371] That is to say, by

---

[364] Or, "Is that to choose the path of safety, think you? Is it not rather to sign his own death-warrant?" L. Dind. cf. Hesiod, *Works and Days*, 293. See Newman, *op. cit.* i. 393-397.

[365] Or, "the noblest study."

[366] (eupraxia, eu prattein)—to do well, in the sense both of well or right doing, and of welfare, and is accordingly opposed to (eutukhia), mere good luck or success. Cf. Plat. *Euthyd.* 281 B.

[367] Lit. "well-doing"; and for the Socratic view see Newman, *op. cit.* i. 305, 401.

[368] Or, "most divinely favoured." Cf. Plat. *Euthyphro*, 7 A.

[369] (alla men kai)... "But indeed the sphere of his helpfulness was not circumscribed; if," etc.

[370] For Parrhasius of Ephesus, the son of Evenor and rival of Zeuxis, see Woltmann and Woermann, *Hist. of Painting*, p. 47 foll.; Cobet, *Pros. Xen.* p. 50 (cf. in particular Quint. XII. x. 627). At the date of conversation (real or ideal) he may be supposed to have been a young man.

[371] Reading with Schneider, L. Dind., etc., after Stobaeus, (e graphike estin eikasia), or if the vulg. (graphike estin e eikasia), trans. "Painting is the term applied to a particular

means of colours and palette you painters represent and reproduce as closely as possible the ups and downs, lights and shadows, hard and soft, rough and smooth surfaces, the freshness of youth and the wrinkles of age, do you not?

You are right (he answered), that is so.

Soc. Further, in portraying ideal types of beauty, seeing it is not easy to light upon any one human being who is absolutely devoid of blemish, you cull from many models the most beautiful traits of each, and so make your figures appear completely beautiful?[372]

Parrh. Yes, that is how we do.[373]

Well, but stop (Socrates continued); do you also pretend to represent in similar perfection the characteristic moods of the soul, its captivating charm and sweetness, with its deep wells of love, its intensity of yearning, its burning point of passion? or is all this quite incapable of being depicted?

Nay (he answered), how should a mood be other than inimitable, Socrates, when it possesses neither linear proportion[374] nor colour, nor any of those qualities which you named just now; when, in a word, it is not even visible?

Soc. Well, but the kindly look of love, the angry glance of hate at any one, do find expression in the human subject, do they not?[375]

Parrh. No doubt they do.

Soc. Then this look, this glance, at any rate may be imitated in the eyes, may it not?

Undoubtedly (he answered).

Soc. And do anxiety and relief of mind occasioned by the good or evil fortune of those we love both wear the same expression?

By no means (he answered); at the thought of good we are radiant, at that of evil a cloud hangs on the brow.

Soc. Then here again are looks with it is possible to represent?

Parrh. Decidedly.

Soc. Furthermore, as through some chink or crevice, there pierces through the countenance of a man, through the very posture of his body as he stands or moves, a glimpse of his nobility and freedom, or again of something in him low and grovelling—the calm of self-restraint, and wisdom, or the swagger of insolence and vulgarity?

You are right (he answered).

---

representation," etc.

[372] Cf. Cic. *de Invent.* ii. 1 ad in. of Zeuxis; Max. Tur. *Dissert.* 23, 3, ap. Schneider *ad loc.*

[373] Or, "that is the secret of our creations," or "our art of composition."

[374] Lit. "symmetry." Cf. Plin. xxxv. 10, "primus symmetriam picturae dedit," etc.

[375] Or, "the glance of love, the scowl of hate, which one directs towards another, are recognised expressions of human feeling." Cf. the description of Parrhasius's own portrait of Demos, ap. Plin. *loc. cit.*

Soc. Then these too may be imitated?

No doubt (he said).

Soc. And which is the pleasanter type of face to look at, do you think—one on which is imprinted the characteristics of a beautiful, good, and lovable disposition, or one which bears the impress of what is ugly, and bad, and hateful?[376]

Parrh. Doubtless, Socrates, there is a vast distinction between the two.

At another time he entered the workshop of the sculptor Cleiton,[377] and in course of conversation with him said:

You have a gallery of handsome people here,[378] Cleiton, runners, and wrestlers, and boxers, and pancratiasts—that I see and know; but how do you give the magic touch of life to your creations, which most of all allures the soul of the beholder through his sense of vision?

As Cleiton stood perplexed, and did not answer at once, Socrates added: Is it by closely imitating the forms of living beings that you succeed in giving that touch of life to your statues?

No doubt (he answered).

Soc. It is, is it not, by faithfully copying the various muscular contractions of the body in obedience to the play of gesture and poise, the wrinklings of flesh and the sprawl of limbs, the tensions and the relaxations, that you succeed in making your statues like real beings—make them "breathe" as people say?

Cleit. Without a doubt.

Soc. And does not the faithful imitation of the various affections of the body when engaged in any action impart a particular pleasure to the beholder?

Cleit. I should say so.

Soc. Then the threatenings in the eyes of warriors engaged in battle should be carefully copied, or again you should imitate the aspect of a conqueror radiant with success?

Cleit. Above all things.

Soc. It would seem then that the sculptor is called upon to incorporate in his ideal form the workings and energies also of the soul?

---

[376] For this theory cp. Ruskin, "Mod. P." ii. 94 foll. and indeed passim.

[377] An unknown artist. Coraes conj. (Kleona). Cf. Plin. xxxiv. 19; Paus. v. 17, vi. 3. He excelled in portrait statues. See Jowett, *Plato,* iv.; "Laws," p. 123.

[378] Reading after L. Dind. (kaloi ous), or if vulg. (alloious), translate "You have a variety of types, Cleiton, not all of one mould, but runners," etc.; al. "I see quite well how you give the diversity of form to your runners," etc.

Xenophon

Paying a visit to Pistias,[379] the corselet maker, when that artist showed him some exquisite samples of his work, Socrates exclaimed:

By Hera! a pretty invention this, Pistias, by which you contrive that the corselet should cover the parts of the person which need protection, and at the same time leave free play to the arms and hands.... but tell me, Pistias (he added), why do you ask a higher price for these corselets of yours if they are not stouter or made of costlier material than the others?

Because, Socrates (he answered), mine are of much finer proportion.

Soc. Proportion! Then how do you make this quality apparent to the customer so as to justify the higher price—by measure or weight? For I presume you cannot make them all exactly equal and of one pattern—if you make them fit, as of course you do?

Fit indeed! that I most distinctly do (he answered), take my word for it: no use in a corselet without that.

But then are not the wearer's bodies themselves (asked Socrates) some well proportioned and others ill?

Decidedly so (he answered).

Soc. Then how do you manage to make the corselet well proportioned if it is to fit an ill-proportioned body?[380]

Pist. To the same degree exactly as I make it fit. What fits is well proportioned.

Soc. It seems you use the term "well-proportioned" not in an absolute sense, but in reference to the wearer, just as you might describe a shield as well proportioned to the individual it suits; and so of a military cloak, and so of the rest of things, in your terminology? But maybe there is another considerable advantage in this "fitting"?

Pist. Pray instruct me, Socrates, if you have got an idea.

Soc. A corselet which fits is less galling by its weight than one which does *not* fit, for the latter must either drag from the shoulders with a dead weight or press upon some other part of the body, and so it becomes troublesome and uncomfortable; but that which fits, having its weight distributed partly along the collar-bone and shoulder-blade, partly over the shoulders and chest, and partly the back and belly, feels like another natural integument rather than an extra load to carry.[381]

Pist. You have named the very quality which gives my work its exceptional value, as I consider; still there are customers, I am bound to

---

[379] Cf. Athen. iv. 20, where the same artist is referred to apparently as (Piston), and for the type of person see the "Portrait of a Tailor" by Moroni in the National Gallery—see *Handbook*, Edw. T. Cook, p. 152.

[380] Or, "how do you make a well-proportioned corselet fit an ill-proportioned body? how well proportioned?"

[381] Schneider *ad loc.* cf. Eur. *Electr.* 192, (prosthemata aglaias), and for the weight cf. Aristoph. *Peace*, 1224.

say, who look for something else in a corselet—they must have them ornamental or inlaid with gold.

For all that (replied Socrates), if they end by purchasing an ill-fitting article, they only become the proprietors of a curiously-wrought and gilded nuisance, as it seems to me. But (he added), as the body is never in one fixed position, but is at one time curved, at another raised erect how can an exactly-modelled corselet fit?

Pist. It cannot fit at all.

You mean (Socrates continued) that it is not the exactly-modelled corselet which fits, but that which does not gall the wearer in the using?

Pist. There, Socrates, you have hit the very point. I see you understand the matter most precisely.[382]

XI

There was once in the city a fair woman named Theodoté.[383] She was not only fair, but ready to consort with any suitor who might win her favour. Now it chanced that some one of the company mentioned her, saying that her beauty beggared description. "So fair is she," he added, "that painters flock to draw her portrait, to whom, within the limits of decorum, she displays the marvels of her beauty." "Then there is nothing for it but to go and see her," answered Socrates, "since to comprehend by hearsay what is beyond description is clearly impossible." Then he who had introduced the matter replied: "Be quick then to follow me"; and on this wise they set off to seek Theodoté. They found her "posing" to a certain painter; and they took their stand as spectators. Presently the painter had ceased his work; whereupon Socrates:

"Do you think, sirs, that we ought to thank Theodoté for displaying her beauty to us, or she us for coming to gaze at her?... It would seem, would it not, that if the exhibition of her charms is the more profitable to her, the debt is on her side; but if the spectacle of her beauty confers the greater benefit on us, then we are her debtors."

Some one answered that "was an equitable statement of the case."

Well then (he continued), as far as she is concerned, the praise we bestow on her is an immediate gain; and presently, when we have spread her fame abroad, she will be further benefited; but for ourselves the immediate effect on us is a strong desire to touch what we have seen; by and by, too, we shall go away with a sting inside us, and when we are fairly gone we shall be consumed with longing. Consequently it

---

[382] Or, "There, Socrates, you have hit the very phrase. I could not state the matter more explicitly myself."

[383] For Theodoté see Athen. v. 200 F, xiii. 574 F; Liban. i. 582. Some say that it was Theodoté who stood by Alcibiades to the last, though there are apparently other better claimants to the honour. Plut. *Alc.* (Clough, ii. p. 50).

seems that we should do her service and she accept our court.

Whereupon Theodoté: Oh dear! if that is how the matter stands, it is I who am your debtor for the spectacle.[384]

At this point, seeing that the lady herself was expensively attired, and that she had with her her mother also, whose dress and style of attendance[385] were out of the common, not to speak of the waiting-women—many and fair to look upon, who presented anything but a forlorn appearance; while in every respect the whole house itself was sumptuously furnished—Socrates put a question:

Pray tell me, Theodoté, have you an estate in the country?

Theod. Not I indeed.

Soc. Then perhaps you possess a house and large revenues along with it?

Theod. No, nor yet a house.

Soc. You are not an employer of labour on a large scale?[386]

Theod. No, nor yet an employer of labour.

Soc. From what source, then, do you get your means of subsistence?[387]

Theod. My friends are my life and fortune, when they care to be kind to me.

Soc. By heaven, Theodoté, a very fine property indeed, and far better worth possessing than a multitude of sheep or goats or cattle. A flock of friends!... But (he added) do you leave it to fortune whether a friend lights like a fly on your hand at random, or do you use any artifice[388] yourself to attract him?

Theod. And how might I hit upon any artifice to attract him?

Soc. Bless me! far more naturally than any spider. You know how they capture the creatures on which they live;[389] by weaving webs of gossamer, is it not? and woe betide the fly that tumbles into their toils! They eat him up.

Theod. So then you would counsel me to weave myself some sort of net?

Soc. Why, surely you do not suppose you are going to ensnare that noblest of all game—a lover, to wit—in so artless a fashion? Do you not see (to speak of a much less noble sort of game) what a number of devices are needed to bag a hare?[390] The creatures range for their food at night; therefore the hunter must provide himself with night dogs. At

---

[384] In reference to the remark of Socrates above; or, "have to thank you for coming to look at me."

[385] Or, "her mother there with her in a dress and general get-up (therapeia) which was out of the common." See Becker, *Charicles*, p. 247 (Eng. tr.).

[386] *Lit.* "You have not (in your employ) a body of handicraftsmen of any sort?"

[387] Or, *Anglice*, "derive your income."

[388] Or, "means and appliances," "machinery."

[389] *Lit.* "the creatures on which they live."

[390] See the author's own treatise on "Hunting," vi. 6 foll.

peep of dawn they are off as fast as they can run. He must therefore have another pack of dogs to scent out and discover which way they betake them from their grazing ground to their forms;[391] and as they are so fleet of foot that they run and are out of sight in no time, he must once again be provided with other fleet-footed dogs to follow their tracks and overtake them;[392] and as some of them will give even these the slip, he must, last of all, set up nets on the paths at the points of escape, so that they may fall into the meshes and be caught.

Theod. And by what like contrivance would you have me catch my lovers?

Soc. Well now! what if in place of a dog you can get a man who will hunt up your wealthy lover of beauty and discover his lair, and having found him, will plot and plan to throw him into your meshes?

Theod. Nay, what sort of meshes have I?

Soc. One you have, and a close-folding net it is,[393] I trow; to wit, your own person; and inside it sits a soul that teaches you[394] with what looks to please and with what words to cheer; how, too, with smiles you are to welcome true devotion, but to exclude all wantons from your presence.[395] It tells you, you are to visit your beloved in sickness with solicitude, and when he has wrought some noble deed you are greatly to rejoice with him; and to one who passionately cares for you, you are to make surrender of yourself with heart and soul. The secret of true love I am sure you know: not to love softly merely, but devotedly.[396] And of this too I am sure: you can convince your lovers of your fondness for them not by lip phrases, but by acts of love.

Theod. No, upon my word, I have none of these devices.

Soc. And yet it makes all the difference whether you approach a human being in the natural and true way, since it is not by force certainly that you can either catch or keep a friend. Kindness and pleasure are the only means to capture this fearful wild-fowl man and keep him constant.

Theod. You are right.

Soc. In the first place you must make such demands only of your well-wisher as he can grant without repentance; and in the next place you must make requital, dispensing your favours with a like economy. Thus you will best make friends whose love shall last the longest and their generosity know no stint.[397] And for your favours you will best

---

[391] Lit. "from pasture to bed."

[392] Or, "close at their heels and run them down." See *Hunting*; cf. *Cyrop.* I. vi. 40.

[393] Or, "right well woven."

[394] Lit. "by which you understand."

[395] Or, "with what smiles to lie in wait for (cf. *Cyrop.* II. iv. 20; Herod. vi. 104) the devoted admirer, and how to banish from your presence the voluptuary."

[396] Or, "that it should be simply soft, but full of tender goodwill."

[397] Or, "This is the right road to friendship—permanent and open-handed friendship."

win your friends if you suit your largess to their penury; for, mark you, the sweetest viands presented to a man before he wants them are apt to prove insipid, or, to one already sated, even nauseous; but create hunger, and even coarser stuff seems honey-sweet.

Theod. How then shall I create this hunger in the heart of my friends?

Soc. In the first place you must not offer or make suggestion of your dainties to jaded appetites until satiety has ceased and starvation cries for alms. Even then shall you make but a faint suggestion to their want, with modest converse—like one who would fain bestow a kindness... and lo! the vision fades and she is gone—until the very pinch of hunger; for the same gifts have then a value unknown before the moment of supreme desire.

Then Theodoté: Oh why, Socrates, why are you not by my side (like the huntsman's assistant) to help me catch my friends and lovers?

Soc. That will I be in good sooth if only you can woo and win me.

Theod. How shall I woo and win you?

Soc. Seek and you will find means, if you truly need me.

Theod. Come then in hither and visit me often.

And Socrates, poking sly fun at his own lack of business occupation, answered: Nay, Theodoté, leisure is not a commodity in which I largely deal. I have a hundred affairs of my own too, private or public, to occupy me; and then there are my lady-loves, my dear friends, who will not suffer me day or night to leave them, for ever studying to learn love-charms and incantations at my lips.

Theod. Why, are you really versed in those things, Socrates?

Soc. Of course, or else how is it, do you suppose, that Apollodorus[398] here and Antisthenes never leave me; or why have Cebes and Simmias come all the way from Thebes to stay with me? Be assured these things cannot happen without diverse love-charms and incantations and magic wheels.

Theod. I wish you would lend me your magic-wheel,[399] then, and I will set it spinning first of all for you.

Soc. Ah! but I do not wish to be drawn to you. I wish you to come to me.

Theod. Then I will come. Only, will you be "at home" to me?

Soc. Yes, I will welcome you, unless some one still dearer holds me engaged, and I must needs be "not at home."

---

[398] For Apollodorus see *Apol.* 28; Plat. *Symp.* 172 A; *Phaed.* 59 A, 117 D. For Antisthenes see above. For Cebes and Simmias see above, I. ii. 48; Plat. *Crit.* 45 B; *Phaed.* passim.

[399] Cf. Theocr. ii. 17; Schneider *ad loc.*

XII

Seeing one of those who were with him, a young man, but feeble of body, named Epigenes,[400] he addressed him.

Soc. You have not the athletic appearance of a youth in training,[401] Epigenes.

And he: That may well be, seeing I am an amateur and not in training.

Soc. As little of an amateur, I take it, as any one who ever entered the lists of Olympia, unless you are prepared to make light of that contest for life and death against the public foe which the Athenians will institute when the day comes.[402] And yet they are not a few who, owing to a bad habit of body, either perish outright in the perils of war, or are ignobly saved. Many are they who for the self-same cause are taken prisoners, and being taken must, if it so betide, endure the pains of slavery for the rest of their days; or, after falling into dolorous straits,[403] when they have paid to the uttermost farthing of all, or may be more than the worth of all, that they possess, must drag on a miserable existence in want of the barest necessaries until death release them. Many also are they who gain an evil repute through infirmity of body, being thought to play the coward. Can it be that you despise these penalties affixed to an evil habit? Do you think you could lightly endure them? Far lighter, I imagine, nay, pleasant even by comparison, are the toils which he will undergo who duly cultivates a healthy bodily condition. Or do you maintain that the evil habit is healthier, and in general more useful than the good? Do you pour contempt upon those blessings which flow from the healthy state? And yet the very opposite of that which befalls the ill attends the sound condition. Does not the very soundness imply at once health and strength?[404] Many a man with no other talisman than this has passed safely through the ordeal of war; stepping, not without dignity,[405] through all its horrors unscathed. Many with no other support than this have come to the rescue of friends, or stood forth as benefactors of their fatherland; whereby they were thought worthy of gratitude, and obtained a great renown and

---

[400] Epigenes, possibly the son of Antiphon. See Plat. *Apol.* 33 E; *Phaed.* 59 B.

[401] (idiotikos), lit. of the person untrained in gymnastics. See A. R. Cluer *ad loc.* Cf. Plat. "Laws," 839 E; I. ii. 4; III. v. 15; *Symp.* ii. 17.

[402] Or, "should chance betide." Is the author thinking of a life-and-death struggle with Thebes?

[403] *e.g.* the prisoners in the Latomiae. Thuc. vii. 87.

[404] It is almost a proverb—"Sound of body and limb is hale and strong." "Qui valet praevalebit."

[405] *e.g.* Socrates himself, according to Alcibiades, ap. Plat. *Symp.* 221 B; and for the word (euskhemonos) see Arist. *Wasps*, 1210, "like a gentleman"; L. and S.; *Cyr.* I. iii. 8; Aristot. *Eth. N.* i. 10, 13, "gracefully."

received as a recompense the highest honours of the State; to whom is also reserved a happier and brighter passage through what is left to them of life, and at their death they leave to their children the legacy of a fairer starting-point in the race of life.

Because our city does not practise military training in public,[406] that is no reason for neglecting it in private, but rather a reason for making it a foremost care. For be you assured that there is no contest of any sort, nor any transaction, in which you will be the worse off for being well prepared in body; and in fact there is nothing which men do for which the body is not a help. In every demand, therefore, which can be laid upon the body it is much better that it should be in the best condition; since, even where you might imagine the claims upon the body to be slightest—in the act of reasoning—who does not know the terrible stumbles which are made through being out of health? It suffices to say that forgetfulness, and despondency, and moroseness, and madness take occasion often of ill-health to visit the intellectual faculties so severely as to expel all knowledge[407] from the brain. But he who is in good bodily plight has large security. He runs no risk of incurring any such catastrophe through ill-health at any rate; he has the expectation rather that a good habit must procure consequences the opposite to those of an evil habit;[408] and surely to this end there is nothing a man in his senses would not undergo.... It is a base thing for a man to wax old in careless self-neglect before he has lifted up his eyes and seen what manner of man he was made to be, in the full perfection of bodily strength and beauty. But these glories are withheld from him who is guilty of self-neglect, for they are not wont to blaze forth unbidden.[409]

XII

Once when some one was in a fury of indignation because he had bidden a passer-by good-day and the salutation was not returned, Socrates said: "It is enough to make one laugh! If you met a man in a wretched condition of body, you would not fall into a rage; but because you stumble upon a poor soul somewhat boorishly disposed, you feel annoyed."

To the remark of another who complained that he did not take his foot with pleasure, he said: "Acumenus[410] has a good prescription for

---

[406] Cf. *Pol. Ath.* i. 13; and above, III. v. 15.

[407] Or, "whole branches of knowledge" (tas epistemas).

[408] Or, "he may well hope to be insured by his good habit against the evils attendant on its opposite."

[409] Or, "to present themselves spontaneously."

[410] A well-known physician. See Plat. *Phaedr.* 227 A, 269 A; *Symp.* 176 B. A similar story is told of Dr. Abernethy, I think.

that." And when the other asked: "And what may that be?" "To stop eating," he said. "On the score of pleasure, economy, and health, total abstinence has much in its favour."[411]

And when some one else lamented that "the drinking-water in his house was hot," he replied: "Then when you want a warm bath you will not have to wait."

The Other. But for bathing purposes it is cold.

Soc. Do you find that your domestics seem to mind drinking it or washing in it?

The Other. Quite the reverse; it is a constant marvel to me how contentedly they use it for either purpose.

Soc. Which is hotter to the taste—the water in your house or the hot spring in the temple of Asclepius?[412]

The Other. The water in the temple of Asclepius.

Soc. And which is colder for bathing—yours or the cold spring in the cave of Amphiaraus?[413]

The Other. The water in the cave of Amphiaraus.

Soc. Then please to observe: if you do not take care, they will set you down as harder to please than a domestic servant or an invalid.[414]

A man had administered a severe whipping to the slave in attendance on him, and when Socrates asked: "Why he was so wroth with his own serving-man?" excused himself on the ground that "the fellow was a lazy, gourmandising, good-for-nothing dolt—fonder of money than of work." To which Socrates: "Did it ever strike you to consider which of the two in that case the more deserves a whipping—the master or the man?"

When some one was apprehending the journey to Olympia, "Why are you afraid of the long distance?" he asked. "Here at home you spend nearly all your day in taking walks.[415] Well, on your road to Olympia you will take a walk and breakfast, and then you will take another walk and dine, and go to bed. Do you not see, if you take and tack together five or six days' length of walks, and stretch them out in one long line, it will soon reach from Athens to Olympia? I would recommend you, however, to set off a day too soon rather than a day too late. To be forced to lengthen the day's journey beyond a reasonable amount may well be a nuisance; but to take one day's journey beyond what is necessary is pure relaxation. Make haste to start, I say, and not while on the road."[416]

When some one else remarked "he was utterly prostrated after a

---

[411] Lit. "he would live a happier, thriftier, and healthier life, if he stopped eating."

[412] In the Hieron at Epidauros probably. See Baedeker, *Greece*, p. 240 foll.

[413] Possibly at Oropos. Cf. Paus. i. 34. 3.

[414] *i.e.* "the least and the most fastidious of men."

[415] (peripateis), "promenading up and down."

[416] "Festina lente"—that is your motto.

long journey," Socrates asked him: "Had he had any baggage to carry?"
"Not I," replied the complainer; "only my cloak."
Soc. Were you travelling alone, or was your man-servant with you?
He. Yes, I had my man.
Soc. Empty-handed, or had he something to carry?
He. Of course; carrying my rugs and other baggage.
Soc. And how did he come off on the journey?
He. Better than I did myself, I take it.
Soc. Well, but now suppose you had had to carry his baggage, what would your condition have been like?
He. Sorry enough, I can tell you; or rather, I could not have carried it at all.
Soc. What a confession! Fancy being capable of so much less toil than a poor slave boy! Does that sound like the perfection of athletic training?

XIV

On the occasion of a common dinner-party[417] where some of the company would present themselves with a small, and others with a large supply of viands, Socrates would bid the servants[418] throw the small supplies into the general stock, or else to help each of the party to a share all round. Thus the grand victuallers were ashamed in the one case not to share in the common stock, and in the other not to throw in their supplies also.[419] Accordingly in went the grand supplies into the common stock. And now, being no better off than the small contributors, they soon ceased to cater for expensive delicacies.

At a supper-party one member of the company, as Socrates chanced to note, had put aside the plain fare and was devoting himself to certain dainties.[420] A discussion was going on about names and definitions, and the proper applications of terms to things.[421] Whereupon Socrates, appealing to the company: "Can we explain why we call a man a 'dainty fellow'? What is the particular action to which the term applies?[422]—since every one adds some dainty to his food when he can get it.[423] But we have not quite hit the definition yet, I think. Are we to be called dainty eaters because we like our bread

---

[417] For the type of entertainment see Becker, *Charicles*, p. 315 (Eng. tr.)
[418] "The boy."
[419] Or, "were ashamed not to follow suit by sharing in the common stock and contributing their own portion."
[420] For the distinction between (sitos) and (opson) see Plat. *Rep.* 372 C.
[421] Or, "The conversation had fallen upon names: what is the precise thing denoted under such and such a term? Define the meaning of so and so."
[422] (opsophagos) = (opson) (or relish) eater, and so a "gourmand" or "epicure"; but how to define a gourmand?
[423] Lit. "takes some (opson) (relish) to his (sitos) (food)."

buttered?"[424]

No! hardly! (some member of the company replied).

Soc. Well, but now suppose a man confine himself to eating venison or other dainty without any plain food at all, not as a matter of training,[425] but for the pleasure of it: has such a man earned the title? "The rest of the world would have a poor chance against him,"[426] some one answered. "Or," interposed another, "what if the dainty dishes he devours are out of all proportion to the rest of his meal—what of him?"[427]

Soc. He has established a very fair title at any rate to the appellation, and when the rest of the world pray to heaven for a fine harvest: "May our corn and oil increase!" he may reasonably ejaculate, "May my fleshpots multiply!"

At this last sally the young man, feeling that the conversation set somewhat in his direction, did not desist indeed from his savoury viands, but helped himself generously to a piece of bread. Socrates was all-observant, and added: Keep an eye on our friend yonder, you others next him, and see fair play between the sop and the sauce.[428]

Another time, seeing one of the company using but one sop of bread[429] to test several savoury dishes, he remarked: Could there be a more extravagant style of cookery, or more murderous to the dainty dishes themselves, than this wholesale method of taking so many dishes together?—why, bless me, twenty different sorts of seasoning at one swoop![430] First of all he mixes up actually more ingredients than the cook himself prescribes, which is extravagant; and secondly, he has the audacity to commingle what the *chef* holds incongruous, whereby if the cooks are right in their method he is wrong in his, and consequently the destroyer of their art. Now is it not ridiculous first to procure the greatest virtuosi to cook for us, and then without any claim to their skill to take and alter their procedure? But there is a worse thing in store for

---

[424] Lit. "simply for that" (sc. the taking of some sort of (opson). For (epi touto) cf. Plat. *Soph.* 218 C; *Parmen.* 147 D.)

[425] Lit. "(opson) (relish) by itself, not for the sake of training," etc. The English reader wil bear in mind that a raw beefsteak or other meat prescribed by the gymnastic trainer in preference to farinaceous food (sitos) would be (opson).

[426] Or, more lit. "Hardly any one could deserve the appellation better."

[427] Lit. "and what of the man who eats much (opson) on the top of a little (sitos)?" (epesthion) = follows up one course by another, like the man in a fragment of Euripides, *Incert.* 98: (kreasi boeiois khlora suk' epesthien), who "followed up his beefsteak with a garnish of green figs."

[428] Lit. "see whether he will make a relish of the staple or a staple of the relish" ("butter his bread or bread his butter").

[429] (psomos), a sop or morsel of bread (cf. (psomion), N. T., in mod. Greek = "bread").

[430] Huckleberry Finn (p. 2 of that young person's *Adventures*) propounds the *rationale* of the system: "In a barrel of odds and ends it is different; things get mixed up, and the juice kind of swaps around, and the things go better."

the bold man who habituates himself to eat a dozen dishes at once: when there are but few dishes served, out of pure habit he will feel himself half starved, whilst his neighbour, accustomed to send his sop down by help of a single relish, will feast merrily, be the dishes never so few.

He had a saying that (euokheisthai), to "make *good* cheer,"[431] was in Attic parlance a synonym for "eating," and the affix (eu) (the attributive "good") connoted the eating of such things as would not trouble soul or body, and were not far to seek or hard to find. So that to "make good cheer" in his vocabulary applied to a modest and well-ordered style of living.[432]

BOOK IV

I

Such was Socrates; so helpful under all circumstances and in every way that no observer, gifted with ordinary sensibility, could fail to appreciate the fact, that to be with Socrates, and to spend long time in his society (no matter where or what the circumstances), was indeed a priceless gain. Even the recollection of him, when he was no longer present, was felt as no small benefit by those who had grown accustomed to be with him, and who accepted him. Nor indeed was he less helpful to his acquaintance in his lighter than in his graver moods.

Let us take as an example that saying of his, so often on his lips: "I am in love with so and so"; and all the while it was obvious the going-forth of his soul was not towards excellence of body in the bloom of beauty, but rather towards faculties of the soul unfolding in virtue.[433] And these "good natures" he detected by certain tokens: a readiness to learn that to which the attention was directed; a power of retaining in the memory the lessons learnt; and a passionate predilection for those studies in particular which serve to good administration of a house or of a state,[434] and in general to the proper handling of man and human affairs. Such beings, he maintained, needed only to be educated[435] to become not only happy themselves and happy administrators of their private households, but to be capable of rendering other human beings

---

[431] (euokheisthai), cf. *Cyrop.* IV. v. 7; *Pol. Ath.* ii. 9; Kühner cf. Eustah. "ad Il." ii. p. 212, 37, ('Akhaioi ten trophen okhen legousin oxutonos). Athen. viii. 363 B. See *Hipparch*, viii. 4, of horses. Cf. Arist. *H. A.* viii. 6.

[432] See *Symp.* vi. 7; and for similar far-fetched etymologies, Plat. *Crat.* passim.

[433] Or, "not excellence of body in respect of beauty, but of the soul as regards virtue; and this good natural disposition might be detected by the readiness of its possessor to learn," etc. Cf. Plat. *Rep.* 535 B.

[434] Cf. above, I. i. 7.

[435] Or, "A person of this type would, if educated, not only prove a fortune-favoured individual himself and," etc. Al. Kühner, "Eos, qui ita instituti sunt, ut tales sint."

as states or individuals happy also.

He had indeed a different way of dealing with different kinds of people.[436] Those who thought they had good natural ability and despised learning he instructed that the most highly-gifted nature stands most in need of training and education;[437] and he would point out how in the case of horses it is just the spirited and fiery thoroughbred which, if properly broken in as a colt, will develop into a serviceable and superb animal, but if left unbroken will turn out utterly intractable and good for nothing. Or take the case of dogs: a puppy exhibiting that zest for toil and eagerness to attack wild creatures which are the marks of high breeding,[438] will, if well brought up, prove excellent for the chase or for any other useful purpose; but neglect his education and he will turn out a stupid, crazy brute, incapable of obeying the simplest command. It is just the same with human beings; here also the youth of best natural endowments—that is to say, possessing the most robust qualities of spirit and a fixed determination to carry out whatever he has laid his hand to—will, if trained and taught what it is right to do, prove a superlatively good and useful man. He achieves, in fact, what is best upon the grandest scale. But leave him in boorish ignorance untrained, and he will prove not only very bad but very mischievous,[439] and for this reason, that lacking the knowledge to discern what is right to do, he will frequently lay his hand to villainous practices; whilst the very magnificence and vehemence of his character render it impossible either to rein him in or to turn him aside from his evil courses. Hence in his case also his achievements are on the grandest scale but of the worst.[440]

Or to take the type of person so eaten up with the pride of riches that he conceives himself dispensed from any further need of education—since it is "money makes the man," and his wealth will amply suffice him to carry out his desires and to win honours from admiring humanity.[441] Socrates would bring such people to their senses by pointing out the folly of supposing that without instruction it was possible to draw the line of demarcation[442] between what is gainful and

---

[436] Or, "His method of attack was not indeed uniformly the same. It varied with the individual."

[437] Or, "If any one was disposed to look down upon learning and study in reliance upon his own natural ability, he tried to lesson him that it is just the highly-gifted nature which stands," etc. See Newman, *op. cit.* i. 397.

[438] Cf. Aristot. *H. A.* ix. 1; and *Hunting*, iii. 11.

[439] Or, "and the same man may easily become a master villain of the most dangerous sort."

[440] Kühner *ad loc.* after Fr. Hermann cf. Plato. *Crito*, 44 E; *Hipp. min.* 375 E; *Rep.* vi. 491 E; *Gorg.* 526 A; *Polit.* 303 A.

[441] Or, "and to be honoured by mankind."

[442] Or, "that without learning the distinction it was possible to distinguish between," etc.

what is hurtful in conduct; and the further folly of supposing that, apart from such discrimination, a man could help himself by means of wealth alone to whatever he liked or find the path of expediency plain before him; and was it not the veriest simplicity to suppose that, without the power of labouring profitably, a man can either be doing well or be in any sort of way sufficiently equipped for the battle of life? and again, the veriest simplicity to suppose that by mere wealth without true knowledge it was possible either to purchase a reputation for some excellence, or without such reputation to gain distinction and celebrity?

II

Or to come to a third kind—the class of people who are persuaded that they have received the best education, and are proud of their wisdom: his manner of dealing with these I will now describe.

Euthydemus[443] "the beautiful" had (Socrates was given to understand) collected a large library, consisting of the most celebrated poets and philosophers,[444] by help of which he already believed himself to be more than a match for his fellows in wisdom, and indeed might presently expect to out-top them all in capacity of speech and action.[445] At first, as Socrates noted, the young man by reason of his youth had not as yet set foot in the agora,[446] but if he had anything to transact, his habit was to seat himself in a saddler's shop hard by. Accordingly to this same saddler's shop Socrates betook himself with some of those who were with him. And first the question was started by some one: "Was it through consorting with the wise,[447] or by his own unaided talent, that Themistocles came so to surpass his fellow-citizens that when the services of a capable man were needed the eyes of the whole community instinctively turned to him?" Socrates, with a view to stirring[448] Euthydemus, answered: There was certainly an ingenuous simplicity in the belief that superiority in arts of comparatively little worth could only be attained by aid of qualified teachers, but that the leadership of the state, the most important concern of all, was destined to drop into the lap of anybody, no matter whom, like an accidental windfall.[449]

---

[443] Euthydemus, the son of Diocles perhaps. See Plat. *Symp.* 222 B, and Jowet *ad loc.*; Cobet, *Prosop. Xen.* s.n.; K. Joel, *op. cit.* p. 372 foll. For (ton kalon) cf. "Phaedr." 278 E, "Isocrates the fair." For the whole chapter cf. Plat. "Alc." i.; *Lys.* 210 E. See above, *Mem.* I. ii. 29; Grote, *Plato,* i. ch. x. *passim.*

[444] Lit. "sophists." See Grote, *H. G.* viii. p. 480, note. For private libraries see Becker, *Char.* p. 272 foll. (Eng. tr.)

[445] See *Hipparch,* i. 24; *Cyrop.* V. v. 46.

[446] See above, III. vi. 1; Schneid. cf. Isocr. *Areop.* 149 C.

[447] Cf. Soph. fr. 12, (sophoi turannoi ton sophon xunousia).

[448] L. and S. cf. Plat. "Lys." 223 A; *Rep.* 329 B: "Wishing to draw him out."

[449] Cf. Plat. *Alc.* i. 118 C: "And Pericles is said not to have got his wisdom by the

On a subsequent occasion, Euthydemus being present, though, as was plain to see, somewhat disposed to withdraw from the friendly concourse,[450] as if he would choose anything rather than appear to admire Socrates on the score of wisdom, the latter made the following remarks.

Soc. It is clear from his customary pursuits, is it not, sirs, that when our friend Euthydemus here is of full age, and the state propounds some question for solution, he will not abstain from offering the benefit of his advice? One can imagine the pretty exordium to his parliamentary speeches which, in his anxiety not to be thought to have learnt anything from anybody, he has ready for the occasion.[451] Clearly at the outset he will deliver himself thus: "Men of Athens, I have never at any time learnt anything from anybody; nor, if I have ever heard of any one as being an able statesman, well versed in speech and capable of action, have I sought to come across him individually. I have not so much as been at pains to provide myself with a teacher from amongst those who have knowledge;[452] on the contrary, I have persistently avoided, I will not say learning from others, but the very faintest suspicion of so doing. However, anything that occurs to me by the light of nature I shall be glad to place at your disposal."... How appropriate[453] would such a preface sound on the lips of any one seeking, say, the office of state physician,[454] would it not? How advantageously he might begin an address on this wise: "Men of Athens, I have never learnt the art of healing by help of anybody, nor have I sought to provide myself with any teacher among medical men. Indeed, to put it briefly, I have been ever on my guard not only against learning anything from the profession, but against the very notion of having studied medicine at all. If, however, you will be so good as to confer on me this post, I promise I will do my best to acquire skill by experimenting on your persons." Every one present laughed at the exordium (and there the matter dropped).

Presently, when it became apparent that Euthydemus had got so far that he was disposed to pay attention to what was said, though he was still at pains not to utter a sound himself, as if he hoped by silence to attach to himself some reputation for sagacity, Socrates, wishing to cure him of that defect, proceeded.

---

light of nature, but to have associated with several of the philosophers" (Jowett).

[450] (sunedrias), "the council."

[451] Or, "the pretty exordium... now in course of composition. He must at all hazards avoid the suspicion of having picked up any crumb of learning from anybody; how can he help therefore beginning his speech thus?"

[452] Or, "scientific experts."

[453] *Al.* "Just as if one seeking the office of state physician were to begin with a like exordium." (armoseie) = "it would be consistent (with what has gone before)."

[454] Schneider cf. Plat. *Laws,* iv. 720 A; *Gorg.* 456 A; and for "the parish doctor," *Polit.* 259 A; Arist. *Acharn.* 1030.

Soc. Is it not surprising that people anxious to learn to play the harp or the flute, or to ride, or to become proficient in any like accomplishment, are not content to work unremittingly in private by themselves at whatever it is in which they desire to excel, but they must sit at the feet of the best-esteemed teachers, doing all things and enduring all things for the sake of following the judgment of those teachers in everything, as though they themselves could not otherwise become famous; whereas, among those who aspire to become eminent politically as orators and statesmen,[455] there are some who cannot see why they should not be able to do all that politics demand, at a moment's notice, by inspiration as it were, without any preliminary pains or preparations whatever? And yet it would appear that the latter concerns must be more difficult of achievement than the former, in proportion as there are more competitors in the field but fewer who reach the goal of their ambition, which is as much as to say that a more sustained effort of attention is needed on the part of those who embark upon the sea of politics than is elsewhere called for.

Such were the topics on which Socrates was wont in the early days of their association to dilate in the hearing of Euthydemus; but when the philosopher perceived that the youth not only could tolerate the turns of the discussion more readily but was now become a somewhat eager listener, he went to the saddler's shop alone,[456] and when Euthydemus was seated by his side the following conversation took place.

Soc. Pray tell me, Euthydemus, is it really true what people tell me, that you have made a large collection of the writings of "the wise," as they are called?[457]

Euthydemus answered: Quite true, Socrates, and I mean to go on collecting until I possess all the books I can possibly lay hold of.

Soc. By Hera! I admire you for wishing to possess treasures of wisdom rather than of gold and silver, which shows that you do not believe gold and silver to be the means of making men better, but that the thoughts[458] of the wise alone enrich with virtue their possessions.

And Euthydemus was glad when he heard that saying, for, thought he to himself, "In the eyes of Socrates I am on the high road to the acquisition of wisdom." But the latter, perceiving him to be pleased with the praise, continued.

Soc. And what is it in which you desire to excel, Euthydemus, that you collect books?

And when Euthydemus was silent, considering what answer he should make, Socrates added: Possibly you want to be a great doctor?

---

[455] Or, more lit. "powerful in speech and action within the sphere of politics."
[456] The question arises: how far is the conversation historical or imaginary?
[457] Or, "have collected several works of our classical authors and philosophers."
[458] Lit. "gnomes," maxims, *sententiae.* Cf. Aristot. *Rhet.* ii. 21.

Why, the prescriptions[459] of the Pharmacopoeia would form a pretty large library by themselves.

No, indeed, not I! (answered Euthydemus).

Soc. Then do you wish to be an architect? That too implies a man of well-stored wit and judgment.[460]

I have no such ambition (he replied).

Soc. Well, do you wish to be a mathematician, like Theodorus?[461]

Euth. No, nor yet a mathematician.

Soc. Then do you wish to be an astronomer?[462] or (as the youth signified dissent) possibly a rhapsodist?[463] (he asked), for I am told you have the entire works of Homer in your possession.[464]

Nay, God forbid! not I! (ejaculated the youth). Rhapsodists have a very exact acquaintance with epic poetry, I know, of course; but they are empty-pated creatures enough themselves.[465]

At last Socrates said: Can it be, Euthydemus, that you are an aspirant to that excellence through which men become statesmen and administrators fit to rule and apt to benefit[466] the rest of the world and themselves?

Yes (replied he), that is the excellence I desire—beyond measure.

Upon my word (said Socrates), then you have indeed selected as the object of your ambition the noblest of virtues and the greatest of the arts, for this is the property of kings, and is entitled "royal"; but (he continued) have you considered whether it is possible to excel in these matters without being just and upright?[467]

Euth. Certainly I have, and I say that without justice and uprightness it is impossible to be a good citizen.

No doubt (replied Socrates) you have accomplished that initial step?

Euth. Well, Socrates, I think I could hold my own against all comers as an upright man.

And have upright men (continued Socrates) their distinctive and appropriate works like those of carpenters or shoe-makers?

Euth. To be sure they have.

---

[459] (suggrammata), "medical treatises." See Aristot. *Eth.* x. 9, 21.

[460] Or, "To be that implies a considerable store of well-packed wisdom."

[461] Of Cyrene (cf. Plat. *Theaet.*) taught Plato. Diog. Laert. ii. 8, 19.

[462] Cf. below, IV. vii. 4.

[463] See *Symp.* iii. 6; Plat. "Ion."

[464] See Jowett, *Plato*, i. 229; Grote, *Plato*, i. 455.

[465] Or, "are simply perfect in the art of reciting epic poetry, but are apt to be the veriest simpletons themselves."

[466] Or, "statesmen, and economists, and rules, and benefactors of the rest of the world and themselves."

[467] Just, (dikaios) = upright, righteous. Justice, (dikaiosune) = social uprightness = righteousness, N.T. To quote a friend: "The Greek (dikaios) combines the active dealing out of justice with the self-reflective idea of preserving justice in our conduct, which is what we mean by 'upright.'"

Soc. And just as the carpenter is able to exhibit his works and products, the righteous man should be able to expound and set forth his, should he not?

I see (replied Euthydemus) you are afraid I cannot expound the works of righteousness! Why, bless me! of course I can, and the works of unrighteousness into the bargain, since there are not a few of that sort within reach of eye and ear every day.

Shall we then (proceeded Socrates) write the letter R on this side,[468] and on that side the letter W; and then anything that appears to us to be the product of righteousness we will place to the R account, and anything which appears to be the product of wrong-doing and iniquity to the account of W?

By all means do so (he answered), if you think that it assists matters.

Accordingly Socrates drew the letters, as he had suggested, and continued.

Soc. Lying exists among men, does it not?
Euth. Certainly.
To which side of the account then shall we place it? (he asked).
Euth. Clearly on the side of wrong and injustice.
Soc. Deceit too is not uncommon?
Euth. By no means.
Soc. To which side shall we place *deceit*?
Euth. Deceit clearly on the side of wrong.
Soc. Well, and *chicanery*[469] or mischief of any sort?
Euth. That too.
Soc. And the *enslavement* of free-born men?[470]
Euth. That too.
Soc. And we cannot allow any of these to lie on the R side of the account, to the side of right and justice, can we, Euthydemus?

It would be monstrous (he replied).

Soc. Very good. But supposing a man to be elected general, and he succeeds in enslaving an unjust, wicked, and hostile state, are we to say that he is doing wrong?
Euth. By no means.
Soc. Shall we not admit that he is doing what is right?
Euth. Certainly.
Soc. Again, suppose he deceives the foe while at war with them?
Euth. That would be all fair and right also.

---

[468] The letter R (to stand for *Right, Righteous, Upright, Just*).
The letter W (to stand for *Wrong, Unrighteous, Unjust*).

[469] Reading (to kakourgein) (= furari, Sturz); al. (kleptein), Stob.

[470] Or, "the kidnapping of men into slavery." (to andrapodizesthai) = the reduction of a free-born man to a state of slavery. Slavery itself (douleia) being regarded as the normal condition of a certain portion of the human race and not in itself immoral.

Soc. Or steals and pillages their property? would he not be doing what is right?

Euth. Certainly; when you began I thought you were limiting the question to the case of friends.

Soc. So then everything which we set down on the side of Wrong will now have to be placed to the credit of Right?

Euth. Apparently.

Soc. Very well then, let us so place them; and please, let us make a new definition—that while it is right to do such things to a foe, it is wrong to do them to a friend, but in dealing with the latter it behoves us to be as straightforward as possible.[471]

I quite assent (replied Euthydemus).

So far so good (remarked Socrates); but if a general, seeing his troops demoralised, were to invent a tale to the effect that reinforcements were coming, and by means of this false statement should revive the courage of his men, to which of the two accounts shall we place that act of fraud?[472]

On the side of right, to my notion (he replied).

Soc. Or again, if a man chanced to have a son ill and in need of medicine, which the child refused to take, and supposing the father by an act of deceit to administer it under the guise of something nice to eat, and by service of that lie to restore the boy to health, to which account shall we set down this fraud?

Euth. In my judgment it too should be placed to the same account.

Soc. Well, supposing you have a friend in deplorably low spirits, and you are afraid he will make away with himself—accordingly you rob him of his knife or other such instrument: to which side ought we to set the theft?

Euth. That too must surely be placed to the score of right behaviour.

Soc. I understand you to say that a straightforward course is not in every case to be pursued even in dealing with friends?

Heaven forbid! (the youth exclaimed). If you will allow me, I rescind my former statement.[473]

Soc. Allow you! Of course you may—anything rather than make a false entry on our lists.... But there is just another point we ought not to leave uninvestigated. Let us take the case of deceiving a friend to his detriment: which is the more wrongful—to do so voluntarily or unintentionally?

Euth. Really, Socrates, I have ceased to believe in my own answers, for all my former admissions and conceptions seem to me

---

[471] Or, "an absolutely straightforward course is necessary."
[472] Cf. *Hell.* IV. iii. 10; *Cyrop.* I. vi. 31.
[473] See above, I. ii. 44 (anatithemai).

Xenophon 113

other than I first supposed them.⁴⁷⁴ Still, if I may hazard one more opinion, the intentional deceiver, I should say, is worse than the involuntary.

Soc. And is it your opinion that there is a lore and science of Right and Justice just as there is of letters and grammar?⁴⁷⁵

Euth. That is my opinion.

Soc. And which should you say was more a man of letters⁴⁷⁶—he who intentionally misspells or misreads, or he who does so unconsciously?

Euth. He who does so intentionally, I should say, because he can spell or read correctly whenever he chooses.

Soc. Then the voluntary misspeller may be a lettered person, but the involuntary offender is an illiterate?⁴⁷⁷

Euth. True, he must be. I do not see how to escape from that conclusion.

Soc. And which of the two knows what is right—he who intentionally lies and deceives, or he who lies and deceives unconsciously?⁴⁷⁸

Euth. Clearly he does.

Euth. The intentional and conscious liar clearly.

Soc. Well then, your statement is this: on the one hand, the man who has the knowledge of letters is more lettered than he who has no such knowledge?⁴⁷⁹

Euth. Yes.

Soc. And he who has the (episteme) of things rightful is more righteous than he who lacks the (episteme)? See Plat. *Hipp. min.*; Arist. *Eth. Eud.* VI. v. 7.

Euth. Yes.

Soc. And, on the other, he who has the knowledge of what is right is more righteous than he who lacks that knowledge?

Euth. I suppose it is, but for the life of me I cannot make head or tail of my own admission.⁴⁸⁰

Soc. Well (look at it like this). Suppose a man to be anxious to

---

⁴⁷⁴ Or, "all my original positions seem to me now other than I first conceived them"; or, "everything I first asserted seems now to be twisted topsy-turvy."

⁴⁷⁵ (mathesis kai episteme tou dikaiou)—a doctrine and a knowledge of the Just.

⁴⁷⁶ Or, "more grammatical"; "the better grammarian."

⁴⁷⁷ Or, "In fact, he who sins against the lore of grammar intentionally may be a good grammarian and a man of letters, but he who does so involuntarily is illiterate and a bad grammarian?"

⁴⁷⁸ Or, *Soc.* And does he who lies and deceives with intent know what is right rather than he who does either or both unconsciously?

⁴⁷⁹ Or, *Soc.* It is a fair inference, is it not, that he who has the (episteme) of grammar is more grammatical than he who has no such (episteme)?

⁴⁸⁰ Lit. "Apparently; but I appear to myself to be saying this also, heaven knows how." See Jowett, *Plato*, ii. p. 416 (ed. 2).

speak the truth, but he is never able to hold the same language about a thing for two minutes together. First he says: "The road is towards the east," and then he says, "No, it's towards the west"; or, running up a column of figures, now he makes the product this, and again he makes it that, now more, now less—what do you think of such a man?

Euth. Heaven help us! clearly he does not know what he thought he knew.

Soc. And you know the appellation given to certain people— "slavish,"[481] or, "little better than a slave?"

Euth. I do.

Soc. Is it a term suggestive of the wisdom or the ignorance of those to whom it is applied?

Euth. Clearly of their ignorance.

Soc. Ignorance, for instance, of smithying?

Euth. No, certainly not.

Soc. Then possibly ignorance of carpentering?

Euth. No, nor yet ignorance of carpentering.

Soc. Well, ignorance of shoemaking?

Euth. No, nor ignorance of any of these: rather the reverse, for the majority of those who do know just these matters are "little better than slaves."

Soc. You mean it is a title particularly to those who are ignorant of the beautiful, the good, the just?[482]

It is, in my opinion (he replied).

Soc. Then we must in every way strain every nerve to avoid the imputation of being slaves?

Euth. Nay, Socrates, by all that is holy, I did flatter myself that at any rate I was a student of philosophy, and on the right road to be taught everything essential to one who would fain make beauty and goodness his pursuit.[483] So that now you may well imagine my despair when, for all my pains expended, I cannot even answer the questions put to me about what most of all a man should know; and there is no path of progress open to me, no avenue of improvement left.

Thereupon Socrates: Tell me, Euthydemus, have you ever been to Delphi?

Yes, certainly; twice (said he).

Soc. And did you notice an inscription somewhere on the temple: (ΓΝΩΘΙ ΣΕΑΥΤΟΝ)—KNOW THYSELF?

---

[481] (andropododeis), which has the connotation of mental dulness, and a low order of intellect, cf. "boorish," "rustic," "loutish," ("pariah," conceivably). "Slavish," "servile," with us connote moral rather than intellectual deficiency, I suppose. Hence it is impossible to preserve the humour of the Socratic argument. See Newman, *op. cit.* i. 107.

[482] Cf. Goethe's "Im Ganzen Guten Schönen resolut zu leben."

[483] (tes kalokagathias), the virtue of the (kalos te kagathos)—nobility of soul. Cf. above, I. vi. 14.

Euth. I did.

Soc. Did you, possibly, pay no regard to the inscription? or did you give it heed and try to discover who and what you were?

I can safely say I did not (he answered). That much I made quite sure I knew, at any rate; since if I did not know even myself, what in the world did I know?

Soc. Can a man be said, do you think, to know himself who knows his own name and nothing more? or must he not rather set to work precisely like the would-be purchaser of a horse, who certainly does not think that he has got the knowledge he requires until he has discovered whether the beast is tractable or stubborn, strong or weak, quick or slow, and how it stands with the other points, serviceable or the reverse, in reference to the use and purpose of a horse? So, I say, must a man in like manner interrogate his own nature in reference to a man's requirements, and learn to know his own capacities, must he not?

Euth. Yes, so it strikes me: he who knows not his own ability knows not himself.

Soc. And this too is plain, is it not: that through self-knowledge men meet with countless blessings, and through ignorance of themselves with many evils? Because, the man who knows himself knows what is advantageous to himself; he discerns the limits of his powers, and by doing what he knows, he provides himself with what he needs and so does well; or, conversely, by holding aloof from what he knows not, he avoids mistakes and thereby mishaps. And having now a test to gauge other human beings he uses their need as a stepping-stone to provide himself with good and to avoid evil. Whereas he who does not know himself, but is mistaken as to his own capacity, is in like predicament to the rest of mankind and all human matters else; he neither knows what he wants, nor what he is doing, nor the people whom he deals with; and being all abroad in these respects, he misses what is good and becomes involved in what is ill.

Again, he that knows what he is doing through the success of his performance attains to fame and honour; his peers and co-mates are glad to make use of him, whilst his less successful neighbours, failing in their affairs, are anxious to secure his advice, his guidance, his protection;[484] they place their hopes of happiness in him, and for all these causes[485] single him out as the chief object of their affection. He, on the contrary, who knows not what he does, who chooses amiss and fails in what he puts his hands to, not only incurs loss and suffers chastisement through his blunders, but step by step loses reputation and becomes a laughing-stock, and in the end is doomed to a life of dishonour and contempt.

---

[484] Cf. Dante, "Tu duca, tu maestro, tu signore."
[485] Reading, (dia panta tauta), or if (dia tauta), translate "and therefore."

What is true of individuals is true also of communities.[486] That state which in ignorance of its power goes to war with a stronger than itself ends by being uprooted or else reduced to slavery.

Thereupon Euthydemus: Be assured I fully concur in your opinion; the precept KNOW THYSELF cannot be too highly valued; but what is the application? What the starting-point of self-examination? I look to you for an explanation, if you would kindly give one.[487]

Well (replied Socrates), I presume you know quite well the distinction between good and bad things: your knowledge may be relied upon so far?

Why, yes, to be sure (replied the youth); for without that much discernment I should indeed be worse than any slave.[488]

Come then (said he), do you give me an explanation of the things so termed.

That is fortunately not hard (replied the youth). First of all, health in itself I hold to be a good, and disease in itself an evil; and in the next place the sources of either of those aforenamed, meats and drinks, and habits of life,[489] I regard as good or evil according as they contribute either to health or to disease.

Soc. Then health and disease themselves when they prove to be sources of any good are good, but when of any evil, evil?

And when (asked he), can health be a source of evil, or disease a source of good?

Why, bless me! often enough (replied Socrates). In the event, for instance, of some ill-starred expedition or of some disastrous voyage or other incident of the sort, of which veritably there are enough to spare—when those who owing to their health and strength take a part in the affair are lost; whilst those who were left behind—as *hors de combat*, on account of ill-health of other feebleness—are saved.

Euth. Yes, you are right; but you will admit that there are advantages to be got from strength and lost through weakness.

Soc. Even so; but ought we to regard those things which at one moment benefit and at another moment injure us in any strict sense good rather than evil?

Euth. No, certainly not, according to that line of argument. But wisdom,[490] Socrates, you must on your side admit, is irrefragably a good; since there is nothing which or in which a wise man would not do better than a fool.

---

[486] Or, more lit. "A law which applies, you will observe, to bodies politic."

[487] Or, "at what point to commence the process of self-inspection?—there is the mystery. I look to you, if you are willing, to interpret it."

[488] Lit. "if I did not know even that."

[489] Or, "pursuits and occupations"; "manners and customs."

[490] See above, III. ix. 5. Here (sophia) is not = (sophrosune).

Soc. What say you? Have you never heard of Daedalus,[491] how he was seized by Minos on account of his wisdom, and forced to be his slave, and robbed of fatherland and freedom at one swoop? and how, while endeavouring to make his escape with his son, he caused the boy's death without effecting his own salvation, but was carried off among barbarians and again enslaved?

Yes, I know the old story (he answered).[492]

Soc. Or have you not heard of the "woes of Palamedes,"[493] that commonest theme of song, how for his wisdom's sake Odysseus envied him and slew him?

Euth. That tale also is current.

Soc. And how many others, pray, do you suppose have been seized on account of their wisdom, and despatched to the great king and at his court enslaved?[494]

Well, prosperity, well-being[495] (he exclaimed), must surely be a blessing, and that the most indisputable, Socrates?

It might be so (replied the philosopher) if it chanced not to be in itself a compound of other questionable blessings.

Euth. And which among the components of happiness and well-being can possibly be questionable?

None (he retorted), unless of course we are to include among these components beauty, or strength, or wealth, or reputation, or anything else of that kind?

Euth. By heaven! of course we are to include these, for what would happiness be without these?

Soc. By heaven! yes; only then we shall be including the commonest sources of mischief which befall mankind. How many are ruined by their fair faces at the hand of admirers driven to distraction[496] by the sight of beauty in its bloom! how many, tempted by their strength to essay deeds beyond their power, are involved in no small evils! how many, rendered effeminate by reason of their wealth, have been plotted against and destroyed![497] how many through fame and political power have suffered a world of woe!

Well (the youth replied) if I am not even right in praising happiness, I must confess I know not for what one ought to supplicate the gods in prayer.[498]

Nay, these are matters (proceeded Socrates) which perhaps,

---

[491] See Ovid. *Met.* viii. 159 foll., 261 foll.; Hygin. *Fab.* 39, 40; Diod. Sic. iv. 79; Paus. vii. 4. 6.
[492] Or, "Ah yes, of course; the tale is current."
[493] See Virg. *Aen.* ii. 90; Hygin. 105; Philostr. *Her.* x.
[494] Cf. Herod. iii. 129.
[495] (to eudaimonein), "happiness." Cf. Herod. i. 86.
[496] Cf. Plat. *Rep.* vii. 517 D; "Phaedr." 249 D.
[497] *e.g.* Alcibiades.
[498] See above for Socrates' own form of supplication.

through excessive confidence in your knowledge of them, you have failed to examine into; but since the state, which you are preparing yourself to direct, is democratically constituted,[499] of course you know what a democracy is.

Euth. I presume I do, decidedly.

Soc. Well, now, is it possible to know what a popular state is without knowing who the people are?

Euth. Certainly not.

Soc. And whom do you consider to be the people?

Euth. The poor citizens, I should say.

Soc. Then you know who the poor are, of course?

Euth. Of course I do.

Soc. I presume you also know who the rich are?

Euth. As certainly as I know who are the poor.

Soc. Whom do you understand by poor and rich?

Euth. By poor I mean those who have not enough to pay for their necessaries,[500] and by rich those who have more means than sufficient for all their needs.

Soc. Have you noticed that some who possess a mere pittance not only find this sufficient, but actually succeed in getting a surplus out of it; while others do not find a large fortune large enough?

I have, most certainly; and I thank you for the reminder (replied Euthydemus). One has heard of crowned heads and despotic rulers being driven by want to commit misdeeds like the veriest paupers.

Then, if that is how matters stand (continued Socrates), we must class these same crowned heads with the commonalty; and some possessors of scant fortunes, provided they are good economists, with the wealthy?

Then Euthydemus: It is the poverty of my own wit which forces me to this admission. I bethink me it is high time to keep silence altogether; a little more, and I shall be proved to know absolutely nothing. And so he went away crestfallen, in an agony of self-contempt, persuaded that he was verily and indeed no better than a slave.

Amongst those who were reduced to a like condition by Socrates, many refused to come near him again, whom he for his part looked upon as dolts and dullards.[501] But Euthydemus had the wit to understand that, in order to become worthy of account, his best plan was to associate as much as possible with Socrates; and from that moment, save for some necessity, he never left him—in some points

---

[499] Or, "popularly governed."

[500] *Al.* "who cannot contribute their necessary quota to the taxes (according to the census)."

[501] Or, "as people of dull intelligence and sluggish temperament." Cf. Plat. *Gorg.* 488 A.

even imitating him in his habits and pursuits. Socrates, on his side, seeing that this was the young man's disposition, disturbed him as little as possible, but in the simplest and plainest manner initiated him into everything which he held to be needful to know or important to practise.

III

It may be inferred that Socrates was in no hurry for those who were with him to discover capacities for speech and action or as inventive geniuses,[502] without at any rate a well-laid foundation of self-control.[503] For those who possessed such abilities without these same saving virtues would, he believed, only become worse men with greater power for mischief. His first object was to instil into those who were with him a wise spirit in their relation to the gods.[504] That such was the tenor of his conversation in dealing with men may be seen from the narratives of others who were present on some particular occasion.[505] I confine myself to a particular discussion with Euthydemus at which I was present.

Socrates said:[506] Tell me, Euthydemus, has it ever struck you to observe what tender pains the gods have taken to furnish man with all his needs?

Euth. No indeed, I cannot say that it has ever struck me.

Well (Socrates continued), you do not need to be reminded that, in the first place, we need light, and with light the gods supply us.

Euth. Most true, and if we had not got it we should, as far as our own eyes could help us, be like men born blind.

Soc. And then, again, seeing that we stand in need of rest and relaxation, they bestow upon us "the blessed balm of silent night."[507]

Yes (he answered), we are much beholden for that boon.

Soc. Then, forasmuch as the sun in his splendour makes manifest to us the hours of the day and bathes all things in brightness, but anon night in her darkness obliterates distinctions, have they not displayed aloft the starry orbs, which inform us of the watches of the night,

---

[502] Or, "as speakers" (see ch. vi. below), "and men of action" (see ch. v. below), "or as masters of invention" (see ch. vii. below).

[503] Or, "but as prior to those excellences must be engrafted in them (sophrosune) (the virtues of temperance and sanity of soul)."

[504] Lit. "His first object and endeavour was to make those who were with him (sophronas) (sound of soul) as regards the gods."

[505] Reading after Herbst, Cobet, etc., (diegountai), or if vulg. (diegounto), translate, "from the current accounts penned during his lifetime by the other witnesses." For (alloi) see K. Joel, *op. cit.* pp. 15, 23; above, *Mem.* I. iv. 1.

[506] For the subject matter of this "teleological" chapter, see above, I. iv.; K. Joel, *op. cit.* Appendix, p. 547 foll. in ref. to Dümmler's views.

[507] (kalliston anapauterion). The diction throughout is "poetical."

whereby we can accomplish many of our needs?[508]

It is so (he answered).

Soc. And let us not forget that the moon herself not only makes clear to us the quarters of the night, but of the month also?

Certainly (he answered).

Soc. And what of this: that whereas we need nutriment, this too the heavenly powers yield us? Out of earth's bosom they cause good to spring up[509] for our benefit; and for our benefit provide appropriate seasons to furnish us in turn not only with the many and diverse objects of need, but with the sources also of our joy and gladness?[510]

Yes (he answered eagerly), these things bear token truly to a love for man.[511]

Soc. Well, and what of another priceless gift, that of water, which conspires with earth and the seasons to give both birth and increase to all things useful to us; nay, which helps to nurture our very selves, and commingling with all that feeds us, renders it more digestible, more wholesome, and more pleasant to the taste; and mark you in proportion to the abundance of our need the superabundance of its supply. What say you concerning such a boon?

Euth. In this again I see a sign of providential care.

Soc. And then the fact that the same heavenly power has provided us with fire[512]—our assistant against cold, our auxiliary in darkness, our fellow-workman in every art and every instrument which for the sake of its utility mortal man may invent or furnish himself withal. What of this, since, to put it compendiously, there is nothing serviceable to the life of man worth speaking of but owes its fabrication to fire?[513]

Euth. Yes, a transcendent instance of benevolent design.[514]

Soc. Again, consider the motions of the Sun,[515] how when he has turned him about in winter[516] he again draws nigh to us, ripening some fruits, and causing others whose time is past to dry up; how when he has fulfilled his work he comes no closer, but turns away as if in fear to scorch us to our hurt unduly; and again, when he has reached a point

---

[508] *e.g.* for temple orientation see Dr. Penrose quoted by Norman Lockyer, *Nature*, August 31. 1893.

[509] Cf. Plat. *Laws*, 747 D.

[510] Or, "pleasure."

[511] Cf. Plat. *Laws*, 713 D; *Symp.* 189 D. "These things are signs of a beneficent regard for man."

[512] Lit. "and then the fact that they made provision for us of even fire"; the credit of this boon, according to Hesiod, being due to Prometheus.

[513] Or, "no life-aiding appliance worthy of the name."

[514] Or, "Yes, that may be called an extreme instance of the divine 'philanthropy.'" Cf. Cic. *de N. D.* ii. 62.

[515] A single MS. inserts a passage (to de kai era... 'Anekphraston).

[516] *i.e.* as we say, "after the winter solstice."

where if he should prolong his retreat we should plainly be frozen to death with cold, note how he turns him about and resumes his approach, traversing that region of the heavens where he may shed his genial influence best upon us.

Yes, upon my word (he answered), these occurrences bear the impress of being so ordered for the sake of man.

Soc. And then, again, it being manifest that we could not endure either scorching heat or freezing cold if they came suddenly upon us, note how gradually the sun approaches, and how gradually recedes, so that we fail to notice how we come at last to either extreme.[517]

For my part (he replied), the question forces itself upon my mind, whether the gods have any other occupation save only to minister to man; and I am only hindered from saying so, because the rest of animals would seem to share these benefits along with man.

Soc. Why, to be sure; and is it not plain that these animals themselves are born and bred for the sake of man? At any rate, no living creature save man derives so many of his enjoyments from sheep and goats, horses and cattle and asses, and other animals. He is more dependent, I should suppose, on these than even on plants and vegetables. At any rate, equally with these latter they serve him as means of subsistence or articles of commerce; indeed, a large portion of the human family do not use the products of the soil as food at all, but live on the milk and cheese and flesh of their flocks and herds, whilst all men everywhere tame and domesticate the more useful kinds of animals, and turn them to account as fellow-workers in war and for other purposes.

Yes, I cannot but agree with what you say (he answered), when I see that animals so much stronger than man become so subservient to his hand that he can use them as he lists.

Soc. And as we reflect on the infinite beauty and utility and the variety of nature, what are we to say of the fact that man has been endowed with sensibilities which correspond with this diversity, whereby we take our fill of every blessing;[518] or, again, this implanted faculty of reasoning, which enables us to draw inferences concerning the things which we perceive, and by aid of memory to understand how each set of things may be turned to our good, and to devise countless contrivances with a view to enjoying the good and repelling the evil; or lastly, when we consider the faculty bestowed upon us of interpretative speech, by which we are enabled to instruct one another, and to

---

[517] Or, "note the gradual approach and gradual recession of the sun- god, so gradual that we reach either extreme in a manner imperceptibly, and before we are aware of its severity."

[518] Or, "Again, when we consider how many beautiful objects there are serviceable to man, and yet how unlike they are to one another, the fact that man has been endowed with senses adapted to each class of things, and so has access to a world of happiness."

participate in all the blessings fore-named: to form societies, to establish laws, and to enter upon a civilised existence[519]—what are we to think?

Euth. Yes, Socrates, decidedly it would appear that the gods do manifest a great regard, nay, a tender care, towards mankind.

Soc. Well, and what do you make of the fact that where we are powerless to take advantageous forethought for our future, at this stage they themselves lend us their co-operation, imparting to the inquirer through divination knowledge of events about to happen, and instructing him by what means they may best be turned to good account?

Euth. Ay, and you, Socrates, they would seem to treat in a more friendly manner still than the rest of men, if, without waiting even to be inquired of by you, they show you by signs beforehand what you must, and what you must not do.[520]

Soc. Yes, and you will discover for yourself the truth of what I say, if, without waiting to behold the outward and visible forms[521] of the gods themselves, you will be content to behold their works; and with these before you, to worship and honour the Divine authors of them.[522] I would have you reflect that the very gods themselves suggest this teaching.[523] Not one of these but gives us freely of his blessings; yet they do not step from behind their veil in order to grant one single boon.[524] And pre-eminently He who orders and holds together the universe,[525] in which are all things beautiful and good;[526] who fashions and refashions it to never-ending use unworn, keeping it free from sickness or decay,[527] so that swifter than thought it ministers to his will unerringly—this God is seen to perform the mightiest operations, but in the actual administration of the same abides himself invisible to mortal ken. Reflect further, this Sun above our heads, so visible to all—as we suppose—will not suffer man to regard him too narrowly, but should any essay to watch him with a shameless stare he will snatch away their power of vision. And if the gods themselves are thus unseen, so too shall you find their ministers to be hidden also; from the height of heaven above the thunderbolt is plainly hurled, and triumphs over all

---

[519] Cf. Aristot. *Pol.* III. ix. 5.

[520] See above, I. iv. 14, for a parallel to the train of thought on the part of Aristodemus "the little," and of Euthydemus; and for Socrates' (daimonion), see above; Grote, *Plato*, i. 400.

[521] Cf. Cic. *de N. D.* I. xii. 31; Lactantius, *de Ira*, xi. 13.

[522] See L. Dindorf *ad loc.* (ed. Ox. 1862), (theous); G. Sauppe, vol. iii. "An. crit." p. xxix; R. Kühner; C. Schenkl.

[523] *i.e.* "that man must walk by faith." For (upodeiknunai) cf. *Econ.* xii. 18.

[524] Schneid. cf. Plat. *Crat.* 396.

[525] Or, "the co-ordinator and container of the universe."

[526] Or, "in whom all beauty and goodness is."

[527] Cf. *Cyrop.* VIII. vii. 22; above, I. iv. 13.

that it encounters, yet it is all-invisible, no eye may detect its coming or its going at the moment of its swoop. The winds also are themselves unseen, though their works are manifest, and through their approach we are aware of them. And let us not forget, the soul of man himself, which if aught else human shares in the divine—however manifestly enthroned within our bosom, is as wholly as the rest hidden from our gaze. These things you should lay to mind, and not despise the invisible ones, but learn to recognise their power, as revealed in outward things, and to know the divine influence.[528]

Nay, Socrates (replied Euthydemus), there is no danger I shall turn a deaf ear to the divine influence even a little; of that I am not afraid, but I am out of heart to think that no soul of man may ever requite the kindness of the gods with fitting gratitude.

Be not out of heart because of that (he said); you know what answer the god at Delphi makes to each one who comes asking "how shall I return thanks to heaven?"—"According to the law and custom of your city"; and this, I presume, is law and custom everywhere that a man should please the gods with offerings according to the ability which is in him.[529] How then should a man honour the gods with more beautiful or holier honour than by doing what they bid him? but he must in no wise slacken or fall short of his ability, for when a man so does, it is manifest, I presume, that at the moment he is not honouring the gods. You must then honour the gods, not with shortcoming but according to your ability; and having so done, be of good cheer and hope to receive the greatest blessings. For where else should a man of sober sense look to receive great blessings if not from those who are able to help him most, and how else should he hope to obtain them save by seeking to please his helper, and how may he hope to please his helper better than by yielding him the amplest obedience?

By such words—and conduct corresponding to his words—did Socrates mould and fashion the hearts of his companions, making them at once more devout and more virtuous.[530]

---

[528] (to daimonion), the divinity.

[529] Or, "and that law, I presume, is universal which says, Let a man," etc.; and for the maxim see above; "Anab." III. ii. 9.

[530] Or, "sounder of soul and more temperate as well as more pious."

IV

But indeed[531] with respect to justice and uprightness he not only made no secret of the opinion he held, but gave practical demonstration of it, both in private by his law-abiding and helpful behaviour to all,[532] and in public by obeying the magistrates in all that the laws enjoined, whether in the life of the city or in military service, so that he was a pattern of loyalty to the rest of the world, and on three several occasions in particular: first, when as president (Epistates) of the assembly he would not suffer the sovereign people to take an unconstitutional vote,[533] but ventured, on the side of the laws, to resist a current of popular feeling strong enough, I think, to have daunted any other man. Again, when the Thirty tried to lay some injunction on him contrary to the laws, he refused to obey, as for instance when they forbade his conversing with the young;[534] or again, when they ordered him and certain other citizens to arrest a man to be put to death,[535] he stood out single-handed on the ground that the injunctions laid upon him were contrary to the laws. And lastly, when he appeared as defendant in the suit instituted by Melêtus,[536] notwithstanding that it was customary for litigants in the law courts to humour the judges in the conduct of their arguments by flattery and supplications contrary to the laws,[537] notwithstanding also that defendants owed their acquittal by the court to the employment of such methods, he refused to do a single thing however habitual in a court of law which was not strictly legal; and though by only a slight deflection from the strict path he might easily have been acquitted by his judges,[538] he preferred to abide by the laws and die rather than transgress them and live.

These views he frequently maintained in conversation, now with one and now with another, and one particular discussion with Hippias of Elis[539] on the topic of justice and uprightness has come to my knowledge.[540]

Hippias had just arrived at Athens after a long absence, and

---

[531] L. Dindorf suspects [§§. 1-6, 'Alla men... pollakis], ed. Lips. 1872. See also Praef. to Ox. ed. p. viii.

[532] Or, "by his conduct to all, which was not merely innocent in the eye of law and custom but positively helpful."

[533] See above, I. i. 18; *Hell.* I. vii. 14, 15; Grote, *H. G.* viii. 272.

[534] See above, I. ii. 35.

[535] Leon of Salamis. See *Hell.* II. iii. 39; Plat. *Apol.* 32 C; Andoc. *de Myst.* 46.

[536] See above, I. i. 1; Plat. *Apol.* 19 C.

[537] Kühner cf. Quintil. VI. i. 7: "Athenis affectus movere etiam per praeconem prohibatur orator"; *Apol.* 4; Plat. *Apol.* 38 D, E.

[538] See Grote, *H. G.* viii. p. 663 foll.

[539] For this famous person see Cob. *Pros. Xen.* s.n.; Plat. *Hipp. maj.* 148; Quint. xii. 11, 21; Grote, *H. G.* viii. 524.

[540] Or, "I can personally vouch for."

chanced to be present when Socrates was telling some listeners how astonishing it was that if a man wanted to get another taught to be a shoemaker or carpenter or coppersmith or horseman, he would have no doubt where to send him for the purpose: "People say,"[541] he added, "that if a man wants to get his horse or his ox taught in the right way,[542] the world is full of instructors; but if he would learn himself, or have his son or his slave taught in the way of right, he cannot tell where to find such instruction."

Hippias, catching the words, exclaimed in a bantering tone: What! still repeating the same old talk,[543] Socrates, which I used to hear from you long ago?

Yes (answered Socrates), and what is still more strange, Hippias, it is not only the same old talk but about the same old subjects. Now you, I daresay, through versatility of knowledge,[544] never say the same thing twice over on the same subject?

To be sure (he answered), my endeavour is to say something new on all occasions.

What (he asked) about things which you know, as for instance in a case of spelling, if any one asks you, "How many letters in Socrates, and what is their order?"[545] I suppose you try to run off one string of letters to-day and to-morrow another? or to a question of arithmetic, "Does twice five make ten?" your answer to-day will differ from that of yesterday?

Hipp. No; on these topics, Socrates, I do as you do and repeat myself. However, to revert to justice (and uprightness),[546] I flatter myself I can at present furnish you with some remarks which neither you nor any one else will be able to controvert.

By Hera![547] (he exclaimed), what a blessing to have discovered![548] Now we shall have no more divisions of opinion on points of right and wrong; judges will vote unanimously; citizens will cease wrangling; there will be no more litigation, no more party faction, states will reconcile their differences, and wars are ended. For my part I do not know how I can tear myself away from you, until I have heard from

---

[541] L. Dindorf, after Ruhnken and Valckenar, omits this sentence (phasi de tines... didaxonton). See Kühner *ad loc*. For the sentiment see Plat. *Apol.* 20 A.
[542] Cf. *Cyrop.* II. ii. 26; VIII. iii. 38; also *Horsem.* iii. 5; *Hunting*, vii. 4.
[543] This tale is repeated by Dio Chrys. *Or.* III. i. 109. Cf. Plat. *Gorg.* 490 E.
[544] Or, "such is the breadth of your learning," (polumathes). Cf. Plat. *Hipp. maj.*
[545] Cf. "Econ." viii. 14; Plat. *Alc.* i. 113 A.
[546] Or, "on the topic of the just I have something to say at present which," etc.
[547] See above, I. v. 5.
[548] Or, "what a panacea are you the inventor of"; lit. "By Hera, you have indeed discovered a mighty blessing, if juries are to cease recording their verdicts 'aye' and 'no'; if citizens are to cease their wranglings on points of justice, their litigations, and their party strifes; if states are to cease differing on matters of right and wrong and appealing to the arbitrament of war."

your own lips all about the grand discovery you have made.

You shall hear all in good time (Hippias answered), but not until you make a plain statement of your own belief. What is justice? We have had enough of your ridiculing all the rest of the world, questioning and cross-examining first one and then the other, but never a bit will you render an account to any one yourself or state a plain opinion upon a single topic.[549]

What, Hippias (Socrates retorted), have you not observed that I am in a chronic condition of proclaiming what I regard as just and upright?

Hipp. And pray what is this theory[550] of yours on the subject? Let us have it in words.

Soc. If I fail to proclaim it in words, at any rate I do so in deed and in fact. Or do you not think that a fact is worth more as evidence than a word?[551]

Worth far more, I should say (Hippias answered), for many a man with justice and right on his lips commits injustice and wrong, but no doer of right ever was a misdoer or could possibly be.

Soc. I ask then, have you ever heard or seen or otherwise perceived me bearing false witness or lodging malicious information, or stirring up strife among friends or political dissension in the city, or committing any other unjust and wrongful act?

No, I cannot say that I have (he answered).

Soc. And do you not regard it as right and just to abstain from wrong?[552]

Hipp. Now you are caught, Socrates, plainly trying to escape from a plain statement. When asked what you believe justice to be, you keep telling us not what the just man does, but what he does not do.

Why, I thought for my part (answered Socrates) that the refusal to do wrong and injustice was a sufficient warrant in itself of righteousness and justice, but if you do not agree, see if this pleases you better: I assert that what is "lawful" is "just and righteous."

Do you mean to assert (he asked) that lawful and just are synonymous terms?

Soc. I do.

I ask (Hippias added), for I do not perceive what you mean by *lawful*, nor what you mean by *just*.[553]

Soc. You understand what is meant by laws of a city or state?

Yes (he answered).

Soc. What do you take them to be?

Hipp. The several enactments drawn up by the citizens or members

---

[549] See Plat. *Gorg.* 465 A.
[550] (o logos).
[551] Or, "is of greater evidential value," "ubi res adsunt, quid opus est verbis?"
[552] Or, "is not abstinence from wrongdoing synonymous with righteous behaviour?"
[553] Lit. "what sort of lawful or what sort of just is spoken of."

of a state in agreement as to what things should be done or left undone. Then I presume (Socrates continued) that a member of a state who regulates his life in accordance with these enactments will be law-abiding, while the transgressor of the same will be law-less?

Certainly (he answered).

Soc. And I presume the law-loving citizen will do what is just and right, while the lawless man will do what is unjust and wrong?

Hipp. Certainly.

Soc. And I presume that he who does what is just is just, and he who does what is unjust is unjust?

Hipp. Of course.

Soc. It would appear, then, that the *law-loving* man is just, and the *lawless unjust?*

Then Hippias: Well, but laws, Socrates, how should any one regard as a serious matter either the laws themselves, or obedience to them, which laws the very people who made them are perpetually rejecting and altering?

Which is also true of war (Socrates replied); cities are perpetually undertaking war and then making peace again.

Most true (he answered).

Soc. If so, what is the difference between depreciating obedience to law because laws will be repealed, and depreciating good discipline in war because peace will one day be made? But perhaps you object to enthusiasm displayed in defence of one's home and fatherland in war?

No, indeed I do not! I heartily approve of it (he answered).

Soc. Then have you laid to heart the lesson taught by Lycurgus to the Lacedaemonians,[554] and do you understand that if he succeeded in giving Sparta a distinction above other states, it was only by instilling into her, beyond all else, a spirit of obedience to the laws? And among magistrates and rulers in the different states, you would scarcely refuse the palm of superiority to those who best contribute to make their fellow-citizens obedient to the laws? And you would admit that any particular state in which obedience to the laws is the paramount distinction of the citizens flourishes most in peace time, and in time of war is irresistible? But, indeed, of all the blessings which a state may enjoy, none stands higher than the blessing of unanimity. "Concord among citizens"—that is the constant theme of exhortation emphasised by the councils of elders[555] and by the choice spirits of the community;[556] at all times and everywhere through the length and breadth of all Hellas it is an established law that the citizens be bound together by an oath of concord;[557] everywhere they do actually swear

---

[554] Cf. *Pol. Lac.* viii. See Newman, *op. cit.* i. 396.
[555] Lit. "the Gerousiai." (S) or (X S) uses the Spartan phraseology.
[556] Lit. "the best men." (S) or (X S) speaks as an "aristocrat."
[557] Cf. *Hell.* II. iv. 43; Lys. xxv. 21 foll.; Schneid. cf. Lycurg. *u Leocr.* 189.

this oath; not of course as implying that citizens shall all vote for the same choruses, or give their plaudits to the same flute-players, or choose the same poets, or limit themselves to the same pleasures, but simply that they shall pay obedience to the laws, since in the end that state will prove most powerful and most prosperous in which the citizens abide by these; but without concord neither can a state be well administered nor a household well organised.

And if we turn to private life, what better protection can a man have than obedience to the laws? This shall be his safeguard against penalties, his guarantee of honours at the hands of the community; it shall be a clue to thread his way through the mazes of the law courts unbewildered, secure against defeat, assured of victory.[558] It is to him, the law-loving citizen, that men will turn in confidence when seeking a guardian of the most sacred deposits, be it of money or be it their sons or daughters. He, in the eyes of the state collectively, is trustworthy—he and no other; who alone may be depended on to render to all alike their dues—to parents and kinsmen and servants, to friends and fellow-citizens and foreigners. This is he whom the enemy will soonest trust to arrange an armistice, or a truce, or a treaty of peace. They would like to become the allies of this man, and to fight on his side. This is he to whom the allies[559] of his country will most confidently entrust the command of their forces, or of a garrison, or their states themselves. This, again, is he who may be counted on to recompense kindness with gratitude, and who, therefore, is more sure of kindly treatment than another whose sense of gratitude is fuller.[560] The most desirable among friends, the enemy of all others to be avoided, clearly he is not the person whom a foreign state would choose to go to war with; encompassed by a host of friends and exempt from foes, his very character has a charm to compel friendship and alliance, and before him hatred and hostility melt away.

And now, Hippias, I have done my part; that is my proof and demonstration that the "lawful" and "law-observant" are synonymous with the "upright" and the "just"; do you, if you hold a contrary view, instruct us.[561]

Then Hippias: Nay, upon my soul, Socrates, I am not aware of holding any contrary opinion to what you have uttered on the theme of justice.[562]

---

[558] Or, "ignorant of hostile, assured of favourable verdict."

[559] Lit. "the Allies," e.g. of Sparta or of Athens, etc.

[560] Lit. "From whom may the doer of a deed of kindness more confidently expect the recompense of gratitude than from your lover of the law? and whom would one select as the recipient of kindness rather than a man susceptible of gratitude?"

[561] For the style of this enconium (of the nomimos) cf. *Ages.* i. 36; and for the "Socratic" reverence for law cf. Plat. *Crito.*

[562] Lit. "the just and upright," (tou dikaiou).

Soc. But now, are you aware, Hippias, of certain unwritten laws?[563]

Yes (he answered), those held in every part of the world, and in the same sense.

Can you then assert (asked Socrates) of these unwritten laws that men made them?

Nay, how (he answered) should that be, for how could they all have come together from the ends of the earth? and even if they had so done, men are not all of one speech?[564]

Soc. Whom then do you believe to have been the makers of these laws.

Hipp. For my part, I think that the gods must have made these laws for men, and I take it as proof that first and foremost it is a law and custom everywhere to worship and reverence the gods.

Soc. And, I presume, to honour parents is also customary everywhere?

Yes, that too (he answered).

Soc. And, I presume, also the prohibition of intermarriage between parents and children?

Hipp. No; at that point I stop, Socrates. That does not seem to me to be a law of God.

Now, why? (he asked).

Because I perceive it is not infrequently transgressed (he answered).[565]

Soc. Well, but there are a good many other things which people do contrary to law; only the penalty, I take it, affixed to the transgression of the divine code is certain; there is no escape for the offender after the manner in which a man may transgress the laws of man with impunity, slipping through the fingers of justice by stealth, or avoiding it by violence.

Hipp. And what is the inevitable penalty paid by those who, being related as parents and children, intermingle in marriage?

Soc. The greatest of all penalties; for what worse calamity can human beings suffer in the production of offspring than to misbeget?[566]

Hipp. But how or why should they breed them ill where nothing hinders them, being of a good stock themselves and producing from stock as good?

Soc. Because, forsooth, in order to produce good children, it is not simply necessary that the parents should be good and of a good stock, but that both should be equally in the prime and vigour of their

---

[563] See Soph. *Antig. Oed. T.* 865, and Prof. Jebb *ad loc.*; Dem. *de Cor.* 317, 23; Aristot. *Rhet.* I. xiii.

[564] Or, "there would be difficulty of understanding each other, and a babel of tongues."

[565] Or, "as I perceive, it is not of universal application, some transgress it."

[566] Or, "in the propagation of the species than to produce misbegotten children."

bodies.[567] Do you suppose that the seed of those who are at their prime is like theirs who either have not yet reached their prime, or whose prime has passed?

Hipp. No, it is reasonable to expect that the seed will differ.

Soc. And for the better—which?

Hipp. Theirs clearly who are at their prime.

Soc. It would seem that the seed of those who are not yet in their prime or have passed their prime is not good?

Hipp. It seems most improbable it should be.

Soc. Then the right way to produce children is not that way?

Hipp. No, that is not the right way.

Soc. Then children who are so produced are produced not as they ought to be?

Hipp. So it appears to me.

What offspring then (he asked) will be ill produced, ill begotten, and ill born, if not these?

I subscribe to that opinion also (replied Hippias).

Soc. Well, it is a custom universally respected, is it not, to return good for good, and kindness with kindness?

Hipp. Yes, a custom, but one which again is apt to be transgressed.

Soc. Then he that so transgresses it pays penalty in finding himself isolated; bereft of friends who are good, and driven to seek after those who love him not. Or is it not so that he who does me kindness in my intercourse with him is my good friend, but if I requite not this kindness to my benefactor, I am hated by him for my ingratitude, and yet I must needs pursue after him and cling to him because of the great gain to me of his society?

Hipp. Yes, Socrates. In all these cases, I admit, there is an implication of divine authority;[568] that a law should in itself be loaded with the penalty of its transgression does suggest to my mind a higher than human type of legislator.

Soc. And in your opinion, Hippias, is the legislation of the gods just and righteous, or the reverse of what is just and righteous?

Hipp. Not the reverse of what is just and righteous, Socrates, God forbid! for scarcely could any other legislate aright, of not God himself.

Soc. It would seem then, Hippias, the gods themselves are well pleased that "the lawful" and "the just" should be synonymous?[569]

By such language and by such conduct, through example and precept alike, he helped to make those who approached him more upright and more just.

---

[567] Cf. Plat. *Laws*, viii. 839 A; Herbst, etc., cf. Grotius, *de Jure*, ii. 5, xii. 4.

[568] Lit. "Yes, upon my word, Socrates, all these cases look very like (would seem to point to) the gods."

[569] Or, "it is well pleasing also to the gods that what is lawful is just and what is just is lawful."

V

And now I propose to show in what way he made those who were with him more vigorous in action.[570] In the first place, as befitted one whose creed was that a basis of self-command is indispensable to any noble performance, he manifested himself to his companions as one who had pre-eminently disciplined himself;[571] and in the next place by conversation and discussion he encouraged them to a like self-restraint beyond all others.[572] Thus it was that he continued ever mindful himself, and was continually reminding all whom he encountered, of matters conducive to virtue; as the following discussion with Euthydemus, which has come to my knowledge,[573] will serve to illustrate—the topic of the discussion being self-command.

Tell me, Euthydemus (he began), do you believe *freedom* to be a noble and magnificent acquisition, whether for a man or for a state?

I cannot conceive a nobler or more magnificent (he answered).

Soc. Then do you believe him to be a free man who is ruled by the pleasures of the body, and thereby cannot perform what is best?

Certainly not (he answered).

Soc. No! for possibly to perform what is best appears to you to savour of freedom? And, again, to have some one over you who will prevent you doing the like seems a loss of freedom?

Most decidedly (he answered).

Soc. It would seem you are decidedly of opinion that the incontinent are the reverse of free?[574]

Euth. Upon my word, I much suspect so.

Soc. And does it appear to you that the incontinent man is merely hindered from doing what is noblest, or that further he is impelled to do what is most shameful?

Euth. I think he is as much driven to the one as he is hindered from the other.

Soc. And what sort of lords and masters are those, think you, who at once put a stop to what is best and enforce what is worst?

Euth. Goodness knows, they must be the very worst of masters.

Soc. And what sort of slavery do you take to be the worst?

I should say (he answered) slavery to the worst masters.

It would seem then (pursued Socrates) that the incontinent man is

---

[570] Lit. "more *practical,*" *i.e.* more energetic and effective.

[571] "If any one might claim to be a prince of ascetics, it was Socrates; such was the ineffaceable impression left on the minds of his associates."

[572] Or, "he stimulated in these same companions a spirit of self- restraint beyond all else."

[573] Or, "which I can vouch for."

[574] Or, "incontinency is illiberal."

bound over to the worst sort of slavery, would it not?

So it appears to be (the other answered).

Soc. And does it not appear to you that this same beldame incontinence shuts out wisdom, which is the best of all things,[575] from mankind, and plunges them into the opposite? Does it not appear to you that she hinders men from attending to things which will be of use and benefit, and from learning to understand them; that she does so by dragging them away to things which are pleasant; and often though they are well aware of the good and of the evil, she amazes and confounds[576] their wits and makes them choose the worse in place of the better?

Yes, so it comes to pass (he answered).

Soc. And[577] *soundness of soul,* the spirit of temperate modesty? Who has less claim to this than the incontinent man? The works of the temperate spirit and the works of incontinency are, I take it, diametrically opposed?

That too, I admit (he answered).

Soc. If this then be so concerning these virtues,[578] what with regard to *carefulness* and *devotion* to all that ought to occupy us? Can anything more seriously militate against these than this same incontinence?

Nothing that I can think of (he replied).

Soc. And can worse befall a man, think you? Can he be subjected to a more baleful influence than that which induces him to choose what is hurtful in place of what is helpful; which cajoles him to devote himself to the evil and to neglect the good; which forces him, will he nill he, to do what every man in his sober senses would shrink from and avoid?

I can imagine nothing worse (he replied).

Soc. Self-control, it is reasonable to suppose, will be the cause of opposite effects upon mankind to those of its own opposite, the want of self-control?

Euth. It is to be supposed so.

Soc. And this, which is the source of opposite effects to the very worst, will be the very best of things?

Euth. That is the natural inference.

Soc. It looks, does it not, Euthydemus, as if self-control were the best thing a man could have?

It does indeed, Socrates (he answered).

---

[575] "Wisdom, the greatest good which men can possess."

[576] Schneid. cf. Plat. "Protag." 355 A; and *Symp.* iv. 23.

[577] "And if this be so concerning wisdom, (sophia), what of (sophrasune), soundness of soul—sobriety?"

[578] Or add, "If this be so concerning not *wisdom* only, but concerning *temperance* and *soundness of soul,* what," etc.

Soc. But now, Euthydemus, has it ever occurred to you to note one fact?

What fact? (he asked).

Soc. That, after all, incontinency is powerless to bring us to that realm of sweetness which some look upon[579] as her peculiar province; it is not incontinency but self-control alone which has the passport to highest pleasures.

In what way? (he asked). How so?

Why, this way (Socrates answered): since incontinency will not suffer us to resist hunger and thirst, or to hold out against sexual appetite, or want of sleep (which abstinences are the only channels to true pleasure in eating and drinking, to the joys of love, to sweet repose and blissful slumber won by those who will patiently abide and endure till each particular happiness is at the flood)[580]—it comes to this: by incontinency we are cut off from the full fruition of the more obvious and constantly recurring pleasures.[581] To self-control, which alone enables us to endure the pains aforesaid, alone belongs the power to give us any pleasure worth remembering in these common cases.

You speak the words of truth[582] (he answered).

Soc. Furthermore,[583] if there be any joy in learning aught "beautiful and good," or in patient application to such rules as may enable a man to manage his body aright, or to administer his household well, or to prove himself useful to his friends and to the state, or to dominate his enemies—which things are the sources not only of advantage but of deepest satisfaction[584]—to the continent and self-controlled it is given to reap the fruits of them in their performance. It is the incontinent who have neither part nor lot in any one of them. Since we must be right in asserting that he is least concerned with such things who has least ability to do them, being tied down to take an interest in the pleasure which is nearest to hand.

Euthydemus replied: Socrates, you would say, it seems to me, that a man who is mastered by the pleasures of the body has no concern at all with virtue.

And what is the distinction, Euthydemus (he asked), between a man devoid of self-control and the dullest of brute beasts? A man who foregoes all height of aim, who gives up searching for the best and

---

[579] Or, "which we are apt to think of as."

[580] Or, "at its season." Lit. "is as sweet as possible."

[581] Or, "from tasting to any extent worth speaking of the most necessary and all-pervading sources of happiness."

[582] Lit. "What you say is absolutely and entirely true" (the *vraie vérité* of the matter).

[583] Or, "But indeed, if there be joy in the pursuit of any noble study or of such accomplishments as shall enable," etc.

[584] Or, "of the highest pleasures."

strives only to gratify his sense of pleasure,[585] is he better than the silliest of cattle?[586] ... But to the self-controlled alone is it given to discover the hid treasures. These, by word and by deed, they will pick out and make selection of them according to their kinds, choosing deliberately the good and holding aloof from the evil.[587] Thus (he added) it is that a man reaches the zenith, as it were, of goodness and happiness, thus it is that he becomes most capable of reasoning and discussion.[588] The very name discussion (dialegesthai) is got from people coming together and deliberating in common by picking out and selecting things (dialegein) according to their kinds.[589] A man then is bound to prepare himself as much as possible for this business, and to pursue it beyond all else with earnest resolution; for this is the right road to excellence, this will make a man fittest to lead his fellows and be a master in debate.[590]

VI

At this point I will endeavour to explain in what way Socrates fostered this greater "dialectic" capacity among his intimates.[591] He held firmly to the opinion that if a man knew what each reality was, he would be able to explain this knowledge to others; but, failing the possession of that knowledge, it did not surprise him that men should stumble themselves and cause others to stumble also.[592] It was for this reason that he never ceased inquiring with those who were with him into the true nature of things that are.[593] It would be a long business certainly to go through in detail all the definitions at which he arrived; I will therefore content myself with such examples as will serve to show his method of procedure. As a first instance I will take the question of piety. The mode of investigation may be fairly represented as follows.

---

[585] Or, "and seeks by hook and by crook to do what is pleasantest."

[586] *i.e.* he becomes an animal "feeding a blind life within the brain."

[587] Or, "selecting the ore and repudiating the dross." Kühner cf. Plat. *Laws*, v. 735 B.

[588] Or, "draws nearer to happiness and perfection, and is most capable of truth-disclosing conversation." Cf. Plat. *Apol.* 41: "What would not a man give, O judges, to be able to examine the leaders of the great Trojan expedition, or Odysseus, or Sisyphus, or numberless others, men and women too! What infinite delight would there be in conversing with them and asking them questions!" (Jowett).

[589] For (dialegein kata gene) = (dialegesthai), cf. Grote, *H. G.* viii. 590.

[590] Cf. Plat. *Rep.* 534 D; *Phaedr.* 252 E; *Crat.* 390 C; *Statesm.* 286 D foll.

[591] Lit. "essayed to make those who were with him more potent in dialectic."

[592] Or, "Socrates believed that any one who knew the nature of anything would be able to let others into his secret; but, failing that knowledge, he thought the best of men would be but blind leaders of the blind, stumbling themselves and causing others to stumble also."

[593] Or add, "'What is this among things? and what is its definition?'—such was the ever-recurrent question for which he sought an answer."

Tell me (said he), Euthydemus, what sort of thing you take *piety* to be?

Something most fair and excellent, no doubt (the other answered).[594]

Soc. And can you tell me what sort of person the pious man is?[595]

I should say (he answered) he is a man who honours the gods.

Soc. And is it allowable to honour the gods in any mode or fashion one likes?

Euth. No; there are laws in accordance with which one must do that.

Soc. Then he who knows these laws will know how he must honour the gods?

I think so (he answered).

Soc. And he who knows how he must honour the gods conceives that he ought not to do so except in the manner which accords with his knowledge?[596] Is it not so?

Euth. That is so.[597]

Soc. And does any man honour the gods otherwise than he thinks he ought?[598]

I think not (he answered).

Soc. It comes to this then: he who knows what the law requires in reference to the gods will honour the gods in the lawful way?[599]

Euth. Certainly.

Soc. But now, he who honours lawfully honours as he ought?[600]

Euth. I see no alternative.

Soc. And he who honours as he ought is a pious man?

Euth. Certainly.

Soc. It would appear that he who knows what the law requires with respect to the gods will correctly be defined as a pious man, and that is our definition?

So it appears to me, at any rate (he replied).[601]

---

[594] Or, "A supreme excellence, no doubt."

[595] Or, "can you give me a definition of the pious man?"; "tell me who and what the pious man is."

[596] *i.e.* "his practice must square with his knowledge and be the outward expression of his belief?"

[597] "That is so; you rightly describe his frame of mind and persuasion."

[598] "As he should and must." See K. Joel, *op. cit.* p. 322 foll.

[599] Or, "he who knows what is lawful with regard to Heaven pays honour to Heaven lawfully."

[600] "As he should and must."

[601] "I accept it at any rate as mine." *N.B.*—in reference to this definition of Piety, the question is never raised (poion ti esti nomos); nor yet (poioi tines eisin oi theoi); but clearly there is a growth in (ta nomima). Cf. the conversation recorded in St. John iv. 7 foll., and the words (verse 23) (pneuma o Theos kai tous proskunountas auton en pneumati kai aletheia dei proskunein), which the philosopher Socrates would perhaps readily have assented to.

Soc. But now, with regard to human beings; is it allowable to deal with men in any way one pleases?[602]

Euth. No; with regard to men also, he will be a law-observing man[603] who knows what things are lawful as concerning men, in accordance with which our dealings with one another must be conducted.[604]

Soc. Then those who deal with one another in this way, deal with each other as they ought?[605]

Obviously (he answered).

Soc. And they who deal with one another as they ought, deal well and nobly—is it not so?

Certainly (he answered).

Soc. And they who deal well and nobly by mankind are well-doers in respect of human affairs?

That would seem to follow (he replied).

Soc. I presume that those who obey the laws do what is just and right?

Without a doubt, (he answered).

Soc. And by things right and just you know what sort of things are meant?

What the laws ordain (he answered).

Soc. It would seem to follow that they who do what the laws ordain both do what is right and just and what they ought?[606]

Euth. I see no alternative.

Soc. But then, he who does what is just and right is upright and just?[607]

I should say so myself (he answered).

Soc. And should you say that any one obeys the laws without knowing what the laws ordain?

I should not (he answered).

---

[602] Or, "may a man deal with his fellow-men arbitrarily according to his fancy?" See above, II. vii. 8.

[603] Or, "he is a man full of the law (lawful) and law-abiding who knows," etc.

[604] Reading (kath' a dei pros allelous khresthai), subaud. (allelois), or if vulg. (kath' a dei pos allelois khresthai), translate "must be specifically conducted."

[605] "As they should and must."

[606] "What they should and must."

[607] This proposition, as Kühner argues (*ad loc.*), is important as being the middle term of the double syllogism (A and B)—
   A. Those who do what the law demands concerning men do what is just and right.
   Those who do what is just and right are righteous and just.
   Ergo—Those who do what the law demands concerning men are righteous and just.
   B. Those who know what is just and right ought (and are bound, cf. above, III. ix. 4) to do also what is just and right.
   Those who do what is just and right are righteous and just.
   Ergo—*Righteous and Just* (dikaioi) may be defined as "Those who know what the law demands (*aliter* things right and just) concerning men."

Soc. And do you suppose that any one who knows what things he ought to do supposes that he ought not to do them?[608]

No, I suppose not (he answered).

Soc. And do you know of anybody doing other than what he feels bound to do?[609]

No, I do not (he answered).

Soc. It would seem that he who knows what things are lawful[610] as concerning men does the things that are just and right?

Without a doubt (he answered).

Soc. But then, he who does what is just and right is upright and just?[611]

Who else, if not? (he replied).

Soc. It would seem, then, we shall have got to a right definition if we name as just and upright those who know the things which are lawful as concerning men?

That is my opinion (he answered).

Soc. And what shall we say that *wisdom* is? Tell me, does it seem to you that the wise are wise in what they know,[612] or are there any who are wise in what they know not?

Euth. Clearly they are wise in what they know;[613] for how could a man have wisdom in that which he does not know?

Soc. In fact, then, the wise are wise in knowledge?

Euth. Why, in what else should a man be wise save only in knowledge?

Soc. And is wisdom anything else than that by which a man is wise, think you?

Euth. No; that, and that only, I think.

Soc. It would seem to follow that knowledge and wisdom are the same?

Euth. So it appears to me.

Soc. May I ask, does it seem to you possible for a man to know all the things that are?

Euth. No, indeed! not the hundredth part of them, I should say.

Soc. Then it would seem that it is impossible for a man to be all-wise?

---

[608] Or, "and no one who knows what he must and should do imagines that he must and should not do it?"

[609] Or, "and nobody that you know of does the contrary of what he thinks he should do?"

[610] Or, "of lawful obligation."

[611] *N.B.*—In reference to this definition of justice, see K. Joel, *op. cit.* p. 323 foll., "Das ist eine Karrikatur des Sokratischen Dialogs."

[612] Or, "in that of which they have the knowledge (episteme)."

[613] Or, "their wisdom is confined to that of which they have the (episteme). How could a man be wise in what he lacks the knowledge of?"

Quite impossible (he answered).

Soc. It would seem the wisdom of each is limited to his knowledge; each is wise only in what he knows?

Euth. That is my opinion.[614]

Soc. Well! come now, Euthydemus, as concerning *the good*: ought we to search for the good in this way?

What way? (he asked).

Soc. Does it seem to you that the same thing is equally advantageous to all?

No, I should say not (he answered).

Soc. You would say that a thing which is beneficial to one is sometimes hurtful to another?

Decidedly (he replied).

Soc. And is there anything else good except that which is beneficial, should you say?[615]

Nothing else (he answered).

Soc. It would seem to follow that the beneficial is good relatively to him to whom it is beneficial?

That is how it appears to me (he answered).

Soc. And *the beautiful*: can we speak of a thing as beautiful in any other way than relatively? or can you name any beautiful thing, body, vessel, or whatever it be, which you know of as universally beautiful?[616]

Euth. I confess I do not know of any such myself.[617]

Soc. I presume to turn a thing to its proper use is to apply it beautifully?

Euth. Undoubtedly it is a beautiful appliance.[618]

Soc. And is this, that, and the other thing beautiful for aught else except that to which it may be beautifully applied?

---

[614] Cf. Plat. *Theaet.* 145 D. N.B.—For this definition of wisdom see K. Joel, *ib.* p. 324 foll.

[615] Or reading (1) (allo d' an ti phaies e agathon einai to ophelimon); or else (2) (allo d' an ti phaies agathon einai to ophelimon); (in which case (alloti) = (allo ti e);) translate (1) "and what is beneficial is good (or a good), should you not say?" lit. "could you say that the beneficial is anything else than good (or a good)?" or else (2) "and what is beneficial is good (or a good)? or is it anything else?"

[616] *i.e.* "beautiful in all relations into which it enters." Reading (to de kalon ekhoimen an pos allos eipein e estin onomazein kalon e soma e skeuos e all' otioun, o oistha pros tanta kalon on; Ma Di', ouk egog', ephe). For other emendations of the vulg., and the many interpretations which have been given to the passage, see R. Kühner *ad loc.*

[617] Or, adopting the reading (ekhois an) in place of (ekhoimen an) above, translate "I certainly cannot, I confess."

[618] Or, "I presume it is well and good and beautiful to use this, that, and the other thing for the purpose for which the particular thing is useful?"—"That nobody can deny (he answered)." It is impossible to convey simply the verbal play and the quasi-argumentative force of the Greek (kalos ekhei pros ti tini khresthai). See K. Joel, p. 426.

Euth. No single thing else.

Soc. It would seem that the useful is beautiful relatively to that for which it is of use?

So it appears to me (he answered).

Soc. And what of *courage*,[619] Euthydemus? I presume you rank courage among things beautiful? It is a noble quality?[620]

Nay, one of the most noble (he answered).

Soc. It seems that you regard courage as useful to no mean end?

Euth. Nay, rather the greatest of all ends, God knows.

Soc. Possibly in face of terrors and dangers you would consider it an advantage to be ignorant of them?

Certainly not (he answered).

Soc. It seems that those who have no fear in face of dangers, simply because they do not know what they are, are not courageous?

Most true (he answered); or, by the same showing, a large proportion of madmen and cowards would be courageous.

Soc. Well, and what of those who are in dread of things which are not dreadful, are they—

Euth. Courageous, Socrates?—still less so than the former, goodness knows.

Soc. Possibly, then, you would deem those who are good in the face of terrors and dangers to be courageous, and those who are bad in the face of the same to be cowards?

Certainly I should (he answered).

Soc. And can you suppose any other people to be good in respect of such things except those who are able to cope with them and turn them to noble account?[621]

No; these and these alone (he answered).

Soc. And those people who are of a kind to cope but badly with the same occurrences, it would seem, are bad?

Who else, if not they? (he asked).

Soc. May it be that both one and the other class do use these circumstances as they think they must and should?[622]

Why, how else should they deal with them? (he asked).

Soc. Can it be said that those who are unable to cope well with them or to turn them to noble account know how they must and should deal with them?[623]

---

[619] Or, perhaps better, *fortitude.* See H. Sidgwick, *Hist. of Ethics,* p. 43.

[620] It is one of (ta kala). See K. Joel, ib. p. 325, and in reference to the definitions of the *Good* and of the *Beautiful,* ib. p. 425 foll.

[621] (kalos khresthai), lit. "make a beautiful use of them."

[622] Or, "feel bound and constrained to do."

[623] Or, "Can it be said that those who are unable to cope nobly with their perilous surroundings know how they ought to deal with them?"

I presume not (he answered).

Soc. It would seem to follow that those who have the knowledge how to behave are also those who have the power?[624]

Yes; these, and these alone (he said).

Soc. Well, but now, what of those who have made no egregious blunder (in the matter); can it be they cope ill with the things and circumstances we are discussing?

I think not (he answered).

Soc. It would seem, conversely, that they who cope ill have made some egregious blunder?

Euth. Probably; indeed, it would appear to follow.

Soc. It would seem, then, that those who know[625] how to cope with terrors and dangers well and nobly are courageous, and those who fail utterly of this are cowards?

So I judge them to be (he answered).[626]

A *kingdom* and a *tyranny*[627] were, he opined, both of them forms of government, but forms which differed from one another, in his belief; a kingdom was a government over willing men in accordance with civil law, whereas a tyranny implied the government over unwilling subjects not according to law, but so as to suit the whims and wishes of the ruler.

There were, moreover, three forms of citizenship or polity; in the case where the magistrates were appointed from those who discharged the obligations prescribed by law, he held the polity to be an *aristocracy* (or rule of the best);[628] where the title to office depended on rateable property, it was a *plutocracy* (or rule of wealth); and lastly, where all the citizens without distinction held the reins of office, that was a *democracy* (or rule of the people).

Let me explain his method of reply where the disputant had no clear statement to make, but without attempt at proof chose to contend that such or such a person named by himself was wiser, or more of a statesman, or more courageous, and so forth, than some other person.[629] Socrates had a way of bringing the whole discussion back to the underlying proposition,[630] as thus:

Soc. You state that so and so, whom you admire, is a better citizen

---

[624] "He who kens can."

[625] "Who have the (episteme)."

[626] *N.B.*—For this definition of *courage* see Plat. *Laches*, 195 A and passim; K. Joel, *op. cit.* p. 325 foll.

[627] Or, "despotism."

[628] Or, "in which the due discharge of lawful (law-appointed) obligations gave the title to magisterial office and government, this form of polity he held to be an *aristocracy* (*or rule of the best*)." See Newman, *op. cit.* i. 212, 235.

[629] Or, "if any one encountered him in argument about any topic or person without any clear statement, but a mere *ipse dixit*, devoid of demonstration, that so and so," etc.

[630] Or, "question at bottom." Cf. Plat. *Laws*, 949 B.

that this other whom I admire?
The Disputant. Yes; I repeat the assertion.
Soc. But would it not have been better to inquire first what is the work or function of a good citizen?
The Disputant. Let us do so.
Soc. To begin, then, with the matter of expenditure: his superiority will be shown by his increasing the resources and lightening the expenditure of the state?[631]
Certainly (the disputant would answer).
Soc. And in the event of war, by rendering his state superior to her antagonists?
The Disputant. Clearly.
Soc. Or on an embassy as a diplomatist, I presume, by securing friends in place of enemies?
That I should imagine (replies the disputant).
Soc. Well, and in parliamentary debate, by putting a stop to party strife and fostering civic concord?
The Disputant. That is my opinion.

By this method of bringing back the argument to its true starting-point, even the disputant himself would be affected and the truth become manifest to his mind.

His own—that is, the Socratic—method of conducting a rational discussion[632] was to proceed step by step from one point of general agreement to another: "Herein lay the real security of reasoning,"[633] he would say; and for this reason he was more successful in winning the common assent of his hearers than any one I ever knew. He had a saying that Homer had conferred on Odysseus the title of a safe, unerring orator,[634] because he had the gift to lead the discussion from one commonly accepted opinion to another.

VII

The frankness and simplicity with which Socrates endeavoured to declare his own opinions, in dealing with those who conversed with him,[635] is, I think, conclusively proved by the above instances; at the same time, as I hope now to show, he was no less eager to cultivate a spirit of independence in others, which would enable them to stand

---

[631] Or, "In the management of moneys, then, his strength will consist in his rendering the state better provided with ways and means?"

[632] Of, "of threading the mazes of an argument."

[633] Reading (tauten asphaleian); *aliter.* (tauten ten asphaleian) = "that this security was part and parcel of reasoning."

[634] *Od.* viii. 171, (o d' asphaleos agoreuei), "and his speech runs surely on its way" (Butcher and Lang), where Odysseus is describing himself. Cf. Dion. Hal. *de Arte Rhet.* xi. 8.

[635] Or, "who frequented his society, is, I hope, clear from what has been said."

alone in all transactions suited to their powers.

Of all the men I have ever known, he was most anxious to ascertain in what any of those about him was really versed; and within the range of his own knowledge he showed the greatest zeal in teaching everything which it befits the true gentleman[636] to know; or where he was deficient in knowledge himself,[637] he would introduce his friends to those who knew.[638] He did not fail to teach them also up to what point it was proper for an educated man to acquire empiric knowledge of any particular matter.[639]

To take geometry as an instance: Every one (he would say) ought to be taught geometry so far, at any rate, as to be able, if necessary, to take over or part with a piece of land, or to divide it up or assign a portion of it for cultivation,[640] and in every case by geometric rule.[641] That amount of geometry was so simple indeed, and easy to learn, that it only needed ordinary application of the mind to the method of mensuration, and the student could at once ascertain the size of the piece of land, and, with the satisfaction of knowing its measurement, depart in peace. But he was unable to approve of the pursuit of geometry up to the point at which it became a study of unintelligible diagrams.[642] What the use of these might be, he failed, he said, to see; and yet he was not unversed in these recondite matters himself.[643] These things, he would say, were enough to wear out a man's life, and to hinder him from many other more useful studies.[644]

Again, a certain practical knowledge of astronomy, a certain skill in the study of the stars, he strongly insisted on. Every one should know enough of the science to be able to discover the hour of the night or the season of the month or year, for the purposes of travel by land or sea—the march, the voyage, and the regulations of the watch;[645] and in general, with regard to all matters connected with the night season, or with the month, or the year,[646] it was well to have such reliable data to

---

[636] Lit. "a *beautiful and good* man."

[637] Or, "where he lacked acquaintance with the matter himself." See, for an instance, *Econ.* iii. 14.

[638] "To those who had the special knowledge"; "a connoisseur in the matter."

[639] Or, "of any particular branch of learning"; "in each department of things."

[640] (e ergon apodeixasthai), or "and to explain the process." Cf. Plat. *Rep.* vii. 528 D. See R. Kühner *ad loc.* for other interpretations of the phrase. Cf. Max. Tyr. xxxvii. 7.

[641] Or, "by correct measurement"; lit. "by measurement of the earth."

[642] Cf. Aristot. *Pol.* v. (viii.) 2; Cic. *Acad. Post.* I. iv. 15. For the attitude compare the attitude of a philosopher in other respects most unlike Socrates—August Comte, *e.g.* as to the futility of sidereal astronomy, *Pos. Pol.* i. 412 (Bridges).

[643] Cf. Isocr. *On the Antidosis*, 258-269, as to the true place of "Eristic" in education. See above, IV. ii. 10.

[644] Cf. A. Comte as to "perte intellectuelle" in the pursuit of barren studies.

[645] Schneid. cf. Plat. *Rep.* vii. 527 D.

[646] "Occurrences connected with the night, the month, or year." *e.g.* the festival of the Karneia, the (tekmerion) (*point de repère*) of which is the full moon of August. Cf.

go upon as would serve to distinguish the various times and seasons. But these, again, were pieces of knowledge easily learnt from night sportsmen,[647] pilots of vessels, and many others who make it their business to know such things. As to pushing the study of astronomy so far as to include a knowledge of the movements of bodies outside our own orbit, whether planets or stars of eccentric movement,[648] or wearing oneself out endeavouring to discover their distances from the earth, their periods, and their causes,[649] all this he strongly discountenanced; for he saw (he said) no advantage in these any more than in the former studies. And yet he was not unversed[650] in the subtleties of astronomy any more than in those of geometry; only these, again, he insisted, were sufficient to wear out a man's lifetime, and to keep him away from many more useful pursuits.

And to speak generally, in regard of things celestial he set his face against attempts to excogitate the machinery by which the divine power formed its several operations.[651] Not only were these matters beyond man's faculties to discover, as he believed, but the attempt to search out what the gods had not chosen to reveal could hardly (he supposed) be well pleasing in their sight. Indeed, the man who tortured his brains about such subjects stood a fair chance of losing his wits entirely, just as Anaxagoras,[652] the headiest speculator of them all, in his attempt to explain the divine mechanism, had somewhat lost his head. Anaxagoras took on himself to assert that sun and fire are identical,[653] ignoring the fact that human beings can easily look at fire, but to gaze steadily into the face of the sun is given to no man; or that under the influence of his rays the colour of the skin changes, but under the rays of fire not.[654] He forgot that no plant or vegetation springs from earth's bosom with healthy growth without the help of sunlight, whilst the influence of fire is to parch up everything, and to destroy life; and when he came to speak of the sun as being a "red-hot stone" he ignored another fact, that a stone in fire neither lights up nor lasts, whereas the sun-god abides for ever with intensest brilliancy undimmed.

Eur. *Alc.* 449.

[647] See Plat. *Soph.* 220 D; above, III. xi. 8; *Cyrop.* I. vi. 40; *Hunting*, xii. 6; Hippocr. *Aër.* 28.

[648] See Lewis, *Astron. of the Ancients*; cf. Diog. Laert. vii. 1. 144.

[649] Or, "the causes of these."

[650] (oude touton ge anekoos en). He had "heard," it is said, Archelaus, a pupil of Anaxagoras. Cf. Cic. *Tusc.* V. iv. 10.

[651] Or, "he tried to divert one from becoming overly-wise in heavenly matters and the *mécanique céleste* of the Godhead in His several operations." See above, I. i. 11. See Grote, *Plato*, i. 438.

[652] Of Clazomenae. Cf. Plat. *Apol.* 14; Diog. Laert. II. vi; Cic. *Tusc.* V. iv. 10; Cobet, *Prosop. Xen.* s.n.; Grote, *H. G.* i. 501.

[653] Or, "that the sun was simply a fire, forgetting so simple a fact as that."

[654] Or, "the complexion darkens, whereas fire has no such effect."

Socrates inculcated the study of reasoning processes,[655] but in these, equally with the rest, he bade the student beware of vain and idle over-occupation. Up to the limit set by utility, he was ready to join in any investigation, and to follow out an argument with those who were with him; but there he stopped. He particularly urged those who were with him to pay the utmost attention to health. They would learn all it was possible to learn from adepts, and not only so, but each one individually should take pains to discover, by a lifelong observation of his own case, what particular regimen, what meat or drink, or what kind of work, best suited him; these he should turn to account with a view to leading the healthiest possible life. It would be no easy matter for any one who would follow this advice, and study his own idiosyncrasy, to find a doctor to improve either on the diagnosis or the treatment requisite.[656]

Where any one came seeking for help which no human wisdom could supply, he would counsel him to give heed to "divination." He who has the secret of the means whereby the gods give signs to men touching their affairs can never surely find himself bereft of heavenly guidance.

VIII

Now if any one should be disposed to set the statement of Socrates touching the divinity[657] which warned him what he ought to do or not to do, against the fact that he was sentenced to death by the board of judges, and argue that thereby Socrates stood convicted of lying and delusion in respect of this "divinity" of his, I would have him to note in the first place that, at the date of his trial, Socrates was already so far advanced in years that had he not died then his life would have reached its natural term soon afterwards; and secondly, as matters went, he escaped life's bitterest load[658] in escaping those years which bring a diminution of intellectual force to all—instead of which he was called upon to exhibit the full robustness of his soul and acquire glory in addition,[659] partly by the style of his defence—felicitous alike in its truthfulness, its freedom, and its rectitude[660]—and partly by the manner

---

[655] (logismous) = [1] "arithmetic," [2] "calculation," [3] "syllogistic reasoning." See L. Dind. *Index. Gr.* s.v., and Kühner *ad loc.*; cf. Plat. *Gorg.* 451 C. It is important to decide which form of "logism" is meant here.

[656] Or, "to find a doctor better able than himself to 'diagnose' and prescribe a treatment congenial to health." Cf. Tac. *Ann.* vi. 46; Plut. *de San.* 136 E, ap. Schneid. *ad loc.*

[657] Or, "the words of Socrates with regard to a divine something which warned him," etc.

[658] The phraseology is poetical.

[659] Or, "in a manner which redounded to his glory."

[660] Or, "marvellous alike for the sincerity of its language, the free unbroken spirit of

Xenophon 145

in which he bore the sentence of condemnation with infinite gentleness and manliness. Since no one within the memory of man, it is admitted, ever bowed his head to death more nobly. After the sentence he must needs live for thirty days, since it was the month of the "Delia,"[661] and the law does not suffer any man to die by the hand of the public executioner until the sacred embassy return from Delos. During the whole of that period (as his acquaintances without exception can testify) his life proceeded as usual. There was nothing to mark the difference between now and formerly in the even tenour of its courage; and it was a life which at all times had been a marvel of cheerfulness and calm content.[662]

[Let us pause and ask how could man die more nobly and more beautifully than in the way described? or put it thus: dying so, then was his death most noble and most beautiful; and being the most beautiful, then was it also the most fortunate and heaven-blest; and being most blessed of heaven, then was it also most precious in the sight of God.][663]

And now I will mention further certain things which I have heard from Hermogenes, the son of Hipponicus,[664] concerning him. He said that even after Melêtus[665] had drawn up the indictment, he himself used to hear Socrates conversing and discussing everything rather than the suit impending, and had ventured to suggest that he ought to be considering the line of his defence, to which, in the first instance, the master answered: "Do I not seem to you to have been practising that my whole life long?" And upon his asking "How?" added in explanation that he had passed his days in nothing else save in distinguishing between what is just and what is unjust (right and wrong), and in doing what is right and abstaining from what is wrong; "which conduct" (he added) "I hold to be the finest possible practice for my defence"; and when he (Hermogenes), returning to the point again, pleaded with Socrates: "Do you not see, Socrates, how commonly it happens that an Athenian jury, under the influence of argument, condemns innocent people to death and acquits real criminals?"—Socrates replied, "I assure you, Hermogenes, that each time I have essayed to give my thoughts to the defence which I am to

---

its delivery, and the absolute rectitude of the speaker."
    [661] *i.e.* the lesser "Delian" solemnities, an annual festival instituted, it was said, by Theseus. See Plut. *Theseus*, 23 (Clough, i. 19); and for the whole matter see Plat. "Phaed." 58 foll.
    [662] Cf. Arist. "Frogs," 82; of Sophocles, (o d' eukolos men enthad', eukolos d' ekei).
    [663] This §3 is bracketed as spurious by Sauppe and other commentators. But see *Cyrop.* VIII. ii. 7, 8, for similar ineptitude of style. R. Kühner defends the passage as genuine.
    [664] See above, II. x. 3; *Symp.* i. 3; iii. 14; iv. 47 foll.; vi. 2; *Apol.* 2; Plat. *Crat.* 384.
    [665] See above, I. i. 1.

make before the court, the divinity[666] has opposed me." And when he (Hermogenes) exclaimed, "How strange!"—"Do you find it strange" (he continued), "that to the Godhead it should appear better for me to close my life at once? Do you not know that up to the present moment there is no man whom I can admit to have spent a better or happier life than mine. Since theirs I regard as the best of lives who study best to become as good as may be, and theirs the happiest who have the liveliest sense of growth in goodness; and such, hitherto, is the happy fortune which I perceive to have fallen to my lot. To such conclusion I have come, not only in accidental intercourse with others, but by a strict comparison drawn between myself and others, and in this faith I continue to this day; and not I only, but my friends continue in a like persuasion with regard to me, not for the lame reason that they are my friends and love me (or else would others have been in like case as regards their friends), but because they are persuaded that by being with me they will attain to their full height of goodness. But, if I am destined to prolong my days, maybe I shall be enforced to pay in full the penalties of old age—to see and hear less keenly, to fail in intellectual force, and to leave school, as it were, more of a dunce than when I came, less learned and more forgetful—in a word, I shall fall from my high estate, and daily grow worse in that wherein aforetime I excelled. But indeed, were it possible to remain unconscious of the change, the life left would scarcely be worth living; but given that there is a consciousness of the change, then must the existence left to live be found by comparison insipid, joyless, a death in life, devoid of life's charm. But indeed, if it is reserved for me to die unjustly, then on those who unjustly slay me lies the shame (since, given injustice is base, how can any unjust action whatsoever fail of baseness?)[667] But for me what disgrace is it that others should fail of a just decision and right acts concerning me?... I see before me a long line of predecessors on this road, and I mark the reputation also among posterity which they have left.[668] I note how it varies according as they did or suffered wrong, and for myself I know that I too, although I die to-day, shall obtain from mankind a consideration far different from that which will be accorded to those who put me to death. I know that undying witness will be borne me to this effect, that I never at any time did wrong to any man, or made him a worse man, but ever tried to make those better who were with me."

Such are the words which he spoke in conversation with Hermogenes and the rest. But amongst those who knew Socrates and recognised what manner of man he was, all who make virtue and

---

[666] (to daimonion)—"the divine (voice)."
[667] This passage also may, perhaps, be regarded as spurious.
[668] Or, "There floats before my eyes a vision of the many who have gone this same gate. I note their legacies of fame among posterity."

perfection their pursuit still to this day cease not to lament his loss with bitterest regret, as for one who helped them in the pursuit of virtue as none else could.

To me, personally, he was what I have myself endeavoured to describe: so pious and devoutly religious[669] that he would take no step apart from the will of heaven; so just and upright that he never did even a trifling injury to any living soul; so self-controlled, so temperate, that he never at any time chose the sweeter in place of the better; so sensible, and wise, and prudent that in distinguishing the better from the worse he never erred; nor had he need of any helper, but for the knowledge of these matters, his judgment was at once infallible and self-sufficing. Capable of reasonably setting forth and defining moral questions,[670] he was also able to test others, and where they erred, to cross-examine and convict them, and so to impel and guide them in the path of virtue and noble manhood. With these characteristics, he seemed to be the very impersonation of human perfection and happiness.[671]

Such is our estimate. If the verdict fail to satisfy I would ask those who disagree with it to place the character of any other side by side with this delineation, and then pass sentence.

The Economist

A Treatise on the Science of the Household in the form of a Dialogue

INTERLOCUTORS

SOCRATES AND CRITOBULUS

At Chapter VII. a prior discussion held between Socrates and Ischomachus is introduced: On the life of a "beautiful and good" man.

In these chapters (vii.-xxi.) Socrates is represented by the author as repeating for the benefit of Critobulus and the rest certain conversations which he had once held with the beautiful and good Ischomachus on the essentials of economy. It was a *tête-à-tête* discussion, and in the original Greek the remarks of the two speakers are denoted by such phrases as (ephe o 'Iskhomakhos—ephen egio)—"said (he) Ischomachus," "said I." (Socrates) To save the repetition of expressions tedious in English, I have, whenever it seemed help to do so, ventured to throw parts of the reported conversations into dramatic form,

---

[669] Or, "of such piety and religious devotedness... of such rectitude... of such sobriety and self-control... of such sound sense and wisdom..."

[670] Or, "gifted with an ability logically to set forth and to define moral subtleties."

[671] Or, "I look upon him as at once the best and happiest of men."

inserting "*Isch.*" "*Soc.*" in the customary way to designate the speakers; but these, it must be borne in mind, are merely "asides" to the reader, who will not forget that Socrates is the narrator throughout—speaking of himself as "*I*," and of Ischomachus as "*he*," or by his name.— *Translator's note, addressed to the English reader.*

THE ECONOMIST[672]

I

I once heard him[673] discuss the topic of economy[674] after the following manner. Addressing Critobulus,[675] he said: Tell me, Critobulus, is "economy," like the words "medicine," "carpentry," "building," "smithying," "metal-working," and so forth, the name of a particular kind of knowledge or science?

Crit. Yes, I think so.

Soc. And as, in the case of the arts just named, we can state the proper work or function of each, can we (similarly) state the proper work and function of economy?

Crit. It must, I should think, be the business of the good economist[676] at any rate to manage his own house or estate well.

Soc. And supposing another man's house to be entrusted to him, he would be able, if he chose, to manage it as skilfully as his own, would he not? since a man who is skilled in carpentry can work as well for another as for himself: and this ought to be equally true of the good economist?

Crit. Yes, I think so, Socrates.

Soc. Then there is no reason why a proficient in this art, even if he does not happen to possess wealth of his own, should not be paid a salary for managing a house, just as he might be paid for building one?

Crit. None at all: and a large salary he would be entitled to earn if, after paying the necessary expenses of the estate entrusted to him, he can create a surplus and improve the property.

Soc. Well! and this word "house," what are we to understand by it? the domicile merely? or are we to include all a man's possessions outside the actual dwelling-place?[677]

---

[672] By "economist" we now generally understand "political economist," but the use of the word as referring to *domestic economy*, the subject matter of the treatise, would seem to be legitimate.

[673] "The master."

[674] Lit. "the management of a household and estate." See Plat. *Rep.* 407 B; Aristot. *Eth. N.* v. 6; *Pol.* i. 3.

[675] See *Mem.* I. iii. 8; *Symp.* p. 292.

[676] Or, "manager of a house or estate."

[677] Lit. "is it synonymous with dwelling-place, or is all that a man possesses outside his dwelling-place part of his house or estate?"

Crit. Certainly, in my opinion at any rate, everything which a man has got, even though some portion of it may lie in another part of the world from that in which he lives,[678] forms part of his estate.

Soc. "Has got"? but he may have got enemies?

Crit. Yes, I am afraid some people have got a great many.

Soc. Then shall we say that a man's enemies form part of his possessions?

Crit. A comic notion indeed! that some one should be good enough to add to my stock of enemies, and that in addition he should be paid for his kind services.

Soc. Because, you know, we agreed that a man's estate was identical with his possessions?

Crit. Yes, certainly! the good part of his possessions; but the evil portion! no, I thank you, that I do not call part of a man's possessions.

Soc. As I understand, *you* would limit the term to what we may call a man's useful or advantageous possessions?

Crit. Precisely; if he has things that injure him, *I* should regard these rather as a loss than as wealth.

Soc. It follows apparently that if a man purchases a horse and does not know how to handle him, but each time he mounts he is thrown and sustains injuries, the horse is not part of his wealth?

Crit. Not, if wealth implies weal, certainly.

Soc. And by the same token land itself is no wealth to a man who so works it that his tillage only brings him loss?

Crit. True; mother earth herself is not a source of wealth to us if, instead of helping us to live, she helps us to starve.

Soc. And by a parity of reasoning, sheep and cattle may fail of being wealth if, through want of knowledge how to treat them, their owner loses by them; to him at any rate the sheep and the cattle are not wealth?

Crit. That is the conclusion I draw.

Soc. It appears, *you* hold to the position that wealth consists of things which benefit, while things which injure are not wealth?

Crit. Just so.

Soc. The same things, in fact, are wealth or not wealth, according as a man knows or does not know the use to make of them? To take an instance, a flute may be wealth to him who is sufficiently skilled to play upon it, but the same instrument is no better than the stones we tread under our feet to him who is not so skilled... unless indeed he chose to sell it?

Crit. That is precisely the conclusion we should come to.[679] To

---

[678] Lit. "not even in the same state or city."

[679] Reading (tout auto), or if (tout au) with Sauppe, transl. "Yes, that is another position we may fairly subscribe to."

persons ignorant of their use[680] flutes are wealth as saleable, but as possessions not for sale they are no wealth at all; and see, Socrates, how smoothly and consistently the argument proceeds,[681] since it is admitted that things which benefit are wealth. The flutes in question unsold are not wealth, being good for nothing: to become wealth they must be sold.

Yes! (rejoined Socrates), presuming the owner knows how to sell them; since, supposing again he were to sell them for something which he does not know how to use,[682] the mere selling will not transform them into wealth, according to your argument.

Crit. You seem to say, Socrates, that money itself in the pockets of a man who does not know how to use it is not wealth?

Soc. And I understand *you* to concur in the truth of our proposition so far: wealth is that, and that only, whereby a man may be benefited. Obviously, if a man used his money to buy himself a mistress, to the grave detriment of his body and soul and whole estate, how is that particular money going to benefit him now? What good will he extract from it?

Crit. None whatever, unless we are prepared to admit that hyoscyamus,[683] as they call it, is wealth, a poison the property of which is to drive those who take it mad.

Soc. Let money then, Critobulus, if a man does not know how to use it aright—let money, I say, be banished to the remote corners of the earth rather than be reckoned as wealth.[684] But now, what shall we say of friends? If a man knows how to use his friends so as to be benefited by them, what of these?

Crit. They are wealth indisputably, and in a deeper sense than cattle are, if, as may be supposed, they are likely to prove of more benefit to a man than wealth of cattle.

Soc. It would seem, according to your argument, that the foes of a man's own household after all may be wealth to him, if he knows how to turn them to good account?[685]

Crit. That is my opinion, at any rate.

Soc. It would seem, it is the part of a good economist[686] to know how to deal with his own or his employer's foes so as to get profit out of them?

Crit. Most emphatically so.

---

[680] *i.e.* "without knowledge of how to use them."

[681] Or, "our discussion marches on all-fours, as it were."

[682] Reading (pros touto o), or if (pros touton, os), transl. "to a man who did not know how to use them."

[683] "A dose of henbane, 'hogs'-bean,' so called." Diosc. 4. 69; 6. 15; Plut. *Demetr.* xx. (Clough, v. 114).

[684] Or, "then let it be relegated... and there let it lie in the category of non-wealth."

[685] Vide *supra*.

[686] "A good administrator of an estate."

Xenophon

Soc. In fact, you need but use your eyes to see how many private persons, not to say crowned heads, do owe the increase of their estates to war.

Crit. Well, Socrates, I do not think, so far, the argument could be improved on;[687] but now comes a puzzle. What of people who have got the knowledge and the capital[688] required to enhance their fortunes, if only they will put their shoulders to the wheel; and yet, if we are to believe our senses, that is just the one thing they will not do, and so their knowledge and accomplishments are of no profit to them? Surely in their case also there is but one conclusion to be drawn, which is, that neither their knowledge nor their possessions are wealth.

Soc. Ah! I see, Critobulus, you wish to direct the discussion to the topic of slaves?

Crit. No indeed, I have no such intention—quite the reverse. I want to talk about persons of high degree, of right noble family[689] some of them, to do them justice. These are the people I have in my mind's eye, gifted with, it may be, martial or, it may be, civil accomplishments, which, however, they refuse to exercise, for the very reason, as I take it, that they have no masters over them.

Soc. No masters over them! but how can that be if, in spite of their prayers for prosperity and their desire to do what will bring them good, they are still so sorely hindered in the exercise of their wills by those that lord it over them?

Crit. And who, pray, are these lords that rule them and yet remain unseen?

Soc. Nay, not unseen; on the contrary, they are very visible. And what is more, they are the basest of the base, as you can hardly fail to note, if at least you believe idleness and effeminacy and reckless negligence to be baseness. Then, too, there are other treacherous beldames giving themselves out to be innocent pleasures, to wit, dicings and profitless associations among men.[690] These in the fulness of time appear in all their nakedness even to them that are deceived, showing themselves that they are after all but pains tricked out and decked with pleasures. These are they who have the dominion over those you speak of and quite hinder them from every good and useful work.

Crit. But there are others, Socrates, who are not hindered by these indolences—on the contrary, they have the most ardent disposition to exert themselves, and by every means to increase their revenues; but in spite of all, they wear out their substance and are involved in endless

---

[687] Or, "Thanks, Socrates. Thus far the statement of the case would seem to be conclusive—but what are we to make of this? Some people..."

[688] Lit. "the right kinds of knowledge and the right starting-points."

[689] "Eupatrids."

[690] Or, "frivolous society."

difficulties.[691]

Soc. Yes, for they too are slaves, and harsh enough are their taskmasters; slaves are they to luxury and lechery, intemperance and the wine-cup along with many a fond and ruinous ambition. These passions so cruelly belord it over the poor soul whom they have got under their thrall, that so long as he is in the heyday of health and strong to labour, they compel him to fetch and carry and lay at their feet the fruit of his toils, and to spend it on their own heart's lusts; but as soon as he is seen to be incapable of further labour through old age, they leave him to his gray hairs and misery, and turn to seize on other victims.[692] Ah! Critobulus, against these must we wage ceaseless war, for very freedom's sake, no less than if they were armed warriors endeavouring to make us their slaves. Nay, foemen in war, it must be granted, especially when of fair and noble type, have many times ere now proved benefactors to those they have enslaved. By dint of chastening, they have forced the vanquished to become better men and to lead more tranquil lives in future.[693] But these despotic queens never cease to plague and torment their victims in body and soul and substance until their sway is ended.

II

The conversation was resumed by Critobulus, and on this wise. He said: I think I take your meaning fully, Socrates, about these matters; and for myself, examining my heart, I am further satisfied, I have sufficient continence and self-command in those respects. So that if you will only advise me on what I am to do to improve my estate, I flatter myself I shall not be hindered by those despotic dames, as you call them. Come, do not hesitate; only tender me what good advice you can, and trust me I will follow it. But perhaps, Socrates, you have already passed sentence on us—we are rich enough already, and not in need of any further wealth?

Soc. It is to myself rather, if I may be included in your plural "we," that I should apply the remark. I am not in need of any further wealth, if you like. I am rich enough already, to be sure. But you, Critobulus, I look upon as singularly poor, and at times, upon my soul, I feel a downright compassion for you.

At this view of the case, Critobulus fell to laughing outright, retorting: And pray, Socrates, what in the name of fortune do you suppose our respective properties would fetch in the market, yours and

---

[691] Or, "become involved for want of means."

[692] "To use others as their slaves."

[693] Lit. "Enemies for the matter of that, when, being beautiful and good, they chance to have enslaved some other, have ere now in many an instance chastened and compelled the vanquished to be better and to live more easily for the rest of time."

mine?

If I could find a good purchaser (he answered), I suppose the whole of my effects, including the house in which I live, might very fairly realise five minae[694] (say twenty guineas). Yours, I am positively certain, would fetch at the lowest more than a hundred times that sum.

Crit. And with this estimate of our respective fortunes, can you still maintain that you have no need of further wealth, but it is I who am to be pitied for my poverty?

Soc. Yes, for my property is amply sufficient to meet my wants, whereas you, considering the parade you are fenced about with, and the reputation you must needs live up to, would be barely well off, I take it, if what you have already were multiplied by three.

Pray, how may that be? Critobulus asked.

Why, first and foremost (Socrates explained), I see you are called upon to offer many costly sacrifices, failing which, I take it, neither gods nor men would tolerate you; and, in the next place, you are bound to welcome numerous foreigners as guests, and to entertain them handsomely; thirdly, you must feast your fellow-citizens and ply them with all sorts of kindness, or else be cut adrift from your supporters.[695] Furthermore, I perceive that even at present the state enjoins upon you various large contributions, such as the rearing of studs,[696] the training of choruses, the superintendence of gymnastic schools, or consular duties,[697] as patron of resident aliens, and so forth; while in the event of war you will, I am aware, have further obligations laid upon you in the shape of pay[698] to carry on the trierarchy, ship money, and war taxes[699] so onerous, you will find difficulty in supporting them. Remissness in respect of any of these charges will be visited upon you by the good citizens of Athens no less strictly than if they caught you stealing their own property. But worse than all, I see you fondling the notion that you are rich. Without a thought or care how to increase your revenue, your fancy lightly turns to thoughts of love,[700] as if you had some special license to amuse yourself.... That is why I pity and compassionate you, fearing lest some irremediable mischief overtake you, and you find yourself in desperate straits. As for me, if I ever stood in need of anything, I am sure you know I have friends who would assist me. They would make some trifling contribution—trifling to themselves, I mean—and deluge my humble living with a flood of plenty. But your

---

[694] 5 x L4:1:3. See Boeckh, *P. E. A.* (Bk. i. ch. xx.), p. 109 f. (Eng. ed.)

[695] See Dr. Holden *ad loc.*, Boeckh (Bk. iii. ch. xxiii.), p. 465 f.

[696] Cf. Lycurg. *c. Leocr.* 139.

[697] Al. "presidential duties."

[698] (trierarkhias (misthous)). The commentators in general "suspect" (misthous). See Boeckh, *P. E. A.* p. 579.

[699] See Boeckh, p. 470 f.; *Revenues*, iii. 9, iv. 40.

[700] Or, "to childish matters," "frivolous affairs"; but for the full import of the phrase (paidikois pragmasi) see *Ages.* viii. 2.

friends, albeit far better off than yourself, considering your respective styles of living, persist in looking to you for assistance.

Then Critobulus: I cannot gainsay what you have spoken, Socrates, it is indeed high time that you were constituted my patronus, or I shall become in very truth a pitiable object.

To which appeal Socrates made answer: Why, you yourself must surely be astonished at the part you are now playing. Just now, when I said that I was rich, you laughed at me as if I had no idea what riches were, and you were not happy till you had cross-examined me and forced me to confess that I do not possess the hundredth part of what you have; and now you are imploring me to be your patron, and to stint no pains to save you from becoming absolutely and in very truth a pauper.[701]

Crit. Yes, Socrates, for I see that you are skilled in one lucrative operation at all events—the art of creating a surplus. I hope, therefore, that a man who can make so much out of so little will not have the slightest difficulty in creating an ample surplus out of an abundance.

Soc. But do not you recollect how just now in the discussion you would hardly let me utter a syllable[702] while you laid down the law: if a man did not know how to handle horses, horses were not wealth to him at any rate; nor land, nor sheep, nor money, nor anything else, if he did not know how to use them? And yet these are the very sources of revenue from which incomes are derived; and how do you expect me to know the use of any of them who never possessed a single one of them since I was born?

Crit. Yes, but we agreed that, however little a man may be blest with wealth himself, a science of economy exists; and that being so, what hinders you from being its professor?

Soc. Nothing, to be sure,[703] except what would hinder a man from knowing how to play the flute, supposing he had never had a flute of his own and no one had supplied the defect by lending him one to practise on: which is just my case with regard to economy,[704] seeing I never myself possessed the instrument of the science which is wealth, so as to go through the pupil stage, nor hitherto has any one proposed to hand me over his to manage. You, in fact, are the first person to make so generous an offer. You will bear in mind, I hope, that a learner of the harp is apt to break and spoil the instrument; it is therefore probable, if I take in hand to learn the art of economy on your estate, I shall ruin it outright.

Critobulus retorted: I see, Socrates, you are doing your very best to escape an irksome task: you would rather not, if you can help it, stretch

---

[701] Or, "literally beggared."
[702] Cf. Aristoph. *Clouds*, 945; *Plut.* 17; Dem. 353; and Holden *ad loc.*
[703] Lit. "The very thing, God help me! which would hinder..."
[704] Lit. "the art of administering an estate."

out so much as your little finger to help me to bear my necessary burthens more easily.

Soc. No, upon my word, I am not trying to escape: on the contrary, I shall be ready, as far as I can, to expound the matter to you.[705] ... Still it strikes me, if you had come to me for fire, and I had none in my house, you would not blame me for sending you where you might get it; or if you had asked me for water, and I, having none to give, had led you elsewhere to the object of your search, you would not, I am sure, have disapproved; or did you desire to be taught music by me, and I were to point out to you a far more skilful teacher than myself, who would perhaps be grateful to you moreover for becoming his pupil, what kind of exception could you take to my behaviour?

Crit. None, with any show of justice, Socrates.

Soc. Well, then, my business now is, Critobulus, to point out[706] to you some others cleverer than myself about those matters which you are so anxious to be taught by me. I do confess to you, I have made it long my study to discover who among our fellow-citizens in this city are the greatest adepts in the various branches of knowledge.[707] I had been struck with amazement, I remember, to observe on some occasion that where a set of people are engaged in identical operations, half of them are in absolute indigence and the other half roll in wealth. I bethought me, the history of the matter was worth investigation. Accordingly I set to work investigating, and I found that it all happened very naturally. Those who carried on their affairs in a haphazard manner I saw were punished by their losses; whilst those who kept their wits upon the stretch and paid attention I soon perceived to be rewarded by the greater ease and profit of their undertakings.[708] It is to these I would recommend you to betake yourself. What say you? Learn of them: and unless the will of God oppose,[709] I venture to say you will become as clever a man of business as one might hope to see.

III

Critobulus, on hearing that, exclaimed: Be sure, Socrates, I will not let you go now until you give the proofs which, in the presence of our friends, you undertook just now to give me.

Well then,[710] Critobulus (Socrates replied), what if I begin by

---

[705] Or, "to play the part of (exegetes), 'legal adviser,' or 'spiritual director,' to be in fact your 'guide, philosopher, and friend.'"

[706] *Al.* "to show you that there are others."

[707] Or, "who are gifted with the highest knowledge in their respective concerns." Cf. *Mem.* IV. vii. 1.

[708] Lit. "got no quicker, easier, and more profitably."

[709] Or, "short of some divine interposition."

[710] Lincke [brackets as an editorial interpolation iii. 1, (ti oun, ephe)—vi. 11, (poiomen)]. See his edition *Xenophons Dialog.* (peri oikonomias) *in seiner*

showing[711] you two sorts of people, the one expending large sums on money in building useless houses, the other at far less cost erecting dwellings replete with all they need; will you admit that I have laid my finger here on one of the essentials of economy?

Crit. An essential point most certainly.

Soc. And suppose in connection with the same, I next point out to you[712] two other sets of persons:—The first possessors of furniture of various kinds, which they cannot, however, lay their hands on when the need arises; indeed they hardly know if they have got all safe and sound or not: whereby they put themselves and their domestics to much mental torture. The others are perhaps less amply, or at any rate not more amply supplied, but they have everything ready at the instant for immediate use.

Crit. Yes, Socrates, and is not the reason simply that in the first case everything is thrown down where it chanced, whereas those others have everything arranged, each in its appointed place?

Quite right (he answered), and the phrase implies that everything is orderly arranged, not in the first chance place, but in that to which it naturally belongs.

Crit. Yes, the case is to the point, I think, and does involve another economic principle.

Soc. What, then, if I exhibit to you a third contrast, which bears on the condition of domestic slaves? On the one side you shall see them fettered hard and fast, as I may say, and yet for ever breaking their chains and running away. On the other side the slaves are loosed, and free to move, but for all that, they choose to work, it seems; they are constant to their masters. I think you will admit that I here point out another function of economy[713] worth noting.

Crit. I do indeed—a feature most noteworthy.

Soc. Or take, again, the instance of two farmers engaged in cultivating farms[714] as like as possible. The one had never done asserting that agriculture has been his ruin, and is in the depth of despair; the other has all he needs in abundance and of the best, and how acquired?—by this same agriculture.

Yes (Critobulus answered), to be sure; perhaps[715] the former spends both toil and money not simply on what he needs, but on things which cause an injury to house alike and owner.

---

ursprünglichen Gestalt; and for a criticism of his views, an article by Charles D. Morris, "Xenophon's Oeconomicus," in the *American Journal of Philology*, vol. i. p. 169 foll.

[711] As a demonstrator.

[712] "As in a mirror, or a picture."

[713] Or, "economical result."

[714] (georgias). See Hartman, "An. Xen." p. 193. Hold. cf. Plat. *Laws*, 806 E. Isocr. *Areop.* 32.

[715] Or, "like enough in the one case the money and pains are spent," etc.

Soc. That is a possible case, no doubt, but it is not the one that I refer to; I mean people pretending they are farmers, and yet they have not a penny to expend on the real needs of their business.

Crit. And pray, what may be the reason of that, Socrates?

Soc. You shall come with me, and see these people also; and as you contemplate the scene, I presume you will lay to heart the lesson.

Crit. I will, if possibly I can, I promise you.

Soc. Yes, and while you contemplate, you must make trial of yourself and see if you have wit to understand. At present, I will bear you witness that if it is to go and see a party of players performing in a comedy, you will get up at cock-crow, and come trudging a long way, and ply me volubly with reasons why I should accompany you to see the play. But you have never once invited me to come and witness such an incident as those we were speaking of just now.

Crit. And so I seem to you ridiculous?[716]

Soc. Far more ridiculous to yourself, I warrant. But now let me point out to you another contrast: between certain people whose dealing with horses has brought them to the brink of poverty, and certain others who have found in the same pursuit the road to affluence,[717] and have a right besides to plume themselves upon their gains.[718]

Crit. Well, then, I may tell you, I see and know both characters as well as you do; but I do not find myself a whit the more included among those who gain.

Soc. Because you look at them just as you might at the actors in a tragedy or comedy, and with the same intent—your object being to delight the ear and charm the eye, but not, I take it, to become yourself a poet. And there you are right enough, no doubt, since you have no desire to become a playwright. But, when circumstances compel you to concern yourself with horsemanship, does it not seem to you a little foolish not to consider how you are to escape being a mere amateur in the matter, especially as the same creatures which are good for use are profitable for sale?

Crit. So you wish me to set up as a breeder of young horses,[719] do you, Socrates?

Soc. Not so, no more than I would recommend you to purchase lads and train them up from boyhood as farm-labourers. But in my opinion there is a certain happy moment of growth which must be seized, alike in man and horse, rich in present service and in future

---

[716] Or, "a comic character in the performance." *Soc.* "Not so comic as you must appear to yourself (*i.e.* with your keen sense of the ludicrous)."

[717] Or, "who have not only attained to affluence by the same pursuit, but can hold their heads high, and may well pride themselves on their thrift."

[718] Cf. Hom. *Il.* xii. 114, (ippoisin kai okhesphin agallomenos), et passim; *Hiero*, viii. 5; *Anab.* II. vi. 26.

[719] See *Horsemanship*, ii. 1.

promise. In further illustration, I can show you how some men treat their wedded wives in such a way that they find in them true helpmates to the joint increase of their estate, while others treat them in a way to bring upon themselves wholesale disaster.[720]

Crit. Ought the husband or the wife to bear the blame of that?

Soc. If it goes ill with the sheep we blame the shepherd, as a rule, or if a horse shows vice we throw the blame in general upon the rider. But in the case of women, supposing the wife to have received instruction from her husband and yet she delights in wrong-doing,[721] it may be that the wife is justly held to blame; but supposing he has never tried to teach her the first principles of "fair and noble" conduct,[722] and finds her quite an ignoramus[723] in these matters, surely the husband will be justly held to blame. But come now (he added), we are all friends here; make a clean breast of it, and tell us, Critobulus, the plain unvarnished truth: Is there an one to whom you are more in the habit of entrusting matters of importance than to your wife?

Crit. There is no one.

Soc. And is there any one with whom you are less in the habit of conversing than with your wife?

Crit. Not many, I am forced to admit.

Soc. And when you married her she was quite young, a mere girl— at an age when, as far as seeing and hearing go, she had the smallest acquaintance with the outer world?

Crit. Certainly.

Soc. Then would it not be more astonishing that she should have real knowledge how to speak and act than that she should go altogether astray?

Crit. But let me ask you a question, Socrates: have those happy husbands, you tell us of, who are blessed with good wives educated them themselves?

Soc. There is nothing like investigation. I will introduce you to Aspasia,[724] who will explain these matters to you in a far more scientific way than I can. My belief is that a good wife, being as she is the partner in a common estate, must needs be her husband's counterpoise and counterpart for good; since, if it is through the transactions of the husband, as a rule, that goods of all sorts find their way into the house, yet it is by means of the wife's economy and thrift that the greater part of the expenditure is checked, and on the successful issue or the mishandling of the same depends the increase or impoverishment of a whole estate. And so with regard to the remaining

---

[720] Reading (e os pleista), al. (e oi pleistoi) = "to bring about disaster in most cases."

[721] Cf. *Horsemanship*, vi. 5, of a horse "to show vice."

[722] Or, "things beautiful and of good report."

[723] Al. "has treated her as a dunce, devoid of this high knowledge."

[724] Aspasia. See *Mem.* II. vi. 36.

arts and sciences, I think I can point out to you the ablest performers in each case, if you feel you have any further need of help.[725]

IV

But why need you illustrate all the sciences, Socrates? (Critobulus asked): it would not be very easy to discover efficient craftsmen of all the arts, and quite impossible to become skilled in all one's self. So, please, confine yourself to the nobler branches of knowledge as men regard them, such as it will best befit me to pursue with devotion; be so good as to point me out these and their performers, and, above all, contribute as far as in you lies the aid of your own personal instruction.

Soc. A good suggestion, Critobulus, for the base mechanic arts, so called, have got a bad name; and what is more, are held in ill repute by civilised communities, and not unreasonably; seeing they are the ruin of the bodies of all concerned in them, workers and overseers alike, who are forced to remain in sitting postures and to hug the loom, or else to crouch whole days confronting a furnace. Hand in hand with physical enervation follows apace enfeeblement of soul: while the demand which these base mechanic arts makes on the time of those employed in them leaves them no leisure to devote to the claims of friendship and the state. How can such folk be other than sorry friends and ill defenders of the fatherland? So much so that in some states, especially those reputed to be warlike, no citizen[726] is allowed to exercise any mechanical craft at all.

Crit. Then which are the arts you would counsel us to engage in?

Soc. Well, we shall not be ashamed, I hope, to imitate the kings of Persia?[727] That monarch, it is said, regards amongst the noblest and most necessary pursuits two in particular, which are the arts of husbandry and war, and in these two he takes the strongest interest.

What! (Critobulus exclaimed); do you, Socrates, really believe that the king of Persia pays a personal regard to husbandry, along with all his other cares?

Soc. We have only to investigate the matter, Critobulus, and I daresay we shall discover whether this is so or not. We are agreed that he takes strong interest in military matters; since, however numerous the tributary nations, there is a governor to each, and every governor has orders from the king what number of cavalry, archers, slingers and

---

[725] *Al.* "there are successful performers in each who will be happy to illustrate any point in which you think you need," etc.

[726] "In the strict sense," *e.g.* the Spartiates in Sparta. See *Pol. Lac.* vii.; Newman, *op. cit.* i. 99, 103 foll.

[727] "It won't make us blush actually to take a leaf out of the great king's book." As to the Greek text at this point see the commentators, and also a note by Mr. H. Richards in the *Classical Review*, x. 102.

targeteers[728] it is his business to support, as adequate to control the subject population, or in case of hostile attack to defend the country. Apart from these the king keeps garrisons in all the citadels. The actual support of these devolves upon the governor, to whom the duty is assigned. The king himself meanwhile conducts the annual inspection and review of troops, both mercenary and other, that have orders to be under arms. These all are simultaneously assembled (with the exception of the garrisons of citadels) at the mustering ground,[729] so named. That portion of the army within access of the royal residence the king reviews in person; the remainder, living in remoter districts of the empire, he inspects by proxy, sending certain trusty representatives.[730] Wherever the commandants of garrisons, the captains of thousands, and the satraps[731] are seen to have their appointed members complete, and at the same time shall present their troops equipped with horse and arms in thorough efficiency, these officers the king delights to honour, and showers gifts upon them largely. But as to those officers whom he finds either to have neglected their garrisons, or to have made private gain of their position, these he heavily chastises, deposing them from office, and appointing other superintendents[732] in their stead. Such conduct, I think we may say, indisputably proves the interest which he takes in matters military.

Further than this, by means of a royal progress through the country, he has an opportunity of inspecting personally some portion of his territory, and again of visiting the remainder in proxy as above by trusty representatives; and wheresoever he perceives that any of his governors can present to him a district thickly populated, and the soil in a state of active cultivation, full of trees and fruits, its natural products, to such officers he adds other territory, adorning them with gifts and distinguishing them by seats of honour. But those officers whose land he sees lying idle and with but few inhabitants, owing either to the harshness of their government, their insolence, or their neglect, he punishes, and making them to cease from their office he appoints other rulers in their place.... Does not this conduct indicate at least as great an anxiety to promote the active cultivation of the land by its inhabitants as to provide for its defence by military occupation?[733]

Moreover, the governors appointed to preside over these two departments of state are not one and the same. But one class governs the inhabitants proper including the workers of the soil, and collects the tribute from them, another is in command of the armed garrisons. If the

---

[728] Or, *Gerrophoroi*, "wicker-shield bearers."
[729] Or, "rendezvous"; "the 'Champ de Mars' for the nonce." Cf. *Cyrop.* VI. ii. 11.
[730] Lit. "he sends some of *the faithful* to inspect." Cf. our "trusty and well-beloved."
[731] See, for the system, Herod. iii. 89 foll.; *Cyrop.* VIII. vi. 11.
[732] Or, as we say, "inspecting officers." Cf. *Cyrop.* VIII. i. 9.
[733] Lit. "by those who guard and garrison it."

commandant[734] protects the country insufficiently, the civil governor of the population, who is in charge also of the productive works, lodges accusation against the commandant to the effect that the inhabitants are prevented working through deficiency of protection. Or if again, in spite of peace being secured to the works of the land by the military governor, the civil authority still presents a territory sparse in population and untilled, it is the commandant's turn to accuse the civil ruler. For you may take it as a rule, a population tilling their territory badly will fail to support their garrisons and be quite unequal to paying their tribute. Where a satrap is appointed he has charge of both departments.[735]

Thereupon Critobulus: Well, Socrates (said he), if such is his conduct, I admit that the great king does pay attention to agriculture no less than to military affairs.

And besides all this (proceeded Socrates), nowhere among the various countries which he inhabits or visits does he fail to make it his first care that there shall be orchards and gardens, parks and "paradises," as they are called, full of all fair and noble products which the earth brings forth; and within these chiefly he spends his days, when the season of the year permits.

Crit. To be sure, Socrates, it is a natural and necessary conclusion that when the king himself spends so large a portion of his time there, his paradises should be furnished to perfection with trees and all else beautiful that earth brings forth.

Soc. And some say, Critobulus, that when the king gives gifts, he summons in the first place those who have shown themselves brave warriors, since all the ploughing in the world were but small gain in the absence of those who should protect the fields; and next to these he summons those who have stocked their countries best and rendered them productive, on the principle that but for the tillers of the soil the warriors themselves could scarcely live. And there is a tale told of Cyrus, the most famous prince, I need not tell you, who ever wore a crown,[736] how on one occasion he said to those who had been called to receive the gifts, "it were no injustice, if he himself received the gifts due to warriors and tillers of the soil alike," for "did he not carry off the palm in stocking the country and also in protecting the goods with which it had been stocked?"

Crit. Which clearly shows, Socrates, if the tale be true, that this same Cyrus took as great a pride in fostering the productive energies of

---

[734] Or, "garrison commandant." Lit. "Phrourarch."

[735] The passage reads like a gloss. See about the Satrap, *Hell.* III. i. 10; *Cyrop.* VIII. vi. 1; *Anab.* I. ix. 29 foll.

[736] Lit. "the most glorious king that ever lived." The remark would seem to apply better to Cyrus the Great. Nitsche and others regard these §§ 18, 19 as interpolated. See Schenkl *ad loc.*

his country and stocking it with good things, as in his reputation as a warrior.

Soc. Why, yes indeed, had Cyrus lived, I have no doubt he would have proved the best of rulers, and in support of this belief, apart from other testimony amply furnished by his life, witness what happened when he marched to do battle for the sovereignty of Persia with his brother. Not one man, it is said,[737] deserted from Cyrus to the king, but from the king to Cyrus tens of thousands. And this also I deem a great testimony to a ruler's worth, that his followers follow him of their own free will, and when the moment of danger comes refuse to part from him.[738] Now this was the case with Cyrus. His friends not only fought their battles side by side with him while he lived, but when he died they too died battling around his dead body, one and all, excepting only Ariaeus, who was absent at his post on the left wing of the army.[739] But there is another tale of this same Cyrus in connection with Lysander, who himself narrated it on one occasion to a friend of his in Megara.[740]

Lysander, it seems, had gone with presents sent by the Allies to Cyrus, who entertained him, and amongst other marks of courtesy showed him his "paradise" at Sardis.[741] Lysander was astonished at the beauty of the trees within, all planted[742] at equal intervals, the long straight rows of waving branches, the perfect regularity, the rectangular[743] symmetry of the whole, and the many sweet scents which hung about them as they paced the park. In admiration he exclaimed to Cyrus: "All this beauty is marvellous enough, but what astonishes me still more is the talent of the artificer who mapped out and arranged for you the several parts of this fair scene."[744] Cyrus was pleased by the remark, and said: "Know then, Lysander, it is I who measured and arranged it all. Some of the trees," he added, "I planted with my own hands." Then Lysander, regarding earnestly the speaker, when he saw the beauty of his apparel and perceived its fragrance, the splendour[745] also of the necklaces and armlets, and other ornaments which he wore, exclaimed: "What say you, Cyrus? did you with your own hands plant some of these trees?" whereat the other: "Does that surprise you,

---

[737] Cf. *Anab.* I. ix. 29 foll.
[738] Cf. *Hiero,* xi. 12, and our author passim.
[739] See *Anab.* ib. 31.
[740] Possibly to Xenophon himself (who may have met Lysander on his way back after the events of the "Anabasis," and implying this dialogue is concocted, since Socrates died before Xenophon returned to Athens, if he did return at that period.)
[741] See *Hell.* I. v. 1.
[742] Reading (oi' isou pephuteumena), or if (ta pephuteumena), transl. "the various plants ranged."
[743] Cf. Dion. Hal. *de Comp.* p. 170; Cic. *de Senect.* S. 59.
[744] Lit. "of these" (deiktikos), *i.e.* pointing to the various beauties of the scenery.
[745] Reading (to kallos).

Lysander? I swear to you by Mithres,[746] when in ordinary health I never dream of sitting down to supper without first practising some exercise of war or husbandry in the sweat of my brow, or venturing some strife of honour, as suits my mood." "On hearing this," said Lysander to his friend, "I could not help seizing him by the hand and exclaiming, 'Cyrus, you have indeed good right to be a happy man,[747] since you are happy in being a good man.'"[748]

V

All this I relate to you (continued Socrates) to show you that quite high and mighty[749] people find it hard to hold aloof from agriculture, devotion to which art would seem to be thrice blest, combining as it does a certain sense of luxury with the satisfaction of an improved estate, and such a training of physical energies as shall fit a man to play a free man's part.[750] Earth, in the first place, freely offers to those that labour all things necessary to the life of man; and, as if that were not enough, makes further contribution of a thousand luxuries.[751] It is she who supplies with sweetest scent and fairest show all things wherewith to adorn the altars and statues of the gods, or deck man's person. It is to her we owe our many delicacies of flesh or fowl or vegetable growth;[752] since with the tillage of the soil is closely linked the art of breeding sheep and cattle, whereby we mortals may offer sacrifices well pleasing to the gods, and satisfy our personal needs withal.

And albeit she, good cateress, pours out her blessings upon us in abundance, yet she suffers not her gifts to be received effeminately, but inures her pensioners to suffer gladly summer's heat and winter's cold. Those that labour with their hands, the actual delvers of the soil, she trains in a wrestling school of her own, adding strength to strength; whilst those others whose devotion is confined to the overseeing eye and to studious thought, she makes more manly, rousing them with cock-crow, and compelling them to be up and doing in many a long day's march.[753] Since, whether in city or afield, with the shifting

---

[746] The Persian "Sun-God." See *Cyrop.* VII. v. 53; Strab. xv. 3. 13.
[747] Or, "fortunate."
[748] Or, "you are a good man, and thereby fortunate."
[749] Lit. "Not even the most blessed of mankind can abstain from." See Plat. *Rep.* 344 B, "The superlatively best and well-to-do."
[750] Lit. "Devotion to it would seem to be at once a kind of luxury, an increase of estate, a training of the bodily parts, so that a man is able to perform all that a free man should."
[751] *Al.* "and further, to the maintenance of life she adds the sources of pleasure in life."
[752] Lit. "she bears these and rears those."
[753] See *Hellenica Essays*, p. 341.

seasons each necessary labour has its hour of performance.[754]

Or to turn to another side. Suppose it to be a man's ambition to aid his city as a trooper mounted on a charger of his own: why not combine the rearing of horses with other stock? it is the farmer's chance.[755] Or would your citizen serve on foot? It is husbandry that shall give him robustness of body. Or if we turn to the toil-loving fascination of the chase,[756] here once more earth adds incitement, as well as furnishing facility of sustenance for the dogs as by nurturing a foster brood of wild animals. And if horses and dogs derive benefit from this art of husbandry, they in turn requite the boon through service rendered to the farm. The horse carries his best of friends, the careful master, betimes to the scene of labour and devotion, and enables him to leave it late. The dog keeps off the depredations of wild animals from fruits and flocks, and creates security in the solitary place.

Earth, too, adds stimulus in war-time to earth's tillers; she pricks them on to aid the country under arms, and this she does by fostering her fruits in open field, the prize of valour for the mightiest.[757] For this also is the art athletic, this of husbandry; as thereby men are fitted to run, and hurl the spear, and leap with the best.[758]

This, too, is that kindliest of arts which makes requital tenfold in kind for every work of the labourer.[759] She is the sweet mistress who, with smile of welcome and outstretched hand, greets the approach of her devoted one, seeming to say, Take from me all thy heart's desire. She is the generous hostess; she keeps open house for the stranger.[760] For where else, save in some happy rural seat of her devising, shall a man more cheerily cherish content in winter, with bubbling bath and blazing fire? or where, save afield, in summer rest more sweetly, lulled by babbling streams, soft airs, and tender shades?[761]

Her high prerogative it is to offer fitting first-fruits to high heaven, hers to furnish forth the overflowing festal board.[762] Hers is a kindly presence in the household. She is the good wife's favourite, the children long for her, she waves her hand winningly to the master's friends.

For myself, I marvel greatly if it has ever fallen to the lot of

---

[754] Lit. "each most necessary operation must ever be in season."

[755] Lit. "farming is best adapted to rearing horses along with other produce."

[756] Lit. "to labour willingly and earnestly at hunting earth helps to incite us somewhat."

[757] Cf. *Hipparch*, viii. 8.

[758] Cf. *Hunting*, xii. 1 foll.

[759] Lit. "What art makes an ampler return for their labour to those who work for her? What art more sweetly welcomes him that is devoted to her?"

[760] Lit. "What art welcomes the stranger with greater prodigality?"

[761] See *Hellenica Essays*, p. 380; and as still more to the point, Cowley's Essays: *Of Agriculture*, passim.

[762] Or, "to appoint the festal board most bounteously."

freeborn man to own a choicer possession, or to discover an occupation more seductive, or of wider usefulness in life than this.

But, furthermore, earth of her own will[763] gives lessons in justice and uprightness to all who can understand her meaning, since the nobler the service of devotion rendered, the ampler the riches of her recompense.[764] One day, perchance, these pupils of hers, whose conversation in past times was in husbandry,[765] shall, by reason of the multitude of invading armies, be ousted from their labours. The work of their hands may indeed be snatched from them, but they were brought up in stout and manly fashion. They stand, each one of them, in body and soul equipped; and, save God himself shall hinder them, they will march into the territory of those their human hinderers, and take from them the wherewithal to support their lives. Since often enough in war it is surer and safer to quest for food with sword and buckler than with all the instruments of husbandry.

But there is yet another lesson to be learnt in the public school of husbandry[766]—the lesson of mutual assistance. "Shoulder to shoulder" must we march to meet the invader;[767] "shoulder to shoulder" stand to compass the tillage of the soil. Therefore it is that the husbandman, who means to win in his avocation, must see that he creates enthusiasm in his workpeople and a spirit of ready obedience; which is just what a general attacking an enemy will scheme to bring about, when he deals out gifts to the brave and castigation[768] to those who are disorderly.

Nor will there be lacking seasons of exhortation, the general haranguing his troops and the husbandman his labourers; nor because they are slaves do they less than free men need the lure of hope and happy expectation,[769] that they may willingly stand to their posts.

It was an excellent saying of his who named husbandry "the mother and nurse of all the arts," for while agriculture prospers all other arts like are vigorous and strong, but where the land is forced to remain desert,[770] the spring that feeds the other arts is dried up; they dwindle, I had almost said, one and all, by land and sea.

These utterances drew from Critobulus a comment:

Socrates (he said), for my part I agree with all you say; only, one must face the fact that in agriculture nine matters out of ten are beyond

---

[763] Reading (thelousa), vulg., or if after Cobet, (theos ousa), transl. "by sanction of her divinity." With (thelousa) Holden aptly compares Virgil's "volentia rura," *Georg.* ii. 500.

[764] "That is, her *lex talionis.*"

[765] "Engaged long time in husbandry."

[766] Lit. "But again, husbandry trains up her scholars side by side in lessons of..."

[767] (sun anthropois), "man with his fellow-man," is the *mot d'order* (cf. the author's favourite (sun theois)); "united human effort."

[768] "Lashes," "punishment." Cf. *Anab.* II. vi. 10, of Clearchus.

[769] "The lure of happy prospects." See *Horsemanship,* iii. 1.

[770] Or, "lie waste and barren as the blown sea-sand."

man's calculation. Since at one time hailstones and another frost, at another drought or a deluge of rain, or mildew, or other pest, will obliterate all the fair creations and designs of men; or behold, his fleecy flocks most fairly nurtured, then comes murrain, and the end most foul destruction.[771]

To which Socrates: Nay, I thought, Critobulus, you full surely were aware that the operations of husbandry, no less than those of war, lie in the hands of the gods. I am sure you will have noted the behaviour of men engaged in war; how on the verge of military operations they strive to win the acceptance of the divine powers;[772] how eagerly they assail the ears of heaven, and by dint of sacrifices and omens seek to discover what they should and what they should not do. So likewise as regards the processes of husbandry, think you the propitiation of heaven is less needed here? Be well assured (he added) the wise and prudent will pay service to the gods on behalf of moist fruits and dry,[773] on behalf of cattle and horses, sheep and goats; nay, on behalf of all their possessions, great and small, without exception.

VI

Your words (Critobulus answered) command my entire sympathy, when you bid us endeavour to begin each work with heaven's help,[774] seeing that the gods hold in their hands the issues alike of peace and war. So at any rate will we endeavour to act at all times; but will you now endeavour on your side to continue the discussion of economy from the point at which you broke off, and bring it point by point to its conclusion? What you have said so far has not been thrown away on me. I seem to discern already more clearly, what sort of behaviour is necessary to anything like real living.[775]

Socrates replied: What say you then? Shall we first survey the ground already traversed, and retrace the steps on which we were agreed, so that, if possible we may conduct the remaining portion of the argument to its issue with like unanimity?[776]

Crit. Why, yes! If it is agreeable for two partners in a business to run through their accounts without dispute, so now as partners in an argument it will be no less agreeable to sum up the points under discussion, as you say, with unanimity.

---

[771] See Virg. *Georg.* iii. 441 foll.: "Turpis oves tentat scabies, ubi frigidus imber."

[772] See *Hell.* III. i. 16 foll., of Dercylidas.

[773] "Every kind of produce, succulent (like the grape and olive) or dry (like wheat and barley, etc.)"

[774] Lit. "with the gods," and for the sentiment see below, x. 10; *Cyrop.* III. i. 15; *Hipparch*, ix. 3.

[775] For (bioteuein) cf. Pind. *Nem.* iv. 11, and see Holden *ad loc.*

[776] Lit. "try whether we can go through the remaining steps with like..."

Soc. Well, then, we agreed that economy was the proper title of a branch of knowledge, and this branch of knowledge appeared to be that whereby men are enabled to enhance the value of their houses or estates; and by this word "house or estate" we understood the whole of a man's possessions; and "possessions" again we defined to include those things which the possessor should find advantageous for the purposes of his life; and things advantageous finally were discovered to mean all that a man knows how to use and turn to good account. Further, for a man to learn all branches of knowledge not only seemed to us an impossibility, but we thought we might well follow the example of civil communities in rejecting the base mechanic arts so called, on the ground that they destroy the bodies of the artisans, as far as we can see, and crush their spirits.

The clearest proof of this, we said,[777] could be discovered if, on the occasion of a hostile inroad, one were to seat the husbandmen and the artisans apart in two divisions, and then proceed to put this question to each group in turn: "Do you think it better to defend our country districts or to retire from the fields[778] and guard the walls?" And we anticipated that those concerned with the soil would vote to defend the soil; while the artisans would vote not to fight, but, in docile obedience to their training, to sit with folded hands, neither expending toil nor venturing their lives.

Next we held it as proved that there was no better employment for a gentleman—we described him as a man beautiful and good—than this of husbandry, by which human beings procure to themselves the necessaries of life. This same employment, moreover, was, as we agreed, at once the easiest to learn[779] and the pleasantest to follow, since it gives to the limbs beauty and hardihood, whilst permitting[780] to the soul leisure to satisfy the claims of friendship and of civic duty.

Again it seemed to us that husbandry acts as a spur to bravery in the hearts of those that till the fields,[781] inasmuch as the necessaries of life, vegetable and animal, under her auspices spring up and are reared outside the fortified defences of the city. For which reason also this way of life stood in the highest repute in the eyes of statesmen and commonwealths, as furnishing the best citizens and those best disposed to the common weal.[782]

Crit. I think I am fully persuaded as to the propriety of making

---

[777] This § 6 has no parallel supra. See Breit. and Schenkl *ad loc.* for attempts to cure the text.

[778] See Cobet, *N. L.* 580, reading (uphemenous), or if (aphemenous) transl. "to abandon."

[779] (raste mathein). *Vide infra*, not *supra*.

[780] Lit. "least allowing the soul no leisure to care for friends and state withal."

[781] Cf. Aristot. *Oec.* I. ii. 1343 B, (pros toutois k.t.l.)

[782] Cf. Aristoph. *Archarnians*.

agriculture the basis of life. I see it is altogether noblest, best, and pleasantest to do so. But I should like to revert to your remark that you understood the reason why the tillage of one man brings him in an abundance of all he needs, while the operations of another fail to make husbandry a profitable employment. I would gladly hear from you an explanation of both these points, so that I may adopt the right and avoid the harmful course.[783]

Soc. Well, Critobulus, suppose I narrate to you from the beginning how I cam in contact with a man who of all men I ever met seemed to me to deserve the appellation of a gentleman. He was indeed a "beautiful and good" man.[784]

Crit. There is nothing I should better like to hear, since of all titles this is the one I covet most the right to bear.

Soc. Well, then, I will tell you how I came to subject him to my inquiry. It did not take me long to go the round of various good carpenters, good bronze-workers, painters, sculptors, and so forth. A brief period was sufficient for the contemplation of themselves and of their most admired works of art. But when it came to examining those who bore the high-sounding title "beautiful and good," in order to find out what conduct on their part justified their adoption of this title, I found my soul eager with desire for intercourse with one of them; and first of all, seeing that the epithet "beautiful" was conjoined with that of "good," every beautiful person I saw, I must needs approach in my endeavour to discover,[785] if haply I might somewhere see the quality of good adhering to the quality of beauty. But, after all, it was otherwise ordained. I soon enough seemed to discover[786] that some of those who in their outward form were beautiful were in their inmost selves the veriest knaves. Accordingly I made up my mind to let go beauty which appeals to the eye, and address myself to one of those "beautiful and good" people so entitled. And since I heard of Ischomachus[787] as one who was so called by all the world, both men and women, strangers and citizens alike, I set myself to make acquaintance with him.

---

[783] Lincke conceives the editor's interpolation as ending here.
[784] Or, "a man 'beautiful and good,' as the phrase goes."
[785] Or, "and try to understand."
[786] Or, "understand."
[787] See Cobet, "Pros. Xen." s.n.

VII

It chanced, one day I saw him seated in the portico of Zeus Eleutherios,[788] and as he appeared to be at leisure, I went up to him and, sitting down by his side, accosted him: How is this, Ischomachus? you seated here, you who are so little wont to be at leisure? As a rule, when I see you, you are doing something, or at any rate not sitting idle in the market-place.

Nor would you see me now so sitting, Socrates (he answered), but that I promised to meet some strangers, friends of mine,[789] at this place.

And when you have no such business on hand (I said) where in heaven's name do you spend your time and how do you employ yourself? I will not conceal from you how anxious I am to learn from your lips by what conduct you have earned for yourself the title "beautiful and good."[790] It is not by spending your days indoors at home, I am sure; the whole habit of your body bears witness to a different sort of life.

Then Ischomachus, smiling at my question, but also, as it seemed to me, a little pleased to be asked what he had done to earn the title "beautiful and good," made answer: Whether that is the title by which folk call me when they talk to you about me, I cannot say; all I know is, when they challenge me to exchange properties,[791] or else to perform some service to the state instead of them, the fitting out of a trireme, or the training of a chorus, nobody thinks of asking for the beautiful and good gentleman, but it is plain Ischomachus, the son of So-and-so,[792] on whom the summons is served. But to answer your question, Socrates (he proceeded), I certainly do not spend my days indoors, if for no other reason, because my wife is quite capable of managing our domestic affairs without my aid.

---

[788] "The god of freedom, or of freed men." See Plat. *Theag.* 259 A. The scholiast on Aristoph. *Plutus* 1176 identifies the god with Zeus Sotêr. See Plut. *Dem.* 859 (Clough, v. 30).

[789] "Foreign friends."

[790] "The sobriquet of 'honest gentleman.'"

[791] On the *antidosis* or compulsory exchange of property, see Boeckh, p. 580, Engl. ed.: "In case any man, upon whom a (leitourgia) was imposed, considered that another was richer than himself, and therefore most justly chargeable with the burden, he might challenge the other to assume the burden, or to make with him an (antidosis) or exchange of property. Such a challenge, if declined, was converted into a lawsuit, or came before a heliastic court for trial." Gow, *Companion*, xviii. "Athenian Finance." See Dem. *Against Midias*, 565, Kennedy, p. 117, and Appendix II. For the various liturgies, *Trierarchy, Choregy,* etc., see *Pol. Ath.* i. 13 foll.

[792] Or, "the son of his father," it being customary at Athens to add the patronymic, *e.g.* Xenophon son of Gryllus, Thucydides son of Olorus, etc. See Herod. vi. 14, viii. 90. In official acts the name of the dême was added, *e.g.* Demosthenes son of Demosthenes of Paianê; or of the tribe, at times. Cf. Thuc. viii. 69; Plat. *Laws*, vi. p. 753 B.

Ah! (said I), Ischomachus, that is just what I should like particularly to learn from you. Did you yourself educate your wife to be all that a wife should be, or when you received her from her father and mother was she already a proficient well skilled to discharge the duties appropriate to a wife?

Well skilled! (he replied). What proficiency was she likely to bring with her, when she was not quite fifteen[793] at the time she wedded me, and during the whole prior period of her life had been most carefully brought up[794] to see and hear as little as possible, and to ask[795] the fewest questions? or do you not think one should be satisfied, if at marriage her whole experience consisted in knowing how to take the wool and make a dress, and seeing how her mother's handmaidens had their daily spinning-tasks assigned them? For (he added), as regards control of appetite and self-indulgence,[796] she had received the soundest education, and that I take to be the most important matter in the bringing-up of man or woman.

Then all else (said I) you taught your wife yourself, Ischomachus, until you had made her capable of attending carefully to her appointed duties?

That did I not (replied he) until I had offered sacrifice, and prayed that I might teach and she might learn all that could conduce to the happiness of us twain.

Soc. And did your wife join in sacrifice and prayer to that effect?

Isch. Most certainly, with many a vow registered to heaven to become all she ought to be; and her whole manner showed that she would not be neglectful of what was taught her.[797]

Soc. Pray narrate to me, Ischomachus, I beg of you, what you first essayed to teach her. To hear that story would please me more than any description of the most splendid gymnastic contest or horse-race you could give me.

Why, Socrates (he answered), when after a time she had become accustomed to my hand, that is, was tamed[798] sufficiently to play her part in a discussion, I put to her this question: "Did it ever strike you to consider, dear wife,[799] what led me to choose you as my wife among all women, and your parents to entrust you to me of all men? It was

---

[793] See Aristot. *Pol.* vii. 16. 1335(a). See Newman, *op. cit.* i. 170 foll.

[794] Or, "surveillance." See *Pol. Lac.* i. 3.

[795] Reading (eroito); or if with Sauppe after Cobet, (eroin), transl. "talk as little as possible."

[796] *Al.* "in reference to culinary matters." See Mahaffy, *Social Life in Greece*, p. 276.

[797] Or, "giving plain proof that, if the teaching failed, it should not be from want of due attention on her part." See *Hellenica Essays,* "Xenophon," p. 356 foll.

[798] (The timid, fawn-like creature.) See Lecky, *Hist. of Eur. Morals*, ii. 305. For the metaphor cf. Dem. *Olynth.* iii. 37. 9.

[799] Lit. "woman." Cf. N. T. (gunai), St. John ii. 4; xix. 26.

certainly not from any difficulty that might beset either of us to find another bedfellow. That I am sure is evident to you. No! it was with deliberate intent to discover, I for myself and your parents in behalf of you, the best partner of house and children we could find, that I sought you out, and your parents, acting to the best of their ability, made choice of me. If at some future time God grant us to have children born to us, we will take counsel together how best to bring them up, for that too will be a common interest,[800] and a common blessing if haply they shall live to fight our battles and we find in them hereafter support and succour when ourselves are old.[801] But at present there is our house here, which belongs like to both. It is common property, for all that I possess goes by my will into the common fund, and in the same way all that you deposited[802] was placed by you to the common fund.[803] We need not stop to calculate in figures which of us contributed most, but rather let us lay to heart this fact that whichever of us proves the better partner, he or she at once contributes what is most worth having."

Thus I addressed her, Socrates, and thus my wife made answer: "But how can I assist you? what is my ability? Nay, everything depends on you. My business, my mother told me, was to be sober-minded!"[804]

"Most true, my wife," I replied, "and that is what my father said to me. But what is the proof of sober-mindedness in man or woman? Is it not so to behave that what they have of good may ever be at its best, and that new treasures from the same source of beauty and righteousness may be most amply added?"

"But what is there that I can do," my wife inquired, "which will help to increase our joint estate?"

"Assuredly," I answered, "you may strive to do as well as possible what Heaven has given you a natural gift for and which the law approves."

"And what may these things be?" she asked.

"To my mind they are not the things of least importance," I replied, "unless the things which the queen bee in her hive presides over are of slight importance to the bee community; for the gods" (so Ischomachus assured me, he continued), "the gods, my wife, would seem to have exercised much care and judgment in compacting that twin system which goes by the name of male and female, so as to secure the greatest possible advantage[805] to the pair. Since no doubt the underlying

---

[800] Or, "our interests will centre in them; it will be a blessing we share in common to train them that they shall fight our battles, and..."

[801] Cf. *Mem.* II. ii. 13. Holden cf. Soph. *Ajax.* 567; Eur. *Suppl.* 918.

[802] Or reading (epenegke) with Cobet, "brought with you in the way of dowry."

[803] Or, "to the joint estate."

[804] "Modest and temperate," and (below) "temperance."

[805] Reading (oti), or if with Br. (eti... auto), "with the further intent it should prove of maximum advantage to itself."

principle of the bond is first and foremost to perpetuate through procreation the races of living creatures;[806] and next, as the outcome of this bond, for human beings at any rate, a provision is made by which they may have sons and daughters to support them in old age.

"And again, the way of life of human beings, not being maintained like that of cattle[807] in the open air, obviously demands roofed homesteads. But if these same human beings are to have anything to bring in under cover, some one to carry out these labours of the field under high heaven[808] must be found them, since such operations as the breaking up of fallow with the plough, the sowing of seed, the planting of trees, the pasturing and herding of flocks, are one and all open-air employments on which the supply of products necessary to life depends.

"As soon as these products of the field are safely housed and under cover, new needs arise. There must be some one to guard the store and some one to perform such necessary operations as imply the need of shelter.[809] Shelter, for instance, is needed for the rearing of infant children; shelter is needed for the various processes of converting the fruits of earth into food, and in like manner for the fabrication of clothing out of wool.

"But whereas both of these, the indoor and the outdoor occupations alike, demand new toil and new attention, to meet the case," I added, "God made provision[810] from the first by shaping, as it seems to me, the woman's nature for indoor and the man's for outdoor occupations. Man's body and soul He furnished with a greater capacity for enduring heat and cold, wayfaring and military marches; or, to repeat, He laid upon his shoulders the outdoor works.

"While in creating the body of woman with less capacity for these things," I continued, "God would seem to have imposed on her the indoor works; and knowing that He had implanted in the woman and imposed upon her the nurture of new-born babies, He endowed her with a larger share of affection for the new-born child than He bestowed upon man.[811] And since He imposed on woman the guardianship of the things imported from without, God, in His wisdom, perceiving that a fearful spirit was no detriment to guardianship,[812] endowed the woman with a larger measure of timidity than He bestowed on man. Knowing further that he to whom the outdoor works

---

[806] Cf. (Aristot.) *Oecon.* i. 3.
[807] "And the beast of the field."
[808] "Sub dis," "in the open air."
[809] Or, "works which call for shelter."
[810] "Straightway from the moment of birth provided." Cf. (Aristot.) *Oecon.* i. 3, a work based upon or at any rate following the lines of Xenophon's treatise.
[811] (edasato), *Cyrop.* IV. ii. 43.
[812] Cf. *Hipparch,* vii. 7; Aristot. *Pol.* iii. 2; *Oecon.* iii.

belonged would need to defend them against malign attack, He endowed the man in turn with a larger share of courage.

"And seeing that both alike feel the need of giving and receiving, He set down memory and carefulness between them for their common use,[813] so that you would find it hard to determine which of the two, the male or the female, has the larger share of these. So, too, God set down between them for their common use the gift of self-control, where needed, adding only to that one of the twain, whether man or woman, which should prove the better, the power to be rewarded with a larger share of this perfection. And for the very reason that their natures are not alike adapted to like ends, they stand in greater need of one another; and the married couple is made more useful to itself, the one fulfilling what the other lacks.[814]

"Now, being well aware of this, my wife," I added, "and knowing well what things are laid upon us twain by God Himself, must we not strive to perform, each in the best way possible, our respective duties? Law, too, gives her consent—law and the usage of mankind, by sanctioning the wedlock of man and wife; and just as God ordained them to be partners in their children, so the law establishes their common ownership of house and estate. Custom, moreover, proclaims as beautiful those excellences of man and woman with which God gifted them at birth.[815] Thus for a woman to bide tranquilly at home rather than roam aborad is no dishonour; but for a man to remain indoors, instead of devoting himself to outdoor pursuits, is a thing discreditable. But if a man does things contrary to the nature given him by God, the chances are,[816] such insubordination escapes not the eye of Heaven: he pays the penalty, whether of neglecting his own works, or of performing those appropriate to woman."[817]

I added: "Just such works, if I mistake not, that same queen-bee we spoke of labours hard to perform, like yours, my wife, enjoined upon her by God Himself."

"And what sort of works are these?" she asked; "what has the queen-bee to do that she seems so like myself, or I like her in what I have to do?"

"Why," I answered, "she too stays in the hive and suffers not the

---

[813] Or, "He bestowed memory and carefulness as the common heritage of both."

[814] Or, "the pair discovers the advantage of duality; the one being strong wherein the other is defective."

[815] Or, "with approving fingers stamps as noble those diverse faculties, those superiorities in either sex which God created in them. Thus for the woman to remain indoors is nobler than to gad about abroad." (ta kala...; kallion... aiskhion...)—These words, which their significant Hellenic connotation, suffer cruelly in translation.

[816] Or, "maybe in some respect this violation of the order of things, this lack of discipline on his part." Cf. *Cyrop.* VII. ii. 6.

[817] Or, "the works of his wife." For the sentiment cf. Soph. *Oed. Col.* 337 foll.; Herod. ii. 35.

other bees to idle. Those whose duty it is to work outside she sends forth to their labours; and all that each of them brings in, she notes and receives and stores against the day of need; but when the season for use has come, she distributes a just share to each. Again, it is she who presides over the fabric of choicely-woven cells within. She looks to it that warp and woof are wrought with speed and beauty. Under her guardian eye the brood of young[818] is nursed and reared; but when the days of rearing are past and the young bees are ripe for work, she sends them out as colonists with one of the seed royal[819] to be their leader."

"Shall I then have to do these things?" asked my wife.

"Yes," I answered, "you will need in the same way to stay indoors, despatching to their toils without those of your domestics whose work lies there. Over those whose appointed tasks are wrought indoors, it will be your duty to preside; yours to receive the stuffs brought in; yours to apportion part for daily use, and yours to make provision for the rest, to guard and garner it so that the outgoings destined for a year may not be expended in a month. It will be your duty, when the wools are introduced, to see that clothing is made for those who need; your duty also to see that the dried corn is rendered fit and serviceable for food.

"There is just one of all these occupations which devolve upon you," I added, "you may not find so altogether pleasing. Should any one of our household fall sick, it will be your care to see and tend them to the recovery of their health."

"Nay," she answered, "that will be my pleasantest of tasks, if careful nursing may touch the springs of gratitude and leave them friendlier than before."

And I (continued Ischomachus) was struck with admiration at her answer, and replied: "Think you, my wife, it is through some such traits of forethought seen in their mistress-leader that the hearts of bees are won, and they are so loyally affectioned towards her that, if ever she abandon her hive, not one of them will dream of being left behind;[820] but one and all must follow her."

And my wife made answer to me: "It would much astonish me (said she) did not these leader's works, you speak of, point to you rather than myself. Methinks mine would be a pretty[821] guardianship and distribution of things indoors without your provident care to see that the importations from without were duly made."

"Just so," I answered, "and mine would be a pretty[822] importation

---

[818] Or, "the growing progeny is reared to maturity."

[819] Or, "royal lineage," reading (ton epigonon) (emend. H. Estienne); or if the vulg. (ton epomenon), "with some leader of the host" (lit. of his followers). So Breitenbach.

[820] *Al.* "will suffer her to be forsaken."

[821] "As laughable an importation."

[822] Or, "ridiculous."

if there were no one to guard what I imported. Do you not see," I added, "how pitiful is the case of those unfortunates who pour water in their sieves for ever, as the story goes,[823] and labour but in vain?"

"Pitiful enough, poor souls," she answered, "if that is what they do."

"But there are other cares, you know, and occupations," I answered, "which are yours by right, and these you will find agreeable. This, for instance, to take some maiden who knows naught of carding wool and to make her proficient in the art, doubling her usefulness; or to receive another quite ignorant of housekeeping or of service, and to render her skilful, loyal, serviceable, till she is worth her weight in gold; or again, when occasion serves, you have it in your power to requite by kindness the well-behaved whose presence is a blessing to your house; or maybe to chasten the bad character, should such an one appear. But the greatest joy of all will be to prove yourself my better; to make me your faithful follower; knowing no dread lest as the years advance you should decline in honour in your household, but rather trusting that, though your hair turn gray, yet, in proportion as you come to be a better helpmate to myself and to the children, a better guardian of our home, so will your honour increase throughout the household as mistress, wife, and mother, daily more dearly prized. Since," I added, "it is not through excellence of outward form,[824] but by reason of the lustre of virtues shed forth upon the life of man, that increase is given to things beautiful and good."[825]

That, Socrates, or something like that, as far as I may trust my memory, records the earliest conversation which I held with her.

VIII

And did you happen to observe, Ischomachus (I asked), whether, as the result of what was said, your wife was stirred at all to greater carefulness?

Yes, certainly (Ischomachus answered), and I remember how piqued she was at one time and how deeply she blushed, when I

---

[823] Or, "how pitiful their case, condemned, as the saying goes, to pour water into a sieve." Lit. "filling a bucket bored with holes." Cf. Aristot. *Oec.* i. 6; and for the Danaids, see Ovid. *Met.* iv. 462; Hor. *Carm.* iii. 11. 25; Lucr. iii. 937; Plaut. *Pseud.* 369. Cp. Coleridge:

> Work without hope draws nectar in a sieve,
> And hope without an object cannot live.

[824] "By reason of the flower on the damask cheek."

[825] Al. "For growth is added to things 'beautiful and good,' not through the bloom of youth but virtuous perfections, an increase coextensive with the life of man." See Breit. *ad loc.*

chanced to ask her for something which had been brought into the house, and she could not give it me. So I, when I saw her annoyance, fell to consoling her. "Do not be at all disheartened, my wife, that you cannot give me what I ask for. It is plain poverty,[826] no doubt, to need a thing and not to have the use of it. But as wants go, to look for something which I cannot lay my hands upon is a less painful form of indigence than never to dream of looking because I know full well that the thing exists not. Anyhow, you are not to blame for this," I added; "mine the fault was who handed over to your care the things without assigning them their places. Had I done so, you would have known not only where to put but where to find them.[827] After all, my wife, there is nothing in human life so serviceable, nought so beautiful as order.[828]

"For instance, what is a chorus?—a band composed of human beings, who dance and sing; but suppose the company proceed to act as each may chance—confusion follows; the spectacle has lost its charm. How different when each and all together act and recite[829] with orderly precision, the limbs and voices keeping time and tune. Then, indeed, these same performers are worth seeing and worth hearing.

"So, too, an army," I said, "my wife, an army destitute of order is confusion worse confounded: to enemies an easy prey, courting attack; to friends a bitter spectacle of wasted power;[830] a mingled mob of asses, heavy infantry, and baggage-bearers, light infantry, cavalry, and waggons. Now, suppose they are on the march; how are they to get along? In this condition everybody will be a hindrance to everybody: 'slow march' side by side with 'double quick,' 'quick march' at cross purposes with 'stand at ease'; waggons blocking cavalry and asses fouling waggons; baggage-bearers and hoplites jostling together: the whole a hopeless jumble. And when it comes to fighting, such an army is not precisely in condition to deliver battle. The troops who are compelled to retreat before the enemy's advance[831] are fully capable of trampling down the heavy infantry detachments in reserve.[832]

"How different is an army well organised in battle order: a splendid sight for friendly eyes to gaze at, albeit an eyesore to the enemy. For who, being of their party, but will feel a thrill of

---

[826] "Vetus proverbium," Cic. ap. Columellam, xii. 2, 3; Nobbe, 236, fr. 6.

[827] Lit. "so that you might know not only where to put," etc.

[828] Or, "order and arrangement." So Cic. ap. Col. xii. 2, 4, "dispositione atque ordine."

[829] Or, "declaim," (phtheggontai), properly of the "recitative" of the chorus. Cf. Plat. *Phaedr.* 238 D.

[830] Reading (agleukestaton), or, if with Breit, (akleestaton), "a most inglorious spectacle of extreme unprofitableness."

[831] Or, "whose duty (or necessity) it is to retire before an attack," *i.e.* the skirmishers. *Al.* "those who have to retreat," *i.e.* the *non-combatants.*

[832] Al. "are quite capable of trampling down the troops behind in their retreat." (tous opla ekhontas) = "the troops proper," "heavy infantry."

satisfaction as he watches the serried masses of heavy infantry moving onwards in unbroken order? who but will gaze with wonderment as the squadrons of the cavalry dash past him at the gallop? And what of the foeman? will not his heart sink within him to see the orderly arrangements of the different arms:[833] here heavy infantry and cavalry, and there again light infantry, there archers and there slingers, following each their leaders, with orderly precision. As they tramp onwards thus in order, though they number many myriads, yet even so they move on and on in quiet progress, stepping like one man, and the place just vacated in front is filled up on the instant from the rear.

"Or picture a trireme, crammed choke-full of mariners; for what reason is she so terror-striking an object to her enemies, and a sight so gladsome to the eyes of friends? is it not that the gallant ship sails so swiftly? And why is it that, for all their crowding, the ship's company[834] cause each other no distress? Simply that there, as you may see them, they sit in order; in order bend to the oar; in order recover the stroke; in order step on board; in order disembark. But disorder is, it seems to me, precisely as though a man who is a husbandman should stow away[835] together in one place wheat and barley and pulse, and by and by when he has need of barley meal, or wheaten flour, or some condiment of pulse,[836] then he must pick and choose instead of laying his hand on each thing separately sorted for use.

"And so with you too, my wife, if you would avoid this confusion, if you would fain know how to administer our goods, so as to lay your finger readily on this or that as you may need, or if I ask you for anything, graciously to give it me: let us, I say, select and assign[837] the appropriate place for each set of things. This shall be the place where we will put the things; and we will instruct the housekeeper that she is to take them out thence, and mind to put them back again there; and in this way we shall know whether they are safe or not. If anything is gone, the gaping space will cry out as if it asked for something back.[838] The mere look and aspect of things will argue what wants mending;[839] and the fact of knowing where each thing is will be like having it put into one's hand at once to use without further trouble or debate."

I must tell you, Socrates, what strikes me as the finest and most accurate arrangement of goods and furniture it was ever my fortune to

---

[833] "Different styles of troops drawn up in separate divisions: hoplites, cavalry, and peltasts, archers, and slingers."

[834] See Thuc. iii. 77. 2.

[835] "Should shoot into one place."

[836] "Vegetable stock," "kitchen." See Holden *ad loc.*, and Prof. Mahaffy, *Old Greek Life*, p. 31.

[837] (dokimasometha), "we will write over each in turn, as it were, 'examined and approved.'"

[838] Lit. "will miss the thing that is not."

[839] "Detect what needs attention."

set eyes on; when I went as a sightseer on board the great Phoenician merchantman,[840] and beheld an endless quantity of goods and gear of all sorts, all separately packed and stowed away within the smallest compass.[841] I need scarce remind you (he said, continuing his narrative) what a vast amount of wooden spars and cables[842] a ship depends on in order to get to moorings; or again, in putting out to sea;[843] you know the host of sails and cordage, rigging[844] as they call it, she requires for sailing; the quantity of engines and machinery of all sorts she is armed with in case she should encounter any hostile craft; the infinitude of arms she carries, with her crew of fighting men aboard. Then all the vessels and utensils, such as people use at home on land, required for the different messes, form a portion of the freight; and besides all this, the hold is heavy laden with a mass of merchandise, the cargo proper, which the master carries with him for the sake of traffic.

Well, all these different things that I have named lay packed there in a space but little larger than a fair-sized dining-room.[845] The several sorts, moreover, as I noticed, lay so well arranged, there could be no entanglement of one with other, nor were searchers needed;[846] and if all were snugly stowed, all were alike get-at-able,[847] much to the avoidance of delay if anything were wanted on the instant.

Then the pilot's mate[848]—"the look-out man at the prow," to give him his proper title—was, I found, so well acquainted with the place for everything that, even off the ship,[849] he could tell you where each set of things was laid and how many there were of each, just as well as any one who knows his alphabet[850] could tell you how many letters there are in Socrates and the order in which they stand.

I saw this same man (continued Ischomachus) examining at leisure[851] everything which could possibly[852] be needful for the service of the ship. His inspection caused me such surprise, I asked him what he was doing, whereupon he answered, "I am inspecting, stranger,"[853] "just considering," says he, "the way the things are lying aboard the

---

[840] See Lucian, lxvi. "The Ship," *ad in.* (translated by S. T. Irwin).
[841] Lit. "in the tiniest receptacle."
[842] See Holden *ad loc.* re (xelina, plekta, kremasta).
[843] "In weighing anchor."
[844] "Suspended tackle" (as opposed to wooden spars and masts, etc.)
[845] Lit. "a symmetrically-shaped dining-room, made to hold ten couches."
[846] Lit. "a searcher"; "an inquisitor." Cf. Shakesp. *Rom. and Jul.* V. ii. 8.
[847] Lit. "not the reverse of easy to unpack, so as to cause a waste of time and waiting."
[848] Cf. *Pol. Ath.* i. 1; Aristoph. *Knights*, 543 foll.
[849] Or, "with his eyes shut, at a distance he could say exactly."
[850] Or, "how to spell." See *Mem.* IV. iv. 7; Plat. *Alc.* i. 113 A.
[851] "Apparently when he had nothing better to do"; "by way of amusement."
[852] (ara), "as if he were asking himself, 'Would this or this possibly be wanted for the ship's service?'"
[853] "Sir."

ship; in case of accidents, you know, to see if anything is missing, or not lying snug and shipshape.[854] There is no time left, you know," he added, "when God makes a tempest in the great deep, to set about searching for what you want, or to be giving out anything which is not snug and shipshape in its place. God threatens and chastises sluggards.[855] If only He destroy not innocent with guilty, a man may be content;[856] or if He turn and save all hands aboard that render right good service,[857] thanks be to Heaven."[858]

So spoke the pilot's mate; and I, with this carefulness of stowage still before my eyes, proceeded to enforce my thesis:

"Stupid in all conscience would it be on our parts, my wife, if those who sail the sea in ships, that are but small things, can discover space and place for everything; can, moreover, in spite of violent tossings up and down, keep order, and, even while their hearts are failing them for fear, find everything they need to hand; whilst we, with all our ample storerooms[859] diversely disposed for divers objects in our mansion, an edifice firmly based[860] on solid ground, fail to discover fair and fitting places, easy of access for our several goods! Would not that argue great lack of understanding in our two selves? Well then! how good a thing it is to have a fixed and orderly arrangement of all furniture and gear; how easy also in a dwelling-house to find a place for every sort of goods, in which to stow them as shall suit each best— needs no further comment. Rather let me harp upon the string of beauty—image a fair scene: the boots and shoes and sandals, and so forth, all laid in order row upon row; the cloaks, the mantles, and the rest of the apparel stowed in their own places; the coverlets and bedding; the copper cauldrons; and all the articles for table use! Nay, though it well may raise a smile of ridicule (not on the lips of a grave man perhaps, but of some facetious witling) to hear me say it, a beauty like the cadence of sweet music[861] dwells even in pots and pans set out in neat array: and so, in general, fair things ever show more fair when orderly bestowed. The separate atoms shape themselves to form a choir, and all the space between gains beauty by their banishment. Even

---

[854] Or, "things not lying handy in their places."
[855] Or, "them that are slack." Cf. *Anab.* V. viii. 15; *Mem.* IV. ii. 40; Plat. *Gorg.* 488 A: "The dolt and good-for-nothing."
[856] "One must not grumble."
[857] "The whole ship's crew right nobly serving." (uperetein) = "to serve at the oar" (metaphorically = to do service to heaven).
[858] Lit. "great thanks be to the gods."
[859] Or, "coffers," "cupboards," "safes."
[860] Cf. *Anab.* III. ii. 19, "firmly planted on *terra firma*."
[861] Or, "like the rhythm of a song," (euruthmon). See Mr. Ruskin's most appropriate note (*Bib. Past.* i. 59), "A remarkable word, as significant of the complete rhythm ((ruthmos)) whether of sound or motion, that was so great a characteristic of the Greek ideal (cf. xi. 16, (metarruthmizo))," and much more equally to the point.

so some sacred chorus,[862] dancing a roundelay in honour of Dionysus, not only is a thing of beauty in itself, but the whole interspace swept clean of dancers owns a separate charm.[863]

"The truth of what I say, we easily can test, my wife," I added, "by direct experiment, and that too without cost at all or even serious trouble.[864] Nor need you now distress yourself, my wife, to think how hard it will be to discover some one who has wit enough to learn the places for the several things and memory to take and place them there. We know, I fancy, that the goods of various sorts contained in the whole city far outnumber ours many thousand times; and yet you have only to bid any one of your domestics go buy this, or that, and bring it you from market, and not one of them will hesitate. The whole world knows both where to go and where to find each thing.

"And why is this?" I asked. "Merely because they lie in an appointed place. But now, if you are seeking for a human being, and that too at times when he is seeking you on his side also, often and often shall you give up the search in sheer despair: and of this again the reason? Nothing else save that no appointed place was fixed where one was to await the other." Such, so far as I can now recall it, was the conversation which we held together touching the arrangement of our various chattels and their uses.

IX

Well (I replied), and did your wife appear, Ischomachus, to lend a willing ear to what you tried thus earnestly to teach her?

Isch. Most certainly she did, with promise to pay all attention. Her delight was evident, like some one's who at length has found a pathway out of difficulties; in proof of which she begged me to lose no time in making the orderly arrangement I had spoken of.

And how did you introduce the order she demanded, Ischomachus? (I asked).

Isch. Well, first of all I thought I ought to show her the capacities of our house. Since you must know, it is not decked with ornaments and fretted ceilings,[865] Socrates; but the rooms were built expressly with a view to forming the most apt receptacles for whatever was intended to be put in them, so that the very look of them proclaimed

---

[862] "Just as a chorus, the while its dancers weave a circling dance."

[863] Or, "contrasting with the movement and the mazes of the dance, a void appears serene and beautiful."

[864] Lit. "now whether these things I say are true (*i.e.* are facts), we can make experiment of the things themselves (*i.e.* of actual facts to prove to us)."

[865] Or, "curious workmanship and paintings." See *Mem.* III. viii. 10. Cf. Plat. *Rep.* vii. 529 B; *Hipp. maj.* 298 A. See Becker, *Charicles,* Exc. i. 111.

what suited each particular chamber best. Thus our own bedroom,[866] secure in its position like a stronghold, claimed possession of our choicest carpets, coverlets, and other furniture. Thus, too, the warm dry rooms would seem to ask for our stock of bread-stuffs; the chill cellar for our wine; the bright and well-lit chambers for whatever works or furniture required light, and so forth.

Next I proceeded to point out to her the several dwelling-rooms, all beautifully fitted up for cool in summer and for warmth in winter.[867] I showed her how the house enjoyed a southern aspect, whence it was plain, in winter it would catch the sunlight and in summer lie in shade.[868] Then I showed her the women's apartments, separated from the men's apartments by a bolted door,[869] whereby nothing from within could be conveyed without clandestinely, nor children born and bred by our domestics without our knowledge and consent[870]—no unimportant matter, since, if the act of rearing children tends to make good servants still more loyally disposed,[871] cohabiting but sharpens ingenuity for mischief in the bad.

When we had gone over all the rooms (he continued), we at once set about distribution our furniture[872] in classes; and we began (he said) by collecting everything we use in offering sacrifice.[873] After this we proceeded to set apart the ornaments and holiday attire of the wife, and the husband's clothing both for festivals and war; then the bedding used in the women's apartments, and the bedding used in the men's apartments; then the women's shoes and sandals, and the shoes and sandals of the men.[874] There was one division devoted to arms and armour; another to instruments used for carding wood; another to implements for making bread; another to utensils for cooking condiments; another to utensils for the bath; another connected with the kneading trough; another with the service of the table. All these we

---

[866] Or, "the bridal chamber." See Becker, *op. cit.* p. 266. Al. "our store-chamber." See Hom. *Od.* xxi. 9:

(be d' imenai thalamonde sun amphipoloisi gunaixin eskhaton, k.t.l.)

"And she (Penelope) betook her, with her handmaidens, to the treasure-chamber in the uttermost part of the house, where lay the treasures of her lord, bronze and gold and iron well wrought."—Butcher and Lang. Cf. *Od.* ii. 337; *Il.* vi. 288.

[867] See *Mem.* III. viii. 8.

[868] See *Mem.* ib. 9.

[869] "By bolts and bars." Lit. "a door fitted with a bolt-pin." See Thuc. ii. 4; Aristoph. *Wasps*, 200.

[870] Cf. (Aristot.) *Oecon.* i. 5, (dei de kai exomereuein tais teknopoiiais).

[871] Lit. "since (you know) if the good sort of servant is rendered, as a rule, better disposed when he becomes a father, the base, through intermarrying, become only more ripe for mischief."

[872] "Movable property," *meubles.*

[873] Holden cf. Plut. *De Curios.* 515 E, (os gar Xenophon legei toi Oikonomikois, k.t.l.)

[874] Cf. *Cyrop.* VIII. ii. 5. See Becker, *op. cit.* p. 447.

assigned to separate places, distinguishing one portion for daily and recurrent use and the rest for high days and holidays. Next we selected and set aside the supplies required for the month's expenditure; and, under a separate head,[875] we stored away what we computed would be needed for the year.[876] For in this way there is less chance of failing to note how the supplies are likely to last to the end.

And so having arranged the different articles of furniture in classes, we proceeded to convey them to their appropriate places. That done, we directed our attention to the various articles needed by our domestics for daily use, such as implements or utensils for making bread, cooking relishes, spinning wool, and anything else of the same sort. These we consigned to the care of those who would have to use them, first pointing out where they must stow them, and enjoining on them to return them safe and sound when done with.

As to the other things which we should only use on feast-days, or for the entertainment of guests, or on other like occasions at long intervals, we delivered them one and all to our housekeeper. Having pointed out to her their proper places, and having numbered and registered[877] the several sets of articles, we explained that it was her business to give out each thing as required; to recollect to whom she gave them; and when she got them back, to restore them severally to the places from which she took them. In appointing our housekeeper, we had taken every pains to discover some one on whose self-restraint we might depend, not only in the matters of food and wine and sleep, but also in her intercourse with men. She must besides, to please us, be gifted with no ordinary memory. She must have sufficient forethought not to incur displeasure through neglect of our interests. It must be her object to gratify us in this or that, and in return to win esteem and honour at our hands. We set ourselves to teach and train her to feel a kindly disposition towards us, by allowing her to share our joys in the day of gladness, or, if aught unkind befell us, by inviting her to sympathise in our sorrow. We sought to rouse in her a zeal for our interests, an eagerness to promote the increase of our estate, by making her intelligent of its affairs, and by giving her a share in our successes. We instilled in her a sense of justice and uprightness, by holding the just in higher honour than the unjust, and by pointing out that the lives of the righteous are richer and less servile than those of the unrighteous; and this was the position in which she found herself installed in our household.[878]

And now, on the strength of all that we had done, Socrates (he

---

[875] See Cic. ap. Col. who curiously mistranslates (dikha).

[876] Schneider, etc., cf. Aristot. *Oecon.* i. 6.

[877] Or, "having taken an inventory of the several sets of things." Cf. *Ages.* i. 18; *Cyrop.* VII. iv. 12. See Newman, *op. cit.* i. 171.

[878] Or, "and this was the position in which we presently established her herself."

added), I addressed my wife, explaining that all these things would fail of use unless she took in charge herself to see that the order of each several part was kept. Thereupon I taught her that in every well-constituted city the citizens are not content merely to pass good laws, but they further choose them guardians of the laws,[879] whose function as inspectors is to praise the man whose acts are law-abiding, or to mulct some other who offends against the law. Accordingly, I bade her believe that she, the mistress, was herself to play the part of *guardian of the laws* to her whole household, examining whenever it seemed good to her, and passing in review the several chattels, just as the officer in command of a garrison[880] musters and reviews his men. She must apply her scrutiny and see that everything was well, even as the Senate[881] tests the condition of the Knights and of their horses.[882] Like a queen, she must bestow, according to the power vested in her, praise and honour on the well-deserving, but blame and chastisement on him who stood in need thereof.

Nor did my lessons end here (added he); I taught her that she must not be annoyed should I seem to be enjoining upon her more trouble than upon any of our domestics with regard to our possessions; pointing out to her that these domestics have only so far a share in their master's chattels that they must fetch and carry, tend and guard them; nor have they the right to use a single one of them except the master grant it. But to the master himself all things pertain to use as he thinks best. And so I pointed the conclusion: he to whom the greater gain attaches in the preservation of the property or loss in its destruction, is surely he to whom by right belongs the larger measure of attention.[883]

When, then (I asked), Ischomachus, how fared it? was your wife disposed at all to lend a willing ear to what you told her?[884]

Bless you,[885] Socrates (he answered), what did she do but forthwith answer me, I formed a wrong opinion if I fancied that, in teaching her the need of minding our property, I was imposing a painful task upon her. A painful task it might have been[886] (she added), had I bade her neglect her personal concerns! But to be obliged to fulfil the duty of attending to her own domestic happiness,[887] that was easy. After all it

---

[879] See Plat. *Laws*, vi. 755 A, 770 C; Aristot. *Pol.* iii. 15, 1287 A; iv. 14, 1298 B; vi. 8, 1323 A; *Ath. Pol.* viii. 4; and Cic. ap. Col. xii. 3. 10 f. Holden cf. Cic. *de Legg.* iii. 20, S. 46; *C. I. G.* 3794.
[880] Lit. Phrourarch, "the commandant."
[881] Or, "Council" at Athens.
[882] Cf. *Hipparch.* i. 8, 13.
[883] Or, "he it is on whom devolves as his concern the duty of surveillance."
[884] Lit. "when she heard did she give ear at all?"
[885] Lit. "By Hera!" Cf. the old formula "Marry!" or "By'r lakin!"
[886] Lit. "more painful had it been, had I enjoined her to *neglect* her own interests than to be obliged..."
[887] (ton oikeion agathon), cp. "charity begins at home." See Joel, *op. cit.* p. 448.

would seem to be but natural (added he); just as any honest[888] woman finds it easier to care for her own offspring than to neglect them, so, too, he could well believe, an honest woman might find it pleasanter to care for than to neglect possessions, the very charm of which is that they are one's very own.

X

So (continued Socrates), when I heard his wife had made this answer, I exclaimed: By Hera, Ischomachus, a brave and masculine intelligence the lady has, as you describe her.

(To which Ischomachus) Yes, Socrates, and I would fain narrate some other instances of like large-mindedness on her part: shown in the readiness with which she listened to my words and carried out my wishes.

What sort of thing? (I answered). Do, pray, tell me, since I would far more gladly learn about a living woman's virtues than that Zeuxis[889] should show me the portrait of the loveliest woman he has painted.

Whereupon Ischomachus proceeded to narrate as follows: I must tell you, Socrates, I one day noticed she was much enamelled with white lead,[890] no doubt to enhance the natural whiteness of her skin; she had rouged herself with alkanet[891] profusely, doubtless to give more colour to her cheeks than truth would warrant; she was wearing high-heeled shoes, in order to seem taller than she was by nature.[892]

Accordingly I put to her this question:[893] "Tell me, my wife, would you esteem me a less lovable co-partner in our wealth, were I to show you how our fortune stands exactly, without boasting of unreal possessions or concealing what we really have? Or would you prefer that I should try to cheat you with exaggeration, exhibiting false money to you, or sham[894] necklaces, or flaunting purples[895] which will lose their colour, stating they are genuine the while?"

She caught me up at once: "Hush, hush!" she said, "talk not such talk. May heaven forfend that you should ever be like that. I could not

---

[888] Or, "true and honest"; "any woman worthy of the name." (sophroni) = with the (sophrosune) of womanhood; possibly transl. "discreet and sober-minded."

[889] See *Mem.* I. iv. 3.

[890] Cf. Aristoph. *Eccl.* 878; ib. 929, (egkhousa mallon kai to son psimuthion): ib. 1072; *Plut.* 1064.

[891] Lit. "enamelled or painted with *anchusa* or *alkanet*," a plant, the wild bugloss, whose root yields a red dye. Cf. Aristoph. *Lys.* 48; Theophr. *H. Pl.* vii. 8. 3.

[892] See Becker, *op. cit.* p. 452; Breit. cf. *Anab.* III. ii. 25; *Mem.* II. i. 22; Aristot. *Eth. Nic.* iv. 3, 5, "True beauty requires a great body."

[893] Lit. "So I said to her, 'Tell me, my wife, after which fashion would you find me the more delectable partner in our joint estate—were I to...? or were I to...?'"

[894] Lit. "only wood coated with gold."

[895] See Becker, *op. cit.* p. 434 f; Holden cf. Athen. ix. 374, xii. 525; Ael. *V. H.* xii. 32; Aristoph. *Plut.* 533.

love you with my whole heart were you really of that sort."

"And are we two not come together," I continued, "for a closer partnership, being each a sharer in the other's body?"

"That, at any rate, is what folk say," she answered.

"Then as regards this bodily relation," I proceeded, "should you regard me as more lovable or less did I present myself, my one endeavour and my sole care being that my body should be hale and strong and thereby well complexioned, or would you have me first anoint myself with pigments,[896] smear my eyes with patches[897] of 'true flesh colour,'[898] and so seek your embrace, like a cheating consort presenting to his mistress's sight and touch vermillion paste instead of his own flesh?"

"Frankly," she answered, "it would not please me better to touch paste than your true self. Rather would I see your own 'true flesh colour' than any pigment of that name; would liefer look into your eyes and see them radiant with health than washed with any wash, or dyed with any ointment there may be."

"Believe the same, my wife, of me then," Ischomachus continued (so he told me); "believe that I too am not better pleased with white enamel or with alkanet than with your own natural hue; but as the gods have fashioned horses to delight in horses, cattle in cattle, sheep in their fellow sheep, so to human beings the human body pure and undefiled is sweetest;[899] and as to these deceits, though they may serve to cheat the outside world without detection, yet if intimates try to deceive each other, they must one day be caught; in rising from their beds, before they make their toilet; by a drop of sweat they stand convicted; tears are an ordeal they cannot pass; the bath reveals them as they truly are."

What answer (said I) did she make, in Heaven's name, to what you said?

What, indeed (replied the husband), save only, that thenceforward she never once indulged in any practice of the sort, but has striven to display the natural beauty of her person in its purity. She did, however, put to me a question: Could I advise her how she might become not in false show but really fair to look upon?

This, then, was the counsel which I gave her, Socrates: Not to be for ever seated like a slave;[900] but, with Heaven's help, to assume the attitude of a true mistress standing before the loom, and where her knowledge gave her the superiority, bravely to give the aid of her instruction; where her knowledge failed, as bravely try to learn. I counselled her to oversee the baking woman as she made the bread; to

---

[896] "Red lead."
[897] Cf. Aristoph. *Ach.* 1029.
[898] (andreikelon). Cf. Plat. *Rep.* 501 B, "the human complexion"; *Crat.* 424 E.
[899] See *Mem.* II. i. 22.
[900] See Becker, p. 491. Breit., etc., cf. Nicostr. ap. Stob. *Tit.* lxxiv. 61.

stand beside the housekeeper as she measured out her stores; to go tours of inspection to see if all things were in order as they should be. For, as it seemed to me, this would at once be walking exercise and supervision. And, as an excellent gymnastic, I recommended her to knead the dough and roll the paste; to shake the coverlets and make the beds; adding, if she trained herself in exercise of this sort she would enjoy her food, grow vigorous in health, and her complexion would in very truth be lovelier. The very look and aspect of the wife, the mistress, seen in rivalry with that of her attendants, being as she is at once more fair[901] and more beautifully adorned, has an attractive charm,[902] and not the less because her acts are acts of grace, not services enforced. Whereas your ordinary fine lady, seated in solemn state, would seem to court comparison with painted counterfeits of womanhood.

And, Socrates, I would have you know that still to-day, my wife is living in a style as simple as that I taught her then, and now recount to you.

XI

The conversation was resumed as follows: Thanking Ischomachus for what he had told me about the occupations of his wife; on that side I have heard enough (I said) perhaps for a beginning; the facts you mention reflect the greatest credit on both wife and husband; but would you now in turn describe to me your work and business? In doing so you will have the pleasure of narrating the reason of your fame. And I, for my part, when I have heard from end to end the story of a beautiful and good man's works, if only my wits suffice and I have understood it, shall be much indebted.

Indeed (replied Ischomachus), it will give me the greatest pleasure to recount to you my daily occupations, and in return I beg you to reform me, where you find some flaw or other in my conduct.[903]

The idea of my reforming you! (I said). How could I with any show of justice hope to reform you, the perfect model[904] of a beautiful, good man—I, who am but an empty babbler,[905] and measurer of the air,[906] who have to bear besides that most senseless imputation of being

---

[901] Lit. "more spotless"; "like a diamond of purest water." Cf. Shakesp. *Lucr.* 394, "whose perfect white Showed like an April daisy in the grass."

[902] Or, "is wondrous wooing, and all the more with this addition, hers are acts of grace, theirs services enforced."

[903] Lit. "in order that you on your side may correct and set me right where I seem to you to act amiss." (metarruthmises)—remodel. Cf. Aristot. *Nic. Eth.* x. 9. 5.

[904] Cf. Plat. *Rep.* 566 A, "a tyrant full grown" (Jowett).

[905] Cf. Plat. *Phaed.* 70 C; Aristoph. *Clouds*, 1480.

[906] Or rather, "a measurer of air"—*i.e.* devoted not to good sound solid "geometry," but the unsubstantial science of "aerometry." See Aristoph. *Clouds*, i. 225; Plat. *Apol.* 18

poor—an imputation which, I assure you, Ischomachus, would have reduced me to the veriest despair, except that the other day I chanced to come across the horse of Nicias,[907] the foreigner? I saw a crowd of people in attendance staring, and I listened to a story which some one had to tell about the animal. So then I stepped up boldly to the groom and asked him, "Has the horse much wealth?" The fellow looked at me as if I were hardly in my right mind to put the question, and retorted, "How can a horse have wealth?" Thereat I dared to lift my eyes from earth, on learning that after all it is permitted a poor penniless horse to be a noble animal, if nature only have endowed him with good spirit. If, therefore, it is permitted even to me to be a good man, please recount to me your works from first to last, I promise, I will listen, all I can, and try to understand, and so far as in me lies to imitate you from tomorrow. To-morrow is a good day to commence a course of virtue, is it not?

You are pleased to jest, Socrates (Ischomachus replied), in spite of which I will recount to you those habits and pursuits by aid of which I seek to traverse life's course. If I have read aright life's lesson, it has taught me that, unless a man first discover what he needs to do, and seriously study to bring the same to good effect, the gods have placed prosperity[908] beyond his reach; and even to the wise and careful they give or they withhold good fortune as seemeth to them best. Such being my creed, I begin with service rendered to the gods; and strive to regulate my conduct so that grace may be given me, in answer to my prayers, to attain to health, and strength of body, honour in my own city, goodwill among my friends, safety with renown in war, and of riches increase, won without reproach.

I, when I heard these words, replied: And are you then indeed so careful to grow rich, Ischomachus?—amassing wealth but to gain endless trouble in its management?

Most certainly (replied Ischomachus), and most careful must I needs be of the things you speak of. So sweet I find it, Socrates, to honour God magnificently, to lend assistance to my friends in answer to their wants, and, so far as lies within my power, not to leave my city unadorned with anything which riches can bestow.

Nay (I answered), beautiful indeed the works you speak of, and powerful the man must be who would essay them. How can it be otherwise, seeing so many human beings need the help of others merely to carry on existence, and so many are content if they can win enough to satisfy their wants. What of those therefore who are able, not only to administer their own estates, but even to create a surplus sufficient to

---

B, 19 B; Xen. *Symp.* vi. 7.
[907] Nothing is known of this person.
[908] "The gods have made well-doing and well-being a thing impossible." Cf. *Mem.* III. ix. 7, 14.

adorn their city and relieve the burthen of their friends? Well may we regard such people as men of substance and capacity. But stay (I added), most of us are competent to sing the praises of such heroes. What I desire is to hear from you, Ischomachus, in your own order,[909] first how you study to preserve your health and strength of body; and next, how it is granted to you[910] to escape from the perils of war with honour untarnished. And after that (I added), it will much content me to learn from your own lips about your money-making.

Yes (he answered), and the fact is, Socrates, if I mistake not, all these matters are in close connection, each depending on the other. Given that a man have a good meal to eat, he has only to work off the effect by toil[911] directed rightly; and in the process, if I mistake not, his health will be confirmed, his strength added to. Let him but practise the arts of war and in the day of battle he will preserve his life with honour. He needs only to expend his care aright, sealing his ears to weak and soft seductions, and his house shall surely be increased.[912]

I answered: So far I follow you, Ischomachus. You tell me that by labouring to his full strength,[913] by expending care, by practice and training, a man may hope more fully to secure life's blessings. So I take your meaning. But now I fain would learn of you some details. What particular toil do you impose on yourself in order to secure good health and strength? After what particular manner do you practise the arts of war? How do you take pains to create a surplus which will enable you to benefit your friends and to gratify the state?

Why then (Ischomachus replied), my habit is to rise from bed betimes, when I may still expect to find at home this, that, or the other friend, whom I may wish to see. Then, if anything has to be done in town, I set off to transact the business and make that my walk;[914] or, if there is no business to do in town, my serving-boy leads my horse to the farm; I follow, and so make the country-road my walk, which suits my purpose quite as well, or better, Socrates, perhaps, than pacing up and down the colonnade.[915] Then when I have reached the farm, where mayhap some of my men are planting trees, or breaking fallow, sowing or getting in the crops, I inspect their various labours with an eye to

---

[909] "And from your own starting-point."

[910] As to the construction (themis einai) see Jebb ad *Oed. Col.* 1191, Appendix.

[911] See *Mem.* I. ii. 4; *Cyrop.* I. ii. 16. *Al.* "bring out the effect of it by toil."

[912] Lit. "it is likely his estate will increase more largely."

[913] Or, "by working off ill-humours," as we should say.

[914] See *Mem.* III. xiii. 5.

[915] (xusto)—the xystus, "a covered corridor in the gymnasium where the athletes exercised in winter." Vitruv. v. 11. 4; vi. 7. 5. See Rich, *Companion*, s.n.; Becker, *op. cit.* p. 309. Cf. Plat. *Phaedr.* 227—Phaedrus loq.: "I have come from Lysias the son of Cephalus, and I am going to take a walk outside the wall, for I have been sitting with him the whole morning; and our common friend Acumenus advises me to walk in the country, which he says is more invigorating than to walk in the courts."—Jowett.

every detail, and, whenever I can improve upon the present system, I introduce reform. After this, as a rule, I mount my horse and take a canter. I put him through his paces, suiting these, as far as possible, to those inevitable in war[916]—in other words, I avoid neither steep slope[917] nor sheer incline, neither trench nor runnel, only giving my utmost heed the while so as not to lame my horse while exercising him. When that is over, the boy gives the horse a roll,[918] and leads him homewards, taking at the same time from the country to town whatever we may chance to need. Meanwhile I am off for home, partly walking, partly running, and having reached home I take a bath and give myself a rub;[919] and then I breakfast—a repast which leaves me neither empty nor replete,[920] and will suffice to last me through the day.

By Hera (I replied), Ischomachus, I cannot say how much your doings take my fancy. How you have contrived, to pack up portably for use—together at the same time—appliances for health and recipes for strength, exercises for war, and pains to promote your wealth! My admiration is raised at every point. That you do study each of these pursuits in the right way, you are yourself a standing proof. Your look of heaven-sent health and general robustness we note with our eyes, while our ears have heard your reputation as a first-rate horseman and the wealthiest of men.

Isch. Yes, Socrates, such is my conduct, in return for which I am rewarded with—the calumnies of half the world. You thought, I daresay, I was going to end my sentence different, and say that a host of people have given me the enviable title "beautiful and good."

I was indeed myself about to ask, Ischomachus (I answered), whether you take pains also to acquire skill in argumentative debate, the cut and thrust and parry of discussion,[921] should occasion call?

Isch. Does it not strike you rather, Socrates, that I am engaged in one long practice of this very skill,[922] now pleading as defendant that, as far as I am able, I do good to many and hurt nobody? And then, again, you must admit, I play the part of prosecutor when accusing

---

[916] See *Horsemanship*, iii. 7 foll.; ib. viii.; *Hipparch*, i. 18.
[917] "Slanting hillside."
[918] See *Horsemanship*, v. 3; Aristoph. *Clouds*, 32.
[919] Lit. "scrape myself clean" (with the (stleggis) or strigil). Cf. Aristoph. *Knights*, 580. See Becker, *op. cit.* p. 150.
[920] See *Lac. Pol.* ii. 5. Cf. Hor. *Sat.* i. 6. 127:

pransus non avide, quantum interpellet inani
ventre diem durare.

Then eat a temperate luncheon, just to stay
A sinking stomach till the close of day (Conington).

[921] Lit. "to give a reason and to get a reason from others." Cf. *Cyrop.* I. iv. 3.
[922] "The arts of the defendant, the apologist; and of the plaintiff, the prosecutor."

people whom I recognise to be offenders, as a rule in private life, or possibly against the state, the good-for-nothing fellows?

But please explain one other thing, Ischomachus (I answered). Do you put defence and accusation into formal language?[923]

Isch. "Formal language," say you, Socrates? The fact is, I never cease to practise speaking; and on this wise: Some member of my household has some charge to bring, or some defence to make,[924] against some other. I have to listen and examine. I must try to sift the truth. Or there is some one whom I have to blame or praise before my friends, or I must arbitrate between some close connections and endeavour to enforce the lesson that it is to their own interests to be friends not foes.[925] ... We are present to assist a general in court;[926] we are called upon to censure some one; or defend some other charged unjustly; or to prosecute a third who has received an honour which he ill deserves. It frequently occurs in our debates[927] that there is some course which we strongly favour: naturally we sound its praises; or some other, which we disapprove of: no less naturally we point out its defects.

He paused, then added: Things have indeed now got so far, Socrates, that several times I have had to stand my trial and have judgment passed upon me in set terms, what I must pay or what requital I must make.[928]

And at whose bar (I asked) is the sentence given? That point I failed to catch.[929]

Whose but my own wife's? (he answered).

And, pray, how do you conduct your own case? (I asked).[930]

Not so ill (he answered), when truth and interest correspond, but when they are opposed, Socrates, I have no skill to make the worse appear the better argument.[931]

Perhaps you have no skill, Ischomachus, to make black white or

---

[923] "Does your practice include the art of translating into words your sentiments?" Cf. *Mem.* I. ii. 52.

[924] Or, "One member of my household appears as plaintiff, another as defendant. I must listen and cross-question."

[925] The "asyndeton" would seem to mark a pause, unless some words have dropped out. See the commentators *ad loc.*

[926] The scene is perhaps that of a court-martial (cf. *Anab.* V. viii.; Dem. *c. Timocr.* 749. 16). (*Al.* cf. Sturz, *Lex.* s.v. "we are present (as advocates) and censure some general"), or more probably, I think, that of a civil judicial inquiry of some sort, conducted at a later date by the Minister of Finance ((to stratego to epi tas summorias eremeno)).

[927] Or, "Or again, a frequent case, we sit in council" (as members of the Boulê). See Aristot. *Pol.* iv. 15.

[928] See *Symp.* v. 8. Al. (dielemmenos) = "to be taken apart and have..."

[929] Or, "so dull was I, I failed to catch the point."

[930] See *Mem.* III. vii. 4; Plat. *Euth.* 3 E.

[931] See Plat. "Apol." 19-23 D; Aristoph. *Clouds,* 114 foll.

falsehood truth (said I).[932]

XII

But (I continued presently), perhaps I am preventing you from going, as you long have wished to do, Ischomachus?

To which he: By no means, Socrates. I should not think of going away until the gathering in the market is dispersed.[933]

Of course, of course (I answered), you are naturally most careful not to forfeit the title they have given you of "honest gentleman";[934] and yet, I daresay, fifty things at home are asking your attention at this moment; only you undertook to meet your foreign friends, and rather than play them false you go on waiting.

Isch. Let me so far correct you, Socrates; in no case will the things you speak of be neglected, since I have stewards and bailiffs[935] on the farms.

Soc. And, pray, what is your system when you need a bailiff? Do you search about, until you light on some one with a natural turn for stewardship; and then try to purchase him?—as, I feel certain, happens when you want a carpenter: first, you discover some one with a turn for carpentry, and then do all you can to get possession of him.[936] Or do you educate your bailiffs yourself?

Isch. Most certainly the latter, Socrates; I try to educate them, as you say, myself; and with good reason. He who is properly to fill my place and manage my affairs when I am absent, my "alter ego,"[937] needs but to have my knowledge; and if I am fit myself to stand at the head of my own business, I presume I should be able to put another in possession of my knowledge.[938]

Soc. Well then, the first thing he who is properly to take your place when absent must possess is goodwill towards you and yours; for without goodwill, what advantage will there be in any knowledge whatsoever which your bailiff may possess?

Isch. None, Socrates; and I may tell you that a kindly disposition towards me and mine is precisely what I first endeavour to instil.

Soc. And how, in the name of all that is holy, do you pick out whom you will and teach him to have kindly feeling towards yourself

---

[932] Or, "It may well be, Ischomachus, you cannot manufacture falsehood into truth." Lit. "Like enough you cannot make an untruth true."

[933] Lit. "until the market is quite broken up," *i.e.* after mid-day. See *Anab.* I. viii. 1; II. i. 7; *Mem.* I. i. 10. Cf. Herod. ii. 173; iii. 104; vii. 223.

[934] Lit. "beautiful and good."

[935] Cf. Becker, *op. cit.* p. 363.

[936] The steward, like the carpenter, and the labourers in general, would, as a rule, be a slave. See below, xxi. 9.

[937] Or, "my other self."

[938] Lit. "to teach another what I know myself."

and yours?

Isch. By kindly treatment of him, to be sure, whenever the gods bestow abundance of good things upon us.

Soc. If I take your meaning rightly, you would say that those who enjoy your good things grow well disposed to you and seek to render you some good?

Isch. Yes, for of all instruments to promote good feeling this I see to be the best.

Soc. Well, granted the man is well disposed to you does it therefore follow, Ischomachus, that he is fit to be your bailiff? It cannot have escaped your observation that albeit human beings, as a rule, are kindly disposed towards themselves, yet a large number of them will not apply the attention requisite to secure for themselves those good things which they fain would have.

Isch. Yes, but believe me, Socrates, when I seek to appoint such men as bailiffs, I teach them also carefulness and application.[939]

Soc. Nay, now in Heaven's name, once more, how can that be? I always thought it was beyond the power of any teacher to teach these virtues.[940]

Isch. Nor is it possible, you are right so far, to teach such excellences to every single soul in order as simply as a man might number off his fingers.

Soc. Pray, then, what sort of people have the privilege?[941] Should you mind pointing them out to me with some distinctness?

Isch. Well, in the first place, you would have some difficulty in making intemperate people diligent—I speak of intemperance with regard to wine, for drunkenness creates forgetfulness of everything which needs to be done.

Soc. And are persons devoid of self-control in this respect the only people incapable of diligence and carefulness? or are there others in like case?

Isch. Certainly, people who are intemperate with regard to sleep, seeing that the sluggard with his eyes shut cannot do himself or see that others do what is right.

Soc. What then?[942] Are we to regard these as the only people incapable of being taught this virtue of carefulness? or are there others in a like condition?

---

[939] (epimeleia) is a cardinal virtue with the Greeks, or at any rate with Xenophon, but it has no single name in English.

[940] For the Socratic problem (ei arete didakte) see Grote, *H. G.* viii. 599.

[941] Lit. "what kind of people can be taught them? By all means signify the sort to me distinctly."

[942] Or, "What then—is the list exhausted? Are we to suppose that these are the sole people..."

Isch. Surely we must include the slave to amorous affection.[943] Your woeful lover[944] is incapable of being taught attention to anything beyond one single object.[945] No light task, I take it, to discover any hope or occupation sweeter to him than that which now employs him, his care for his beloved, nor, when the call for action comes,[946] will it be easy to invent worse punishment than that he now endures in separation from the object of his passion.[947] Accordingly, I am in no great hurry to appoint a person of this sort to manage[948] my affairs; the very attempt to do so I regard as futile.

Soc. Well, and what of those addicted to another passion, that of gain? Are they, too, incapable of being trained to give attention to field and farming operations?

Isch. On the contrary, there are no people easier to train, none so susceptible of carefulness in these same matters. One needs only to point out to them that the pursuit is gainful, and their interest is aroused.

Soc. But for ordinary people? Given they are self-controlled to suit your bidding,[949] given they possess a wholesome appetite for gain, how will you lesson them in carefulness? how teach them growth in diligence to meet your wishes?

Isch. By a simple method, Socrates. When I see a man intent on carefulness, I praise and do my best to honour him. When, on the other hand, I see a man neglectful of his duties, I do not spare him: I try in every way, by word and deed, to wound him.

Soc. Come now, Ischomachus, kindly permit a turn in the discussion, which has hitherto concerned the persons being trained to carefulness themselves, and explain a point in reference to the training process. Is it possible for a man devoid of carefulness himself to render others more careful?

No more possible (he answered) than for a man who knows no music to make others musical.[950] If the teacher sets but an ill example, the pupil can hardly learn to do the thing aright.[951] And if the master's conduct is suggestive of laxity, how hardly shall his followers attain to

---

[943] See *Mem.* I. iii. 8 foll.; II. vi. 22.
[944] (duserotes). Cf. Thuc. vi. 13, "a desperate craving" (Jowett).
[945] Cf. *Symp.* iv. 21 foll.; *Cyrop.* V. i. 7-18.
[946] Or, "where demands of business present themselves, and something must be done."
[947] Cf. Shakesp. *Sonnets*, passim.
[948] Or, "I never dream of appointing as superintendent." See above, iv. 7.
[949] Or, "in matters such as you insist on."
[950] Or, "to give others skill in 'music.'" See Plat. *Rep.* 455 E; *Laws*, 802 B. *Al.* "a man devoid of letters to make others scholarly." See Plat. *Phaedr.* 248 D.
[951] Lit. "when the teacher traces the outline of the thing to copy badly." For (upodeiknuontos) see *Mem.* IV. iii. 13; *Horsem.* ii. 2. Cf. Aristot. *Oecon.* i. 6; *Ath. Pol.* 41. 17; and Dr. Sandys' note *ad loc.*

carefulness! Or to put the matter concisely, "like master like man." I do not think I ever knew or heard tell of a bad master blessed with good servants. The converse I certainly have seen ere now, a good master and bad servants; but they were the sufferers, not he.[952] No, he who would create a spirit of carefulness in others[953] must have the skill himself to supervise the field of labour; to test, examine, scrutinise.[954] He must be ready to requite where due the favour of a service well performed, nor hesitate to visit the penalty of their deserts upon those neglectful of their duty.[955] Indeed (he added), the answer of the barbarian to the king seems apposite. You know the story,[956] how the king had met with a good horse, but wished to give the creature flesh and that without delay, and so asked some one reputed to be clever about horses: "What will give him flesh most quickly?" To which the other: "The master's eye." So, too, it strikes me, Socrates, there is nothing like "the master's eye" to call forth latent qualities, and turn the same to beautiful and good effect.[957]

XIII

But now (I ventured), suppose you have presented strongly to the mind of some one[958] the need of carefulness to execute your wishes, is a person so qualified to be regarded as fit at once to be your bailiff? or is there aught else which he must learn in order to play the part of an efficient bailiff?

Most certainly there is (he answered): it still remains for him to learn particulars—to know, that is, what things he has to do, and when and how to do them; or else, if ignorant of these details, the profit of this bailiff in the abstract may prove no greater than the doctor's who pays a most precise attention to a sick man, visiting him late and early, but what will serve to ease his patient's pains[959] he knows not.

Soc. But suppose him to have learnt the whole routine of business, will he need aught else, or have we found at last your bailiff

---

[952] Or, "but they did not go scot-free"; "punishments then were rife."

[953] Cf. Plat. *Polit.* 275 E: "If we say either tending the herds, or managing the herds, or *having the care of them,* that will include all, and then we may wrap up the statesman with the rest, as the argument seems to require."—Jowett.

[954] Or, "he must have skill to over-eye the field of labour, and be scrutinous."

[955] "For every boon of service well performed he must be eager to make requital to the author of it, nor hesitate to visit on the heads of those neglectful of their duty a just recompense." (The language is poetical.)

[956] See Aristot. *Oecon.* i. 6; Aesch. *Pers.* 165; Cato ap. Plin. *H. N.* xviii. 5. Cic. ap. Colum. iv. 18; *ib.* vi. 21; La Fontaine, *L'Oeil du Maitre.*

[957] Or, "so, too, in general it seems to me 'the master's eye' is aptest to elicit energy to issue beautiful and good."

[958] Breit. cf. *Pol. Lac.* xv. 8. Holden cf. Plat. *Rep.* 600 C.

[959] Lit. "what it is to the advantage of his patient to do, is beyond his ken."

absolute?[960]

Isch. He must learn at any rate, I think, to rule his fellow-workmen.

What! (I exclaimed): you mean to say you educate your bailiffs to that extent? Actually you make them capable of rule?

At any rate I try to do so (he replied).

And how, in Heaven's name (I asked), do you contrive to educate another in the skill to govern human beings?

Isch. I have a very simple system, Socrates; so simple, I daresay, you will simply laugh at me.

Soc. The matter, I protest, is hardly one for laughter. The man who can make another capable of rule, clearly can teach him how to play the master; and if can make him play the master, he can make him what is grander still, a kingly being.[961] Once more, therefore, I protest: A man possessed of such creative power is worthy, not of ridicule, far from it, but of the highest praise.

Thus, then, I reason,[962] Socrates (he answered): The lower animals are taught obedience by two methods chiefly, partly through being punished when they make attempts to disobey, partly by experiencing some kindness when they cheerfully submit. This is the principle at any rate adopted in the breaking of young horses. The animal obeys its trainer, and something sweet is sure to follow; or it disobeys, and in place of something sweet it finds a peck of trouble; and so on, until it comes at last to yield obedience to the trainer's every wish. Or to take another instance: Young dogs,[963] however far inferior to man in thought and language,[964] can still be taught to run on errands and turn somersaults,[965] and do a host of other clever things, precisely on this same principle of training. Every time the animal obeys it gets something or other which it wanted, and every time it misbehaves it gets a whipping. But when it comes to human beings: in man you have a creature still more open to persuasion through appeals to reason;[966] only make it plain to him "it is his interest to obey." Or if they happen to be slaves,[967] the more ignoble training of wild animals tamed to the lure will serve to teach obedience. Only gratify their bellies in the

---

[960] Cf. Plat. *Rep.* 566 D. Or, "the perfect and consummate type of bailiff."

[961] *i.e.* (arkhikos) includes (1) (despotikos), *i.e.* an arbitrary head of any sort, from the master of one's own family to the (turannos kai despotes) (Plat. *Laws,* 859 A), despotic lord or owner; (2) (basilikos), the king or monarch gifted with regal qualities.

[962] (oukoun). "This, then, is my major premiss: the dumb animal..." (lit. "the rest of animals").

[963] (ta kunidia) possibly implies "performing poodles."

[964] (te gnome... te glotte), *i.e.* mental impression and expression, "mind and tongue."

[965] Or, "to run round and round and turn heels over head." *Al.* "dive for objects."

[966] "Logic, argument." Or, "a creature more compliant; merely by a word demonstrate to him..."

[967] Cf. Plat. *Rep.* 591 C.

matter of appetite, and you will succeed in winning much from them.[968] But ambitious, emulous natures feel the spur of praise,[969] since some natures hunger after praise no less than others crave for meats and drinks. My practice then is to instruct those whom I desire to appoint as my bailiffs in the various methods which I have found myself to be successful in gaining the obedience of my fellows. To take an instance: There are clothes and shows and so forth, with which I must provide my workfolk.[970] Well, then, I see to it that these are not all alike in make;[971] but some will be of better, some of less good quality: my object being that these articles for use shall vary with the service of the wearer; the worse man will receive the worse things as a gift, the better man the better as a mark of honour. For I ask you, Socrates, how can the good avoid despondency seeing that the work is wrought by their own hands alone, in spite of which these villains who will neither labour nor face danger when occasion calls are to receive an equal guerdon with themselves? And just as I cannot bring myself in any sort of way to look upon the better sort as worthy to receive no greater honour than the baser, so, too, I praise my bailiffs when I know they have apportioned the best things among the most deserving. And if I see that some one is receiving preference by dint of flatteries or like unworthy means, I do not let the matter pass; I reprimand my bailiff roundly, and so teach him that such conduct is not even to his interest.

XIV

Soc. Well, then, Ischomachus, supposing the man is now so fit to rule that he can compel obedience,[972] is he, I ask once more, your bailiff absolute? or even though possessed of all the qualifications you have named, does he still lack something?[973]

Most certainly (replied Ischomachus). One thing is still required of him, and that is to hold aloof from property and goods which are his master's; he must not steal. Consider, this is the very person through whose hands the fruits and produce pass, and he has the audacity to make away with them! perhaps he does not leave enough to cover the expenses of the farming operations! Where would be the use of farming the land by help of such an overseer?

What (I exclaimed), can I believe my ears? You actually undertake

---

[968] See Pater, *Plato and Platonism*, "Lacedaemon," p. 196 foll.

[969] See *Cyrop.* passim.

[970] (ergastersi), Xenophontic for the common Attic (ergatais). See Hold. *ad loc.* for similar forms, and cf. Rutherford, *New Phrynichus*, 59.

[971] Cf. Aristot. *Oecon.* i. 5 (where the thesis is developed further).

[972] Or, "that discipline flows from him;" al. "he presents you with obedient servants."

[973] Lit. "will he still need something further to complete him?"

to teach them virtue! What really, justice!

Isch. To be sure, I do. but it does not follow therefore that I find all equally apt to lend an ear to my instruction. However, what I do is this. I take a leaf now out of the laws of Draco and again another out of the laws of Solon,[974] and so essay to start my household on the path of uprightness. And indeed, if I mistake not (he proceeded), both those legislators enacted many of their laws expressly with a view to teaching this branch of justice.[975] It is written, "*Let a man be punished for a deed of theft*"; "*Let whosoever is detected in the act be bound and thrown in prison*"; "*If he offer violence,[976] let him be put to death.*" It is clear that the intention of the lawgivers in framing these enactments was to render the sordid love of gain[977] devoid of profit to the unjust person. What I do, therefore, is to cull a sample of their precepts, which I supplement with others from the royal code[978] where applicable; and so I do my best to shape the members of my household into the likeness of just men concerning that which passes through their hands. And now observe—the laws first mentioned act as penalties, deterrent to transgressors only; whereas the royal code aims higher: by it not only is the malefactor punished, but the righteous and just person is rewarded.[979] The result is, that many a man, beholding how the just grow ever wealthier than the unjust, albeit harbouring in his heart some covetous desires, is constant still to virtue. To abstain from unjust dealing is engrained in him.[980]

Those of my household (he proceeded) whom, in spite of kindly treatment, I perceive to be persistently bent on evil-doing, in the end I treat as desperate cases. Incurable self-seekers,[981] plain enough to see, whose aspiration lifts them from earth, so eager are they to be reckoned just men, not by reason only of the gain derivable from justice, but

---

[974] Cobet, *Pros. Xen.* cf. Plut. *Solon*, xvii. (proton men oun tous Drakontos nomous aneile k.t.l.) "First, then, he repealed all Draco's laws, except those concerning homicide, because they were too severe and the punishments too great; for death was appointed for almost all offences, insomuch that those that were convicted of idleness were to die, and those that stole a cabbage or an apple to suffer even as villains that committed sacrilege or murder" (Clough, i. 184). See Aul. Gell. *N. A.* xi. 13.

[975] "The branch of justice which concerns us, viz. righteous dealing between man and man."

[976] For this sense of (tous egkheirountas) cf. Thuc. iv. 121; *Hell.* IV. v. 16. *Al.* (dedesthai tous egkheirountas kai thanatousthai en tis alo poion) (Weiske), "let the attempt be punished with imprisonment"; "let him who is caught in the act be put to death."

[977] Cf. Plat. *Laws,* 754 E.

[978] Or, "the royal laws," *i.e.* of Persia. Cf. *Anab.* I. ix. 16; *Cyrop.* I. ii. 2, 3. Or possibly = "regal"; cf. Plat. *Minos,* 317 C; (to men orthon nomos esti basilikos).

[979] Lit. "benefited."

[980] Lit. "Whereby, beholding the just becoming wealthier than the unjust, many albeit covetous at heart themselves most constantly abide by abstinence from evil-doing."

[981] Lit. "Those, on the other hand, whom I discover to be roused" (to honesty—not solely because honesty is the best policy).

through passionate desire to deserve my praise—these in the end I treat as free-born men. I make them wealthy, and not with riches only, but in honour, as befits their gentle manliness.[982] For if, Socrates, there be one point in which the man who thirsts for honour differs from him who thirsts for gain, it is, I think, in willingness to toil, face danger, and abstain from shameful gains—for the sake of honour only and fair fame.[983]

XV

Soc. But now, suppose, Ischomachus, you have created in the soul of some one a desire for your welfare; have inspired in him not a mere passive interest, but a deep concern to help you to achieve prosperity; further, you have obtained for him a knowledge of the methods needed to give the operations of the field some measure of success; you have, moreover, made him capable of ruling; and, as the crowning point of all your efforts, this same trusty person shows no less delight, than you might take yourself, in laying at your feet[984] earth's products, each in due season richly harvested—I need hardly ask concerning such an one, whether aught else is lacking to him. It is clear to me[985] an overseer of this sort would be worth his weight in gold. But now, Ischomachus, I would have you not omit a topic somewhat lightly handled by us in the previous argument.[986]

What topic, pray, was that? (he asked).

Soc. You said, if I mistake not, that it was most important to learn the methods of conducting the several processes of husbandry; for, you added, unless a man knows what things he has to do and how to do them, all the care and diligence in the world will stand him in no stead.

At this point[987] he took me up, observing: So what you now command me is to teach the art itself of tillage, Socrates?

Yes (I replied), for now it looks as if this art were one which made the wise and skilled possessor of it wealthy, whilst the unskilled, in spite of all the pains he takes, must live in indigence.

Isch. Now shall you hear, then,[988] Socrates, the generous nature of

---

[982] Or, "men of fair and noble type"; "true gentlemen." This passage suggests the "silver lining to the cloud" of slavery.

[983] Cf. Hom. *Il.* ix. 413, (oleto men moi nostos, atar kleos aphthiton estai), "but my fame shall be imperishable."

[984] (apodeiknuon), *i.e.* in presenting the inventory of products for the year. Cf. *Hell.* V. iii. 17; "Revenues," ii. 7.

[985] (ede), at this stage of the discussion.

[986] Or, "that part of the discussion which we ran over in a light and airy fashion," in reference to xiii. 2.

[987] Keeping the vulg. order of §§ 3-9, which many commentators would rearrange in various ways. See Breit. *ad loc.*; Lincke, *op. cit.* p. 111 foll.

[988] Or, "Listen, then, and whilst I recount to you at once the loving-kindness of this

Xenophon 199

this human art. For is it not a proof of something noble in it, that being of supreme utility, so sweet a craft to exercise, so rich in beauty, so acceptable alike to gods and men, the art of husbandry may further fairly claim to be the easiest of all the arts to learn? Noble I name it! this, at any rate, the epithet we give to animals which, being beautiful and large and useful, are also gentle towards the race of man.[989]

Allow me to explain, Ischomachus (I interposed). Up to a certain point I fully followed what you said. I understand, according to your theory, how a bailiff must be taught. In other words, I follow your descriptions both as to how you make him kindly disposed towards yourself; and how, again, you make him careful, capable of rule, and upright. But at that point you made the statement that, in order to apply this diligence to tillage rightly, the careful husbandman must further learn what are the different things he has to do, and not alone *what* things he has to do, but *how* and *when* to do them. These are the topics which, in my opinion, have hitherto been somewhat lightly handled in the argument. Let me make my meaning clearer by an instance: it is as if you were to tell me that, in order to be able to take down a speech in writing,[990] or to read a written statement, a man must know his letters. Of course, if not stone deaf, I must have garnered that for a certain object knowledge of letters was important to me, but the bare recognition of the fact, I fear, would not enable me in any deeper sense to know my letters. So, too, at present I am easily persuaded that if I am to direct my care aright in tillage I must have a knowledge of the art of tillage. But the bare recognition of the fact does not one whit provide me with the knowledge how I ought to till. And if I resolved without ado to set about the work of tilling, I imagine, I should soon resemble your physician going on his rounds and visiting his patients without knowing what to prescribe or what to do to ease their sufferings. To save me from the like predicaments, please teach me the actual work and processes of tillage.

Isch. But truly,[991] Socrates, it is not with tillage as with the other arts, where the learner must be well-nigh crushed[992] beneath a load of study before his prentice-hand can turn out work of worth sufficient merely to support him.[993] The art of husbandry, I say, is not so ill to learn and cross-grained; but by watching labourers in the field, by listening to what they say, you will have straightway knowledge

---

art, to man the friendliest."
[989] Schenkl regards this sentence as an interpolation. For the epithet (gennaios) applied to the dog see *Cyrop.* I. iv. 15, 21; *Hunting,* iv. 7.
[990] Or, "something from dictation."
[991] "Nay, if you will but listen, Socrates, with husbandry it is not the same as with the other arts."
[992] (katatribenai), "worn out." See *Mem.* III. iv. 1; IV. vii. 5. Al. "bored to death."
[993] Or, "before the products of his pupilage are worth his keep."

enough to teach another, should the humour take you. I imagine, Socrates (he added), that you yourself, albeit quite unconscious of the fact, already know a vast amount about the subject. The fact is, other craftsmen (the race, I mean, in general of artists) are each and all disposed to keep the most important[994] features of their several arts concealed: with husbandry it is different. Here the man who has the most skill in planting will take most pleasure in being watched by others; and so too the most skilful sower. Ask any question you may choose about results thus beautifully wrought, and not one feature in the whole performance will the doer of it seek to keep concealed. To such height of nobleness (he added), Socrates, does husbandry appear, like some fair mistress, to conform the soul and disposition of those concerned with it.

The proem[995] to the speech is beautiful at any rate (I answered), but hardly calculated to divert the hearer from the previous question. A thing so easy to be learnt, you say? then, if so, do you be all the readier for that reason to explain its details to me. No shame on you who teach, to teach these easy matters; but for me to lack the knowledge of them, and most of all if highly useful to the learner, worse than shame, a scandal.

XVI

Isch. First then, Socrates, I wish to demonstrate to you that what is called[996] "the intricate variety in husbandry"[997] presents no difficulty. I use a phrase of those who, whatever the nicety with which they treat the art in theory,[998] have but the faintest practical experience of tillage. What they assert is, that "he who would rightly till the soil must first be made acquainted with the nature of the earth."

And they are surely right in their assertion (I replied); for he who does not know what the soil is capable of bearing, can hardly know, I fancy, what he has to plant or what to sow.

But he has only to look at his neighbour's land (he answered), at his crops and trees, in order to learn what the soil can bear and what it cannot.[999] After which discovery, it is ill work fighting against heaven. Certainly not by dint of sowing and planting what he himself desires will he meet the needs of life more fully than by planting and sowing

---

[994] Or, "critical and crucial."
[995] Or, "the prelude to the piece."
[996] "They term"; in reference to the author of some treatise.
[997] Or, "the riddling subtlety of tillage." See *Mem.* II. iii. 10; Plat. *Symp.* 182 B; *Phileb.* 53 E.
[998] Theophr. *De Caus.* ii. 4, 12, mentions Leophanes amongst other writers on agriculture preceding himself.
[999] Holden cf. Virg. *Georg.* i. 53; iv. 109. According to the commentator Servius, the poet drew largely upon Xenophon's treatise.

what the earth herself rejoices to bear and nourish on her bosom. Or if, as well may be the case, through the idleness of those who occupy it, the land itself cannot display its native faculty,[1000] it is often possible to derive a truer notion from some neighbouring district that ever you will learn about it from your neighbour's lips.[1001] Nay, even though the earth lie waste and barren, it may still declare its nature; since a soil productive of beautiful wild fruits can by careful tending be made to yield fruits of the cultivated kind as beautiful. And on this wise, he who has the barest knowledge[1002] of the art of tillage can still discern the nature of the soil.

Thank you (I said), Ischomachus, my courage needs no further fanning upon that score. I am bold enough now to believe that no one need abstain from agriculture for fear he will not recognise the nature of the soil. Indeed, I now recall to mind a fact concerning fishermen, how as they ply their business on the seas, not crawling lazily along, nor bringing to, for prospect's sake, but in the act of scudding past the flying farmsteads,[1003] these brave mariners have only to set eyes upon crops on land, and they will boldly pronounce opinion on the nature of the soil itself, whether good or bad: this they blame and that they praise. And these opinions for the most part coincide, I notice, with the verdict of the skilful farmer as to quality of soil.[1004]

Isch. At what point shall I begin then, Socrates, to revive your recollection[1005] of the art of husbandry? since to explain to you the processes employed in husbandry means the statement of a hundred details which you know yourself full well already.

Soc. The first thing I should like to learn, Ischomachus, I think, if only as a point befitting a philosopher, is this: how to proceed and how to work the soil, did I desire to extract the largest crops of wheat and barley.

Isch. Good, then! you are aware that fallow must be broken up in readiness[1006] for sowing?

Soc. Yes, I am aware of that.

Isch. Well then, supposing we begin to plough our land in winter?

Soc. It would not do. There would be too much mud.

Isch. Well then, what would you say to summer?

Soc. The soil will be too hard in summer for a plough and a pair of oxen to break up.

[1000] Or, "cannot prove its natural aptitude."

[1001] Or, "from a neighbouring mortal."

[1002] Or, "a mere empiric in the art of husbandry."

[1003] Or, "the flying coastland, fields and farmyards."

[1004] Lit. "And indeed the opinions they pronounce about 'a good soil' mostly tally with the verdict of the expert farmer."

[1005] Or, "begin recalling to your mind." See Plat. *Meno*, for the doctrine of *Anamênsis* here apparently referred to.

[1006] Or, "ploughed up." Cf. Theophr. *Hist. Pl.* iii. i. 6; Dion. Hal. *Ant.* x. 17.

Isch. It looks as if spring-time were the season to begin this work, then? What do you say?

Soc. I say, one may expect the soil broken up at that season of the year to crumble[1007] best.

Isch. Yes, and grasses[1008] turned over at that season, Socrates, serve to supply the soil already with manure; while as they have not shed their seed as yet, they cannot vegetate.[1009] I am supposing that you recognise a further fact: to form good land, a fallow must be clean and clear of undergrowth and weeds,[1010] and baked as much as possible by exposure to the sun.[1011]

Soc. Yes, that is quite a proper state of things, I should imagine.

Isch. And to bring about this proper state of things, do you maintain there can be any other better system than that of turning the soil over as many times as possible in summer?

Soc. On the contrary, I know precisely that for either object, whether to bring the weeds and quitch grass to the surface and to wither them by scorching heat, or to expose the earth itself to the sun's baking rays, there can be nothing better than to plough the soil up with a pair of oxen during mid-day in midsummer.

Isch. And if a gang of men set to, to break and make this fallow with the mattock, it is transparent that their business is to separate the quitch grass from the soil and keep them parted?

Soc. Just so!—to throw the quitch grass down to wither on the surface, and to turn the soil up, so that the crude earth may have its turn of baking.

XVII

You see, Socrates (he said, continuing the conversation), we hold the same opinion, both of us, concerning fallow.

Why, so it seems (I said)—the same opinion.

Isch. But when it comes to sowing, what is your opinion? Can you suggest a better time for sowing than that which the long experience of former generations, combined with that of men now living, recognises as the best? See, so soon as autumn time has come, the faces of all men everywhere turn with a wistful gaze towards high heaven. "When will God moisten the earth," they ask, "and suffer men to sow their seed?"[1012]

[1007] (kheisthai) = laxari, dissolvi, to be most friable, to scatter readily.

[1008] "Herbage," whether grass or other plants, "grass," "clover," etc; Theophr. *Hist. Pl.* i. 3. 1; Holden, "green crops."

[1009] Lit. "and not as yet have shed their seed so as to spring into blade."

[1010] Or, "quitch."

[1011] Holden cf. Virg. *Georg.* i. 65, *coquat*; ii. 260, *excoquere*. So Lucr. vi. 962.

[1012] See Dr. Holden's interesting note at this point: "According to Virgil (*Georg.* i.

Yes, Ischomachus (I answered), for all mankind must recognise the precept:[1013] "Sow not on dry soil" (if it can be avoided), being taught wisdom doubtless by the heavy losses they must struggle with who sow before God's bidding.

Isch. It seems, then, you and I and all mankind hold one opinion on these matters?

Soc. Why, yes; where God himself is teacher, such accord is apt to follow; for instance, all men are agreed, it is better to wear thick clothes[1014] in winter, if so be they can. We light fires by general consent, provided we have logs to burn.

Yet as regards this very period of seed-time (he made answer), Socrates, we find at once the widest difference of opinion upon one point; as to which is better, the early, or the later,[1015] or the middle sowing?

Soc. Just so, for neither does God guide the year in one set fashion, but irregularly, now suiting it to early sowing best, and now to middle, and again to later.

Isch. But what, Socrates, is your opinion? Were it better for a man to choose and turn to sole account a single sowing season, be it much he has to sow or be it little? or would you have him begin his sowing with the earliest season, and sow right on continuously until the latest?

And I, in my turn, answered: I should think it best, Ischomachus, to use indifferently the whole sowing season.[1016] Far better[1017] to have enough of corn and meal at any moment and from year to year, than first a superfluity and then perhaps a scant supply.

Isch. Then, on this point also, Socrates, you hold a like opinion with myself—the pupil to the teacher; and what is more, the pupil was the first to give it utterance.

So far, so good! (I answered). Is there a subtle art in scattering the seed?

Isch. Let us by all means investigate that point. That the seed must be cast by hand, I presume you know yourself?

Soc. Yes, by the testimony of my eyes.[1018]

Isch. But as to actual scattering, some can scatter evenly, others

---

215), spring is the time," etc.

[1013] Or, "it is a maxim held of all men."

[1014] Or, "a thick cloak." See Rich, s.v. *Pallium* (= (imation)).

[1015] See Holden *ad loc.* Sauppe, *Lex. Xen.*, notes (opsimos) as Ionic and poet. See also Rutherford, *New Phryn.* p. 124: "First met with in a line of the *Iliad* (ii. 325), (opsimos) does not appear till late Greek except in the *Oeconomicus*, a disputed work of Xenophon."

[1016] Or, "share in the entire period of seed time." Zeune cf. *Geop.* ii. 14. 8; Mr. Ruskin's translators, *Bibl. Past.* vol. i.; cf. Eccles. xi. 6.

[1017] Lit. "according to my tenet," (nomizo).

[1018] Lit. "Yes, for I have seen it done."

cannot.[1019]

Soc. Does it not come to this, the hand needs practice (like the fingers of a harp-player) to obey the will?

Isch. Precisely so, but now suppose the soil is light in one part and heavy in another?

Soc. I do not follow; by "light" do you mean weak? and by "heavy" strong?

Isch. Yes, that is what I mean. And the question which I put to you is this: Would you allow both sorts of soil an equal share of seed? or which the larger?[1020]

Soc. The stronger the wine the larger the dose of water to be added, I believe. The stronger, too, the man the heavier the weight we will lay upon his back to carry: or if it is not porterage, but people to support, there still my tenet holds: the broader and more powerful the great man's shoulders, the more mouths I should assign to him to feed. But perhaps a weak soil, like a lean pack-horse,[1021] grows stronger the more corn you pour into it. This I look to you to teach me.[1022]

With a laugh, he answered: Once more you are pleased to jest. Yet rest assured of one thing, Socrates: if after you have put seed into the ground, you will await the instant when, while earth is being richly fed from heaven, the fresh green from the hidden seed first springs, and take and turn it back again,[1023] this sprouting germ will serve as food for earth: as from manure an inborn strength will presently be added to the soil. But if you suffer earth to feed the seed of corn within it and to bring forth fruit in an endless round, at last[1024] it will be hard for the weakened soil to yield large corn crops, even as a weak sow can hardly rear a large litter of fat pigs.

Soc. I understand you to say, Ischomachus, that the weaker soil must receive a scantier dose of seed?

Isch. Most decidedly I do, and you on your side, Socrates, I understand, give your consent to this opinion in stating your belief that the weaker the shoulders the lighter the burdens to be laid on them.

Soc. But those hoers with their hoes, Ischomachus, tell me for what reason you let them loose[1025] upon the corn.

[1019] Holden cf. W. Harte, *Essays on Husbandry*, p. 210, 2nd ed., "The main perfection of sowing is to disperse the seeds equally."

[1020] See Theophr. *Hist. Pl.* viii. 6. 2; Virg. *Georg.* ii. 275. Holden cf. Adam Dickson, *Husbandry of the Ancients*, vol. ii. 35. 33 f. (Edin. 1788), "Were the poor light land in Britain managed after the manner of the Roman husbandry, it would certainly require much less seed than under its present management."

[1021] Or, "lean cattle."

[1022] Or, "Will you please answer me that question, teacher?"

[1023] "If you will plough the seedlings in again."

[1024] (dia telous... es telos), "continually... in the end." See references in Holden's fifth edition.

[1025] Cf. *Revenues*, iv. 5.

Isch. You know, I daresay, that in winter there are heavy rains?[1026]

Soc. To be sure, I do.

Isch. We may suppose, then, that a portion of the corn is buried by these floods beneath a coat of mud and slime, or else that the roots are laid quite bare in places by the torrent. By reason of this same drench, I take it, oftentimes an undergrowth of weeds springs up with the corn and chokes it.

Soc. Yes, all these ills are likely enough to happen.

Isch. Are you not agreed the corn-fields sorely need relief at such a season?

Soc. Assuredly.

Isch. Then what is to be done, in your opinion? How shall we aid the stricken portion lying mud-bedabbled?

Soc. How better than by lifting up and lightening the soil?

Isch. Yes! and that other portion lying naked to the roots and defenceless, how aid it?

Soc. Possibly by mounding up fresh earth about it.[1027]

Isch. And what when the weeds spring up together with the corn and choke it? or when they rob and ruthlessly devour the corn's proper sustenance, like unserviceable drones[1028] that rob the working bees of honey, pilfering the good food which they have made and stored away with labour: what must we do?

Soc. In good sooth, there can be nothing for it save to cut out the noisome weed, even as drones are cleared out from the hive.

Isch. You agree there is some show of reason for letting in these gangs of hoers?

Soc. Most true. And now I am turning over in my mind,[1029] Ischomachus, how grand a thing it is to introduce a simile or such like figure well and aptly. No sooner had you mentioned the word "drones" than I was filled with rage against those miserable weeds, far more than when you merely spoke of weeds and undergrowth.

[1026] "And melting snows, much water every way."
[1027] "Scraping up a barrier of fresh earth about it."
[1028] Cf. Shakesp. "Lazy yawning drones," *Henry V.* I. ii. 204.
[1029] Or, "I was just this moment pondering the virtue of a happy illustration." Lit. "what a thing it is to introduce an 'image' ((tas eikonas)) well." See Plat. *Rep.* 487 E, (de eikonos), "in a parable" (Jowett); *Phaed.* 87 B, "a figure"; Aristoph. *Clouds,* 559; Plat. *Phaedr.* 267 C; Aristot. *Rhet.* III. iv. As to the drones, J. J. Hartman, *An. X.* 186, aptly cf. Aristoph. *Wasps,* 1114 f.

XVIII

But, not to interrupt you further (I continued), after sowing, naturally we hope to come to reaping. If, therefore, you have anything to say on that head also, pray proceed to teach me.

Isch. Yes, by all means, unless indeed you prove on this head also to know as much yourself already as your teacher. To begin then: You know that corn needs cutting?

Soc. To be sure, I know that much at any rate.

Isch. Well, then, the next point: in the act of cutting corn how will you choose to stand? facing the way the wind blows,[1030] or against the wind?

Soc. Not against the wind, for my part. Eyes and hands must suffer, I imagine, if one stood reaping face to face with husks and particles of straw.[1031]

Isch. And should you merely sever the ears at top, or reap close to the ground?[1032]

If the stalk of corn were short (I answered), I should cut down close, to secure a sufficient length of straw to be of use. But if the stalk be tall, you would do right, I hold, to cut it half-way down, whereby the thresher and the winnower will be saved some extra labour (which both may well be spared).[1033] The stalk left standing in the field, when burnt down (as burnt it will be, I presume), will help to benefit the soil;[1034] and laid on as manure, will serve to swell the volume of manure.[1035]

Isch. There, Socrates, you are detected "in the very act"; you know as much about reaping as I do myself.

It looks a little like it (I replied). But I would fain discover whether I have sound knowledge also about threshing.

Isch. Well, I suppose you are aware of this much: corn is threshed by beasts of burthen?[1036]

Soc. Yes, I am aware of that much, and beast of burthen is a general name including oxen, horses, mules, and so forth.[1037]

[1030] Lit. "(on the side) where the wind blows or right opposite."

[1031] *i.e.* "with particles of straw and beards of corn blowing in one's face."

[1032] See Holden *ad loc.*; Sir Anthony Fitzherbert, *Husbandry*, 27 (ed. 1767), "In Somersetshire... they do share theyr wheate very lowe...."

[1033] Lit. "will be spared superfluous labour on what they do not want."

[1034] *Al.* "if burnt down...; if laid on as manure..."

[1035] "Help to swell the bulk" (Holden). For the custom see Virg. *Georg.* i. 84; J. Tull, *op. cit.* ix. 141: "The custom of burning the stubble on the rich plains about Rome continues to this time."

[1036] Holden cf. Dr. Davy, "Notes and Observations on the Ionian Islands." "The grain is beaten out, commonly in the harvest field, by men, horses, or mules, on a threshing-floor prepared extempore for the purpose, where the ground is firm and dry, and the chaff is separated by winnowing."—Wilkinson, *Ancient Egyptians*, ii. 41 foll.

[1037] See Varro, i. 52, as to *tritura* and *ventilatio.*

Isch. Is it your opinion that these animals know more than merely how to tread the corn while driven with the goad?

Soc. What more can they know, being beasts of burthen?

Isch. Some one must see, then, that the beasts tread out only what requires threshing and no more, and that the threshing is done evenly itself: to whom do you assign that duty, Socrates?

Soc. Clearly it is the duty of the threshers who are in charge.[1038] It is theirs to turn the sheaves, and ever and again to push the untrodden corn under the creatures' feet; and thus, of course, to keep the threshing-floor as smooth, and finish off the work as fast, as possible.

Isch. Your comprehension of the facts thus far, it seems, keeps pace with mine.

Soc. Well, after that, Ischomachus, we will proceed to cleanse the corn by winnowing.[1039]

Isch. Yes, but tell me, Socrates; do you know that if you begin the process from the windward portion (of the threshing-floor), you will find your chaff is carried over the whole area.

Soc. It must be so.

Isch. Then it is more than likely the chaff will fall upon the corn.

Soc. Yes, considering the distance,[1040] the chaff will hardly be carried across the corn into the empty portion of the threshing-floor.

Isch. But now, suppose you begin winnowing on the "lee" side of the threshing-floor?[1041]

Soc. It is clear the chaff will at once fall into the chaff-receiver.[1042]

Isch. And when you have cleansed the corn over half the floor, will you proceed at once, with the corn thus strewn in front of you, to winnow the remainder,[1043] or will you first pack the clean grain into the narrowest space against the central pillar?[1044]

Soc. Yes, upon my word! first pack together the clean grain, and proceed. My chaff will now be carried into the empty portion of the floor, and I shall escape the need of winnowing twice over.[1045]

Isch. Really, Socrates, you are fully competent yourself, it seems,

---

[1038] Or, "to the over-threshers," "the drivers" (Holden).

[1039] Breit. cf. Colum. *de r. r.* ii. 10, 14, 21; vide Rich, s.v. *ventilabrum*.

[1040] Lit. "it is a long space for the chaff to be carried." Al. (1) "It is of great consequence the chaff should be carried beyond the corn." (2) "It often happens that the corn is blown not only on to the corn, but over and beyond it into the empty portion of the threshing-floor." So Breit.

[1041] Or, "on the side of the threshing-floor opposite the wind." Al. "protected from the wind."

[1042] A hollowed-out portion of the threshing-floor, according to Breitenbach.

[1043] Lit. "of the chaff," where we should say "corn," the winnowing process separating chaff from grain and grain from chaff.

[1044] If that is the meaning of (ton polon). Al. "the outer edge or rim of the threshing-floor."

[1045] Or, "the same *chaff* (*i.e.* unwinnowed corn, Angl. *corn*) twice."

to teach an ignorant world[1046] the speediest mode of winnowing.

Soc. It seems, then, as you say, I must have known about these matters, though unconsciously; and here I stand and beat my brains,[1047] reflecting whether or not I may not know some other things—how to refine gold and play the flute and paint pictures—without being conscious of the fact. Certainly, as far as teaching goes, no one ever taught me these, no more than husbandry; while, as to using my own eyes, I have watched men working at the other arts no less than I have watched them till the soil.

Isch. Did I not tell you long ago that of all arts husbandry was the noblest, the most generous, just because it is the easiest to learn?

Soc. That it is without a doubt, Ischomachus. It seems I must have known the processes of sowing, without being conscious of my knowledge.[1048]

XIX

Soc. (continuing). But may I ask, is the planting of trees[1049] a department in the art of husbandry?

Isch. Certainly it is.

Soc. How is it, then, that I can know about the processes of sowing and at the same time have no knowledge about planting?

Isch. Is it so certain that you have no knowledge?

Soc. How can you ask me? when I neither know the sort of soil in which to plant, nor yet the depth of hole[1050] the plant requires, nor the breadth, or length of ground in which it needs to be embedded;[1051] nor lastly, how to lay the plant in earth, with any hope of fostering its growth.[1052]

Isch. Come, then, to lessons, pupil, and be taught whatever you do not know already! You have seen, I know, the sort of trenches which are dug for plants?

Soc. Hundreds of times.

Isch. Did you ever see one more than three feet deep?

Soc. No, I do not think I ever saw one more than two and a half feet deep.

[1046] Lit. "After all, Socrates, it seems you could even teach another how to purge his corn most expeditiously."

[1047] Lit. "all this while, I am thinking whether..."

[1048] Or, "but for all my science, I was ignorant (of knowing my own knowledge)."

[1049] *i.e.* of fruit trees, the vine, olive, fig, etc.

[1050] Reading (to phuto), "nor yet how deep or broad to sink (the hole) for the plant." Holden (ed. 1886) supplies (bothunon). *Al.* (bothron).

[1051] See Loudon, *Encycl. of Agric.* § 407, ap. Holden: "In France plantations of the vine are made by dibbling in cuttings of two feet of length; pressing the earth firmly to their lower end, an essential part of the operation, noticed even by Xenophon."

[1052] Lit. "how, laid in the soil, the plant will best shoot forth or grow."

Isch. Well, as to the breadth now. Did you ever see a trench more than three feet broad?[1053]

Soc. No, upon my word, not even more than two feet broad.

Isch. Good! now answer me this question: Did you ever see a trench less than one foot deep?

Soc. No, indeed! nor even less than one foot and a half. Why, the plants would be no sooner buried than dug out again, if planted so extremely near the surface.

Isch. Here, then, is one matter, Socrates, which you know as well as any one.[1054] The trench is not to be sunk deeper than two feet and a half, or shallower than one foot and a half.

Soc. Obviously, a thing so plain appeals to the eye at once.

Isch. Can you by eyesight recognise the difference between a dry soil and a moist?

Soc. I should certainly select as dry the soil round Lycabettus,[1055] and any that resembles it; and as moist, the soil in the marsh meadows of Phalêrum,[1056] or the like.

Isch. In planting, would you dig (what I may call) deep trenches in a dry soil or a moist?

Soc. In a dry soil certainly; at any rate, if you set about to dig deep trenches in the moist you will come to water, and there and then an end to further planting.

Isch. You could not put it better. We will suppose, then, the trenches have been dug. Does your eyesight take you further?[1057] Have you noticed at what season in either case[1058] the plants must be embedded?

Soc. Certainly.[1059]

Isch. Supposing, then, you wish the plants to grow as fast as possible: how will the cutting strike and sprout, do you suppose, most readily?—after you have laid a layer of soil already worked beneath it, and it merely has to penetrate soft mould? or when it has to force its way through unbroken soil into the solid ground?

Soc. Clearly it will shoot through soil which has been worked more quickly than through unworked soil.

[1053] Or, "width," "wide." The commentators cf. Plin. *H. N.* xvii. 11, 16, 22; Columell. v. 5. 2; *ib.* iii. 15. 2; Virg. *Georg.* ii. 288.

[1054] Lit. "quite adequately."

[1055] See Leake, *Topog. of Athens*, i. 209.

[1056] Or, "the Phaleric marsh-land." See Leake, *ib.* 231, 427; ii. 9.

[1057] Lit. "As soon as the trenches have been dug then, have you further noticed..."

[1058] (1) The vulg. reading (openika... ekatera) = "at what precise time... either (*i.e.* 'the two different' kinds of) plant," *i.e.* "vine and olive" or "vine and fig," I suppose; (2) Breit. emend. (opotera... en ekatera) = "which kind of plant... in either soil..."; (3) Schenkl. etc., (openika... en ekatera) = "at what season... in each of the two sorts of soil..."

[1059] There is an obvious lacuna either before or after this remark, or at both places.

Isch. Well then, a bed of earth must be laid beneath the plant?
Soc. I quite agree; so let it be.
Isch. And how do you expect your cutting to root best?—if set straight up from end to end, pointing to the sky?[1060] or if you set it slantwise under its earthy covering, so as to lie like an inverted *gamma*?[1061]
Soc. Like an inverted *gamma*, to be sure, for so the plant must needs have more *eyes* under ground. Now it is from these same *eyes* of theirs, if I may trust my own,[1062] that plants put forth their shoots above ground. I imagine, therefore, the eyes still underground will do the same precisely, and with so many buds all springing under earth, the plant itself, I argue, as a whole will sprout and shoot and push its way with speed and vigour.
Isch. I may tell you that on these points, too, your judgment tallies with my own. But now, should you content yourself with merely heaping up the earth, or will you press it firmly round your plant?
Soc. I should certainly press down the earth; for if the earth is not pressed down, I know full well that at one time under the influence of rain the unpressed soil will turn to clay or mud; at another, under the influence of the sun, it will turn to sand or dust to the very bottom: so that the poor plant runs a risk of being first rotted with moisture by the rain, and next of being shrivelled up with drought through overheating of the roots.[1063]
Isch. So far as the planting of vines is concerned, it appears, Socrates, that you and I again hold views precisely similar.
And does this method of planting apply also to the fig-tree? (I inquired).
Isch. Surely, and not to the fig-tree alone, but to all the rest of fruit-trees.[1064] What reason indeed would there be for rejecting in the case of other plant-growths[1065] what is found to answer so well with the vine?
Soc. How shall we plant the olive, pray, Ischomachus?

[1060] Lit. "if you set the whole cutting straight up, facing heavenwards."

[1061] *i.e.* Anglice, "like the letter (G) upon its back" (an inverted "upper-case" gamma looks like an L). See Lord Bacon, *Nat. Hist.* Cent. v. 426: "When you would have many new roots of fruit-trees, take a low tree and bow it and lay all his branches aflat upon the ground and cast earth upon them; and every twig will take root. And this is a very profitable experiment for costly trees (for the boughs will make stock without charge), such as are apricots, peaches, almonds, cornelians, mulberries, figs, etc. The like is continually practised with vines, roses, musk roses, etc."

[1062] Lit. "it is from their eyes, I see, that plants..."

[1063] Through "there being too much bottom heat." Holden (ed. 1886).

[1064] (akrodrua) = "edible fruits" in Xenophon's time. See Plat. *Criti.* 115 B; Dem. *c. Nicostr.* 1251; Aristot. *Hist. An.* viii. 28. 8, (out akrodrua out opora khronios); Theophr. *H. Pl.* iv. 4. 11. (At a later period, see "Geopon." x. 74, = "fruits having a hard rind or shell," *e.g.* nuts, acorns, as opposed to pears, apples, grapes, etc., (opora).) See further the interesting regulations in Plat. *Laws*, 844 D, 845 C.

[1065] Lit. "planting in general."

Isch. I see your purpose. You ask that question with a view to put me to the test,[1066] when you know the answer yourself as well as possible. You can see with your own eyes[1067] that the olive has a deeper trench dug, planted as it is so commonly by the side of roads. You can see that all the young plants in the nursery adhere to stumps.[1068] And lastly, you can see that a lump of clay is placed on the head of every plant,[1069] and the portion of the plant above the soil is protected by a wrapping.[1070]

Soc. Yes, all these things I see.

Isch. Granted, you see: what is there in the matter that you do not understand? Perhaps you are ignorant how you are to lay the potsherd on the clay at top?

Soc. No, in very sooth, not ignorant of that Ischomachus, or anything you mentioned. That is just the puzzle, and again I beat my brains to discover why, when you put to me that question a while back: "Had I, in brief, the knowledge how to plant?" I answered, "No." Till then it never would have struck me that I could say at all how planting must be done. But no sooner do you begin to question me on each particular point than I can answer you; and what is more, my answers are, you tell me, accordant with the views of an authority[1071] at once so skilful and so celebrated as yourself. Really, Ischomachus, I am disposed to ask: "Does teaching consist in putting questions?"[1072] Indeed, the secret of your system has just this instant dawned upon me. I seem to see the principle in which you put your questions. You lead me through the field of my own knowledge,[1073] and then by pointing

---

[1066] Plat. *Prot.* 311 B, 349 C; *Theaet.* 157 C: "I cannot make out whether you are giving your own opinion, or only wanting to draw me out" (Jowett).

[1067] For the advantage, see *Geopon.* iii. 11. 2.

[1068] Holden cf. Virg. *Georg.* ii. 30—

quin et caudicibus sectis, mirabile dictu,
truditur e sicco radix oleagina ligno.

The stock in slices cut, and forth shall shoot,
O passing strange! from each dry slice a root (Holden).

See John Martyn *ad loc.*: "La Cerda says, that what the Poet here speaks of was practised in Spain in his time. They take the trunk of an olive, says he, deprive it of its root and branches, and cut it into several pieces, which they put into the ground, whence a root and, soon afterwards, a tree is formed." This mode of propagating by dry pieces of the trunk (with bark on) is not to be confounded with that of "truncheons" mentioned in *Georg.* ii. 63.

[1069] See Theophr. *H. Pl.* ii. 2, 4; *de Caus.* iii. 5. 1; *Geopon.* ix. 11. 4, ap. Hold.; Col. v. 9. 1; xi. 2. 42.

[1070] Or, "covered up for protection."

[1071] Or, "whose skill in farming is proverbial."

[1072] Lit. "Is questioning after all a kind of teaching?" See Plat. *Meno*; *Mem.* IV. vi. 15.

[1073] It appears, then, that the Xenophontean Socrates has (episteme) of a sort.

out analogies[1074] to what I know, persuade me that I really know some things which hitherto, as I believed, I had no knowledge of.

Isch. Do you suppose if I began to question you concerning money and its quality,[1075] I could possibly persuade you that you know the method to distinguish good from false coin? Or could I, by a string of questions about flute-players, painters, and the like, induce you to believe that you yourself know how to play the flute, or paint, and so forth?

Soc. Perhaps you might; for have you not persuaded me I am possessed of perfect knowledge of this art of husbandry,[1076] albeit I know that no one ever taught this art to me?

Isch. Ah! that is not the explanation, Socrates. The truth is what I told you long ago and kept on telling you. Husbandry is an art so gentle, so humane, that mistress-like she makes all those who look on her or listen to her voice intelligent[1077] of herself at once. Many a lesson does she herself impart how best to try conclusions with her.[1078] See, for instance, how the vine, making a ladder of the nearest tree whereon to climb, informs us that it needs support.[1079] Anon it spreads its leaves when, as it seems to say, "My grapes are young, my clusters tender," and so teaches us, during that season, to screen and shade the parts exposed to the sun's rays; but when the appointed moment comes, when now it is time for the swelling clusters to be sweetened by the sun, behold, it drops a leaf and then a leaf, so teaching us to strip it bare itself and let the vintage ripen. With plenty teeming, see the fertile mother shows her mellow clusters, and the while is nursing a new brood in primal crudeness.[1080] So the vine plant teaches us how best to gather in the vintage, even as men gather figs, the juiciest first.[1081]

[1074] Or, "a series of resemblances," "close parallels," reading (epideiknus): or if with Breit. (apodeiknus), transl. "by proving such or such a thing is like some other thing known to me already."

[1075] Lit. "whether it is good or not."

[1076] Or, "since you actually succeeded in persuading me I was scientifically versed in," etc. See Plat. *Statesm.* 301 B; *Theaet.* 208 E; Aristot. *An. Post.* i. 6. 4; *Categ.* 8. 41.

[1077] Or, "gives them at once a perfect knowledge of herself."

[1078] Lit. "best to deal with her," "make use of her."

[1079] Lit. "teaches us to prop it."

[1080] Lit. "yet immature."

[1081] Or, "first one and then another as it swells." Cf. Shakespeare:

> The mellow plum doth fall, the green sticks fast,
> Or being early pluck'd is sour to taste ("V. and A." 527).

XX

At this point in the conversation I remarked: Tell me, Ischomachus, if the details of the art of husbandry are thus easy to learn, and all alike know what needs to be done, how does it happen that all farmers do not fare like, but some live in affluence owning more than they can possibly enjoy, while others of them fail to obtain the barest necessities and actually run into debt?

I will tell you, Socrates (Ischomachus replied). It is neither knowledge nor lack of knowledge in these husbandmen which causes some to be well off, while others are in difficulties; nor will you ever hear such tales afloat as that this or that estate has gone to ruin because the sower failed to sow evenly, or that the planter failed to plant straight rows of plants, or that such an one,[1082] being ignorant what soil was best suited to bear vines, had set his plants in sterile ground, or that another[1083] was in ignorance that fallow must be broken up for purposes of sowing, or that a third[1084] was not aware that it is good to mix manure in with the soil. No, you are much more likely to hear said of So-and-so: No wonder the man gets in no wheat from his farm, when he takes no pains to have it sown or properly manured. Or of some other that he grows no wine: Of course not, when he takes no pains either to plant new vines or to make those he has bear fruit. A third has neither figs nor olives; and again the self-same reason: He too is careless, and takes no steps whatever to succeed in growing either one or other. These are the distinctions which make all the difference to prosperity in farming, far more than the reputed discovery of any clever agricultural method or machine.[1085]

You will find the principle applies elsewhere. There are points of strategic conduct in which generals differ from each other for the better or the worse, not because they differ in respect of wit or judgment, but of carefulness undoubtedly. I speak of things within the cognisance of every general, and indeed of almost every private soldier, which some commanders are careful to perform and others not. Who does not know, for instance, that in marching through a hostile territory an army ought to march in the order best adapted to deliver battle with effect should need arise?[1086]—a golden rule which, punctually obeyed by some, is disobeyed by others. Again, as all the world knows, it is better to place

---

[1082] "Squire This."
[1083] "Squire That."
[1084] "Squire T'other."
[1085] There is something amiss with the text at this point. For emendations see Breit., Schenkl, Holden, Hartman.
[1086] See Thuc. ii. 81: "The Hellenic troops maintained order on the march and kept a look-out until..."—Jowett.

day and night pickets[1087] in front of an encampment. Yet even that is a procedure which, carefully observed at times, is at times as carelessly neglected. Once more: not one man in ten thousand,[1088] I suppose, but knows that when a force is marching through a narrow defile, the safer method is to occupy beforehand certain points of vantage.[1089] Yet this precaution also has been known to be neglected.

Similarly, every one will tell you that manure is the best thing in the world for agriculture, and every one can see how naturally it is produced. Still, though the method of production is accurately known, though there is every facility to get it in abundance, the fact remains that, while one man takes pains to have manure collected, another is entirely neglectful. And yet God sends us rain from heaven, and every hollow place becomes a standing pool, while earth supplies materials of every kind; the sower, too, about to sow must cleanse the soil, and what he takes as refuse from it needs only to be thrown into water and time itself will do the rest, shaping all to gladden earth.[1090] For matter in every shape, nay earth itself,[1091] in stagnant water turns to fine manure.

So, again, as touching the various ways in which the earth itself needs treatment, either as being too moist for sowing, or too salt[1092] for planting, these and the processes of cure are known to all men: how in one case the superfluous water is drawn off by trenches, and in the other the salt corrected by being mixed with various non-salt bodies, moist or dry. Yet here again, in spite of knowledge, some are careful of these matters, others negligent.

But even if a man were altogether ignorant what earth can yield, were he debarred from seeing any fruit or plant, prevented hearing from the lips of any one the truth about this earth: even so, I put it to you, it would be easier far for any living soul to make experiments on a piece of land,[1093] than on a horse, for instance, or on his fellow-man. For there is nought which earth displays with intent to deceive, but in clear and simple language stamped with the seal of truth she informs us what she can and cannot do.[1094] Thus it has ever seemed to me that earth is

---

[1087] See *Cyrop.* I. vi. 43.
[1088] Lit. "it would be hard to find the man who did not know."
[1089] Or, "to seize advantageous positions in advance." Cf. *Hiero,* x. 5.
[1090] Lit. "Time itself will make that wherein Earth rejoices."
[1091] *i.e.* "each fallen leaf, each sprig or spray of undergrowth, the very weeds, each clod." Lit. "what kind of material, what kind of soil does not become manure when thrown into stagnant water?"
[1092] See Anatol. *Geop.* ii. 10. 9; Theophr. *de Caus.* ii. 5. 4, 16. 8, ap. Holden. Cf. Virg. *Georg.* ii. 238:

> salsa autem tellus, et quae perhibetur amara
> frugibus infelix.

[1093] Or, "this fair earth herself."
[1094] Or, "earth our mother reveals her powers and her impotence."

the best discoverer of true honesty,[1095] in that she offers all her stores of knowledge in a shape accessible to the learner, so that he who runs may read. Here it is not open to the sluggard, as in other arts, to put forward the plea of ignorance or lack of knowledge, for all men know that earth, if kindly treated, will repay in kind. No! there is no witness[1096] against a coward soul so clear as that of husbandry;[1097] since no man ever yet persuaded himself that he could live without the staff of life. He therefore that is unskilled in other money-making arts and will not dig, shows plainly he is minded to make his living by picking and stealing, or by begging alms, or else he writes himself down a very fool.[1098]

Presently, Ischomachus proceeded: Now it is of prime importance,[1099] in reference to the profitableness or unprofitableness of agriculture, even on a large estate where there are numerous[1100] workfolk,[1101] whether a man takes any pains at all to see that his labourers are devoted to the work on hand during the appointed time,[1102] or whether he neglects that duty. Since one man will fairly distance ten[1103] simply by working at the time, and another may as easily fall short by leaving off before the hour.[1104] In fact, to let the fellows take things easily the whole day through will make a difference easily of half in the whole work.[1105]

As, on a walking-expedition, it may happen, of two wayfarers, the one will gain in pace upon the other half the distance say in every five-and-twenty miles,[1106] though both alike are young and hale of body. The one, in fact, is bent on compassing the work on which he started, he steps out gaily and unflinchingly; the other, more slack in spirit, stops to recruit himself and contemplate the view by fountain side and shady nook, as though his object were to court each gentle zephyr. So in farm work; there is a vast difference as regards performance between those who do it not, but seek excuse for idleness and are suffered to be listless. Thus, between good honest work and base neglect there is as great a difference as there is between—what shall I say?—why, work

---

[1095] Lit. "of the good and the bad." Cf. Dem. *adv. Phorm.* 918. 18.
[1096] Lit. "no accuser of." Cf. Aesch. *Theb.* 439.
[1097] Reading, with Sauppe, (all' e georgia), or if, with Jacobs, (e en georgia argia), transl. "as that of idleness in husbandry."
[1098] Or, "if not, he must be entirely irrational." Cf. Plat. *Apol.* 37 C.
[1099] Lit. "it made a great difference, he said, with regard to profit and loss in agriculture."
[1100] Or if, after Hertlein, adding (kai meionon), transl. "workmen now more, now less, in number."
[1101] (ergasteron), "poet." L. & S. cf. *Orph. H.* 65. 4. See above, v. 15; xiii. 10.
[1102] Cf. Herod. II. ii. 2.
[1103] Or, "Why! one man in ten makes all the difference by..." (para) = "by comparison with."
[1104] Reading as vulg., or if (to me pro k.t.l.) transl. "by not leaving off, etc."
[1105] *i.e.* "is a difference of fifty per cent on the whole work."
[1106] Lit. "per 200 stades."

and idleness.[1107] The gardeners, look, are hoeing vines to keep them clean and free of weeds; but they hoe so sorrily that the loose stuff grows ranker and more plentiful. Can you call that[1108] anything but idleness?

Such, Socrates, are the ills which cause a house to crumble far more than lack of scientific knowledge, however rude it be.[1109] For if you will consider; on the one hand, there is a steady outflow[1110] of expenses from the house, and, on the other, a lack of profitable works outside to meet expenses; need you longer wonder if the field-works create a deficit and not a surplus? In proof, however, that the man who can give the requisite heed, while straining every nerve in the pursuit of agriculture, has speedy[1111] and effective means of making money, I may cite the instance of my father, who had practised what he preached.[1112]

Now, my father would never suffer me to purchase an estate already under cultivation, but if he chanced upon a plot of land which, owing to the neglect or incapacity of the owner, was neither tilled nor planted,[1113] nothing would satisfy him but I must purchase it. He had a saying that estates already under cultivation cost a deal of money and allowed of no improvement; and where there is no prospect of improvement, more than half the pleasure to be got from the possession vanishes. The height of happiness was, he maintained, to see your purchase, be it dead chattel or live animal,[1114] go on improving daily under your own eyes.[1115] Now, nothing shows a larger increase[1116] than a piece of land reclaimed from barren waste and bearing fruit a hundredfold. I can assure you, Socrates, many is the farm which my father and I made worth I do not know how many times more than its original value. And then, Socrates, this valuable invention[1117] is so easy

---

[1107] Or, "wholly to work and wholly to be idle." Reading as Sauppe, etc., or if with Holden, etc., (to de de kalos kai to kakos ergazesthai e epimeleisthai), transl. "between toil and carefulness well or ill expended there lies all the difference; the two things are sundered as wide apart as are the poles of work and play," etc. A. Jacobs' emend. ap. Hartm. *An. Xen.* p. 211, (to de de kakos ergazesthai e kakos epimeleisthai kei to kalos), seems happy.

[1108] Or, "such a hoer aught but an idle loon."

[1109] Cf. Thuc. v. 7; Plat. *Rep.* 350 A; *Theaet.* 200 B.

[1110] Or, "the expenses from the house are going on at the full rate," (enteleis). Holden cf. Aristoph. *Knights*, 1367: (ton misthon apodoso 'ntele), "I'll have the arrears of seamen's wages paid *to a penny*" (Frere).

[1111] (anutikotaten). Cf. *Hipparch*, ii. 6.

[1112] Or, "who merely taught me what he had himself carried out in practice."

[1113] *i.e.* out of cultivation, whether as corn land or for fruit trees, viz. olive, fig, vine, etc.

[1114] Or, "be it a dead thing or a live pet." Cf. Plat. *Theaet.* 174 B; *Laws*, 789 B, 790 D, 819 B; "C. I." 1709.

[1115] Cf. *Horsem.* iii. 1; and see Cowley's Essay above referred to.

[1116] Or, "is susceptible of greater improvement."

[1117] Or, "discovery." See *Anab.* III. v. 12; *Hell.* IV. v. 4; *Hunting*, xiii. 13.

to learn that you who have but heard it know and understand it as well as I myself do, and can go away and teach it to another if you choose. Yet my father did not learn it of another, nor did he discover it by a painful mental process;[1118] but, as he has often told me, through pure love of husbandry and fondness of toil, he would become enamoured of such a spot as I describe,[1119] and then nothing would content him but he must own it, in order to have something to do, and at the same time, to derive pleasure along with profit from the purchase. For you must know, Socrates, of all Athenians I have ever heard of, my father, as it seems to me, had the greatest love for agricultural pursuits.

When I heard this, I could not resist asking a question; Ischomachus (I said), did your father retain possession of all the farms he put under cultivation, or did he part with them whenever he was offered a good price?

He parted with them, without a doubt (replied Ischomachus), but then at once he bought another in the place of what he sold, and in every case an untilled farm, in order to gratify his love for work.

As you describe him (I proceeded), your father must truly have been formed by nature with a passion for husbandry, not unlike that corn-hunger which merchants suffer from. You know their habits: by reason of this craving after corn,[1120] whenever they hear that corn is to be got, they go sailing off to find it, even if they must cross the Aegean, or the Euxine, or the Sicilian seas. And when they have got as much as ever they can get, they will not let it out of their sight, but store it in the vessel on which they sail themselves, and off they go across the seas again.[1121] Whenever they stand in need of money, they will not discharge their precious cargo,[1122] at least not in haphazard fashion, wherever they may chance to be; but first they find out where corn is at the highest value, and where the inhabitants will set the greatest store by it, and there they take and deliver the dear article. Your father's fondness for agriculture seems to bear a certain family resemblance to this passion.

To these remarks Ischomachus replied: You jest, Socrates; but still I hold to my belief: that man is fond of bricks and mortar who no sooner has built one house than he must needs sell it and proceed to build another.

To be sure, Ischomachus (I answered), and for my part I assure

---

[1118] Or, "nor did he rack his brains to discover it." See *Mem.* III. v. 23. Cf. Aristoph. *Clouds*, 102, (merimnophrontistai), minute philosophers.

[1119] "He could not see an estate of the sort described but he must fall over head and ears in love with it at first sight; have it he must."

[1120] Lit. "of their excessive love for corn."

[1121] Lit. "they carry it across the seas again, and that, too, after having stored it in the hold of the very vessel in which they sail themselves."

[1122] Or, "their treasure." (auton) throughout, which indeed is the humour of the passage. The love of John Barleycorn is their master passion.

you, upon oath, I, Socrates, do verily and indeed believe[1123] you that all men by nature love (or hold they ought to love) those things wherebysoever they believe they will be benefited.

XXI

After a pause, I added: I am turning over in my mind how cleverly you have presented the whole argument to support your thesis: which was, that of all arts the art of husbandry is the easiest to learn. And now, as the result of all that has been stated, I am entirely persuaded that this is so.

Isch. Yes, Socrates, indeed it is. But I, on my side, must in turn admit that as regards that faculty which is common alike to every kind of conduct (tillage, or politics, the art of managing a house, or of conducting war), the power, namely, of command[1124]—I do subscribe to your opinion, that on this score one set of people differ largely from another both in point of wit and judgment. On a ship of war, for instance,[1125] the ship is on the high seas, and the crew must row whole days together to reach moorings.[1126] Now note the difference. Here you may find a captain[1127] able by dint of speech and conduct to whet the souls of those he leads, and sharpen them to voluntary toils; and there another so dull of wit and destitute of feeling that it will take his crew just twice the time to finish the same voyage. See them step on shore. The first ship's company are drenched in sweat; but listen, they are loud in praise of one another, the captain and his merry men alike. And the others? They are come at last; they have not turned a hair, the lazy fellows, but for all that they hate their officer and by him are hated.

Generals, too, will differ (he proceeded), the one sort from the other, in this very quality. Here you have a leader who, incapable of kindling a zest for toil and love of hairbreadth 'scapes, is apt to engender in his followers that base spirit which neither deigns nor chooses to obey, except under compulsion. They even pride and plume themselves,[1128] the cowards, on their opposition to their leader; this same leader who, in the end, will make his men insensible to shame even in presence of most foul mishap. On the other hand, put at their

---

[1123] Reading (e men pisteuein soi phusei (nomizein) philein tauta pantas...); and for the "belief" propounded with so much humorous emphasis, see Adam Smith, *Moral Sentiments*. Hartman, "An. Xen." 180, cf. Plat. *Lysis*.

[1124] See *Mem.* I. i. 7.

[1125] Or, "the crew must row the livelong day..."

[1126] For an instance see *Hell.* VI. ii. 27, Iphicrates' periplûs.

[1127] Or, "one set of boatswains." See Thuc. ii. 84. For the duties of the *Keleustês* see *Dict. Gk. Rom. Ant.* s.v. *portisculus*; and for the type of captain see *Hell.* V. i. 3, Teleutias.

[1128] Lit. "magnify themselves." See *Ages.* x. 2; *Pol. Lac.* viii. 2.

Xenophon 219

head another stamp of general: one who is by right divine[1129] a leader, good and brave, a man of scientific knowledge. Let him take over to his charge those malcontents, or others even of worse character, and he will have them presently ashamed of doing a disgraceful deed. "It is nobler to obey" will be their maxim. They will exult in personal obedience and in common toil, where toil is needed, cheerily performed. For just as an unurged zeal for voluntary service[1130] may at times invade, we know, the breasts of private soldiers, so may like love of toil with emulous longing to achieve great deeds of valour under the eyes of their commander, be implanted in whole armies by good officers.

Happy must that leader be whose followers are thus attached to him: beyond all others he will prove a stout and strong commander. And by strong, I mean, not one so hale of body as to tower above the stoutest of the soldiery themselves; no, nor him whose skill to hurl a javelin or shoot an arrow will outshine the skilfullest; nor yet that mounted on the fleetest charger it shall be his to bear the brunt of danger foremost amid the knightliest horsemen, the nimblest of light infantry. No, not these, but who is able to implant a firm persuasion in the minds of all his soldiers: follow him they must and will through fire, if need be, or into the jaws of death.[1131]

Lofty of soul and large of judgment[1132] may he be designated justly, at whose back there steps a multitude stirred by his sole sentiment; not unreasonably may he be said to march "with a mighty arm,"[1133] to whose will a thousand willing hands are prompt to

---

[1129] Or, "god-like," "with something more than human in him." See Hom. *Il.* xxiv. 259:

(oude eokei andros ge thnetou pais emmenai alla theoio.)

Od. iv. 691; (theioi basilees). Cf. Carlyle, *Heroes*; Plat. *Meno*, 99 D: Soc. And may we not, Meno, truly call those men divine who, having no understanding, yet succeed in many a grand deed and word?" And below: *Soc.* "And the women too, Meno, call good men divine; and the Spartans, when they praise a good man, say, 'that he is a divine man'" (Jowett). Arist. *Eth. N.* vii. 1: "That virtue which transcends the human, and which is of an heroic or godlike type, such as Priam, in the poems of Homer, ascribes to Hector, when wishing to speak of his great goodness:

Not woman-born seemed he, but sprung from gods."

And below: "And exactly as it is a rare thing to find a man of godlike nature—to use the expression of the Spartans, 'a godlike man,' which they apply to those whom they expressively admire—so, too, brutality is a type of character rarely found among men" (Robert Williams).

[1130] Reading (etheloponia tis), or if (philoponia), transl. "just as some strange delight in labour may quicken in the heart of many an individual soldier." See *Anab.* IV. vii. 11.

[1131] Or, "through flood and fire or other desperate strait." Cf. *Anab.* II. vi. 8.

[1132] See *Ages.* ix. 6, "of how lofty a sentiment."

[1133] See Herod. vii. 20, 157; Thuc. iii. 96.

minister; a great man in every deed he is who can achieve great ends by resolution rather than brute force.

So, too, within the field of private industry, the person in authority, be it the bailiff, be it the overseer,[1134] provided he is able to produce unflinching energy, intense and eager, for the work, belongs to those who haste to overtake good things[1135] and reap great plenty. Should the master (he proceeded), being a man possessed of so much power, Socrates, to injure the bad workman and reward the zealous—should he suddenly appear, and should his appearance in the labour field produce no visible effect upon his workpeople, I cannot say I envy or admire him. But if the sight of him is followed by a stir of movement, if there come upon[1136] each labourer fresh spirit, with mutual rivalry and keen ambition, drawing out the finest qualities of each,[1137] of him I should say, Behold a man of kingly disposition. And this, if I mistake not, is the quality of greatest import in every operation which needs the instrumentality of man; but most of all, perhaps, in agriculture. Not that I would maintain that it is a thing to be lightly learnt by a glance of the eye, or hearsay fashion, as a tale that is told. Far from it, I assert that he who is to have this power has need of education; he must have at bottom a good natural disposition; and, what is greatest of all, he must be himself a god-like being.[1138] For if I rightly understand this blessed gift, this faculty of command over willing followers, by no means is it, in its entirety, a merely human quality, but it is in part divine. It is a gift plainly given to those truly initiated[1139] in the mystery of self-command. Whereas despotism over unwilling slaves, the heavenly ones give, as it seems to me, to those whom they deem worthy to live the life of Tantalus in Hades, of whom it is written[1140] "he consumes unending days in apprehension of a second death."

[1134] According to Sturz, "Lex." s.v., the (epitropos) is (as a rule, see *Mem*. II. viii.) a slave or freedman, the (epistates) a free man. See *Mem*. III. v. 18.

[1135] Apparently a homely formula, like "make hay whilst the sun shines," "a stitch in time saves nine."

[1136] Cf. Hom. *Il*. ix. 436, xvii. 625; *Hell*. VII. i. 31.

[1137] Reading (kratiste ousa), or if with Heindorf, (kratisteusai), transl. "to prove himself the best."

[1138] See *Cyrop*. I. i. 3; Grote, *Plato*, vol. iii. 571.

[1139] See Plat. *Phaed*. 69 C; Xen. *Symp*. i. 10.

[1140] Or, "it is said." See Eur. *Orest*. 5, and Porson *ad loc.*

The Symposium

OR, THE BANQUET

I

For myself,[1141] I hold to the opinion that not alone are the serious transactions of "good and noble men"[1142] most memorable, but that words and deeds distinctive of their lighter moods may claim some record.[1143] In proof of which contention, I will here describe a set of incidents within the scope of my experience.[1144]

The occasion was a horse-race[1145] at the great Panathenaic festival.[1146] Callias,[1147] the son of Hipponicus, being a friend and lover of the boy Autolycus,[1148] had brought the lad, himself the winner of the pankration,[1149] to see the spectacle.

As soon as the horse race was over,[1150] Callias proceeded to escort Autolycus and his father, Lycon, to his house in the Piraeus, being attended also by Nicêratus.[1151] But catching sight of Socrates along with certain others (Critobulus,[1152] Hermogenes, Antisthenes, and Charmides), he bade an attendant conduct the party with Autolycus, whilst he himself approached the group, exclaiming:

A happy chance brings me across your path, just when I am about to entertain Autolycus and his father at a feast. The splendour of the entertainment shall be much enhanced, I need not tell you, if my hall[1153] should happily be graced by worthies like yourselves, who have

---

[1141] See Aristid. ii. foll.

[1142] Or, "nature's noblemen."

[1143] Cf. Plut. Ages. 29 (Clough, iv. 35): "And indeed if, as Xenophon says, in conversation good men, even in their sports and at their wine, let fall many sayings that are worth preserving." See Grote, Plato, ii. 228 foll. as to the sportive character of the work.

[1144] Or, "let me describe a scene which I was witness of." See Hug. Plat. Symp. p. xv. foll.

[1145] See Hipparch, ii. 1.

[1146] "Held towards the end of July (Hecatombaeon) every year, and with greater pomp every four years (the third of each Olympiad)."—Gow, 84, 129, n.

[1147] Callias. Cobet, Pros. X. p. 67 foll.; Boeckh, P. E. A. p. 481.

[1148] See Cobet, op. cit. p. 54; Plut. Lysand. 15 (Clough, iii. 120); Grote, H. G. ix. 261.

[1149] 420 B.C., al. 421. The date is fixed by the Autolycus of Eupolis. See Athen. v. 216. For the pankration, which comprised wrestling and boxing, see Aristot. Rhet. i. § 14.

[1150] See A. Martin, op. cit. p. 265.

[1151] Nicêratus. See Cobet, op. cit. 71; Boeckh, P. E. A. 480; Plat. Lach. 200 C; Hell. II. iii. 39; Lys. xviii.; Diod. xiv. 5.

[1152] Critobulus, Hermogenes, Antisthenes, Charmides. See Mem.

[1153] Or, "dining-room." See Becker, Charicles, 265.

attained to purity of soul,[1154] rather than by generals and cavalry commanders[1155] and a crowd of place-hunters.[1156]

Whereat Socrates: When will you have done with your gibes, Callias? Why, because you have yourself spent sums of money on Protagoras,[1157] and Gorgias, and Prodicus, and a host of others, to learn wisdom, must you pour contempt on us poor fellows, who are but self-taught tinkers[1158] in philosophy compared with you?

Hitherto, no doubt (retorted Callias), although I had plenty of wise things to say, I have kept my wisdom to myself; but if only you will honour me with your company to-day, I promise to present myself in quite another light; you will see I am a person of no mean consideration after all.[1159]

Socrates and the others, while thanking Callias politely for the invitation, were not disposed at first to join the dinner party; but the annoyance of the other so to be put off was so obvious that in the end the party were persuaded to accompany their host.

After an interval devoted to gymnastic exercise (and subsequent anointing of the limbs) by some, whilst others of them took a bath, the guests were severally presented to the master of the house.

Autolycus was seated next his father, as was natural,[1160] while the rest reclined on couches. Noting the scene presented, the first idea to strike the mind of any one must certainly have been that beauty has by nature something regal in it; and the more so, if it chance to be combined (as now in the person of Autolycus) with modesty and self-respect. Even as when a splendid object blazes forth at night, the eyes of men are riveted,[1161] so now the beauty of Autolycus drew on him the gaze of all; nor was there one of those onlookers but was stirred to his soul's depth by him who sat there.[1162] Some fell into unwonted silence, while the gestures of the rest were equally significant.

It seems the look betokening divine possession, no matter who the god, must ever be remarkable. Only, whilst the subject of each commoner emotion passion-whirled may be distinguished by flashings of the eye, by terror-striking tones of voice, and by the vehement

---

[1154] See Grote, *H. G.* viii. 619 foll. Cf. Plat. *Rep.* 527 D; *Soph.* 230 E.

[1155] Lit. *Stratêgoi, Hipparchs*.

[1156] Or, "petitioners for offices of state." Reading (spoudarkhiais).

[1157] As to Protagoras of Abdera, Gorgias of Leontini, Prodicus of Ceos, see Plat. *Prot.* 314 C, *Rep.* x. 600 C, *Apol.* 19 E; *Anab.* II. vi. 17; *Mem.* II. i. 21; *Encyc. Brit.* "Sophists," H. Jackson.

[1158] Or, "hand-to-mouth cultivators of philosophy," "roturiers." Cf. Plat. *Rep.* 565 A: "A third class who work for themselves"; Thuc. i. 141: "The Peloponnesians cultivate their own soil, and they have no wealth either public or private." Cf. *Econ.* v. 4.

[1159] Or, "I will prove to you that I am worthy of infinite respect."

[1160] *Al.* "Autolycus found a seat beside his father, while the rest reclined on couches in the usual fashion." See Schneider's note.

[1161] Passage imitated by Max. Tyr. *Or.* xxiv. 4.

[1162] Cf. Plat. *Charm.* 154.

fervour of the man's whole being, so he who is inspired by temperate and harmonious love[1163] will wear a look of kindlier welcome in his eyes; the words he utters fall from his lips with softer intonation; and every gesture of his bodily frame conform to what is truly frank and liber*al*. Such, at any rate, the strange effects now wrought on Callias by love. He was like one transformed, the cynosure of all initiated in the mysteries of this divinity.[1164]

So they supped in silence, the whole company, as if an injunction had been laid upon them by some superior power. But presently there came a knocking on the door! *Philippus the jester* bade the doorkeeper[1165] announce him, *with apologies for seeking a night's lodging:*[1166] *he had come, he said, provided with all necessaries for dining, at a friend's expense: his attendant was much galled with carrying, nothing but an empty bread-basket.*[1167] To this announcement Callias, appealing to his guests, replied: "It would never do to begrudge the shelter of one's roof:[1168] let him come in." And as he spoke, he glanced across to where Autolycus was seated, as if to say: "I wonder how you take the jest."

Meanwhile the jester, standing at the door of the apartment where the feast was spread, addressed the company:

I believe you know, sirs, that being a jester by profession, it is my business to make jokes. I am all the readier, therefore, to present myself, feeling convinced it is a better joke to come to dinner thus unbidden than by solemn invitation.

Be seated,[1169] then (replied the host). The company are fully fed on serious thoughts, you see, if somewhat starved of food for laughter.

The feast proceeded; and, if only to discharge the duty laid upon him at a dinner-party, Philippus must try at once to perpetrate a jest. Failing to stir a smile, poor fellow, he made no secret of his perturbation. Presently he tried again; and for the second time the joke fell flat. Whereat he paused abruptly in the middle of the course, and muffling up his face, fell prostrate on the couch.

Then Callias: What ails you, sirrah? Have you the cramp? the toothache? what?

To which the other heaving a deep groan: Yes, Callias, an

[1163] Cf. Plat. *Rep.* iii. 403 A: "Whereas true love is a love of beauty and order, temperate and harmonious."

[1164] Cf. *Econ.* xxi. 12.

[1165] Lit. "him who answers the knock," "the *concierge*" or hall-porter. Cf. Theophr. *Char.* xiv. 7; Aristot. *Oec.* i. 6.

[1166] Lit. "and why he wished to put up."

[1167] Lit. "and being breakfastless"; cf. Theocr. i. 51. The jester's humour resembles Pistol's (*Merry Wives*, i. 3. 23) "O base Hungarian wight!"

[1168] Or, "How say you, my friends, it would hardly do, methinks, to shut the door upon him." See Becker, *Charicles*, p. 92.

[1169] Lit. "Pray, find a couch then."

atrocious ache; since laughter has died out among mankind, my whole estate is bankrupt.[1170] In old days I would be asked to dinner to amuse the company with jests.[1171] Now all is changed, and who will be at pains to ask me out to dinner any more? I might as well pretend to be immortal as to be serious. Nor will any one invite me in hopes of reclining at my board in his turn. Everyone knows so serious a thing as dinner in my house was never heard of; it's against the rules—the more's the pity.

And as he spoke he blew his nose and snuffled, uttering the while so truly dolorous a moan[1172] that everybody fell to soothing him. "They would all laugh again another day," they said, and so implored him to have done and eat his dinner; till Critobulus could not stand his lamentation longer, but broke into a peal of laughter. The welcome sound sufficed. The sufferer unveiled his face, and thus addressed his inner self:[1173] "Be of good cheer, my soul, there are many battles[1174] yet in store for us," and so he fell to discussing the viands once again.

II

Now the tables were removed, and in due order they had poured out the libation, and had sung the hymn.[1175] To promote the revelry, there entered now a Syracusan, with a trio of assistants: the first, a flute-girl, perfect in her art; and next, a dancing-girl, skilled to perform all kinds of wonders; lastly, in the bloom of beauty, a boy, who played the harp and danced with infinite grace. This Syracusan went about exhibiting his troupe, whose wonderful performance was a source of income to him.

[1170] Cf. *Cyrop.* VI. i. 3; Plat. *Laws*, 677 C.

[1171] Lit. "by the laughter which I stirred in them."

[1172] Philippus would seem to have anticipated Mr. Woodward; see Prologue to *She Stoops to Conquer*:

> Pray, would you know the reason I'm crying?
> The Comic Muse long sick is now a-dying!
> And if she goes...

[1173] Cf. *Cyrop.* I. iv. 13; Eur. *Med.* 1056, 1242; Aristoph. *Ach.* 357, 480.

[1174] Or add, "ere we have expended our last shot." Philippus puns on the double sense of (sumbolai). Cf. Aristoph. *Ach.* 1210, where Lamachus groans (talas ego xumboles bareias), and Dicaeopolis replies (tois Khousi gar tis xumbolas epratteto).

> *Lam.* 'Twas at the final charge; I'd paid before
> A number of the rogues; at least a score.
> *Dic.* It was a most expensive charge you bore:
> Poor Lamachus! he was forced to pay the score.
> H. Frere.

[1175] See Plat. *Symp.* 176 A; Athen. ix. 408.

After the girl had played to them upon the flute, and then the boy in turn upon the harp, and both performers, as it would appear, had set the hearts of every one rejoicing, Socrates turned to Callias:

A feast, upon my word, O princeliest entertainer![1176] Was it not enough to set before your guests a faultless dinner, but you must feast our eyes and ears on sights and sounds the most delicious?

To which the host: And that reminds me, a supply of unguents might not be amiss;[1177] what say you? Shall we feast on perfumes also?[1178]

No, I protest (the other answered). Scents resemble clothes. One dress is beautiful on man and one on woman; and so with fragrance: what becomes the woman, ill becomes the man. Did ever man anoint himself with oil of myrrh to please his fellow? Women, and especially young women (like our two friends' brides, Nicêratus' and Critobulus'), need no perfume, being but compounds themselves of fragrance.[1179] No, sweeter than any perfume else to women is good olive-oil, suggestive of the training-school:[1180] sweet if present, and when absent longed for. And why? Distinctions vanish with the use of perfumes. The freeman and the slave have forthwith both alike one odour. But the scents derived from toils—those toils which every free man loves[1181]—need customary habit first, and time's distillery, if they are to be sweet with freedom's breath, at last.[1182]

Here Lycon interposed: That may be well enough for youths, but what shall we do whose gymnastic days are over? What fragrance is left for us?

Soc. Why, that of true nobility, of course.

Lyc. And whence shall a man obtain this chrism?

Soc. Not from those that sell perfumes and unguents, in good sooth.

Lyc. But whence, then?

Soc. Theognis has told us:

> From the good thou shalt learn good things, but if with the evil
> Thou holdest converse, thou shalt lose the wit that is in thee.[1183]

[1176] Lit. "in consummate style."

[1177] Lit. "suppose I tell the servant to bring in some perfumes, so that we may further feast on fragrance..." Cf. Theophr. *Char.* vii. 6 (Jebb *ad loc.*)

[1178] See Athen. xv. 686.

[1179] Cf. Solomon's Song, iv. 10: "How fair is thy love, my sister, my spouse! how much better is thy love than wine! and the smell of thine ointments than all spices!"

[1180] Lit. "the gymnasium."

[1181] Cf. Aristoph. *Clouds,* 1002 foll. See J. A. Symonds, *The Greek Poets,* 1st s., p. 281.

[1182] See *Mem.* III. x. 5; *Cyrop.* VIII. i. 43.

[1183] Theog. 35 foll. See *Mem.* I. ii. 20; Plat. *Men.* 95 D.

Lyc. (turning to his son). Do you hear that, my son?

That he does (Socrates answered for the boy), and he puts the precept into practice also; to judge, at any rate, from his behaviour. When he had set his heart on carrying off the palm of victory in the pankration, he took you into his counsel;[1184] and will again take counsel to discover the fittest friend to aid him in his high endeavour,[1185] and with this friend associate.

Thereupon several of the company exclaimed at once. "Where will he find a teacher to instruct him in that wisdom?" one inquired. "Why, it is not to be taught!" exclaimed another; to which a third rejoined: "Why should it not be learnt as well as other things?"[1186]

Then Socrates: The question would seem at any rate to be debatable. Suppose we defer it till another time, and for the present not interrupt the programme of proceedings. I see, the dancing-girl is standing ready; they are handing her some hoops.

And at the instant her fellow with the flute commenced a tune to keep her company, whilst some one posted at her side kept handing her the hoops till she had twelve in all. With these in her hands she fell to dancing, and the while she danced she flung the hoops into the air— overhead she sent them twirling—judging the height they must be thrown to catch them, as they fell, in perfect time.[1187]

Then Socrates: The girl's performance is one proof among a host of others, sirs, that woman's nature is nowise inferior to man's. All she wants is strength and judgment;[1188] and that should be an encouragement to those of you who have wives, to teach them whatever you would have them know as your associates.[1189]

Antisthenes rejoined: If that is your conclusion, Socrates, why do you not tutor your own wife, Xanthippe,[1190] instead of letting her[1191] remain, of all the wives that are, indeed that ever will be, I imagine, the most shrewish?

[1184] It looks as if something had been lost intimating that Autolycus would have need of some one to instruct him in spiritual things. For attempts to fill up the lacuna see Schenkl.

[1185] Or, "these high pursuits."

[1186] Cf. for the question (ei arete didakton), *Mem.* I. ii. 19; IV. i; *Cyrop.* III. i. 17; III. iii. 53.

[1187] "In time with the music and the measure of the dance."

[1188] Reading, as vulg. (gnomes de kai iskhuos deitai); *al.* continuing (ouden) from the first half of the sentence, transl. "she has no lack of either judgment or physical strength." Lange conj. (romes) for (gnomes), "all she needs is force and strength of body." See Newman, *op. cit.* i. 419.

[1189] Lit. "so that, if any of you has a wife, he may well take heart and teach her whatever he would wish her to know in dealing with her." Cf. *N. A.* i. 17.

[1190] See Cobet, *Pros. Xen.* p. 56; *Mem.* II. ii. 1; Aul. Gell. *N. A.* i. 17.

[1191] Lit. "dealing with her," "finding in her"; (khro) corresponding to (khrethai) in Socrates' remarks.

Well now, I will tell you (he answered). I follow the example of the rider who wishes to become an expert horseman: "None of your soft-mouthed, docile animals for me," he says; "the horse for me to own must show some spirit":[1192] in the belief, no doubt, if he can manage such an animal, it will be easy enough to deal with every other horse besides. And that is just my case. I wish to deal with human beings, to associate with man in general; hence my choice of wife.[1193] I know full well, if I can tolerate her spirit, I can with ease attach myself to every human being else.

A well-aimed argument, not wide of the mark by any means![1194] the company were thinking.

Hereupon a large hoop studded with a bristling row of upright swords[1195] was introduced; and into the centre of this ring of knives and out of it again the girl threw somersaults backwards, forwards, several times, till the spectators were in terror of some accident; but with the utmost coolness and without mishap the girl completed her performance.

Here Socrates, appealing to Antisthenes: None of the present company, I take it, who have watched this spectacle will ever again deny that courage can be taught,[1196] when the girl there, woman should she be, rushes so boldly into the midst of swords.

He, thus challenged, answered: No; and what our friend, the Syracusan here, should do is to exhibit his dancing-girl to the state.[1197] Let him tell the authorities he is prepared, for a consideration, to give the whole Athenian people courage to face the hostile lances at close quarters.

Whereat the jester: An excellent idea, upon my word; and when it happens, may I be there to see that mighty orator[1198] Peisander learning to throw somersaults[1199] into swords; since incapacity to look a row of lances in the face at present makes him shy of military service.[1200]

[1192] Lit. "Because I see the man who aims at skill in horsemanship does not care to own a soft-mouthed, docile animal, but some restive, fiery creature."

[1193] Lit. "being anxious to have intercourse with all mankind, to deal with every sort of human being, I possess my wife."

[1194] Cf. Plat. *Theaet.* 179 C.

[1195] See Becker, *Char.* p. 101. Cf. Plat. *Symp.* 190; *Euthyd.* 294.

[1196] Cf. *Mem.* III. ix. 1.

[1197] Or, "to the city," *i.e.* of Athens.

[1198] Or, "tribune of the people." Cf. Plat. *Gorg.* 520 B; *Laws*, 908 D.

[1199] Or, "learning to go head over heels into swords."

[1200] For Peisander see Cobet, *Pros. Xen.* p. 46 foll. A thoroughgoing oligarch (Thuc. viii. 90), he was the occasion of much mirth to the comic writers (so Grote, *H. G.* viii. 12). See *re* his "want of spirit" Aristoph. *Birds,* 1556:

(entha kai Peisandros elthe
deomenos psukhen idein, e
zont ekeinon proulipe, k.t.l.)

At this stage of the proceedings the boy danced.

The dance being over, Socrates exclaimed: Pray, did you notice how the beauty of the child, so lovely in repose, became enhanced with every movement of his supple body?

To which Charmides replied: How like a flatterer you are! one would think you had set yourself to puff the dancing-master.[1201]

To be sure (he answered solemnly); and there's another point I could not help observing: how while he danced no portion of his body remained idle; neck and legs and hands together, one and all were exercised.[1202] That is how a man should dance, who wants to keep his body light and healthy.[1203] (Then turning to the Syracusan, he added): I cannot say how much obliged I should be to you, O man of Syracuse, for lessons in deportment. Pray teach me my steps.[1204]

And what use will you make of them? (the other asked).

God bless me! I shall dance, of course (he answered).

The remark was greeted with a peal of merriment.

Then Socrates, with a most serious expression of countenance:[1205] You are pleased to laugh at me. Pray, do you find it so ridiculous my wishing to improve my health by exercise? or to enjoy my victuals better? to sleep better? or is it the sort of exercise I set my heart on? Not like those runners of the long race,[1206] to have my legs grow muscular and my shoulders leaner in proportion; nor like a boxer, thickening chest and shoulders at expense of legs; but by distribution of the toil throughout my limbs[1207] I seek to give an even balance to my body. Or are you laughing to think that I shall not in future have to seek

---

where the poet has a fling at Socrates also:

> Socrates beside the brink,
> Summons from the murky sink
> Many a disembodied ghost;
> *And Peisander reached the coast*
> *To raise the spirit that he lost;*
> With conviction strange and new,
> A gawky camel which he slew,
> Like Ulysses.—Whereupon, etc.
>   H. Frere

Cf. *Peace*, 395; *Lysistr.* 490.
   [1201] See "The Critic," I. ii.
   [1202] Cf. *Pol. Lac.* v. 9.
   [1203] Cf. Aristot. *H. A.* vi. 21. 4.
   [1204] "Gestures," "postures," "figures." See Eur. *Cycl.* 221; Aristoph. *Peace*, 323; Isocr. *Antid.* 183.
   [1205] "Bearing a weighty and serious brow."
   [1206] "Like your runner of the mile race." Cf. Plat. *Prot.* 335 E.
   [1207] Or, "resolute exercise of the whole body." See Aristot. *Pol.* viii. 4. 9; *Rhet.* i. 5. 14.

a partner in the training school,[1208] whereby it will not be necessary for an old man like myself to strip in public?[1209] All I shall need will be a seven-sofa'd chamber,[1210] where I can warm to work,[1211] just like the lad here who has found this room quite ample for the purpose. And in winter I shall do gymnastics[1212] under cover, or when the weather is broiling under shade.... But what is it you keep on laughing at—the wish on my part to reduce to moderate size a paunch a trifle too rotund? Is that the source of merriment?[1213] Perhaps you are not aware, my friends, that Charmides—yes! he there—caught me only the other morning in the act of dancing?

Yes, that I will swear to (the other answered), and at first I stood aghast, I feared me you had parted with your senses; but when I heard your explanation, pretty much what you have just now told us, I went home and—I will not say, began to dance myself (it is an accomplishment I have not been taught as yet), but I fell to sparring,[1214] an art of which I have a very pretty knowledge.

That's true, upon my life! (exclaimed the jester). One needs but look at you to see there's not a dram of difference between legs and shoulders.[1215] I'll be bound, if both were weighed in the scales apart, like "tops and bottoms," the clerks of the market[1216] would let you off scot-free.

Then Callias: O Socrates, do please invite me when you begin your dancing lessons. I will be your *vis-à-vis*,[1217] and take lessons with you.

Come on (the jester shouted), give us a tune upon the pipe, and let me show you how to dance.

So saying up he got, and mimicked the dances of the boy and girl in burlesque fashion, and inasmuch as the spectators had been pleased to think the natural beauty of the boy enhanced by every gesture of his body in the dance, so the jester must give a counter-representation,[1218]

[1208] Or, "be dependent on a fellow-gymnast." *Pol. Lac.* ix. 5; Plat. *Soph.* 218 B; *Laws,* 830 B; *Symp.* 217 B, C.

[1209] Or, "to strip in public when my hair turns gray." Socrates was (421 B.C.) about 50, but is pictured, I think, as an oldish man.

[1210] See Aristot. *H. A.* ix. 45. 1; *Econ.* viii. 13.

[1211] Passage referred to by Diog. Laert. ii. 5. 15; Lucian, *de Salt.* 25; Plut. *Praec. San.* 496.

[1212] "Take my exercise."

[1213] Zeune cf. Max. Tyr. *Diss.* vii. 9; xxxix. 5.

[1214] "Sparring," etc., an art which Quintil. *Inst. Or.* i. 11, 17, attributes to Socrates. Cf. Herod. vi. 129 concerning Hippocleides; and Rich, *Dict. of Antiq.* s.v. *Chironomia.*

[1215] Lit. "your legs are equal in weight with your shoulders." Cf. *Od.* xviii. 373, (elikes... isophoroi boes), "of equal age and force to bear the yoke."—Butcher and Lang.

[1216] See Boeckh, *Public Economy of Athens,* p. 48; Aristoph. *Acharn.* 723; Lys. 165, 34.

[1217] Cf. *Anab.* V. iv. 12.

[1218] Reading (antepedeizen). Cf. Plat. *Theaet.* 162 B; *Ages.* i. 12; if vulg. (antapedeizen), transl. "would prove per contra each bend," etc. Cf. Aristot. *Rhet.* ii. 26. 3.

in which each twist and movement of his body was a comical exaggeration of nature.

And since the girl had bent herself backwards and backwards, till she was nearly doubled into the form of a hoop, so he must try to imitate a hoop by stooping forwards and ducking down his head.

And as finally, the boy had won a round of plaudits for the manner in which he kept each muscle of the body in full exercise whilst dancing, so now the jester, bidding the flute-girl quicken the time (*presto! presto! prestissimo!*), fell to capering madly, tossing legs and arms and head together, until he was fairly tired out, and threw himself dead beat upon the sofa, gasping:

There, that's a proof that my jigs too are splendid exercise; at any rate, I am dying of thirst; let the attendant kindly fill me the mighty goblet.[1219]

Quite right (said Callias), and we will pledge you. Our throats are parched with laughing at you.

At this point Socrates: Nay, gentlemen, if drinking is the order of the day, I heartily approve. Wine it is in very truth that moistens the soul of man,[1220] that lulls at once all cares to sleep, even as mandragora[1221] drugs our human senses, and at the same time kindles light-hearted thoughts,[1222] as oil a flame. Yet it fares with the banquets of men,[1223] if I mistake not, precisely as with plants that spring and shoot on earth. When God gives these vegetable growths too full a draught of rain, they cannot lift their heads nor feel the light air breathe through them; but if they drink in only the glad supply they need, they stand erect, they shoot apace, and reach maturity of fruitage. So we, too, if we drench our throats with over-copious draughts,[1224] ere long may find our legs begin to reel and our thoughts begin to falter;[1225] we shall scarce be able to draw breath, much less to speak a word in

---

[1219] Cf. Plat. *Symp.* 223 C.
[1220] Cf. Plat. *Laws*, 649; Aristoph. *Knights*, 96:

> Come, quick now, bring me a lusty stoup of wine,
> To moisten my understanding and inspire me (H. Frere).

[1221] Cf. Plat. *Rep.* vi. 488 C; Dem. *"Phil."* iv. 133. 1; Lucian v., "Tim." 2; lxxiii., "Dem. Enc." 36. See "Othello," iii. 3. 330:

> Not poppy, nor mandragora,
> Nor all the drowsy syrups of the world;
> *Antony and Cl.* i. 5, 4.

[1222] Cf. 1 Esdras iii. 20: "It turneth also every thought into jollity and mirth," (eis euokhian kai euphrosunen). The whole passage is quoted by Athen. 504. Stob. *Fl.* lvi. 17.
[1223] Reading (sumposia), cf. Theog. 298, 496; or if after Athen. (somata) transl. "persons."
[1224] Or, "if we swallow at a gulp the liquor." Cf. Plat. *Sym.* 176 D.
[1225] See *Cyrop.* I. iii. 10, VIII. viii. 10; Aristoph. *Wasps*, 1324; *Pol. Lac.* v. 7.

season. But if (to borrow language from the mint of Gorgias[1226]), if only the attendants will bedew us with a frequent mizzle[1227] of small glasses, we shall not be violently driven on by wine to drunkenness, but with sweet seduction reach the goal of sportive levity.

The proposition was unanimously carried, with a rider appended by Philippus: The cup-bearers should imitate good charioteers, and push the cups round, quickening the pace each circuit.[1228]

III

During this interval, whilst the cup-bearers carried out their duties, the boy played on the lyre tuned to accompany the flute, and sang.[1229]

The performance won the plaudits of the company, and drew from Charmides a speech as follows: Sirs, what Socrates was claiming in behalf of wine applies in my opinion no less aptly to the present composition. So rare a blending of boyish and of girlish beauty, and of voice with instrument, is potent to lull sorrow to sleep, and to kindle Aphrodite's flame.

Then Socrates, reverting in a manner to the charge: The young people have fully proved their power to give us pleasure. Yet, charming as they are, we still regard ourselves, no doubt, as much their betters. What a shame to think that we should here be met together, and yet make no effort ourselves to heighten the festivity![1230]

Several of the company exclaimed at once: Be our director then yourself. Explain what style of talk we should engage in to achieve that object.[1231]

Nothing (he replied) would please me better than to demand of Callias a prompt performance of his promise. He told us, you recollect, if we would dine with him, he would give us an exhibition of his wisdom.

To which challenge Callias: That I will readily, but you on your side, one and all, must propound some virtue of which you claim to have the knowledge.

[1226] For phrases filed by Gorgias, see Aristot. *Rhet.* iii. 3; "faults of taste in the use of metaphors," Longin. *de Subl.* 3. See also Plat. *Symp.* 198 C.

[1227] Cf. Aristoph. *Peace*, 1141; Theophr. *Lap.* 13; Lucian, xvii., *De merc. cond.* 27; Cic. *Cat. m.* 14, transl. "pocula... minuta atque rorantia."

[1228] Or, "at something faster than a hand-gallop each round." See the drinking song in *Antony and Cl.* i. 7. 120.

[1229] Cf. Plat. *Laws*, 812 C; Aristot. *Poet.* i. 4.

[1230] See Plat. *Prot.* 347 D; "A company like this of ours, and men such as we profess to be, do not require the help of another's voice," etc.—Jowett. Cf. id. *Symp.* 176: "To-day let us have conversation instead; and if you will allow me, I will tell you what sort of conversation."

[1231] (exegou). "Prescribe the form of words we must lay hold of to achieve the object, and we will set to work, arch-casuist."

Socrates replied: At any rate, not one of us will have the least objection to declaring what particular thing he claims to know as best worth having.

Agreed (proceeded Callias); and for my part I proclaim at once what I am proudest of. My firm belief is, I have got the gift to make my fellow-mortals better.

Make men better! (cried Antisthenes); and pray how? by teaching them some base mechanic art? or teaching them nobility of soul?[1232]

The latter (he replied), if justice[1233] be synonymous with that high type of virtue.

Of course it is (rejoined Antisthenes) the most indisputable specimen. Since, look you, courage and wisdom may at times be found calamitous to friends or country,[1234] but justice has no single point in common with injustice, right and wrong cannot commingle.[1235]

Well then (proceeded Callias), as soon[1236] as every one has stated his peculiar merit,[1237] I will make no bones of letting you into my secret. You shall learn the art by which I consummate my noble end.[1238] So now, Nicêratus, suppose you tell us on what knowledge you most pride yourself.

He answered: My father,[1239] in his pains to make me a good man, compelled me to learn the whole of Homer's poems, and it so happens that even now I can repeat the *Iliad* and the *Odyssey* by heart.[1240]

You have not forgotten (interposed Antisthenes), perhaps, that besides yourself there is not a rhapsodist who does not know these epics?

Forgotten! is it likely (he replied), considering I had to listen to them almost daily?

Ant. And did you ever come across a sillier tribe of people than these same rhapsodists?[1241]

Nic. Not I, indeed. Don't ask me to defend their wits.

It is plain (suggested Socrates), they do not know the underlying meaning.[1242] But you, Nicêratus, have paid large sums of money to Anaximander, and Stesimbrotus, and many others,[1243] so that no single

---

[1232] Or, "beauty and nobility of soul" (kalokagathia). See *Mem.* I. vi. 14.

[1233] *i.e.* "social uprightness."

[1234] See *Mem.* IV. ii. 33.

[1235] *i.e.* "the one excludes the other."

[1236] Reading (emon). *Al.* (umon), "when you others."

[1237] Lit. "what he has for which to claim utility."

[1238] Or, "give the work completeness." Cf. Plat. *Charm.* 173 A; *Gorg.* 454 A.

[1239] Nicias.

[1240] Of, "off-hand." See *Mem.* III. vi. 9; Plat. *Theaet.* 142 D.

[1241] Cf. *Mem.* IV. ii. 10.

[1242] *i.e.* "they haven't the key (of knowledge) to the allegorical or spiritual meaning of the sacred text." Cf. Plat. *Crat.* 407; *Ion,* 534; *Rep.* 378, 387; *Theaet.* 180; *Prot.* 316. See Grote, *H. G.* i. 564.

[1243] See Aristot. *Rhet.* iii. 11, 13. "Or we may describe Nicêratus (not improbably

point in all that costly lore is lost upon you.[1244] But what (he added, turning to Critobulus) do you most pride yourself upon?

On beauty (answered Critobulus).

What (Socrates rejoined), shall you be able to maintain that by your beauty you can make us better?

Crit. That will I, or prove myself a shabby sort of person.

Soc. Well, and what is it you pride yourself upon, Antisthenes?

On wealth (he answered).

Whereupon Hermogenes inquired: Had he then a large amount of money?[1245]

Not one sixpence:[1246] that I swear to you (he answered).

Herm. Then you possess large property in land?

Ant. Enough, I daresay, for the youngster there, Autolycus, to dust himself with*al*.[1247]

Well, we will lend you our ears, when your turn comes (exclaimed the others).

Soc. And do you now tell us, Charmides, on what you pride yourself.

Oh, I, for my part, pride myself on poverty (he answered).

Upon my word, a charming business! (exclaimed Socrates). Poverty! of all things the least liable to envy; seldom, if ever, an object of contention;[1248] never guarded, yet always safe; the more you starve it, the stronger it grows.

And you, Socrates, yourself (their host demanded), what is it you pride yourself upon?

Then he, with knitted brows, quite solemnly: On pandering.[1249] And when they laughed to hear him say this,[1250] he continued: Laugh to your hearts content, my friends; but I am certain I could make a fortune, if I chose to practise this same art.

---

our friend) as a 'Philoctetes stung by Pratys,' using the simile of Thrasymachus when he saw Nicêratus after his defeat by Pratys in the rhapsody with his hair still dishevelled and his face unwashed."—Welldon. As to Stesimbrotus, see Plat. *Ion*, 530: "Ion. Very true, Socrates; interpretation has certainly been the most laborious part of my art; and I believe myself able to speak about Homer better than any man; and that neither Metrodorus of Lampsacus, nor Stesimbrotus of Thasos, nor Glaucon, nor any one else who ever was, had as good ideas about Homer, or as many of them, as I have."—Jowett. Anaximander, probably of Lampsacus, the author of a ('Erologia); see Cobet, *Pros. Xen.* p. 8.

[1244] Or, "you will not have forgotten one point of all that precious teaching." Like Sir John Falstaff's page (2 "Henry IV." ii. 2. 100), Nicêratus, no doubt, has got many "a crown's worth of good interpretations."

[1245] *i.e.* "out at interest," or, "in the funds," as we should say.

[1246] Lit. "not an obol" = "a threepenny bit," circa.

[1247] *i.e.* "to sprinkle himself with sand, after anointing." Cf. Lucian, xxxviii., *Amor.* 45.

[1248] Cf. Plat. *Rep.* 521 A; *Laws*, 678 C.

[1249] Or, more politely, "on playing the go-between." See Grote, *H. G.* viii. 457, on the "extremely Aristophanic" character of the *Symposium* of Xenophon.

[1250] "*Him*, the master, thus declare himself."

At this point Lycon, turning to Philippus: We need not ask you what you take the chiefest pride in. What can it be, you laughter-making man, except to set folk laughing?

Yes (he answered), and with better right, I fancy, than Callippides,[1251] the actor, who struts and gives himself such pompous airs, to think that he alone can set the crowds a-weeping in the theatre.[1252]

And now you, Lycon, tell us, won't you (asked Antisthenes), what it is you take the greatest pride in?

You all of you, I fancy, know already what that is (the father answered); it is in my son here.

And the lad himself (some one suggested) doubtless prides himself, beyond all else, on having won the prize of victory.

At that Autolycus (and as he spoke he blushed) answered for himself:[1253] No indeed, not I.

The company were charmed to hear him speak, and turned and looked; and some one asked: On what is it then, Autolycus?

To which he answered: On my father (and leaned closer towards him).

At which sight Callias, turning to the father: Do you know you are the richest man in the whole world, Lycon?

To which Lycon: Really, I was not aware of that before.

Then Callias: Why then, it has escaped you that you would refuse the whole of Persia's wealth,[1254] in exchange for your own son.

Most true (he answered), I plead guilty; here and now I am convicted[1255] of being the wealthiest man in all the world!

And you, Hermogenes, on what do you plume yourself most highly? (asked Nicêratus).

On the virtue and the power of my friends (he answered), and that being what they are, they care for me.

At this remark they turned their eyes upon the speaker, and several spoke together, asking: Will you make them known to us?

I shall be very happy (he replied).

IV

At this point, Socrates took up the conversation: It now devolves on us to prove in turn that what we each have undertaken to defend is really valuable.

[1251] For illustrative tales about him see Plut. *Ages.* xxi.; *Alcib.* xxxii.; Polyaen. vi. 10. Cf. *Hell.* IV. viii. 16.

[1252] Or, "set for their sins a-weeping."

[1253] Cf. Plat. *Charm.* 158 C.

[1254] Lit. "of the Great King." Cf. *Cyrop.* VIII. iii. 26.

[1255] "Caught *flagrante delicto.* I do admit I do out-Croesus Croesus."

Then Callias: Be pleased to listen to me first: My case is this, that while the rest of you go on debating what justice and uprightness are,[1256] I spend my time in making men more just and upright.

Soc. And how do you do that, good sir?

Call. By giving money, to be sure.

Antisthenes sprang to his feet at once, and with the manner of a cross-examiner demanded: Do human beings seem to you to harbour justice in their souls, or in their purses,[1257] Callias?

Call. In their souls.

Ant. And do you pretend to make their souls more righteous by putting money in their pockets?

Call. Undoubtedly.

Ant. Pray how?

Call. In this way. When they know that they are furnished with the means, that is to say, my money, to buy necessaries, they would rather not incur the risk of evil-doing, and why should they?

Ant. And pray, do they repay you these same moneys?

Call. I cannot say they do.

Ant. Well then, do they requite your gifts of gold with gratitude?

Call. No, not so much as a bare "Thank you." In fact, some of them are even worse disposed towards me when they have got my money than before.

Now, here's a marvel! (exclaimed Antisthenes, and as he spoke he eyed the witness with an air of triumph). You can render people just to all the world, but towards yourself you cannot?

Pray, where's the wonder? (asked the other). Do you not see what scores of carpenters and house-builders there are who spend their time in building houses for half the world; but for themselves they simply cannot do it, and are forced to live in lodgings. And so admit that home-thrust, Master Sophist;[1258] and confess yourself confuted.

Upon my soul, he had best accept his fate[1259] (said Socrates). Why, after all, you are only like those prophets who proverbially foretell the future for mankind, but cannot foresee what is coming upon themselves.

And so the first discussion ended.[1260]

Thereupon Nicêratus: Lend me your ears, and I will tell you in what respects you shall be better for consorting with myself. I presume, without my telling you, you know that Homer, being the wisest of mankind, has touched upon nearly every human topic in his poems.[1261]

[1256] (to to dikaion); cf. *Mem.* IV. iv.
[1257] Or, "pockets."
[1258] "Professor of wisdom."
[1259] Or, "the *coup de grâce.*"
[1260] Or, "so ended fytte the first of the word-controversy."
[1261] Or, "his creations are all but coextensive with every mortal thing."

Whosoever among you, therefore, would fain be skilled in economy, or oratory, or strategy; whose ambition it is to be like Achilles, or Ajax, Nestor, or Odysseus—one and all pay court to me, for I have all this knowledge at my fingers' ends.

Pray (interposed Antisthenes),[1262] do you also know the way to be a king?[1263] since Homer praises Agamemnon, you are well aware, as being

> A goodly king and eke a spearman bold.[1264]

Nic. Full well I know it, and full well I know the duty of a skilful charioteer; how he who holds the ribbons must turn his chariot nigh the pillar's edge[1265]

> Himself inclined upon the polished chariot-board
> A little to the left of the twin pair: the right hand horse
> Touch with the prick, and shout a cheery shout, and give him rein.[1266]

I know another thing besides, and you may put it to the test this instant, if you like. Homer somewhere has said:[1267]

> And at his side an onion, which to drink gives relish.

So if some one will but bring an onion, you shall reap the benefit of my sage lore[1268] in less than no time, and your wine will taste the sweeter.

Here Charmides exclaimed: Good sirs, let me explain. Nicêratus is anxious to go home, redolent of onions, so that his fair lady may persuade herself, it never entered into anybody's head to kiss her lord.[1269]

Bless me, that isn't all (continued Socrates); if we do not take care, we shall win ourselves a comic reputation.[1270] A relish must it be, in

---

[1262] Some modern critics (*e.g.* F. Dummler, *Antisthenica*, p. 29 foll.) maintain plausibly that the author is here glancing (as also Plato in the *Ion*) at Antisthenes' own treatises against the Rhapsodists and on a more correct interpretation of Homer, (peri exegeton) and (peri 'Omerou).

[1263] Or, "Have you the knowledge also how to play the king?"

[1264] *Il.* iii. 179. See *Mem.* III. ii. 2.

[1265] *Il.* xxiii. 335; Plat. *Ion*, 537.

[1266] Lit. "yield him the reins with his hands."

[1267] *Il.* xi.630: "And set out a leek savourer of drink" (Purves). Plat. *Ion*, 538 C.

[1268] "My culinary skill."

[1269] See Shakesp. *Much Ado*, v. 2. 51 foll.; *Mids. N. D.* iv. 2.

[1270] Lit. "I warrant you! (quoth Socrates) and there's another funny notion we have every chance of getting fathered on us."

very truth, that can sweeten cup as well as platter, this same onion; and if we are to take to munching onions for desert, see if somebody does not say of us, "They went to dine with Callias, and got more than their deserts, the epicures."[1271]

No fear of that (rejoined Nicêratus). Always take a bite of onion before speeding forth to battle, just as your patrons of the cock-pit give their birds a feed of garlic[1272] before they put them for the fight. But for ourselves our thoughts are less intent perhaps on dealing blows than blowing kisses.[1273]

After such sort the theme of their discourse reached its conclusion.

Then Critobulus spoke: It is now my turn, I think, to state to you the grounds on which I pride myself on beauty.[1274]

A chorus of voices rejoined: Say on.

Crit. To begin with, if I am not beautiful, as methinks I be, you will bring on your own heads the penalty of perjury; for, without waiting to have the oath administered, you are always taking the gods to witness that you find me beautiful. And I must needs believe you, for are you not all honourable men?[1275] If I then be so beautiful and affect you, even as I also am affected by him whose fair face here attracts me,[1276] I swear by all the company of heaven I would not choose the great king's empire in exchange for what I am—the beauty of the world, the paragon of animals.[1277] And at this instant I feast my eyes on Cleinias[1278] gladlier than on all other sights which men deem fair. Joyfully will I welcome blindness to all else, if but these eyes may still behold him and him only. With sleep and night I am sore vexed, which rob me of his sight; but to daylight and the sun I owe eternal thanks, for they restore him to me, my heart's joy, Cleinias.[1279]

Yes, and herein also have we, the beautiful,[1280] just claim to boast.

[1271] Or, "and had a most hilarious and herbaceous time."

[1272] Cf. Aristoph. *Knights*, 494:

> *Chorus.* And here's the garlic. Swallow it down!
> *Sausage Seller....* What for?
> *Chorus.* It will prime you up and make you fight the better.
>
> H. Frere.

[1273] "We are concerned less with the lists of battle than of love"; "we meditate no furious close of battle but of lips." Lit. "how we shall kiss some one rather than do battle with."

[1274] See *Hellenica Essays*, p. 353.

[1275] Or, "beautiful and good."

[1276] Or, "whose fair face draws me." Was Cleinias there as a *muta persona*? Hardly, in spite of (nun). It is the image of him which is present to the mind's eye.

[1277] Lit. "being beautiful"; but there is a touch of bombast infused into the speech by the artist. Cf. the speech of Callias (*Hell.* VI. iii. 3) and, for the humour, *Cyrop.* passim.

[1278] See Cobet, *Pros. Xen.* p. 59. Cf. *Mem.* I. iii. 8.

[1279] Or, "for that they reveal his splendour to me."

[1280] "We beauties."

The strong man may by dint of toil obtain good things; the brave, by danger boldly faced, and the wise by eloquence of speech; but to the beautiful alone it is given to achieve all ends in absolute quiescence. To take myself as an example. I know that riches are a sweet possession, yet sweeter far to me to give all that I have to Cleinias than to receive a fortune from another. Gladly would I become a slave—ay, forfeit freedom—if Cleinias would deign to be my lord. Toil in his service were easier for me than rest from labour: danger incurred in his behalf far sweeter than security of days. So that if you, Callias, may boast of making men more just and upright, to me belongs by juster right than yours to train mankind to every excellence. We are the true inspirers[1281] who infuse some subtle fire into amorous souls, we beauties, and thereby raise them to new heights of being; we render them more liberal in the pursuit of wealth; we give them a zest for toil that mocks at danger, and enables them where honour the fair vision leads, to follow.[1282] We fill their souls with deeper modesty, a self-constraint more staunch; about the things they care for most, there floats a halo of protecting awe.[1283] Fools and unwise are they who choose not beauteous men to be their generals. How merrily would I, at any rate, march through fire by the side of Cleinias;[1284] and so would all of you, I know full well, in company of him who now addresses you.

Cease, therefore, your perplexity, O Socrates, abandon fears and doubts, believe and know that this thing of which I make great boast, my beauty, has power to confer some benefit on humankind.

Once more, let no man dare dishonour beauty, merely because the flower of it soon fades, since even as a child has growth in beauty, so is it with the stripling, the grown man, the reverend senior.[1285] And this the proof of my contention. Whom do we choose to bear the sacred olive-shoot[1286] in honour of Athena?—whom else save beautiful old men? witnessing thereby[1287] that beauty walks hand in hand as a companion with every age of life, from infancy to eld.

Or again, if it be sweet to win from willing hearts the things we seek for, I am persuaded that, by the eloquence of silence, I could win a kiss from yonder girl or boy more speedily than ever you could, O sage! by help of half a hundred subtle arguments.

Eh, bless my ears, what's that? (Socrates broke in upon this final

---

[1281] The (eispnelas) in relation to the (aitas), the Inspirer to the Hearer. Cf. Theocr. xii. 13; Ael. *V. H.* iii. 12. See *Müller, Dorians,* ii. 300 foll.

[1282] (philokaloterous). Cf. Plat. *Phaedr.* 248 D; *Criti.* 111 E; Aristot. *Eth. N.* iv. 4. 4; x. 9. 3.

[1283] Lit. "they feel most awe of what they most desire."

[1284] Cf. *Mem.* I. iii. 9.

[1285] Cf. *ib.* III. iii. 12.

[1286] Cf. Aristoph. *Wasps,* 544.

[1287] Or, "beauty steps in attendance lovingly hand in hand at every season of the life of man." So Walt Whitman, *passim.*

flourish of the speaker). So beautiful you claim to rival me, you boaster?

Crit. Why, yes indeed, I hope so, or else I should be uglier than all the Silenuses in the Satyric drama.[1288]

Good! (Socrates rejoined); the moment the programme of discussion is concluded,[1289] please remember, we must obtain a verdict on the point of beauty. Judgment shall be given—not at the bar of Alexander, son of Priam—but of these[1290] who, as you flatter yourself, have such a hankering to kiss you.

Oh, Socrates (he answered, deprecatingly), will you not leave it to the arbitrament of Cleinias?

Then Socrates: Will you never tire of repeating that one name? It is Cleinias here, there, and everywhere with you.

Crit. And if his name died on my lips, think you my mind would less recall his memory? Know you not, I bear so clear an image of him in my soul, that had I the sculptor's or the limner's skill, I might portray his features as exactly from this image of the mind as from contemplation of his actual self.

But Socrates broke in: Pray, why then, if you bear about this lively image, why do you give me so much trouble, dragging me to this and that place, where you hope to see him?

Crit. For this good reason, Socrates, the sight of him inspires gladness, whilst his phantom brings not joy so much as it engenders longing.

At this point Hermogenes protested: I find it most unlike you, Socrates, to treat thus negligently one so passion-crazed as Critobulus.

Socrates replied: Do you suppose the sad condition of the patient dates from the moment only of our intimacy?

Herm. Since when, then?

Soc. Since when? Why, look at him: the down begins to mantle on his cheeks,[1291] and on the nape[1292] of Cleinias' neck already mounts.

[1288] The MSS. add ["to whom, be it noted, Socrates indeed bore a marked resemblance"]. Obviously a gloss. Cf. Aristoph. *Clouds,* 224; Plat. *Symp.* 215 B.

[1289] Lit. "the arguments proposed have gone the round."

[1290] *i.e.* "the boy and girl." *Al.* "the present company, who are so eager to bestow on you their kisses."

[1291] Lit. "creeping down beside his ears." Cf. *Od.* xi. 319:

(prin sphoin upo krotaphoisin ioulous
anthesai pukasai te genus euanthei lakhne.)

"(Zeus destroyed the twain) ere the curls had bloomed beneath their temples, and darked their chins with the blossom of youth."—Butcher and Lang. Cf. Theocr. xv. 85: (praton ioulon apo krotaphon kataballon), "with the first down upon his cheeks" (Lang); Aesch. *Theb.* 534.

[1292] (pros to opisthen), perhaps = "ad posteriorem capitis partem," which would be more applicable to Critobulus, whose whiskers were just beginning to grow, than to

The fact is, when they fared to the same school together, he caught the fever. This his father was aware of, and consigned him to me, hoping I might be able to do something for him. Ay, and his plight is not so sorry now. Once he would stand agape at him like one whose gaze is fixed upon the Gorgons,[1293] his eyes one stony stare, and like a stone himself turn heavily away. But nowadays I have seen the statue actually blink.[1294] And yet, may Heaven help me! my good sirs, I think, between ourselves, the culprit must have bestowed a kiss on Cleinias, than which love's flame asks no fiercer fuel.[1295] So insatiable a thing it is and so suggestive of mad fantasy. (And for this reason held perhaps in higher honour, because of all external acts the close of lip with lip bears the same name as that of soul with soul in love.)[1296] Wherefore, say I, let every one who wishes to be master of himself and sound of soul abstain from kisses imprinted on fair lips.[1297]

Then Charmides: Oh! Socrates, why will you scare your friends with these hobgoblin terrors,[1298] bidding us all beware of handsome faces, whilst you yourself—yes, by Apollo, I will swear I saw you at the schoolmaster's[1299] that time when both of you were poring over one book, in which you searched for something, you and Critobulus, head to head, shoulder to shoulder bare, as if incorporate?[1300]

As yes, alack the day! (he answered); and that is why, no doubt, my shoulder ached for more than five days afterwards, as if I had been bitten by some fell beast, and methought I felt a sort of scraping at the heart.[1301] Now therefore, in the presence of these witnesses, I warn you, Critobulus, never again to touch me till you wear as thick a crop of hair[1302] upon your chin as on your head.

So pell-mell they went at it, half jest half earnest, and so the medley ended. Callias here called on Charmides.

Callias. Possibly we should read (after Pollux, ii. 10) (peri ten upenen), "on the upper lip." See Plat. *Protag.*309 B; *Il.* xxiv. 348; *Od.* x. 279.

[1293] Cf. Pind. *Pyth.* x. 75.

[1294] See *Cyrop.* I. iv. 28; Shakesp. *Ven. and Ad.* 89: "But when her lips were ready for his pay, he winks, and turns his lips another way."

[1295] Or, "a kiss which is to passion as dry combustious matter is to fire," Shakesp. *ib.* 1162.

[1296] Or, "is namesake of the love within the soul of lovers." The whole passage, involving a play on the words (philein phileisthai), "where kisses rain without, love reigns within," is probably to be regarded as a gloss. Cf. *Mem.* I. iii. 13.

[1297] Cf. *Mem.* I. iii. 8-14.

[1298] Cf. Plat. *Crit.* 46 D; *Hell.* IV. iv. 17; Arist. *Birds*, 1245.

[1299] "Grammarian's." Plat. *Protag.*312 B; 326 D; Dem. 315. 8.

[1300] Like Hermia and Helena, *Mids. N. D.* iii. 2. 208.

[1301] Reading (knisma), "scratching." Plat. *Hipp. maj.* 304 A. *Al.* (knesma).

[1302] See Jebb, *Theophr. Ch.* xxiv. 16.

Call. Now, Charmides, it lies with you to tell us why you pride yourself on poverty.[1303]

Charmides responded: On all hands it is admitted, I believe, that confidence is better than alarm; better to be a freeman than a slave; better to be worshipped than pay court to others; better to be trusted than to be suspected by one's country.

Well now, I will tell you how it fared with me in this same city when I was wealthy. First, I lived in daily terror lest some burglar should break into my house and steal my goods and do myself some injury. I cringed before informers.[1304] I was obliged to pay these people court, because I knew that I could injure them far less than they could injure me. Never-ending the claims upon my pocket which the state enforced upon me; and as to setting foot abroad, that was beyond the range of possibility. But now that I have lost my property across the frontier,[1305] and derive no income from my lands in Attica itself; now that my very household goods have been sold up, I stretch my legs at ease, I get a good night's rest. The distrust of my fellow-citizens has vanished; instead of trembling at threats, it is now my turn to threaten; at last I feel myself a freeman, with liberty to go abroad or stay at home as suits my fancy. The tables now are turned. It is the rich who rise to give *me* their seats, who stand aside and make way for me as I meet them in the streets. To-day I am like a despot, yesterday I was literally a slave; formerly it was I who had to pay my tribute[1306] to the sovereign people, now it is I who am supported by the state by means of general taxation.[1307]

And there is another thing. So long as I was rich, they threw in my teeth as a reproach that I was friends with Socrates, but now that I am become a beggar no one troubles his head two straws about the matter. Once more, the while I rolled in plenty I had everything to lose, and, as a rule, I lost it; what the state did not exact, some mischance stole from me. But now that is over. I lose nothing, having nought to lose; but, on the contrary, I have everything to gain, and live in hope of some day getting something.[1308]

Call. And so, of course, your one prayer is that you may never more be rich, and if you are visited by a dream of luck your one thought is to offer sacrifice to Heaven to avert misfortune.[1309]

Char. No, that I do not. On the contrary, I run my head into each

---

[1303] Zeune, cf. *Cyrop.* VIII. iii. 35-50.
[1304] "And police agents."
[1305] Cf. *Mem.* II. viii. 1.
[1306] (phoros), *tributum. Al.* "property-tax." Cf. *Econ.* ii. 6.
[1307] (telos), *vectigal.* Sturz, *Lex. Xen.* s.v. Cf. *Pol. Ath.* i. 3.
[1308] "I feed on the pleasures of hope, and fortune in the future."
[1309] Or, "you wake up in a fright, and offer sacrifice to the 'Averters.'" For (tois apotropaiois) see Aristoph. *Plutus,* 359; Plat. *Laws,* 854 B; *Hell.* III. iii. 4.

danger most adventurously. I endure, if haply I may see a chance of getting something from some quarter of the sky some day.

Come now (Socrates exclaimed), it lies with you, sir, you, Antisthenes, to explain to us, how it is that you, with means so scanty, make so loud a boast of wealth.

Because (he answered) I hold to the belief, sirs, that wealth and poverty do not lie in a man's estate, but in men's souls. Even in private life how many scores of people have I seen, who, although they roll in wealth, yet deem themselves so poor, there is nothing they will shrink from, neither toil nor danger, in order to add a little to their store.[1310] I have known two brothers,[1311] heirs to equal fortunes, one of whom has enough, more than enough, to cover his expenditure; the other is in absolute indigence. And so to monarchs, there are not a few, I perceive, so ravenous of wealth that they will outdo the veriest vagrants in atrocity. Want[1312] prompts a thousand crimes, you must admit. Why do men steal? why break burglariously into houses? why hale men and women captive and make slaves of them? Is it not from want? Nay, there are monarchs who at one fell swoop destroy whole houses, make wholesale massacre, and oftentimes reduce entire states to slavery, and all for the sake of wealth. These I must needs pity for the cruel malady which plagues them. Their condition, to my mind, resembles that poor creature's who, in spite of all he has[1313] and all he eats, can never stay the wolf that gnaws his vitals.

But as to me, my riches are so plentiful I cannot lay my hands on them myself;[1314] yet for all that I have enough to eat till my hunger is stayed, to drink till my thirst is sated;[1315] to clothe myself withal; and out of doors not Callias there, with all his riches, is more safe than I from shivering; and when I find myself indoors, what warmer shirting[1316] do I need than my bare walls? what ampler greatcoat than the tiles above my head? these seem to suit me well enough; and as to bedclothes, I am not so ill supplied but it is a business to arouse me in the morning.

And as to sexual desire, my body's need is satisfied by what comes first to hand. Indeed, there is no lack of warmth in the caress which greets me, just because it is unsought by others.[1317]

[1310] Cf. *Cyrop.* VIII. ii. 21; Hor. "Epist." i. 2. 26, "semper avarus eget."

[1311] Is Antisthenes thinking of Callias and Hermogenes? (presuming these are sons of Hipponicus and brothers). Cf. *Mem.* II. x. 3.

[1312] Or, "'Tis want that does it." See *Pol. Ath.* i. 5; *Revenues*, i. 1.

[1313] Reading (ekhon), or if (pinon), transl. "who eats and drinks, but never sates himself."

[1314] "That I can scarce discover any portion of it." Zeune cf. *Econ.* viii. 2.

[1315] So "the master" himself. See *Mem.* I. ii. 1, vi. 5.

[1316] Cf. Aristot. *Pol.* ii. 8. 1, of Hippodamus.

[1317] Cf. *Mem.* I. iii. 14, the germ of cynicism and stoicism, the Socratic (XS) form of "better to marry than to burn."

Well then, these several pleasures I enjoy so fully that I am much more apt to pray for less than more of them, so strongly do I feel that some of them are sweeter than what is good for one or profitable. But of all the precious things in my possession, I reckon this the choicest, that were I robbed of my whole present stock, there is no work so mean, but it would amply serve me to furnish me with sustenance. Why, look you, whenever I desire to fare delicately, I have not to purchase precious viands in the market, which becomes expensive, but I open the storehouse of my soul, and dole them out.[1318] Indeed, as far as pleasure goes, I find it better to await desire before I suffer meat or drink to pass my lips, than to have recourse to any of your costly viands, as, for instance, now, when I have chanced on this fine Thasian wine,[1319] and sip it without thirst. But indeed, the man who makes frugality, not wealth of worldly goods, his aim, is on the face of it a much more upright person. And why?—the man who is content with what he has will least of all be prone to clutch at what is his neighbour's.

And here's a point worth noting. Wealth of my sort will make you liberal of soul. Look at Socrates; from him it was I got these riches. He did not supply me with it by weight or by measure, but just as much as I could carry, he with bounteous hand consigned to me. And I, too, grudge it to no man now. To all my friends without distinction I am ready to display my opulence: come one, come all; and whosoever likes to take a share is welcome to the wealth that lies within my soul. Yes, and moreover, that most luxurious of possessions,[1320] unbroken leisure, you can see, is mine, which leaves me free to contemplate things worthy of contemplation,[1321] and to drink in with my ears all charming sounds. And what I value most, freedom to spend whole days in pure scholastic intercourse[1322] with Socrates, to whom I am devoted.[1323] And he, on his side, is not the person to admire those whose tale of gold and silver happens to be the largest, but those who are well-pleasing to him he chooses for companions, and will consort with to the end.

With these words the speaker ended, and Callias exclaimed:

By Hera, I envy you your wealth, Antisthenes, firstly, because the state does not lay burthens on you and treat you like a slave; and secondly, people do not fall into a rage with you when you refuse to be their creditor.

[1318] Or, "turn to the storehouse of a healthy appetite." See *Apol.* 18, the same sentiment "ex ore Socratis."

[1319] See Athen. *Deipnos.* i. 28.

[1320] See Eur. *Ion*, 601. Lit. "at every moment I command it."

[1321] "To gaze upon all fairest shows (like a spectator in the theatre), and to drink in sounds most delectable." So Walt Whitman.

[1322] Aristot. *Rhet.* ii. 4. 12; *Eth. N.* ix. 4. 9.

[1323] See *Mem.* III. xi. 17.

You may stay your envy (interposed Nicêratus), I shall presently present myself to borrow of him this same key of his to independence.[1324] Trained as I am to cast up figures by my master Homer—

> Seven tripods, which ne'er felt the fire, and of gold ten talents
> And burnished braziers twenty, and horses twelve—[1325]

by weight and measure duly reckoned,[1326] I cannot stay my craving for enormous wealth. And that's the reason certain people, I daresay, imagine I am inordinately fond of riches.

The remark drew forth a peal of laughter from the company, who thought the speaker hit the truth exactly.

Then some one: It lies with you, Hermogenes, to tell us who your friends are; and next, to demonstrate the greatness of their power and their care for you, if you would prove to us your right to pride yoruself on them.

Herm. That the gods know all things, that the present and the future lie before their eyes, are tenets held by Hellenes and barbarians alike. This is obvious; or else, why do states and nations, one and all, inquire of the gods by divination what they ought to do and what they ought not? This also is apparent, that we believe them able to do us good and to do us harm; or why do all men pray to Heaven to avert the evil and bestow the good? Well then, my boast is that these gods, who know and can do all things,[1327] deign to be my friends; so that, by reason of their care for me, I can never escape from their sight,[1328] neither by night nor by day, whithersoever I essay to go, whatsoever I take in hand to do.[1329] But because they know beforehand the end and issue of each event, they give me signals, sending messengers, be it some voice,[1330] or vision of the night, with omens of the solitary bird, which tell me what I should and what I should not do. When I listen to their warnings all goes well with me, I have no reason to repent; but if, as ere now has been the case, I have been disobedient, chastisement has overtaken me.

Then Socrates: All this I well believe,[1331] but there is one thing I would gladly learn of you: What service do you pay the gods, so to

---

[1324] Or, "his want-for-nothing," or, "supply-all."

[1325] Nicêratus quotes *Il.* ix. 122, 123, 263, 264.

[1326] Or, "by number and by measure," "so much apiece, so much a pound," in reference to Antisthenes' remark that Socrates does not stint his "good things."

[1327] Cf. *Mem.* I. i. 19; I. iv. 18.

[1328] Schneid. cf. Hom. *Il.* x. 279, (oude se letho kinomenos), "nor doth any motion of mine escape thee" (A. Lang); and see Arrian, *Epictet.* i. 12. 3.

[1329] Cf. Ps. cxxxix. *Domine probasti.*

[1330] See *Mem.* I. i. 3; *Apol.* xii. 13; *Cyrop.* VIII. vii. 3.

[1331] Lit. "Nay, nought of the things you tell us is incredible, but..."

secure their friendship?

Truly it is not a ruinous service, Socrates (he answered)—far from it. I give them thanks, which is not costly. I make return to them of all they give to me from time to time. I speak well of them, with all the strength I have. And whenever I take their sacred names to witness, I do not wittingly falsify my word.

Then God be praised (said Socrates), if being what you are, you have such friends; the gods themselves, it would appear, delight in nobleness of soul.[1332]

Thus, in solemn sort, the theme was handled, thus gravely ended.

But now it was the jester's turn, and so they fell to asking him:[1333] What could he see to pride himself upon so vastly in the art of making people laugh?

Surely I have good reason (he replied). The whole world knows my business is to set them laughing, so when they are in luck's way, they eagerly invite me to a share of it; but if ill betide them, helter-skelter off they go, and never once turn back,[1334] so fearful are they I may set them laughing will he nill he.

Nic. Heavens! you have good reason to be proud; with me it is just the opposite. When any of my friends are doing well, they take good care to turn their backs on me,[1335] but if ever it goes ill with them, they claim relationship by birth,[1336] and will not let their long-lost cousin out of sight.

Charm. Well, well! and you, sir (turning to the Syracusan), what do you pride yourself upon? No doubt, upon the boy?

The Syr. Not I, indeed; I am terribly afraid concerning him. It is plain enough to me that certain people are contriving for his ruin.[1337]

Good gracious![1338] (Socrates exclaimed, when he heard that), what crime can they conceive your boy is guilty of that they should wish to make an end of him?

The Syr. I do not say they want to murder him, but wheedle him away with bribes to pass his nights with them.

Soc. And if that happened, you on your side, it appears, believe the boy will be corrupted?

The Syr. Beyond all shadow of a doubt, most villainously.

[1332] (kalokagathia), "beautiful and gentle manhood."

[1333] Lit. "now that they had come to Philippus (in the 'period' of discussion), they..." Or read, after Hartman, *An. Xen.* p. 242, (eken) (sc. (o logos)).

[1334] Plat. *Rep.* 620 E; *Laws*, 854 C.

[1335] Or, "they take good care to get out of my way," "they hold aloof from me entirely."

[1336] Or, "produce the family-pedigree and claim me for a cousin." Cf. Lucian v., *Tim.* 49; Ter. *Phorm.* ii. 33, 45.

[1337] (diaphtheirai) = (1) to destroy, make away with; (2) to ruin and corrupt, seduce by bribes or otherwise.

[1338] Lit. "Heracles!" "Zounds!"

Soc. And you, of course, you never dream of such a thing. You don't spend nights with him?

The Syr. Of course I do, all night and every night.

Soc. By Hera, what a mighty piece of luck[1339] for you—to be so happily compounded, of such flesh and blood. You alone can't injure those who sleep beside you. You have every right, it seems, to boast of your own flesh, if nothing else.

The Syr. Nay, in sooth, it is not on that I pride myself.

Soc. Well, on what then?

The Syr. Why, on the silly fools who come and see my puppet show.[1340] I live on them.

Phil. Ah yes! and that explains how the other day I heard you praying to the gods to grant you, wheresoe'er you chance to be, great store of corn and wine, but dearth of wits.[1341]

Pass on (said Callias); now it is your turn, Socrates. What have you to say to justify your choice? How can you boast of so discredited an art?[1342]

He answered: Let us first decide[1343] what are the duties of the good go-between;[1344] and please to answer every question without hesitating; let us know the points to which we mutually assent.[1345] Are you agreed to that?

The Company, in chorus. Without a doubt (they answered, and the formula, once started, was every time repeated by the company, full chorus).

Soc. Are you agreed it is the business of a good go-between to make him (or her) on whom he plies his art agreeable to those with them?[1346]

Omnes. Without a doubt.

Soc. And, further, that towards agreeableness, one step at any rate consists in wearing a becoming fashion of the hair and dress?[1347] Are you agreed to that?

[1339] Cf. Plat. *Symp.* 217 A.

[1340] "My marionettes." Cf. Herod. ii. 48; Lucian lxxii., *De Syr. d.* 16; Aristot. *de Mund.* 6.

[1341] Or, "of fruits abundance, but of wits a famine." Cf. Plat. *Rep.* 546 A. His prayer resembles that of the thievish trader in Ovid, *Fast.* v. 675 foll., "Grant me to-day my daily... fraud!" but in spite of himself (like Dogberry), he seems to pray to the gods to "write him down an ass"!

[1342] Sc. "the hold-door trade."

[1343] Or, "define in common." Cf. *Mem.* IV. vi. 15.

[1344] Or, "man-praiser." Cf. *The Manx Witch,* p. 47 (T. E. Brown), "And Harry, more like a dooiney-molla For Jack, lak helpin him to woo." See, too, Mr. Hall Caine's *Manxman,* p. 73.

[1345] See Plat. *Rep.* 342 D, for a specimen of Socratic procedure, "from one point of agreement to another."

[1346] *Al.* "their followers." See *Mem.* II. vi. 36.

[1347] See Becker, *Char.* Exc. iii. to Sc. xi.

Omnes. Without a doubt.

Soc. And we know for certain, that with the same eyes a man may dart a look of love or else of hate[1348] on those he sees. Are you agreed?

Omnes. Without a doubt.

Soc. Well! and with the same tongue and lips and voice may speak with modesty or boastfulnes?

Omnes. Without a doubt.

Soc. And there are words that bear the stamp of hate, and words that tend to friendliness?[1349]

Omnes. Without a doubt.

Soc. The good go-between will therefore make his choice between them, and teach only what conduces to agreeableness?

Omnes. Without a doubt.

Soc. And is he the better go-between who can make his clients pleasing to one person only, or can make them pleasing to a number?[1350]

The company was here divided; the one half answered, "Yes, of course, the largest number," whilst the others still maintained, "Without a doubt."

And Socrates, remarking, "That proposition is agreed to also," thus proceeded: And if further he were able to make them pleasing to the whole community, should we not have found in this accomplished person an arch-go-between?

Clearly so (they answered with one voice).

Soc. If then a man had power to make his clients altogether pleasing; that man, I say, might justly pride himself upon his art, and should by rights receive a large reward?[1351]

And when these propositions were agreed to also, he turned about and said: Just such a man, I take it, is before you in the person of Antisthenes![1352]

Whereupon Antisthenes exclaimed: What! are you going to pass on the business? will you devolve this art of yours on me as your successor, Socrates?[1353]

I will, upon my word, I will (he answered): since I see that you have practised to some purpose, nay elaborated, an art which is the handmaid to this other.

And what may that be? asked Antisthenes.

[1348] See *Mem.* III. x. 5.

[1349] Cf. Ep. St. James iii. 10, "Out of the same mouth proceedeth blessing and cursing."

[1350] Or, "to the many." The question is ambiguous. (e) = "an" or "quam."

[1351] Or, "he deserves to do a rattling business," "to take handsome fees." Cf. Sheridan's Mrs. Coupler, in *A Trip to Scarborough*.

[1352] See Diog. Laert. *Antisth.* VI. i. 8; Plut. *Symp.* ii. 1. 503.

[1353] Or, "going to give up business, and hand on the trade to me as your successor?"

Soc. The art of the procurer.[1354]

The other (in a tone of deep vexation): Pray, what thing of the sort are you aware I ever perpetrated?

Soc. I am aware that it was you who introduced our host here, Callias, to that wise man Prodicus;[1355] they were a match, you saw, the one enamoured of philosophy, and the other in need of money. It was you again, I am well enough aware, who introduced him once again to Hippias[1356] of Elis, from whom he learnt his "art of memory";[1357] since which time he has become a very ardent lover,[1358] from inability to forget each lovely thing he sets his eyes on. And quite lately, if I am not mistaken, it was you who sounded in my ears such praise of our visitor from Heraclea,[1359] that first you made me thirst for his society, and then united us.[1360] For which indeed I am your debtor, since I find him a fine handsome fellow and true gentleman.[1361] And did you not, moreover, sing the praises of Aeschylus of Phlius[1362] in my ears and mine in his?—in fact, affected us so much by what you said, we fell in love and took to coursing wildly in pursuit of one another like two dogs upon a trail.[1363]

With such examples of your wonder-working skill before my eyes, I must suppose you are a first-rate matchmaker. For consider, a man with insight to discern two natures made to be of service to each other, and with power to make these same two people mutually enamoured! That is the sort of man, I take it, who should weld together states in friendship; cement alliances with gain to the contracting parties;[1364] and, in general, be found an acquisition to those several states; to friends and intimates, and partisans in war, a treasure worth possessing.[1365] But you, my friend, you got quite angry. One would suppose I had given you an evil name in calling you a first-rate

---

[1354] Cf. Plat. *Theaet.* 150 A; Aristot. *Eth. N.* v. 2, 13; Aeschin. 3, 7; Plut. *Solon*, 23.

[1355] Or, "the sage," "the sophist." See *Mem.* I. vi. 13; II. i. 21.

[1356] See *Mem.* IV. iv. 5; and for his *art of memory* cf. Plat. *Hipp. min.* 368 D; *Hipp. maj.* 285 E.

[1357] The *memoria technica* (see Aristot. *de An.* iii. 3, 6), said to have been invented by Simonides of Ceos. Cic. *de Or.* ii. 86; *de Fin.* ii. 32; Quinct. xi. 2. 559.

[1358] Or, "has grown amorous to a degree" (*al.* "an adept in love's lore himself." Cf. Plat. *Rep.* 474 D, "an authority in love."—Jowett) "for the simple reason he can't forget each lovely thing he once has seen." Through the *ars memoriae* of Hippias, it becomes an *idée fixe* of the mind.

[1359] Perhaps Zeuxippus. See Plat. *Prot.* 318 B. *Al.* Zeuxis, also a native of Heraclea. See *Mem.* I. iv. 3; *Econ.* x. 1.

[1360] Or, "introduced him to me." Cf. *Econ.* iii. 14; Plat. *Lach.* 200 D.

[1361] "An out-and-out (kalos te kagathos)."

[1362] Who this Phliasian is, no one knows.

[1363] *Al.* "like two hounds chevying after one another."

[1364] *Al.* "and cement desirable matrimonial connections." Cf. Aristot. *Pol.* iii. 9, 13. 1280 B; v. 4, 5-8. 1303 B.

[1365] See the conversation with Critobulus, so often referred to, (peri philias), in *Mem.* II. vi.

matchmaker.

Yes (he answered meekly), but now I am calm. It is clear enough, if I possess these powers I shall find myself surcharged with spiritual riches.

In this fashion the cycle of the speeches was completed.[1366]

V

Then Callias: Our eyes are on you, Critobulus. Yours to enter the lists[1367] against the champion Socrates, who claims the prize of beauty. Do you hesitate?

Soc. Likely enough he does, for possibly he sees Sir Pandarus stands high in their esteem who are the judges of the contest.

In spite of which (retorted Critobulus), I am not for drawing back[1368]. I am ready; so come on, and if you have any subtle argument to prove that you are handsomer than I am, now's your time, instruct us. But just stop one minute; have the goodness, please, to bring the lamp a little closer.

Soc. Well then, I call upon you first of all, as party to this suit, to undergo the preliminary examination.[1369] Attend to what I say, and please be good enough to answer.

Crit. Do you be good enough yourself to put your questions.

Soc. Do you consider that the quality of beauty is confined to man, or is it to be found in other objects also? What is your belief on this point?

Crit. For my part, I consider it belongs alike to animals—the horse, the ox—and to many things inanimate: that is to say, a shield, a sword, a spear are often beautiful.

Soc. How is it possible that things, in no respect resembling one another, should each and all be beautiful?[1370]

Crit. Of course it is, God bless me! if well constructed by the hand of man to suit the sort of work for which we got them, or if naturally adapted to satisfy some want, the things in either case are beautiful.

Soc. Can you tell me, then, what need is satisfied by our eyes?

Crit. Clearly, the need of vision.

Soc. If so, my eyes are proved at once to be more beautiful than

---

[1366] See Hug, *Einleitung*, xxxi. "Quellen des Platonischen Symposion."

[1367] Soph. *Fr.* 234; Thuc. i. 93.

[1368] Or, "I do; but all the same, I am not for shirking." Cf. Aristoph. *Frogs*, 860, (etiomos eum egoge, kouk anaduomai, daknein): "I'm up to it; I am resolved" (Frere); Dem. "de F. Leg." 406 20: "His resolution never reached that point, but shrank back, for his conscience checked it" (Kennedy).

[1369] The (anakrisis), or "previous inquiry" (before one of the archons) of parties concerned in a suit, to see whether the action lay. Cf. Plat. *Charm.* 176 C. See Gow, *Companion*, xiv. 74.

[1370] See *Mem.* III. viii. 5, quoted by Galen, *de Usu Part.* i. 370.

yours.

Crit. How so?

Soc. Because yours can only see just straight in front of them, whereas mine are prominent and so projecting, they can see aslant.[1371]

Crit. And amongst all animals, you will tell us that the crab has loveliest eyes?[1372] Is that your statement?

Soc. Decidedly, the creature has. And all the more so, since for strength and toughness its eyes by nature are the best constructed.

Crit. Well, let that pass. To come to our two noses, which is the more handsome, yours or mine?

Soc. Mine, I imagine, if, that is, the gods presented us with noses for the sake of smelling. Your nostrils point to earth; but mine are spread out wide and flat, as if to welcome scents from every quarter.

Crit. But consider, a snubness of the nose, how is that more beautiful than straightness?[1373]

Soc. For this good reason, that a snub nose does not discharge the office of a barrier;[1374] it allows the orbs of sight free range of vision: whilst your towering nose looks like an insulting wall of partition to shut off the two eyes.[1375]

As to the mouth (proceeded Critobulus), I give in at once; for, given mouths are made for purposes of biting, you could doubtless bite off a much larger mouthful with your mouth than I with mine.

Soc. Yes, and you will admit, perhaps, that I can give a softer kiss than you can, thanks to my thick lips.

Crit. It seems I have an uglier mouth than any ass.

Soc. And here is a fact which you will have to reckon with, if further evidence be needed to prove that I am handsomer than you. The naiads, nymphs, divine, have as their progeny Sileni, who are much more like myself, I take it, than like you. Is that conclusive?

Nay, I give it up (cried Critobulus), I have not a word to say in answer. I am silenced. Let them record the votes. I fain would know at once what I must suffer or must pay.[1376] Only (he added) let them vote

---

[1371] Or, "squint sideways and command the flanks."

[1372] Or, "is best provided in respect of eyeballs."

[1373] Or, "your straight nose." Cf. Plat. *Theaet.* 209 C: *Soc.* "Or, if I had further known you not only as having nose and eyes, but as having a snub nose and prominent eyes, should I have any more notion of you than myself and others who resemble me?" Cf. also Aristot. *Pol.* v. 9, 7: "A nose which varies from the ideal of straightness to a hook or snub may still be a good shape and agreeable to the eye; but if the excess be very great, all symmetry is lost, and the nose at last ceases to be a nose at all on account of some excess in one direction or defect in the other; and this is true of every other part of the human body. The same law of proportion holds in states."—Jowett.

[1374] Or, "the humble snub is not a screen or barricade."

[1375] Cf. *Love's Labour Lost,* v. 2. 568: *Boyet.* "Your nose says no, you are not, for it stands too right"; also *The Song of Solomon,* vii. 4: "Thy nose is the tower of Lebanon, which looketh toward Damascus."

[1376] For this formula see *Dict. Ant*" (timema). Cf. *Econ.* xi. 25; Plat. *Apol.* 36 B;

in secret.[1377] I am afraid your wealth and his (Antisthenes') combined may overpower me.

Accordingly the boy and girl began to register the votes in secret, while Socrates directed the proceedings. He would have the lampstand[1378] this time brought close up to Critobulus; the judges must on no account be taken in; the victor in the suit would get from the two judges, not a wreath of ribands[1379] for a chaplet, but some kisses.

When the urns were emptied, it was found that every vote, without exception, had been cast for Critobulus.[1380]

Whereat Socrates: Bless me! you don't say so? The coin you deal in, Critobulus, is not at all like that of Callias. His makes people just; whilst yours, like other filthy lucre, can corrupt both judge and jury.[1381]

VI

Thereupon some members of the party called on Critobulus to accept the meed of victory in kisses (due from boy and girl); others urged him first to bribe their master; whilst others bandied other jests. Amidst the general hilarity Hermogenes alone kept silence.

Whereat Socrates turned to the silent man, and thus accosted him: Hermogenes, what is a drunken brawl? Can you explain to us?

He answered: If you ask me what it is, I do not know, but I can tell you what it seems to me to be.

Soc. That seems as good. What does it seem?

Her. A drunken brawl, in my poor judgment, is annoyance caused to people over wine.

Soc. Are you aware that you at present are annoying us by silence?

Her. What, whilst you are talking?

Soc. No, when we pause a while.

Her. Then you have not observed that, as to any interval between your talk, a man would find it hard to insert a hair, much more one grain of sense.

Then Socrates: O Callias, to the rescue! help a man severely handled by his cross-examiner.

Statesm. 299 A; *Laws,* freq.; Dem. 529. 23; 533. 2.

[1377] And not as in the case described (Thuc. iv. 74), where the people (at Megara) were compelled to *give sentence* on the political opponents of the oligarchs by an open vote. Cf. Lysias, 133, 12, (ten de psephon ouk eis kadiskous, alla phaneran epi tas trapezas tautas dei tithenai).

[1378] (ton lukhnon) here, above, §. 2, (ton lamptera). Both, I take it, are oil-lamps, and differ merely as "light" and "lamp."

[1379] Cf. Plat. *Symp.* 213; *Hell.* V. i. 3.

[1380] Lit. "When the pebbles were turned out and proved to be with Critobulus, Socrates remarked, 'Papae!'" which is as much to say, "Od's pity!"

[1381] (kai dikastas kai kritas), "both jury and presiding judges," *i.e.* the company and the boy and girl.

Call. With all my heart (and as he spoke he faced Hermogenes). Why, when the flute is talking, we are as silent as the grave.

Her. What, would you have me imitate Nicostratus[1382] the actor, reciting his *tetrameters*[1383] to the music of the fife? Must I discourse to you in answer to the flute?

Then Socrates: By all that's holy, I wish you would, Hermogenes. How delightful it would be. Just as a song sounds sweeter in concert with the flute, so would your talk be more mellifluous attuned to its soft pipings; and particularly if you would use gesticulation like the flute-girl, to suit the tenor of your speech.

Here Callias demanded: And when our friend (Antisthenes) essays to cross-examine people[1384] at a banquet, what kind of piping[1385] should he have?

Ant. The person in the witness-box would best be suited with a serpent-hissing theme.[1386]

Thus the stream of talk flowed on; until the Syracusan, who was painfully aware that while the company amused themselves, his "exhibition" was neglected, turned, in a fit of jealous spleen, at last on Socrates.[1387]

The Syr. They call you Socrates. Are you that person commonly nicknamed the thinker?[1388]

Soc. Which surely is a better fate than to be called a thoughtless person?

The Syr. Perhaps, if you were not thought to split your brains on things above us—transcendental stuff.[1389]

Soc. And is there anything more transcendental than the gods?

The Syr. By heaven! no, it is not the gods above us whom you care for, but for matters void of use and valueless.[1390]

[1382] See Cobet, *Pros. Xen.* p. 53; and cf. Diog. Laert. iv. 3, 4; Polyaen. vi. 10; *Hell.* IV. viii. 18.

[1383] See Aristoph. *Clouds,* where Socrates is giving Strepsiades a lesson in "measures," 639-646: (poteron to trimetron e to tetrametron).

[1384] Or, "a poor body," in reference to the elentic onslaught made on himself by Antisthenes above.

[1385] (to aulema), a composition for reed instruments, "music for the flute." Cf. Aristoph. *Frogs,* 1302.

[1386] Or, "motif on a scrannel pipe." See L. & S. s.v. (puthaules). Cf. Poll. iv. 81, (puthikon aulema), an air (nomos) played on the (puthois aulos), expressing the battle between Apollo and the Python, the hiss of which was imitated.

[1387] "The Syracusan was 'civil as an orange, and of that jealous complexion.'"

[1388] Apparently he has been to see the "Clouds" (exhibited first in 423 B.C.), and has conceived certain ideas concerning Socrates, "a wise man, who speculated about the heaven above, and searched into the earth beneath, and made the worse appear the better cause." Plat. *Apol.* 18 B, 19 C. *Clouds,* 101, 360, (khair o presbuta... ton nun meteorosophiston... ta te meteora phrontistes).

[1389] Or, "if only you were held to be less 'meteoric,' less head-in-airy in your speculations."

[1390] It is impossible to give the play on words. *The Syr.* (anophelestaton). *Soc.* (ano...

Soc. It seems, then, by your showing I do care for them. How valueless the gods, not more, if being above us they make the void of use to send us rain, and cause their light to shine on us? And now, sir, if you do not like this frigid[1391] argument, why do you cause me trouble? The fault is yours.[1392]

Well, let that be (the other answered); answer me one question: How many fleas' feet distance is it, pray, from you to me?[1393] They say you measure them by geometric scale.

But here Antisthenes, appealing to Philippus, interposed: You are a man full of comparisons.[1394] Does not this worthy person strike you as somewhat like a bully seeking to pick a quarrel?[1395]

Yes (replied the jester), he has a striking likeness to that person and a heap of others. He bristles with metaphors.

Soc. For all that, do not you be too eager to draw comparisons at his expense, or you will find yourself the image of a scold and brawler.[1396]

Phil. But what if I compare him to all the primest creatures of the world, to beauty's nonpareils,[1397] to nature's best—I might be justly likened to a flatterer but not a brawler.[1398]

Soc. Why now, you are like a person apt to pick a quarrel, since

---

ophelousin). Schenkl after Madvig emend.: (ton ano en nephelais onton) = "but for things in the clouds above."

[1391] Cf. *Cyrop.* VIII. iv. 22, 23.

[1392] (pho parekhousin... pragmata moi parekhon). Lit. "cause light... causing me trouble."

[1393] See Aristoph. *Clouds,* 144 foll.:
(aneret' arti Khairephonta Sokrates
psullan oposous alloito tous autes podas
dakousa gar...)
Cf. Lucian, ii. *Prom. in Verb.* 6, and *Hudibras, the Second Part of,* canto iii.:
How many scores a Flea will jump
Of his own length from Head to Rump
Which Socrates and Chaerephon
In vain essayed so long agon.

[1394] Like Biron, "L. L. L." v. 2. 854. Or, "you are a clever caricaturist." See Plat. *Symp.* 215 A; Hug, "Enleitung," xiv.; Aristoph. *Birds,* 804 (Frere, p. 173); *Wasps,* 1309.

[1395] Aristoph. *Frogs,* 857, "For it ill beseems illustrious bards to scold like market-women." (Frere, p. 269); *Knights,* 1410, "to bully"; "Eccles." 142:

(kai loidorountai g' osper empepokotes, kai ton paroinount' ekpherous' oi toxotai.)
[1396] Or, "a striking person."

[1397] Lit. "compare him to those in all things beauteous and the best." With (tois pasi kalois kai tois beltistois) cf. Thuc. v. 28, (oi 'Argeioi arista eskhon tois pasi), "The Argives were in excellent condition in all respects." As to Philippus's back-handed compliment to the showman, it reminds one of Peter Quince's commendation of Bottom: "Yea and the best person too; and he is a very paramour for a sweet voice."

[1398] It is not easy to keep pace with the merryman's jests; but if I follow his humour, he says to Socrates: "If the cap is to fit, you must liken me to one who quits 'assault and battery' for 'compliments [*sotto voce,* "lies"] and flattery.'"

you imply they are all his betters.[1399]

Phil. What, would you have me then compare him to worse villains?

Soc. No, not even to worse villains.

Phil. What, then, to nothing, and to nobody?

Soc. To nought in aught. Let him remain his simple self—

Phil. Incomparable. But if my tongue is not to wag, whatever shall I do to earn my dinner?

Soc. Why, that you shall quite easily, if with your wagging tongue you do not try to utter things unutterable.

Here was a pretty quarrel over wine soon kindled and soon burnt.

VII

But on the instant those who had not assisted in the fray gave tongue, the one part urging the jester to proceed with his comparisons, and the other part dissuading.

The voice of Socrates was heard above the tumult: Since we are all so eager to be heard at once, what fitter time than now to sing a song, in chorus.

And suiting the action to the words, he commenced a stave.

The song was barely finished, when a potter's wheel was brought in, on which the dancing-girl was to perform more wonders.

At this point Socrates addressed the man of Syracuse: It seems I am likely to deserve the title which you gave me of a thinker in good earnest. Just now I am speculating by what means your boy and girl may pass a happy time, and we spectators still derive the greatest pleasure from beholding them; and this, I take it, is precisely what you would yourself most wish. Now I maintain, that throwing somersaults in and out of swords is a display of danger uncongenial to a banquet. And as for writing and reading on a wheel that all the while keeps whirling, I do not deny the wonder of it, but what pleasure such a marvel can present, I cannot for the life of me discover. Nor do I see how it is a whit more charming to watch these fair young people twisting about their bodies and imitating wheels than to behold them peacefully reposing.

We need not fare far afield to light on marvels, if that is our object. All about us here is full of marvel; we can begin at once by wondering, why it is the candle gives a light by dint of its bright flame, while side by side with it the bright bronze vessel gives no light, but shows within itself those other objects mirrored.[1400] Or, how is it that oil, being moist

---

[1399] When Socrates says (ei pant' autou beltio phes einai, k.t.l.), the sense seems to be: "No, if you say that all these prime creatures are better than he is, you are an abusive person still."

[1400] Cf. *Mem.* IV. vii. 7. Socrates' criticism of Anaxagoras' theory with regard to the

and liquid, keeps that flame ablaze, but water, just because it is liquid, quenches fire. But no more do these same marvels tend to promote the object of the wine-cup.[1401]

But now, supposing your young people yonder were to tread a measure to the flute, some pantomime in dance, like those which the Graces and the Hours with the Nymphs are made to tread in pictures,[1402] I think they would spend a far more happy time themselves, and our banquet would at once assume a grace and charm unlooked for.

The Syracusan caught the notion readily.

By all that's holy, Socrates (he cried), a capital suggestion, and for my part, I warrant you, I will put a piece upon the stage, which will delight you, one and all.

VIII

With these words the Syracusan made his exit, bent on organising his performance.[1403] As soon as he was gone, Socrates once more essayed a novel argument.[1404] He thus addressed them:

It were but reasonable, sirs, on our part not to ignore the mighty power here present,[1405] a divinity in point of age coequal with the everlasting gods, yet in outward form the youngest,[1406] who in magnitude embraces all things, and yet his shrine is planted in the soul of man. Love[1407] is his name! and least of all should we forget him who are one and all votaries of this god.[1408] For myself I cannot name the time at which I have not been in love with some one.[1409] And

---

sun.
[1401] Lit. "work to the same end as wine."
[1402] Cf. Plat. *Laws*, vii. 815 C; Hor. "Carm." i. 4. 6:

iunctaeque Nymphis Gratiae decentes
alterno terram quatiunt pede.

The Graces and the Nymphs, together knit,
With rhythmic feet the meadow beat (Conington).

Ib. iv. 7. 5.

[1403] (sunekroteito), "on the composition of his piece." *Al.* "amidst a round of plaudits."
[1404] "Struck the keynote of a novel theme." Cf. Plat. *Symp.* 177 E.
[1405] Cf. Shelley, "Hymn to Intellectual Beauty":
The awful shadow of some unseen Power Floats, though unseen, among us....
[1406] Reading with L. D. after Blomfield (Aesch. *Ag.* p. 304), (idrumenou), or if as vulg. (isoumenou), transl. "but in soul is fashioned like to mortal man."
[1407] "Eros."
[1408] Or, "who are each and all of us members of his band." For (thiasotai) cf. Aristot. *Eth. N.* viii. 9. 5; Aristoph. *Frogs*, 327.
[1409] Cf. Plat. *Symp.* 177 D: "No one will vote against you, Erysimachus, said

Charmides here has, to my knowledge, captivated many a lover, while his own soul has gone out in longing for the love of not a few himself.[1410] So it is with Critobulus also; the beloved of yesterday is become the lover of to-day. Ay, and Nicêratus, as I am told, adores his wife, and is by her adored.[1411] As to Hermogenes, which of us needs to be told[1412] that the soul of this fond lover is consumed with passion for a fair ideal—call it by what name you will—the spirit blent of nobleness and beauty.[1413] See you not what chaste severity dwells on his brow;[1414] how tranquil his gaze;[1415] how moderate his words; how gentle his intonation; now radiant his whole character. And if he enjoys the friendship of the most holy gods, he keeps a place in his regard for us poor mortals. But how is it that you alone, Antisthenes, you misanthrope, love nobody?

But there we must stop. Hermogenes is a sort of Sir Percivale, "such a courtesy spake thro' the limbs and in the voice."

Nay, so help me Heaven! (he replied), but I do love most desperately yourself, O Socrates!

Whereat Socrates, still carrying on the jest, with a coy, coquettish air,[1416] replied: Yes; only please do not bother me at present. I have other things to do, you see.

Antisthenes replied: How absolutely true to your own character, arch go-between![1417] It is always either your familiar oracle won't suffer you, that's your pretext, and so you can't converse with me; or you are bent upon something or somebody else.

Then Socrates: For Heaven's sake, don't carbonado[1418] me,

Socrates; on the only subject ((ta erotika)) of which I profess to have any knowledge, I certainly cannot refuse to speak, nor, I presume, Agathon and Pasuanias; and there can be no doubt of Arisophanes, who is the constant servant of Dionysus and Aphrodite; nor will any one disagree of those I see around me" (Jowett).

[1410] Or, "has had many a passionate admirer, and been enamoured of more than one true love himself." See Plat. *Charm.*, ad in.

[1411] For Love and Love-for-Love, (eros) and (anteros), see Plat. *Phaedr.* 255 D. Cf. Aristot. *Eth. N.* ix. 1.

[1412] Lit. "which of us but knows his soul is melting away with passion." Cf. Theocr. xiv. 26.

[1413] Lit. "beautiful and gentle manhood."

[1414] Lit. "how serious are his brows."

[1415] The phrases somehow remind one of Sappho's famous ode:

(phainetai moi kenos isos theoisin
emmen oner, ostis enantios toi
izanei, kai plasion adu phoneusas upakouei
kai gelasas imeroen).

[1416] *Al.* "like a true coquet." Cf. Plat. *Phaedr.* 228 C.

[1417] See *Mem.* III. xi. 14.

[1418] Or, "tear and scratch me."

Antisthenes, that's all. Any other savagery on your part I can stand, and will stand, as a lover should. However (he added), the less we say about your love the better, since it is clearly an attachment not to my soul, but to my lovely person.

And then, turning to Callias: And that you, Callias, do love Autolycus, this whole city knows and half the world besides,[1419] if I am not mistaken; and the reason is that you are both sons of famous fathers, and yourselves illustrious. For my part I have ever admired your nature, but now much more so, when I see that you are in love with one who does not wanton in luxury or languish in effeminacy,[1420] but who displays to all his strength, his hardihood, his courage, and sobriety of soul. To be enamoured of such qualities as these is a proof itself of a true lover's nature.

Whether indeed Aphrodite be one or twain[1421] in personality, the heavenly and the earthly, I cannot tell, for Zeus, who is one and indivisible, bears many titles.[1422] But this thing I know, that these twain have separate altars, shrines, and sacrifices,[1423] as befits their nature—she that is earthly, of a lighter and a laxer sort; she that is heavenly, purer and holier in type. And you may well conjecture, it is the earthly goddess, the common Aphrodite, who sends forth the bodily loves; while from her that is named of heaven, Ourania, proceed those loves which feed upon the soul, on friendship and on noble deeds. It is by this latter, Callias, that you are held in bonds, if I mistake not, Love divine.[1424] This I infer as well from the fair and noble character of your friend, as from the fact that you invite his father to share your life and intercourse.[1425] Since no part of these is hidden from the father by the fair and noble lover.

Hermogenes broke in: By Hera, Socrates, I much admire you for many things, and now to see how in the act of gratifying Callias you are training him in duty and true excellence.[1426]

Why, yes (he said), if only that his cup of happiness may overflow, I wish to testify to him how far the love of soul is better than the love of body.

[1419] Lit. "many a foreign visitor likewise."

[1420] See the Attic type of character, as drawn by Pericles, Thuc. ii. 40.

[1421] For Aphrodite Ourania and Pandêmos see Plat. *Symp.* 180.

[1422] Lit. "that is believed to be the same." See Cic. "De N. D." iii. 16. Cf. Aesch. *Prom.* 210 (of Themis and Gaia), (pollon onomaton morphe mia).

[1423] *e.g.* to Aphrodite Pandêmos a white goat, (mekas leuke), but to Aphrodite Ourania a heifer, and (thusiai nephaliai), offerings without wine, *i.e.* of water, milk, and honey. Schol. to Soph. *Oed. Col.* 100; Lucian, lxvii. "Dial. Mer." 7. 1.

[1424] Lit. "by Eros."

[1425] Cf. Plat. *Prot.* 318 A; Aristoph. *Thesmoph.* 21, "learned conversazioni."

[1426] Lit. "teaching him what sort of man he ought to be." This, as we know, is the very heart and essence of the Socratic (= (XS)) method. See *Mem.* I. ii. 3.

Without friendship,[1427] as we full well know, there is no society of any worth. And this friendship, what is it? On the part of those whose admiration[1428] is bestowed upon the inner disposition, it is well named a sweet and voluntary compulsion. But among those whose desire[1428] is for the body, there are not a few who blame, nay hate, the ways of their beloved ones. And even where attachment[1428] clings to both,[1429] even so the bloom of beauty after all does quickly reach its prime; the flower withers, and when that fails, the affection which was based upon it must also wither up and perish. But the soul, with every step she makes in her onward course towards deeper wisdom, grows ever worthier of love.

Ay, and in the enjoyment of external beauty a sort of surfeit is engendered. Just as the eater's appetite palls through repletion with regard to meats,[1430] so will the feelings of a lover towards his idol. But the soul's attachment, owing to its purity, knows no satiety.[1431] Yet not therefore, as a man might fondly deem, has it less of the character of loveliness.[1432] But very clearly herein is our prayer fulfilled, in which we beg the goddess to grant us words and deeds that bear the impress of her own true loveliness.[1433]

That a soul whose bloom is visible alike in beauty of external form, free and unfettered, and an inner disposition, bashful, generous; a spirit[1434] at once imperial and affable,[1435] born to rule among its fellows—that such a being will, of course, admire and fondly cling to his beloved, is a thesis which needs no further argument on my part. Rather I will essay to teach you, how it is natural that this same type of lover should in turn be loved by his soul's idol.[1436]

How, in the first place, is it possible for him to hate a lover who, he

---

[1427] Lit. "That without love no intercourse is worth regarding, we all know."

[1428] N.B.—(agamenon, epithumounton, sterxosi). Here, as often, the author seems to have studied the (orthoepeia) of Prodicus. See *Mem.* II. i. 24.

[1429] *i.e.* "body and character."

[1430] Cf. *Mem.* III. xi. 13.

[1431] Lit. "is more insatiate." Cf. Charles Wesley's hymn:

O Love Divine, how sweet Thou art!
When shall I find my willing heart
All taken up by Thee?

[1432] Lit. "is she, the soul, more separate from Aphrodite."

[1433] Or, "stamped with the image of Aphrodite." Zeune cf. Lucr. i. 24, addressing Venus, "te sociam studeo scribendis versibus esse," "I would have thee for a helpmate in writing the verses..."; and below, 28, "quo magis aeternum da dictis, diva, leporem," "Wherefore all the more, O lady, lend my lays an ever-living charm" (H. A. J. Munro).

[1434] Cf. Plat. *Phaedr.* 252 E.

[1435] The epithet (philophron) occurs *Mem.* III. i. 6, of a general; *ib.* III. v. 3 (according to the vulg. reading), of the Athenians.

[1436] Or, "the boy whom he cherishes."

knows, regards him as both beautiful and good?[1437] and, in the next place, one who, it is clear, is far more anxious to promote the fair estate of him he loves[1438] than to indulge his selfish joys? and above all, when he has faith and trust that neither dereliction,[1439] nor loss of beauty through sickness, nor aught else, will diminish their affection.

If, then, they own a mutual devotion,[1440] how can it but be, they will take delight in gazing each into the other's eyes, hold kindly converse, trust and be trusted, have forethought for each other, in success rejoice together, in misfortune share their troubles; and so long as health endures make merry cheer, day in day out; or if either of them should fall on sickness, then will their intercourse be yet more constant; and if they cared for one another face to face, much more will they care when parted.[1441] Are not all these the outward tokens of true loveliness?[1442] In the exercise of such sweet offices, at any rate, they show their passion for holy friendship's state, and prove its bliss, continuously pacing life's path from youth to eld.

But the lover who depends upon the body,[1443] what of him? First, why should love-for-love be given to such a lover? because, forsooth, he bestows upon himself what he desires, and upon his minion things of dire reproach? or that what he hastens to exact, infallibly must separate that other from his nearest friends?

If it be pleaded that persuasion is his instrument, not violence; is that no reason rather for a deeper loathing? since he who uses violence[1444] at any rate declares himself in his true colours as a villain, while the tempter corrupts the soul of him who yields to his persuasions.

Ay, and how should he who traffics with his beauty love the purchaser, any more than he who keeps a stall in the market-place and vends to the highest bidder? Love springs not up, I trow, because the one is in his prime, and the other's bloom is withered, because fair is mated with what is not fair, and hot lips are pressed to cold. Between man and woman it is different. There the wife at any rate shares with her husband in their nuptial joys; but here conversely, the one is sober and with unimpassioned eye regards his fellow, who is drunken with

---

[1437] Or, "perfection."
[1438] Lit. "the boy."
[1439] Reading (en para ti poiese). *Al.* "come what come may," lit. "no alteration"; or if reading (parebese) transl. "although his May of youth should pass, and sickness should mar his features, the tie of friendship will not be weakened."
[1440] For beauty of style (in the original) Zeune cf. *Mem.* II. vi. 28 foll.; III. xi. 10.
[1441] "Albeit absent from one another in the body, they are more present in the soul." Cf. Virg. *Aen.* iv. 83, "illum absens absentem auditque videtque."
[1442] Or, "bear the stamp of Aphrodite."
[1443] Or, "is wholly taken up with." Cf. Plat. *Laws,* 831 C.
[1444] Cf. *Hiero,* iii. 3; *Cyrop.* III. i. 39.

the wine of passion.[1445]

Wherefore it is no marvel if, beholding, there springs up in his breast the bitterest contempt and scorn for such a lover. Search and you shall find that nothing harsh was ever yet engendered by attachment based on moral qualities; whilst shameless intercourse, time out of mind, has been the source of countless hateful and unhallowed deeds.[1446]

I have next to show that the society of him whose love is of the body, not the soul, is in itself illiber*al*. The true educator who trains another in the path of virtue, who will teach us excellence, whether of speech or conduct,[1447] may well be honoured, even as Cheiron and Phoenix[1448] were honoured by Achilles. But what can he expect, who stretches forth an eager hand to clutch the body, save to be treated[1449] as a beggar? That is his character; for ever cringing and petitioning a kiss, or some other soft caress,[1450] this sorry suitor dogs his victims.

If my language has a touch of turbulence,[1451] do not marvel: partly the wine exalts me; partly that love which ever dwells within my heart of hearts now pricks me forward to use great boldness of speech[1452] against his base antagonist. Why, yes indeed, it seems to me that he who fixes his mind on outward beauty is like a man who has taken a farm on a short lease. He shows no anxiety to improve its value; his sole object being to take off it the largest crops he can himself. But he whose heart is set on loyal friendship resembles rather a man who has a farmstead of his own. At any rate, he scours the wide world to find what may enhance the value of his soul's delight.[1453]

Again, let us consider the effect upon the object of attachment. Let

---

[1445] Lit. "by Aphrodite." Cf. Plat. *Phaedr.* 240, "But the lover... when he is drunk" (Jowett); *Symp.* 214 C.

[1446] Zeune cf. Ael. *V. H.* viii. 9, re Archelaus king of Macedon, concerning whom Aristotle, *Pol.* v. 10. 1311 B: "Many conspiracies have originated in shameful attempts made by sovereigns on the persons of their subjects. Such was the attack of Crataeus upon Archelaus," etc. (Jowett).

[1447] Phoenix addresses Achilles, *Il.* ix. 443:

(muthon te reter' emenai, prektera te ergon)

Therefore sent he (Peleus) me to thee to teach thee all things,
To be both a speaker of words and a doer of deeds (W. Leaf).

[1448] See *Il.* xi. 831; *Hunting,* ch. i., as to Cheiron and his scholars, the last of whom is Achilles.

[1449] (an periepoito). "He will be scurvily treated." Cf. *Hell.* III. i. 19.

[1450] Cf. *Mem.* I. ii. 29.

[1451] Or, "wantonness"; and for the apology see Plat. *Phaedr.* 238: "I appear to be in a divine fury, for already I am getting into dithyrambics" (Jowett).

[1452] Lit. "to speak openly against that other sort of love which is its riv*al*."

[1453] Cf. Michelet, I think, as to the French peasant-farmer regarding his property as "sa femme."

him but know his beauty is a bond sufficient to enthrall his lover,[1454] and what wonder if he be careless of all else and play the wanton. Let him discover, on the contrary, that if he would retain his dear affection he must himself be truly good and beautiful, and it is only natural he should become more studious of virtue. But the greatest blessing which descends on one beset with eager longing to convert the idol of his soul into a good man and true friend is this: necessity is laid upon himself to practise virtue; since how can he hope to make his comrade good, if he himself works wickedness? Is it conceivable that the example he himself presents of what is shameless and incontinent,[1455] will serve to make the beloved one temperate and modest?

I have a longing, Callias, by mythic argument[1456] to show you that not men only, but gods and heroes, set greater store by friendship of the soul than bodily enjoyment. Thus those fair women[1457] whom Zeus, enamoured of their outward beauty, wedded, he permitted mortal to remain; but those heroes whose souls he held in admiration, these he raised to immortality. Of whom are Heracles and the Dioscuri, and there are others also named.[1458] As I maintain, it was not for his body's sake, but for his soul's, that Ganymede[1459] was translated to Olympus, as the story goes, by Zeus. And to this his very name bears witness, for is it not written in Homer?

And he gladdens (ganutai) to hear his voice.[1460]

This the poet says, meaning "he is pleased to listen to his words."

And again, in another passage he says:

Knowing deep devices (medea) in his mind,[1461]

which is as much as to say, "knowing wise counsels in his mind." Ganymede, therefore, bears a name compounded of the two words, "*joy*" and "*counsel*," and is honoured among the gods, not as one "whose body," but "whose *mind*" "*gives pleasure*."

[1454] Or, "that by largess of beauty he can enthrall his lover."

[1455] See Plat. *Symp.* 182 A, 192 A.

[1456] Or, "I have a desire to romance a little," "for your benefit to explain by legendary lore." Cf. Isocr. 120 C; Plat. *Rep.* 392 B.

[1457] e.g. Leda, Danaë, Europa, Alcmena, Electra, Latona, Laodamia (Zeune).

[1458] See *Hunting*, i.; *Hell.* VI. iii. 6.

[1459] See Plat. *Phaedr.* 255 C; Cic. *Tusc.* i. 26, "nec Homerum audio... divina mallem ad nos," a protest against anthropomorphism in religion.

[1460] Not in "our" version of Homer, but cf. *Il.* xx. 405, (ganutai de te tois 'Enosikhthon); *Il.* xiii. 493, (ganutai d' ara te phrena poimen).

[1461] Partly *Il.* xxiv. 674, (pukina phresi mede' ekhontes); and *Il.* xxiv. 424, (phila phresi medea eidos). Cf. *Od.* vi. 192; xviii. 67, 87; xxii. 476.

Furthermore (I appeal to you, Nicêratus),[1462] Homer makes Achilles avenge Patroclus in that brilliant fashion, not as his favourite, but as his comrade.[1463] Yes, and Orestes and Pylades,[1464] Theseus and Peirithoüs,[1465] with many another noble pair of demigods, are celebrated as having wrought in common great and noble deeds, not because they lay inarmed, but because of the admiration they felt for one another.

Nay, take the fair deeds of to-day: and you shall find them wrought rather for the sake of praise by volunteers in toil and peril, than by men accustomed to choose pleasure in place of honour. And yet Pausanias,[1466] the lover of the poet Agathon,[1467] making a defence in behalf[1468] of some who wallow in incontinence, has stated that an army composed of lovers and beloved would be invincible.[1469] These, in his opinion, would, from awe of one another, have the greatest horror of destruction. A truly marvellous argument, if he means that men accustomed to turn deaf ears to censure and to behave to one another shamelessly, are more likely to feel ashamed of doing a shameful deed. He adduced as evidence the fact that the Thebans and the Eleians[1470] recognise the very principle, and added: Though they sleep inarmed, they do not scruple to range the lover side by side with the beloved one in the field of battle. An instance which I take to be no instance, or at any rate one-sided,[1471] seeing that what they look upon as lawful with us is scandalous.[1472] Indeed, it strikes me that this vaunted battle-order

---

[1462] As an authority on Homer.

[1463] Cf. Plat. *Symp.* 179 E: "The notion that Patroclus was the beloved one is a foolish error into which Aeschylus has fallen," etc. (in his *Myrmidons*). See J. A. Symonds, *The Greek Poets*, 2nd series, "Achilles," p. 66 foll.

[1464] Concerning whom Ovid ("Pont." iii. 2. 70) says, "nomina fama tenet."

[1465] See Plut. *Thes.* 30 foll. (Clough, i. p. 30 foll.); cf. Lucian, xli. *Toxaris*, 10.

[1466] See Cobet, *Pros. Xen.* p. 15; Plat. *Protag.*315 D; Ael. *V. H.* ii. 21.

[1467] Ib.; Aristot. *Poet.* ix.

[1468] Or, "in his 'Apology' for."

[1469] Plat. *Symp.* 179 E, puts the sentiment into the mouth of Phaedrus: "And if there were only some way of contriving that a state or an army should be made up of lovers and their loves, they would be the very best governors of their own city, abstaining from all dishonour, and emulating one another in honour; and when fighting at one another's side, although not a mere handful, they would overcome the world. For what lover would not choose rather to be seen by all mankind than by his beloved, either when abandoning his post or throwing away his arms? He would be ready to die a thousand deaths rather than endure this. Or would desert his beloved or fail him in the hour of danger? The veriest coward would become an inspired hero, equal to the bravest, at such a time; Love would inspire him. That courage which, as Homer says, the god breathes into the soul of heroes, Love of his own nature infuses into the lover" (Jowett). Cf. *Hunting*, xii. 20; *Anab.* VII. iv. 7; *Cyrop.* VII. i. 30.

[1470] Sc. in their institutions. Cf. Plat. *Symp.* 182, "in Elis and Boeotia"; *Pol. Lac.* ii. 13; Ael. *V. H.* iii. 12, xiii. 5; Athen. xiii. 2. For the Theban Sacred Band see Plut. *Pelop.* 18, 19 (Clough, ii. 218).

[1471] Or, "not *in pari materia*, so to speak."

[1472] Is not Xenophon imputing himself to Socrates? Henkel cf. Plat. *Crito*, 52 E. See

would seem to argue some mistrust on their part who adopt it—a suspicion that their bosom friends, once separated from them, may forget to behave as brave men should. But the men of Lacedaemon, holding that "if a man but lay his hand upon the body and for lustful purpose, he shall thereby forfeit claim to what is beautiful and noble"— do, in the spirit of their creed, contrive to mould and fashion their "beloved ones" to such height of virtue,[1473] that should these find themselves drawn up with foreigners, albeit no longer side by side with their own lovers,[1474] conscience will make desertion of their present friends impossible. Self-respect constrains them: since the goddess whom the men of Lacedaemon worship is not "Shamelessness," but "Reverence."[1475]

I fancy we should all agree with one another on the point in question, if we thus approached it. Ask yourself to which type of the two must he[1476] accord, to whom you would entrust a sum of money, make him the guardian of your children, look to find in him a safe and sure depositary of any favour?[1477] For my part, I am certain that the very lover addicted to external beauty would himself far sooner have his precious things entrusted to the keeping of one who has the inward beauty of the soul.[1478]

Ah, yes! and you, my friend (he turned to Callias), you have good reason to be thankful to the gods who of their grace inspired you with love for your Autolycus. Covetous of honour,[1479] beyond all controversy, must he be, who could endure so many toils and pains to hear his name proclaimed[1480] victor in the "pankration."

But what if the thought arose within him:[1481] his it is not merely to add lustre to himself and to his father, but that he has ability, through help of manly virtue, to benefit his friends and to exalt his fatherland, by trophies which he will set up against our enemies in war,[1482]

Newman, *op. cit.* i. 396.

[1473] Or, "shape to so fine a manhood that..."

[1474] Reading (en te aute taxei). *Al.* (... polei), transl. "nor indeed in the same city." Cf. *Hell.* V. iv. 33, re death of Cleonymus at Leuctra.

[1475] Lit. "Aidôs not Anaideia." See Paus. *Lac.* xx. 10; *Attica*, xvii. 1; Cic. *de Leg.* ii. 11, a reference which I owe to M. Eugene Talbot, "Xen." i. 236.

[1476] He (the master-mistress of my passion).

[1477] (kharitas) = "kindly offices," *beneficia.* Cf. *Ages.* iv. 4; *Mem.* IV. iv. 17. *Al.* = *delicias*, "to deposit some darling object."

[1478] Or, "some one truly lovable in soul and heart."

[1479] See *Mem.* II. iii. 16; *Isocr.* 189 C, (ph. kai megalopsukhoi).

[1480] *i.e.* "by the public herald."

[1481] Cf. Theogn. 947:

(patrida kosmeso, liparen polin, out' epi demo
trepsas out' adikois andrasi peithomenos).

[1482] Who in 421 B.C. were of course the Lacedaemonians and the allies. Autolycus was killed eventually by the Thirty to please the Lacedaemonian harmost. See Plut.

whereby he will himself become the admired of all observers, nay, a name to be remembered among Hellenes and barbarians.[1483] Would he not in that case, think you, make much of[1484] one whom he regarded as his bravest fellow-worker, laying at his feet the greatest honours?

If, then, you wish to be well-pleasing in his eyes, you had best inquire by what knowledge Themistocles[1485] was able to set Hellas free. You should ask yourself, what keen wit belonged to Pericles[1485] that he was held to be the best adviser of his fatherland. You should scan[1486] the field of history to learn by what sage wisdom Solon[1487] established for our city her consummate laws. I would have you find the clue to that peculiar training by which the men of Lacedaemon have come to be regarded as the best of leaders.[1488] Is it not at your house that their noblest citizens are lodged as representatives of a foreign state?[1489]

Be sure that our state of Athens would speedily entrust herself to your direction were you willing.[1490] Everything is in your favour. You are of noble family, "eupatrid" by descent, a priest of the divinities,[1491] and of Erechtheus' famous line,[1492] which with Iacchus marched to encounter the barbarian.[1493] And still, at the sacred festival to-day, it is agreed that no one among your ancestors has ever been more fitted to discharge the priestly office than yourself; yours a person the goodliest to behold in all our city, and a frame adapted to undergo great toils.

But if I seem to any of you to indulge a vein more serious than befits the wine-cup, marvel not. It has long been my wont to share our city's passion for noble-natured souls, alert and emulous in pursuit of virtue.

Lysand. 15 (Clough, iii. 120); Paus. i. 18. 3; ix. 32. 8. Cf. *Hell.* II. iii. 14.

[1483] Cf. *Anab.* IV. i. 20; *Mem.* III. vi. 2.

[1484] (periepein). Cf. *Cyrop.* IV. iv. 12; *Mem.* II. ix. 5.

[1485] See *Mem.* II. vi. 13; III. vi. 2; IV. ii. 2.

[1486] For the diction, (skepteon, skepteon, aphreteon, ereuneteon, epistamenos, eidos, philosopheras), Xenophon's rhetorical style imitates the (orthoepeia) of Prodicus.

[1487] See *Econ.* xiv. 4.

[1488] Or, "won for themselves at all hands the reputation of noblest generalship." Cf. *Ages.* i. 3; *Pol. Lac.* xiv. 3.

[1489] Reading as vulg. (proxenoi d' ei...) or if with Schenkl, (proxenos d' ei...) transl. "You are their consul-general; at your house their noblest citizens are lodged from time to time." As to the office, cf. Dem. 475. 10; 1237. 17; Thuc. ii. 29; Boeckh, *P. E. A.* 50. Callias appears as the Lac. (proxenos) (*Hell.* V. iv. 22) 378 B.C., and at Sparta, 371 B.C., as the peace commissioner (*Hell.* VI. iii. 3).

[1490] Cf. *Mem.* III. vii.

[1491] *i.e.* Demeter and Core. Callias (see *Hell.* VI. *l.c.*) was dadouchos (or torch-holder) in the mysteries.

[1492] Or, "whose rites date back to Erechtheus." Cf. Plat. *Theag.* 122.

[1493] At Salamis. The tale is told by Herod. viii. 65, and Plut. *Themist.* 15; cf. Polyaen. *Strat.* iii. 11. 2. Just as Themistocles had won the battle of Salamis by help of Iacchus on the 16th Boedromion, the first day of the mysteries, so Chabrias won the sea-fight of Naxos by help of the day itself, (to 'Alade mustai), 376 B.C.

He ended, and, while the others continued to discuss the theme of his discourse, Autolycus sat regarding Callias. That other, glancing the while at the beloved one, turned to Socrates.

Call. Then, Socrates, be pleased, as go-between,[1494] to introduce me to the state, that I may employ myself in state affairs and never lapse from her good graces.[1495]

Never fear (he answered), if only people see your loyalty to virtue is genuine,[1496] not of mere repute. A false renown indeed is quickly seen for what it is worth, being tested; but true courage[1497] (save only what some god hinder) perpetually amidst the storm and stress of circumstance[1498] pours forth a brighter glory.

IX

On such a note he ended his discourse.

At that, Autolycus, whose hour for walking exercise had now come, arose. His father, Lycon, was about to leave the room along with him, but before so doing, turned to Socrates, remarking:

By Hera, Socrates, if ever any one deserved the appellation "beautiful and good,"[1499] you are that man!

So the pair departed. After they were gone, a sort of throne was first erected in the inner room abutting on the supper chamber. Then the Syracusan entered, with a speech:

With your good pleasure, sirs, Ariadne is about to enter the bridal chamber set apart for her and Dionysus. Anon Dionysus will appear, fresh from the table of the gods, wine-flushed, and enter to his bride. In the last scene the two will play[1500] with one another.

He had scarce concluded, when Ariadne entered, attired like a bride. She crossed the stage and sate herself upon the throne. Meanwhile, before the god himself appeared a sound of flutes was heard; the cadence of the Bacchic air proclaimed his coming.

At this point the company broke forth in admiration of the ballet-master. For no sooner did the sound of music strike upon the ear of Ariadne than something in her action revealed to all the pleasure which it caused her. She did not step forward to meet her lover, she did not rise even from her seat; but the flutter of her unrest was plain to see.[1501]

[1494] Lit. "as pander."
[1495] So Critobulus in the conversation so often referred to. *Mem.* II. vi.
[1496] See *Mem.* I. vii. 1, passim; II. vi. 39; *Econ.* x. 9.
[1497] Cf. Thuc. ii. 42, (andragathia), "true courage in the public service covers a multitude of private shortcomings."
[1498] (en tais praxesi). Cf. Plat. *Phaedr.* 271 D, "in actual life."
[1499] For (kalos ge kalathos) see *Econ.* vii. 2 and passim.
[1500] (paixountai). The Syracusan naturally uses the Doric form. See Cobet, *Pros. Xen.* p. 16, note 23. Rutherford, *N. Phrynicus*, p. 91.
[1501] Lit. "the difficulty she had to keep so still was evident."

When Dionysus presently caught sight of her he loved, lightly he danced towards her, and with show of tenderest passion gently reclined upon her knees; his arms entwined about her lovingly, and upon her lips he sealed a kiss;[1502]—she the while with most sweet bashfulness was fain to wind responsive arms about her lover; till the banqueters, the while they gazed all eyes, clapped hands and cried "Encore!" But when Dionysus rose upon his feet, and rising lifted Ariadne to her full height, the action of those lovers as they kissed and fondled one another was a thing to contemplate.[1503] As to the spectators, they could see that Dionysus was indeed most beautiful, and Ariadne like some lovely blossom; nor were those mocking gestures, but real kisses sealed on loving lips; and so,[1504] with hearts aflame, they gazed expectantly. They could hear the question asked by Dionysus, did she love him? and her answer, as prettily she swore she did. And withal so earnestly, not Dionysus only, but all present, had sworn an oath in common: the boy and girl were verily and indeed a pair of happy lovers. So much less did they resemble actors, trained to certain gestures, than two beings bent on doing what for many a long day they had set their hearts on.

At last when these two lovers, caught in each other's arms, were seen to be retiring to the nuptial couch, the members of the supper party turned to withdraw themselves; and whilst those of them who were unmarried swore that they would wed, those who were wedded mounted their horses and galloped off to join their wives, in quest of married joys.

Only Socrates, and of the rest the few who still remained behind, anon set off with Callias, to see out Lycon and his son, and share the walk.

And so this supper party, assembled in honour of Autolycus, broke up.

[1502] Or, "and encircling his arms about her impressed upon her lips a kiss."
[1503] Or, "then was it possible to see the more than mimic gestures."
[1504] Or, "on the tiptoe of excitement." Cf. *Hell.* III. i. 14, iv. 2.

The Apology

OF SOCRATES[1505]

Among the reminiscences of Socrates, none, as it seems to me, is more deserving of record than the counsel he took with himself[1506] (after being cited to appear before the court), not only with regard to his defence, but also as to the ending of his life. Others have written on this theme, and all without exception have touched upon[1507] the lofty style of the philosopher,[1508] which may be taken as a proof that the language used by Socrates was really of that type. But none of these writers has brought out clearly the fact that Socrates had come to regard death as for himself preferable to life; and consequently there is just a suspicion of foolhardiness in the arrogancy of his address.[1509] We have, however, from the lips of one of his intimate acquaintances, Hermogenes,[1510] the son of Hipponicus, an account of him which shows the high demeanour in question to have been altogether in keeping with the master's rational purpose.[1511] Hermogenes says that, seeing Socrates discoursing on every topic rather than that of his impending trial, he roundly put it to him whether he ought not to be debating the line of his defence, to which Socrates in the first instance answered: "What! do I not seem to you to have spent my whole life in meditating my defence?" And when Hermogenes asked him, "How?" he added: "By a lifelong persistence in doing nothing wrong, and that I take to be the finest practice for his defence which a man could devise." Presently reverting to the topic, Hermogenes demanded: "Do you not see, Socrates, how often Athenian juries[1512] are constrained by arguments to put quite innocent people to death, and not less often to acquit the guilty, either through some touch of pity excited by the pleadings, or that the defendant had skill to turn some charming phrase?" Thus appealed to, Socrates replied: "Nay, solemnly I tell you, twice already I have essayed to consider my

---

[1505] Or, "Socrates' Defence before the Dicasts." For the title of the work see Grote, *H. G.* viii. 641; Schneid. ap. L. Dindorf's note (pros tous dikastas), ed. Ox. 1862, and Dindorf's own note; L. Schmitz, "On the Apology of Socrates, commonly attributed to Xenophon," *Class. Mus.* v. 222 foll.; G. Sauppe, *Praef.* vol. iii. p. 117, ed. ster.; J. J. Hartman, *An. Xen.* p. 111 foll.; E. Richter, *Xen. Stud.* pp. 61-96; M. Schanz, *Platos Apologia*.

[1506] Or possibly, "his deliberate behaviour."

[1507] Or, "have succeeded in hitting off"; "done full justice to."

[1508] Or, "the magniloquence of the master."

[1509] Or, "so that according to them his lofty speech seems rather foolhardy."

[1510] See (*Mem.* IV. viii. 4 foll.), a passage of which this is either an *ébauchement* or a *réchauffé*.

[1511] Or, "the philosopher's cast of thought."

[1512] Dikastêries.

defence, and twice the divinity[1513] hinders me"; and to the remark of Hermogenes, "That is strange!" he answered again: "Strange, do you call it, that to God it should seem better for me to die at once? Do you not know that up to this moment I will not concede to any man to have lived a better life than I have; since what can exceed the pleasure, which has been mine, of knowing[1514] that my whole life has been spent holily and justly? And indeed this verdict of self-approval I found re-echoed in the opinion which my friends and intimates have formed concerning me.[1515] And now if my age is still to be prolonged,[1516] I know that I cannot escape paying[1517] the penalty of old age, in increasing dimness of sight and dulness of hearing. I shall find myself slower to learn new lessons, and apter to forget the lessons I have learnt. And if to these be added the consciousness of failing powers, the sting of self-reproach, what prospect have I of any further joy in living? It may be, you know," he added, "that God out of his great kindness is intervening in my behalf[1518] to suffer me to close my life in the ripeness of age, and by the gentlest of deaths. For if at this time sentence of death be passed upon me, it is plain I shall be allowed to meet an end which, in the opinion of those who have studied the matter, is not only the easiest in itself, but one which will cause the least trouble to one's friends,[1519] while engendering the deepest longing for the departed. For of necessity he will only be thought of with regret and longing who leaves nothing behind unseemly or discomfortable to haunt the imagination of those beside him, but, sound of body, and his soul still capable of friendly repose, fades tranquilly away."

"No doubt," he added, "the gods were right in opposing me at that time (touching the inquiry, what I was to say in my defence),[1520] when you all thought the great thing was to discover some means of acquittal;[1521] since, had I effected that, it is clear I should have prepared for myself, not that surcease from life which is in store for me anon, but to end my days wasted by disease, or by old age, on which a confluent stream of evil things most alien to joyousness converges."[1522]

"No," he added, "God knows I shall display no ardent zeal to bring

---

[1513] (to daimonion).

[1514] (edein), *i.e.* at any moment.

[1515] For the phrase (iskhuros agamenos emauton), cf. *Mem.* II. i. 19.

[1516] L. Dindorf cf. Dio Chrys. "Or." 28, (anagke gar auto en probainonti anti men kallistou aiskhrotero gignesthai k.t.l.)

[1517] (apoteleisthai). In *Mem.* IV. viii. 8, (epiteleisthai).

[1518] Or, "God of his good favour vouchsafes as my protector that I should," etc. For (proxenei) cf. *Anab.* VI. v. 14; Soph. *O. C.* 465, and *O. T.* 1483; and Prof. Jebb's notes *ad loc.* "the god's kindly offices grant to me that I should lose my life."

[1519] Cf. Plat. *Phaed.* 66.

[1520] (te tou logou episkepsei). Cf. Plat. "Rep." 456 C.

[1521] Or, if (emin), transl. "we all were for thinking that the main thing was."

[1522] Or, "that sink into which a confluent stream of evil humours discharge most incompatible with gaiety of mind." Schneid. conj. (eremon) sc. (geras).

that about.[1523] On the contrary, if by proclaiming all the blessings which I owe to god and men; if, by blazoning forth the opinion which I entertain with regard to myself, I end by wearying the court, even so will I choose death rather than supplicate in servile sort for leave to live a little longer merely to gain a life impoverished in place of death."

It was in this determination, Hermogenes states, that, when the prosecution accused him of not recognising the gods recognised by the state, but introducing novel divinities and corrupting the young, Socrates stepped forward and said: "In the first place, sirs, I am at a loss to imagine on what ground[1524] Melêtus asserts that I do not recognise the gods which are recognised by the state, since, as far as sacrificing goes, the rest of the world who have chanced to be present have been in the habit of seeing me so engaged at common festivals, and on the public altars; and so might Melêtus himself, if he had wished. And as to novel divinities, how, pray, am I supposed to introduce them by stating that I have a voice[1525] from God which clearly signifies to me what I ought do? Why, what else do those who make use of the cries of birds or utterances of men draw their conclusions from if not from voices? Who will deny that the thunder has a voice and is a very mighty omen;[1526] and the priestess on her tripod at Pytho,[1527] does not she also proclaim by voice the messages from the god? The god, at any rate, has foreknowledge, and premonishes those whom he will of what is about to be. That is a thing which all the world believes and asserts even as I do. Only, when they describe these premonitions under the name of birds and utterances, tokens[1528] and soothsayers, I speak of a divinity, and in using that designation I claim to speak at once more exactly and more reverentially than they do who ascribe the power of the gods to birds. And that I am not lying against the Godhead I have this as a proof: although I have reported to numbers of friends the counsels of heaven, I have never at any time been shown to be a deceiver or deceived."

As they listened to these words the judges murmured their dissent, some as disbelieving what was said, and others out of simple envy that Socrates should actually receive from heaven more than they themselves; whereupon Socrates returned to the charge. "Come," he said, "lend me your ears while I tell you something more, so that those of you who choose may go to a still greater length in refusing to believe that I am thus highly honoured by the divine powers. Chaerephon[1529]

[1523] Or, "I will give no helping hand to that."
[1524] Cf. *Mem.* I. i. 2.
[1525] Cf. Plat. *Apol.* 19.
[1526] Cf. *Anab.* III. ii. 11; Aristoph. *Birds*, 720.
[1527] Delphi.
[1528] Or, "the objects that meet us." See Prof. Jebb ad Theophr. *Ch.* xxviii. 5.
[1529] L. Dindorf cf. Athen. v. 218 E; Hermesianax ap. Athen. xiii. 599 A; Liban. vol.

once, in the presence of many witnesses, put a question at Delhi concerning me, and Apollo answered that there was no human being more liberal, or more upright, or more temperate than myself." And when once more on hearing these words the judges gave vent, as was only natural, to a fiercer murmur of dissent, Socrates once again spoke: "Yet, sirs, they were still greater words which the god spake in oracle concerning Lycurgus,[1530] the great lawgiver of Lacedaemon, than those concerning me. It is said that as he entered the temple the god addressed him with the words: 'I am considering whether to call thee god or man.' Me he likened not indeed to a god, but in excellence[1531] preferred me far beyond other men."

"Still I would not have you accept this even on the faith of the god too rashly; rather I would have you investigate, point by point, what the god has said. I ask you, is there any one[1532] else, you know of, less enslaved than myself to the appetites[1533] of the body? Can you name another man of more independent spirit than myself, seeing that I accept from no one either gifts or pay? Whom have you any right to believe to be more just[1534] than one so suited with what he has, that the things of others excite no craving in him?[1535] Whom would one reasonably deem wise, rather than such a one as myself, who, from the moment I began to understand things spoken,[1536] have never omitted to inquire into and learn every good thing in my power? And that I laboured not in vain, what more conclusive evidence than the fact that so many of my fellow-citizens who make virtue their pursuit, and many strangers also, choose my society in preference to that of others?[1537] And how are we to explain the fact that though all know well enough that I am wholly unable to repay them in money, so many are eager to

---

iii. pp. 34, 35; Plat. *Apol.* 21 A; Paus. i. 22. 8; Schol. ad Aristoph. *Clouds*, 144; Grote, *H. G.* viii. 567 foll.

[1530] See Herod. i. 65:

(ekeis, o Lukoorge, emon pori piona neon,
Zeni philos kai pasin 'Olumpia domat' ekhousi
dizo e se theon manteusomai e anthropon.
all' eti kai mallon theon elpomai, o Lukoorge.)
Cf. Plut. *Lyc.* 5 (Clough, i. 89).

[1531] Or, "gave judgment beforehand that I far excelled."
[1532] Lit. "whom do you know," and so throughout.
[1533] Cf. Plat. *Phaed.* 66 C.
[1534] Or, "so attempered and adjusted." The phrase savours of "cynic." theory.
[1535] Or, "present no temptation to him"; lit. "that he stands in no further need of what belongs to his neighbours."
[1536] (ta legomena), "the meaning of words and the force of argument."
[1537] (ek panton). Cf. Thuc. i. 120, (osper kai en allois ek panton protimontai (oi egemones)), "as they (leaders) are first in honour, they should be first in the fulfilment of their duties" (Jowett).

present me with some gift?[1538] And what do you make of this—while no one dreams of dunning me for benefits conferred, hosts of people acknowledge debts of gratitude to myself? And what of this, that during the siege,[1539] while others were pitying themselves[1540] I lived in no greater straits than when the city was at the height of her prosperity? and of this, that while others provide themselves with delicacies[1541] of the market at great cost, mine are the dainties of the soul more sweet than theirs,[1542] procured without expense? If in all I have said about myself no one can convict me of lying, is it not obvious that the praise I get from gods and men is justly earned? And yet in spite of all, Melêtus, you will have it that by such habits I corrupt the young. We know, I fancy, what such corrupting influences are; and perhaps you will tell us if you know of any one who, under my influence, has been changed from a religious into an irreligious man; who, from being sober-minded, has become prodigal; from being a moderate drinker has become a wine-bibber and a drunkard; from being a lover of healthy honest toil has become effeminate, or under the thrall of some other wicked pleasure."

"Nay, bless my soul," exclaimed Melêtus, "I know those whom you persuaded to obey yourself rather than the fathers who begat them."[1543]

"I admit it," Socrates replied, "in the case of education, for they know that I have made the matter a study; and with regard to health a man prefers to obey his doctor rather than his parents; in the public assembly the citizens of Athens, I presume, obey those whose arguments exhibit the soundest wisdom rather than their own relations. And is it not the case that, in your choice of generals, you set your fathers and brothers, and, bless me! your own selves aside, by comparison with those whom you believe to be the wisest authorities on military matters?"

"No doubt, Socrates," replied Melêtus, "because it is expedient and customary so to do."

"Well then," rejoined Socrates, "does it not strike even you, Melêtus, as wonderful when in all ordinary concerns the best people should obtain, I do not say only an equal share, but an exclusive

---

[1538] The commentators quote Libanius, *Apol.* vol. iii. p. 39, (kai dia touto ekalei men Eurulokhos o Kharistios, ekalei de Skopas k Kranonios, oukh ekista Iontes, upiskhnoumenoi). Cf. Diog. Laert. ii. 31, (Kharmidou oiketas auto didontos, in' ap' auton prosodeuoito, oukh eileto). Cf. id. 65, 74.

[1539] See *Hell.* II. ii. 10.

[1540] (oikteirein eautous). See L. Dind. *ad loc.* For an incident in point see *Mem.* II. vii.

[1541] Plat. *Rep.* iii. 404 D, "refinements of Attic confectionery."

[1542] (ek tes psukhes), possibly "by a healthy appetite." Cf. *Symp.* iv. 41. The same sentiment *ex ore Antisthenis.* See Joel, *op. cit.* i. 382; Schanz, Plat. *Apol.* p. 88, S. 26.

[1543] Cf. *Mem.* I. ii. 49.

preference; but in my case, simply because I am selected by certain people as an adept in respect of the greatest treasure men possess—education, I am on that account to be prosecuted by you, sir, on the capital charge?"

Much more than this, it stands to reason, was urged, whether by himself or by the friends who advocated his cause.[1544] But my object has not been to mention everything that arose out of the suit. It suffices me to have shown on the one hand that Socrates, beyond everything, desired not to display impiety to heaven,[1545] and injustice to men; and on the other, that escape from death was not a thing, in his opinion, to be clamoured for importunately—on the contrary, he believed that the time was already come for him to die. That such was the conclusion to which he had come was made still more evident later when the case had been decided against him. In the first place, when called upon to suggest a counter-penalty,[1546] he would neither do so himself nor suffer his friends to do so for him, but went so far as to say that to propose a counter-penalty was like a confession of guilt. And afterwards, when his companions wished to steal him out of prison,[1547] he would not follow their lead, but would seem to have treated the idea as a jest, by asking "whether they happened to know of some place outside Attica where death was forbidden to set foot?"

When the trial drew to an end, we are told, the master said:[1548] "Sirs, those who instructed the witnesses that they ought to perjure themselves and bear false witness against me, alike with those who listened to their instruction, must be conscious to themselves of a deep impiety and injustice.[1549] But for myself, what reason have I at the present time to hold my head less high than I did before sentence was passed against me, if I have not been convicted of having done any of those things whereof my accusers accused me? It has not been proved against me that I have sacrificed to novel divinities in place of Zeus and Hera and the gods who form their company. I have not taken oath by any other gods, nor named their name.

"And then the young—how could I corrupt them by habituating them to manliness and frugality? since not even my accusers themselves allege against me that I have committed any of those

---

[1544] (sunagoreuein), L. and S. cf Thuc. vi. 6, "partisans," viii. 84, "pleaded the case of" (Jowett).

[1545] Or, "laid the greatest stress of not being guilty of impiety"; "attached the greatest importance to the fact that he was never guilty of impiety."

[1546] (upotimasthai). See L. Dind. cf. Cic. *Orat.* i. 54; the technical word is (antitimasthai). Cf. Plat. *Apol.* 36 D; Diog. Laert. ii. 41. These authorities tell a different story. Why should these stories, if true, as no doubt they were, be omitted?

[1547] Cf. Plat. "Crit." 44 B.

[1548] (eipein auton [autos(?)]), *i.e.* "according to Hermiogenes."

[1549] Or, "must have a heavy load on their minds in the consciousness of their impiety and injustice."

deeds[1550] of which death is the penalty, such as robbery of temples,[1551] breaking into houses, selling freemen into slavery, or betrayal of the state; so that I must still ask myself in wonderment how it has been proved to you that I have done a deed worthy of death. Nor yet again because I die innocently is that a reason why I should lower my crest, for that is a blot not upon me but upon those who condemned me.

"For me, I find a certain consolation in the case of Palamedes,[1552] whose end was not unlike my own; who still even to-day furnishes a far nobler theme of song than Odysseus who unjustly slew him; and I know that testimony will be borne to me also by time future and time past that I never wronged another at any time or ever made a worse man of him,[1553] but ever tried to benefit those who practised discussion with me, teaching them gratuitously every good thing in my power."

Having so said he turned and went in a manner quite in conformity[1554] with the words which he had spoken—so bright an air was discernible alike in the glance of his eye, his gesture, and his step.

And when he perceived those who followed by his side in tears, "What is this?" he asked. "Why do you weep now?[1555] Do you not know that for many a long day, ever since I was born, sentence of death was passed upon me by nature? If so be I perish prematurely while the tide of life's blessings flows free and fast, certainly I and my well-wishers should feel pained; but if it be that I am bringing my life to a close on the eve of troubles, for my part I think you ought all of you to take heart of grace and rejoice in my good fortune."

Now there was a certain Apollodorus,[1556] who was an enthusiastic lover of the master, but for the rest a simple-minded man. He exclaimed very innocently, "But the hardest thing of all to bear, Socrates, is to see you put to death unjustly."[1557]

Whereupon Socrates, it is said, gently stroked the young man's

---

[1550] Cf. *Mem.* I. ii. 62.

[1551] See Plat. "Rep." iii. 413 A.

[1552] Cf. *Mem.* IV. viii. 9, 10; *ib.* IV. ii. 3. See Plat. *Rep.* v. 476 D, (exomen ti paramutheisthai auton); and *Hunting*, i. 11. The story of Palamedes is told by Ovid, *Met.* xiii. 5.

[1553] Cf. Plat. *Apol.* 25 D, (poteron eme eisageis deuro os diaphtheironta tous neous kai poneroterous poiounta ekonta e akonta).

[1554] (omologoumenos). For the use of the word L. Dind. cf. Diog. Laert. vii. 87, (dioper protos o Zenon en to peri anthropou phuseos telos eipe to omologoumenos te phusei zen) (Cicero's *naturae convenienter vivere*, L. and S.), whereas the regular Attic use is different. Cf. "Oec." i. 11, (kai omologoumenos ge o logos emin khorei) = *consentanea ratione*. "Our argument runs on all-fours." Plat. "Symp." 186 B, (to nasoun omologoumenos eteron te kai anomoion esti), *ut inter omnes conveniet*.

[1555] "Why precisely now?"

[1556] Cf. *Mem.* III. xi. 17; Plut. *Cato min.* 46 (Clough, iv. 417). See Cobet, *Pros. Xen.* s.n.; cf. Plat. *Symp.* 173; *Phaed.* 54 A, 117 D; Aelian, *V. H.* i. 16; Heges. *Delph.* ap. Athen. xi. 507.

[1557] Diog. Laert. ii. 5. 35, ascribes the remark to Xanthippe, and so Val. Max. 7. 2, Ext. 1.

head: "Would you have been better pleased, my dear one, to see me put to death for some just reason rather than unjustly?" and as he spoke he smiled tenderly.[1558]

It is also said that, seeing Anytus[1559] pass by, Socrates remarked: "How proudly the great man steps; he thinks, no doubt, he has performed some great and noble deed in putting me to death, and all because, seeing him deemed worthy of the highest honours of the state, I told him it ill became him to bring up his so in a tan-yard.[1560] What a scamp the fellow is! he appears not to know that of us two whichever has achieved what is best and noblest for all future time is the real victor in this suit. Well! well!" he added, "Homer[1561] has ascribed to some at the point of death a power of forecasting things to be, and I too am minded to utter a prophecy. Once, for a brief space, I associated with the son of Anytus, and he seemed to me not lacking in strength of soul; and what I say is, he will not adhere long to the slavish employment which his father has prepared for him, but, in the absence of any earnest friend and guardian, he is like to be led into some base passion and go to great lengths in depravity."

The prophecy proved true. The young man fell a victim to the pleasures of wine; night and day he never ceased drinking, and at last became a mere good-for-nothing, worthless alike to his city, his friends, and himself. As to Anytus, even though the grave has closed upon him, his evil reputation still survives him, due alike to his son's base bringing-up and his own want of human feeling.

Socrates did, it is true, by his self-laudation draw down upon him the jealousy of the court and caused his judges all the more to record their votes against him. Yet even so I look upon the lot of destiny which he obtained as providential,[1562] chancing as he did upon the easiest amidst the many shapes of death,[1563] and escaping as he did the

---

[1558] See Plat. *Phaed.* 89 B, where a similar action is attributed to Socrates in the case of Phaedo (his beloved disciple). "He stroked my head and pressed the hair upon my neck—he had a way of playing with my air; and then he said: 'To-morrow, Phaedo, I suppose that these fair locks of yours will be severed.'"

[1559] Son of Anthemion. See Plat. *Men.* 90 B, (airountai goun auton epi tas megistas arkhas), Plut. *Alc.* 4; id. *Coriol.* 14; Aristot. *Ath. Pol.* 27, 25, re (to dekazein); 34, 23. A *moderate* oligarch; cf. Xen. *Hell.* II. iii. 42, 44; Schol. Cod. Clarkiani ad Plat. *Apol.* 18 B ap. L. Dind. *ad loc.*; cf. Diod. xiii. 64.

[1560] Cf. Plat. *Apol.* 23 E.

[1561] e.g. Patroclus dying predicts the death of Hector who had slain him, *Il.* xvi. 851 foll.; and Hector that of Achilles, *Il.* xxii. 358 foll. Cf. Cic. *de Div.* 1, 30. Plato, *Apol.* 39 C, making Socrates thus address his judges: (to de de meta touto epithumo umin khresmodesai, o katapsephisamenoi mou' kai gar eimi ede entautha, en o malist' anthropoi khresmodousin, otan mellosin apothaneisthai). "And now, O men who have condemned me, I would fain prophesy to you, for I am about to die, and that is the hour at which all men are gifted with prophetic power" (Jowett).

[1562] Lit. "dear to the gods"; "highly favoured."

[1563] Cf. Hom. *Od.* xii. 341, (pantes men stugeroi thanatoi deiloisi brotoisin).

one grievous portion of existence. And what a glorious chance, moreover, he had to display the full strength of his soul, for when once he had decided that death was better for him than life, just as in the old days he had never harshly opposed himself to the good things of life morosely,[1564] so even in face of death he showed no touch of weakness, but with gaiety welcomed death's embrace, and discharged life's debt.

For myself indeed, as I lay to mind the wisdom of the man and his nobility, I can neither forget him nor, remembering him, forbear to praise him. But if any of those who make virtue their pursuit have ever met a more helpful friend than Socrates, I tender such an one my congratulations as a most enviable man.

Hiero

OR, "THE TYRANT"

A DIALOGUE

I

Once upon a time Simonides the poet paid a visit to Hiero the "tyrant,"[1565] and when both obtained the leisure requisite, Simonides began this conversation:

Would you be pleased to give me information, Hiero, upon certain matters, as to which it is likely you have greater knowledge than myself?[1566]

And pray, what sort of things may those be (answered Hiero), of which I can have greater knowledge than yourself, who are so wise a man?

I know (replied the poet) that you were once a private person,[1567] and are now a monarch. It is but likely, therefore, that having tested both conditions,[1568] you should know better than myself, wherein the life of the despotic ruler differs from the life of any ordinary person, looking to the sum of joys and sorrows to which flesh is heir.

Would it not be simpler (Hiero replied) if you, on your side,[1569]

[1564] (prosantes), *i.e.* "he faced death boldly as he had encountered life's blessings blandly." "As he had been no stoic to repudiate life's blessings, so he was no coward to," etc.

[1565] Or, "came to the court of the despotic monarch *Hiero*." For the *dramatis personae* see Dr. Holden's Introduction to the *Hieron* of Xenophon.

[1566] Or, "would you oblige me by explaining certain matters, as to which your knowledge naturally transcends my own?"

[1567] Or, "a common citizen," "an ordinary mortal," "a private individual."

[1568] Or, "having experienced both lots in life, both forms of existence."

[1569] Simonides is still in the chrysalis or grub condition of private citizenship; he has not broken the shell as yet of ordinary manhood.

who are still to-day a private person, would refresh my memory by recalling the various circumstances of an ordinary mortal's life? With these before me,[1570] I should be better able to describe the points of difference which exist between the one life and the other.

Thus it was that Simonides spoke first: Well then, as to private persons, for my part I observe,[1571] or seem to have observed, that we are liable to various pains and pleasures, in the shape of sights, sounds, odours, meats, and drinks, which are conveyed through certain avenues of sense—to wit, the eyes, ears, nostrils, mouth. And there are other pleasures, those named of Aphrodite, of which the channels are well known. While as to degree of heat and cold, things hard and soft, things light and heavy, the sense appealed to here, I venture to believe, is that of the whole body;[1572] whereby we discern these opposites, and derive from them now pain, now pleasure. But with regard to things named good and evil,[1573] it appears to me that sometimes the mind (or soul) itself is the sole instrument by which we register our pains and pleasures; whilst at other times such pains and pleasures are derived conjointly through both soul and body.[1574] There are some pleasures, further, if I may trust my own sensations, which are conveyed in sleep, though how and by what means and when precisely, are matters as to which I am still more conscious of my ignorance. Nor is it to be wondered at perhaps, if the perceptions of waking life in some way strike more clearly on our senses than do those of sleep.[1575]

To this statement Hiero made answer: And I, for my part, O Simonides, would find it hard to state, outside the list of things which you have named yourself, in what respect the despot can have other channels of perception.[1576] So that up to this point I do not see that the despotic life differs in any way at all from that of common people.

Then Simonides: Only in this respect it surely differs, in that the pleasures which the "tyrant" enjoys through all these several avenues of sense are many times more numerous, and the pains he suffers are far

---

[1570] Lit. "in that case, I think I should best be able to point out the *differentia* of either."

[1571] Or, "if I may trust my powers of observation I would say that common men are capable of pains and pleasures conveyed through certain avenues of sense, as sight through our eyes, sounds through our ears, smells through our noses, and meats and drinks through our mouths."

[1572] Cf. Cic. *de N. D.* ii. 56, § 141.

[1573] Reading (edesthai te kai lupeisthai...) or if with Breit reading (ote d' au lupeisthai), transl. "then as to good and evil we are affected pleasurably or painfully, as the case may be: sometimes, if I am right in my conclusion, through the mind itself alone; at other times..."

[1574] Or, "they are mental partly, partly physical."

[1575] Lit. "the incidents of waking life present sensations of a more vivid character."

[1576] *i.e.* "being like constituted, the autocratic person has no other sources of perception: he has no claim to a wider gamut of sensation, and consequently thus far there is not a pin to choose between the life of the despot and that of a private person."

fewer.

To which Hiero: Nay, that is not so, Simonides, take my word for it; the fact is rather that the pleasures of the despot are far fewer than those of people in a humbler condition, and his pains not only far more numerous, but more intense.

That sounds incredible (exclaimed Simonides); if it were really so, how do you explain the passionate desire commonly displayed to wield the tyrant's sceptre, and that too on the part of persons reputed to be the ablest of men? Why should all men envy the despotic monarch?

For the all-sufficient reason (he replied) that they form conclusions on the matter without experience of the two conditions. And I will try to prove to you the truth of what I say, beginning with the faculty of vision, which, unless my memory betrays me, was your starting-point.

Well then, when I come to reason[1577] on the matter, first of all I find that, as regards the class of objects of which these orbs of vision are the channel,[1578] the despot has the disadvantage. Every region of the world, each country on this fair earth, presents objects worthy of contemplation, in quest of which the ordinary citizen will visit, as the humour takes him, now some city (for the sake of spectacles),[1579] or again, the great national assemblies,[1580] where sights most fitted to entrance the gaze of multitudes would seem to be collected.[1581] But the despot has neither part nor lot in these high festivals,[1582] seeing it is not safe for him to go where he will find himself at the mercy of the assembled crowds;[1583] nor are his home affairs in such security that he can leave them to the guardianship of others, whilst he visits foreign parts. A twofold apprehension haunts him:[1584] he will be robbed of his throne, and at the same time be powerless to take vengeance on his wrongdoer.[1585]

Perhaps you will retort: "Why should he trouble to go abroad to

---

[1577] (logizomenos), "to apply my moral algebra."

[1578] (en tois dia tes opseos theamasi). See Hartman, *An. Xen. Nova*, p. 246. (theamasi) = "spectacular effects," is perhaps a gloss on "all objects apprehensible through vision." Holden (crit. app.) would rather omit (dia tes opseos) with Schneid.

[1579] The words are perhaps a gloss.

[1580] e.g. the games at Olympia, or the great Dionysia at Athens, etc.

[1581] Omitting (einai), or if with Breit. (dokei einai... sunageiresthai), transl. "in which it is recognised that sights are to be seen best fitted to enchain the eyes and congregate vast masses." For other emendations see Holden, crit. app.; Hartm. *op. cit.* p. 258.

[1582] "Religious embassies"; it. *Theôries*. See Thuc. vi. 16; *Mem*. IV. viii. 2.

[1583] Lit. "not stronger than those present."

[1584] Or, "The dread oppresses him, he may be deprived of his empire and yet be powerless."

[1585] Cf. Plat. *Rep*. ix. 579 B: "His soul is dainty and greedy; and yet he only of all men is never allowed to go on a journey, or to see things which other free men desire to see; but he lives in his hole like a woman hidden in the house, and is jealous of any other citizen who goes into foreign parts and sees things of interest" (Jowett).

seek for such things? They are sure to come to him, although he stops at home." Yes, Simonides, that is so far true; a small percentage of them no doubt will, and this scant moiety will be sold at so high a price to the despotic monarch, that the exhibitor of the merest trifle looks to receive from the imperial pocket, within the briefest interval, ten times more than he can hope to win from all the rest of mankind in a lifetime; and then he will be off.[1586]

To which Simonides: Well, granted you have the worst of it in sights and sightseeing; yet, you must admit you are large gainers through the sense of hearing; you who are never stinted of that sweetest of all sounds,[1587] the voice of praise, since all around you are for ever praising everything you do and everything you say. Whilst, conversely, to that most harsh and grating of all sounds, the language of abuse, your ears are sealed, since no one cares to speak evil against a monarch to his face.

Then Hiero: And what pleasure do you suppose mere abstinence from evil words implies, when it is an open secret that those silent persons are cherishing all evil thoughts against the tyrant?[1588] What mirth, do you imagine, is to be extracted from their panegyrics who are suspected of bestowing praise out of mere flattery?

Simonides made answer: Yes, I must indeed admit, I do concede to you, that praise alone is sweetest which is breathed from lips of free men absolutely free. But, look you, here is a point: you will find it hard to persuade another, that you despots, within the limits of those things whereby we one and all sustain our bodies, in respect, that is, of meats and drinks, have not a far wider range of pleasures.

Yes, Simonides (he answered), and what is more, I know the explanation of the common verdict. The majority have come to the conclusion that we monarchs eat and drink with greater pleasure than do ordinary people, because they have got the notion, they themselves would make a better dinner off the viands served at our tables than their own. And doubtless some break in the monotony gives a fillip of pleasure. And that explains why folk in general look forward with pleasure to high days and holy days—mankind at large, but not the despot; his well-stocked table groaning from day to day under its weight of viands admits of no state occasions. So that, as far as this particular pleasure, to begin with, goes, the pleasure of anticipation, the monarch is at disadvantage compared with private people.

[1586] Lit. "to get from the tyrant all in a moment many times more than he will earn from all the rest of mankind in a whole lifetime, and depart."

[1587] Cf. Cic. *pro Arch.* 20, "Themistoclem illum dixisse aiunt cum ex eo quaereretur, 'quod acroama aut cujus vocem libentissime audiret': 'ejus, a quo sua virtus optime praedicaretur.'"

[1588] "One knows plainly that these dumb attendants stand there like mutes, but harbour every evil thought against their autocratic lord."

And in the next place (he continued), I am sure your own experience will bear me out so far: the more viands set before a man at table (beyond what are sufficient),[1589] the more quickly will satiety of eating overtake him. So that in actual duration of the pleasure, he with his many dishes has less to boast of than the moderate liver.

Yes, but good gracious! surely (broke in Simonides), during the actual time,[1590] before the appetite is cloyed, the gastronomic pleasure derived from the costlier bill of fare far exceeds that of the cheaper dinner-table.

But, as a matter of plain logic (Hiero retorted), should you not say, the greater the pleasure a man feels in any business, the more enthusiastic his devotion to it?

That is quite true (he answered).

Hiero. Then have you ever noticed that crowned heads display more pleasure in attacking the bill of fare provided them, than private persons theirs?

No, rather the reverse (the poet answered); if anything, they show a less degree of gusto,[1591] unless they are vastly libelled.

Well (Hiero continued), and all these wonderfully-made dishes which are set before the tyrant, or nine-tenths of them, perhaps you have observed, are combinations of things acid to the taste, or pungent, or astringent, or akin to these?[1592]

To be sure they are (he answered), unnatural viands, one and all, in my opinion, most alien to ordinary palates.[1593]

Hiero. In fact, these condiments can only be regarded as the cravings[1594] of a stomach weakened by luxurious living; since I am quite sure that keen appetites (and you, I fancy, know it well too) have not the slightest need for all these delicate made things.

It is true, at any rate (observed Simonides), about those costly perfumes, with which your persons are anointed, that your neighbours rather than yourselves extract enjoyment from them; just as the unpleasant odour of some meats is not so obvious to the eater as to those who come in contact with him.

[1589] (ta peritta ton ikanon). These words Hartm. *op. cit.* p. 254, regards as an excrescence.

[1590] Lit. "so long as the soul (*i.e.* the appetite) accepts with pleasure the viands"; *i.e.* there's an interval, at any rate, during which "such as my soul delights in" can still apply and for so long.

[1591] "No, not more pleasure, but exceptional fastidiousness, if what people say is true." (agleukesteron), said ap. Suid. to be a Sicilian word = "more sourly."

[1592] Lit. "and their congeners," "their analogues," *e.g.* "curries, pickles, bitters, peppery condiments."

[1593] Or, "unsuited to man's taste," "'*caviare* to the general' I name them."

[1594] Cf. Plat. *Laws,* 687 C; *Hipp.* ii. 44. Lit. "can you in fact regard these condiments as other than..." See Holden *ad loc.* (ed. 1888); Hartm. *op. cit.* p. 259, suggests (enthumemata), "inventions."

Hiero. Good, and on this principle we say of meats, that he who is provided with all sorts on all occasions brings no appetite to any of them. He rather to whom these things are rarities, that is the man who, when some unfamiliar thing is put before him, will take his fill of it with pleasure.[1595]

It looks very much (interposed Simonides) as if the sole pleasure left you to explain the vulgar ambition to wear a crown, must be that named after Aphrodite. For in this field it is your privilege to consort with whatever fairest fair your eyes may light on.

Hiero. Nay, now you have named that one thing of all others, take my word for it, in which we princes are worse off than lesser people.[1596]

To name marriage first. I presume a marriage[1597] which is contracted with some great family, superior in wealth and influence, bears away the palm, since it confers upon the bridegroom not pleasure only but distinction.[1598] Next comes the marriage made with equals; and last, wedlock with inferiors, which is apt to be regarded as degrading and disserviceable.

Now for the application: a despotic monarch, unless he weds some foreign bride, is forced to choose a wife from those beneath him, so that the height of satisfaction is denied him.[1599]

The tender service of the proudest-souled of women, wifely rendered, how superlatively charming![1600] and by contrast, how little welcome is such ministration where the wife is but a slave—when present, barely noticed; or if lacking, what fell pains and passions will it not engender!

And if we come to masculine attachments, still more than in those whose end is procreation, the tyrant finds himself defrauded of such mirthfulness,[1601] poor monarch! Since all of us are well aware, I fancy, that for highest satisfaction,[1602] amorous deeds need love's strong

---

[1595] (meta kharas). Cf. Aesch. Fr. 237, (stomatos en prote khara), of a hungry man; *Od.* xvii. 603.

[1596] Reading (saph' isthi), or if as Cobet conj. (saphestata), transl. "are at a disadvantage most clearly by comparison with ordinary folk."

[1597] Cf. *Hunting,* i. 9. Holden cf. Eur. *Rhes.* 168; *Androm.* 1255.

[1598] Cf. Dem. *in Lept.* § 69, p. 499. See Plat. *Rep.* 553 C.

[1599] *Al.* "supreme content, the quintessential bliss, is quite unknown to him."

[1600] Or, "the gentle ministrations of loftiest-thoughted women and fair wives possess a charm past telling, but from slaves, if tendered, the reverse of welcome, or if not forthcoming..."

[1601] "Joys sacred to that goddess fair and free in Heaven yclept Euphrosyne."

[1602] For (polu diaphncrontos) cf. Browning (*Abt Vogler*), not indeed of Aphrodisia conjoined with Eros, but of the musician's gift:

That out of three sounds he frame not a fourth sound, but a star.

passion.[1603]

But least of all is true love's passion wont to lodge in the hearts of monarchs, for love delights not to swoop on ready prey; he needs the lure of expectation.[1604]

Well then, just as a man who has never tasted thirst can hardly be said to know the joy of drinking,[1605] so he who has never tasted Passion is ignorant of Aphrodite's sweetest sweets.

So Hiero ended.

Simonides answered laughingly: How say you, Hiero? What is that? Love's strong passion for his soul's beloved incapable of springing up in any monarch's heart? What of your own passion for Daïlochus, surnamed of men "most beautiful"?

Hiero. That is easily explained, Simonides. What I most desire of him is no ready spoil, as men might reckon it, but rather what it is least of all the privilege of a tyrant to obtain.[1606] I say it truly, I—the love I bear Daïlochus is of this high sort. All that the constitution of our souls and bodies possibly compels a man to ask for at the hands of beauty, that my fantasy desires of him; but what my fantasy demands, I do most earnestly desire to obtain from willing hands and under seal of true affection. To clutch it forcibly were as far from my desire as to do myself some mortal mischief.

Were he my enemy, to wrest some spoil from his unwilling hands would be an exquisite pleasure, to my thinking. But of all sweet favours the sweetest to my notion is the free-will offering of a man's beloved. For instance, how sweet the responsive glance of love for love; how sweet the questions and the answers;[1607] and, most sweet of all, most love-enkindling, the battles and the strifes of faithful lovers.[1608] But to enjoy[1609] one's love perforce (he added) resembles more an act of robbery, in my judgment, than love's pastime. And, indeed, the robber derives some satisfaction from the spoils he wins and from the pain he causes to the man he hates. But to seek pleasure in the pain of one we love devoutly, to kiss and to be hated, to touch[1610] and to be loathed—

[1603] *i.e.* "Eros, the Lord of Passion, must lend his hand." "But," he proceeds, "the god is coy; he has little liking for the breasts of kings. He is more likely to be found in the cottage of the peasant than the king's palace."

[1604] Or, "even on the heels of hoped-for bliss he follows."

[1605] Reading with Holden (after H. Steph.) (osper oun an tis...) or with Hartm. (*op. cit.* p. 259) (osper ouk an tis...)

[1606] Lit. "of tyrant to achieve," a met. from the chase. Cf. *Hunting,* xii. 22.

[1607] "The *innere Unterhaltung*"; the (oarismoi). Cf. Milton, *P. L.*:

With thee conversing, I forget all time.

[1608] Cf. Ter. *Andr.* iii. 3. 23, "amantium irae amoris intergratiost."

[1609] "To make booty of."

[1610] For (aptesthai) L. & S. cf. Plat. *Laws,* 840 A; Aristot. *H. A.* v. 14. 27; Ep. 1 Cor. vii. 1.

can one conceive a state of things more odious or more pitiful? For, it is a certainty, the ordinary person may accept at once each service rendered by the object of his love as a sign and token of kindliness inspired by affection, since he knows such ministry is free from all compulsion. Whilst to the tyrant, the confidence that he is loved is quite foreclosed. On the contrary,[1611] we know for certain that service rendered through terror will stimulate as far as possible the ministrations of affection. And it is a fact, that plots and conspiracies against despotic rulers are oftenest hatched by those who most of all pretend to love them.[1612]

II

To these arguments Simonides replied: Yes, but the topics you have named are to my thinking trifles; drops, as it were, in the wide ocean. How many men, I wonder, have I seen myself, men in the deepest sense,[1613] true men, who choose to fare but ill in respect of meats and drinks and delicacies; ay, and what is more, they voluntarily abstain from sexual pleasures. No! it is in quite a different sphere, which I will name at once, that you so far transcend us private citizens.[1614] It is in your vast designs, your swift achievements; it is in the overflowing wealth of your possessions; your horses, excellent for breed and mettle; the choice beauty of your arms; the exquisite finery of your wives; the gorgeous palaces in which you dwell, and these, too, furnished with the costliest works of art; add to which the throng of your retainers, courtiers, followers, not in number only but accomplishments a most princely retinue; and lastly, but not least of all, in your supreme ability at once to afflict your foes and benefit your friends.

To all which Hiero made answer: That the majority of men, Simonides, should be deluded by the glamour of a despotism in no respect astonishes me, since it is the very essence of the crowd, if I am not mistaken, to rush wildly to conjecture touching the happiness or wretchedness of people at first sight.

Now the nature of a tyranny is such: it presents, nay flaunts, a show of costliest possessions unfolded to the general gaze, which rivets the

---

[1611] Reading (au). "If we do know anything it is this, that," etc.

[1612] Or, "do oftenest issue from treacherous make-believe of warmest friendship." Cf. Grote, *H. G.* xi. 288; *Hell.* VI. iv. 36.

[1613] Lit. "many among those reputed to be *men*." Cf. *Cyrop.* V. v. 33; *Hell.* i. 24, "their hero"; and below, viii. 3. Aristoph. "Ach." 78, (oi barbaroi gar andras egountai monous) | (tous pleista dunamenous phagein te kai piein): "To the Barbarians 'tis the test of manhood: there the great drinkers are the greatest men" (Frere); id. *Knights,* 179; *Clouds,* 823; so Latin *vir.* See Holden *ad loc.*

[1614] "Us lesser mortals."

attention;[1615] but the real troubles in the souls of monarchs it keeps concealed in those hid chambers where lie stowed away the happiness and the unhappiness of mankind.

I repeat then, I little marvel that the multitude should be blinded in this matter. But that you others also, you who are held to see with the mind's eye more clearly than with the eye of sense the mass of circumstances,[1616] should share its ignorance, does indeed excite my wonderment. Now, I know it all too plainly from my own experience, Simonides, and I assure you, the tyrant is one who has the smallest share of life's blessings, whilst of its greater miseries he possesses most.

For instance, if peace is held to be a mighty blessing to mankind, then of peace despotic monarchs are scant sharers. Or is war a curse? If so, of this particular pest your monarch shares the largest moiety. For, look you, the private citizen, unless his city-state should chance to be engaged in some common war,[1617] is free to travel wheresoe'er he chooses without fear of being done to death, whereas the tyrant cannot stir without setting his foot on hostile territory. At any rate, nothing will persuade him but he must go through life armed, and on all occasions drag about with him armed satellites. In the next place, the private citizen, even during an expedition into hostile territory,[1618] can comfort himself in the reflection that as soon as he gets back home he will be safe from further peril. Whereas the tyrant knows precisely the reverse; as soon as he arrives in his own city, he will find himself in the centre of hostility at once. Or let us suppose that an invading army, superior in force, is marching against a city: however much the weaker population, whilst they are still outside their walls, may feel the stress of danger, yet once within their trenches one and all expect to find themselves in absolute security. But the tyrant is not out of danger, even when he has passed the portals of his palace. Nay! there of all places most, he feels, he must maintain the strictist watch.[1619] Again, to the private citizen there will come eventually, either through truce or terms of peace, respite from war; but for the tyrant, the day of peace will never dawn. What peace can he have with those over whom he exercises his despotic sway?[1620] Nor have the terms of truce been yet devised, on

---

[1615] There is some redundancy in the phraseology.
[1616] Lit. "the majority of things"; al. "the thousand details of a thing."
[1617] (koinon), *i.e.* making demands upon the energies of *all the citizens in common*, as opposed to the *personal* character of war as conducted by a despot = "public," "patriotic," "national" war. *Al.* borne by the particular (polis) as member of a league, whether of states united for the time being in a (summakhia), or permanently in a confederacy = a "federal" war.
[1618] "Even if serving on a campaign in the enemy's country."
[1619] Or, "he has to exercise the utmost vigilance."
[1620] "With those who are 'absolutely governed,' not to say tyrannically ruled."

which the despotic ruler may rely with confidence.[1621]

Wars doubtless there are,[1622] wars waged by states and wars waged by autocratic monarchs against those whom they have forcibly enslaved, and in respect of these wars there is no hardship which any member of the states at war[1623] can suffer but the tyrant will feel it also. That is to say, both must alike be under arms, keep guard, run risks; and whatever the pains of defeat may be, they are equally sustained by both. Up to this point there is no distinction. The "bitters" are equal. But when we come to estimate the "sweets" derivable from warfare between states,[1624] the parallel ceases. The tyrant, if he shared the pains before, no longer shares the pleasures now. What happens when a state has gained the mastery in battle over her antagonist? It would be hard (I take it) to describe the joy of that occurrence: joy in the rout, joy in the pursuit, joy in the slaughter of their enemies; and in what language shall I describe the exultation of these warriors at their feats of arms? With what assumption they bind on their brows the glittering wreath of glory;[1625] with what mirth and jollity congratulate themselves on having raised their city to newer heights of fame. Each several citizen claims to have shared in the plan of the campaign,[1626] and to have slain the largest number. Indeed it would be hard to find where false embellishment will not creep in,[1627] the number stated to be the slain exceeding that of those that actually perished. So truly glorious a thing it seems to them to have won a great victory.[1628]

But the tyrant, when he forebodes, or possibly perceives in actual fact, some opposition brewing, and puts the suspects[1629] to the sword, knows he will not thereby promote the welfare of the state collectively.

[1621] Or, "which the tyrant may accept in faith and go his way rejoicing."

[1622] Lit. "and further, wars there are, waged against forcibly-subjected populations whether by free states"—e.g. of Olynthus, *Hell.* V. ii. 23, or Athens against her "subject allies" during the Pel. war—"or by despotic rules"—Jason of Pherae (*Hell.* VI.) *Al.* "wars waged by free states against free states, and wars waged by tyrants against enslaved peoples."

[1623] Does (o en tais polesi) = "the citizen"? So some commentators; or (sub. polemos) = "the war among states" (see Hartman, *op. cit.* p. 248)? in which case transl. "all the hardships involved in international war come home to the tyrant also." The same obscurity attaches to (oi en tais polesi) below (the commonly adopted emend. of the MS. (oi sunontes polesi)) = "the citizens," or else = "international wars."

[1624] "The pleasures incidental to warfare between states"; al. "the sweets which citizens engaged in warfare as against rival states can count upon."

[1625] Reading (analambanousin), or, if after Cobet, etc., (lambanousin), transl. "what brilliant honour, what bright credit they assume."

[1626] "To have played his part in counsel." See *Anab.* passim, and M. Taine, *Essais de Critique*, "Xenophon," p. 128.

[1627] Lit. "they do not indulge in false additions, pretending to have put more enemies to death than actually fell."

[1628] Cf. *Hipparch*, viii. 11; *Cyrop.* VIII. iii. 25; *Thuc.* i. 49.

[1629] See Hold. (crit. app.); Hartman, *op. cit.* p. 260.

The cold clear fact is, he will have fewer subjects to rule over.[1630] How can he show a cheerful countenance?[1631] how magnify himself on his achievement? On the contrary, his desire is to lessen the proportions of what has taken place, as far as may be. He will apologise for what he does, even in the doing of it, letting it appear that what he has wrought at least was innocent;[1632] so little does his conduct seem noble even to himself. And when those he dreaded are safely in their graves, he is not one whit more confident of spirit, but still more on his guard than heretofore. That is the kind of war with which the tyrant is beset from day to day continually, as I do prove.[1633]

III

Turn now and contemplate the sort of friendship whereof it is given to tyrants to partake. And first, let us examine with ourselves and see if friendship is truly a great boon to mortal man.

How fares it with the man who is beloved of friends? See with what gladness his friends and lovers hail his advent! delight to do him kindness! long for him when he is absent from them![1634] and welcome him most gladly on his return![1635] In any good which shall betide him they rejoice together; or if they see him overtaken by misfortune, they rush to his assistance as one man.[1636]

Nay! it has not escaped the observation of states and governments that friendship is the greatest boon, the sweetest happiness which men may taste. At any rate, the custom holds[1637] in many states "to slay the adulterer" alone of all "with impunity,"[1638] for this reason clearly that such miscreants are held to be destroyers of that friendship[1639] which

---

[1630] Cf. *Mem.* I. ii. 38.

[1631] Cf. *Anab.* II. vi. 11; *Hell.* VI. iv. 16.

[1632] "Not of malice prepense."

[1633] Or, "Such then, as I describe it, is the type of war," etc.

[1634] Reading (an ate), or if (an apie), transl. "have yearning hearts when he must leave them."

[1635] See Anton Rubinstein, *Die Musik und ihre Meister*, p. 8, "Some Remarks on Beethoven's Sonata Op. 81."

[1636] Cf. *Cyrop.* I. vi. 24 for a repetition of the sentiment and phraseology.

[1637] Lit. "many of the states have a law and custom to," etc. Cf. "Pol. Lac." ii. 4.

[1638] Cf. Plat. *Laws*, 874 C, "if a man find his wife suffering violence he may kill the violator and be guiltless in the eye of the law." Dem. *in Aristocr.* 53, (ean tis apokteine en athlois akon... e epi damarti, k.t.l.... touton eneka me pheugein kteinanta).

[1639] See Lys. "de caed Eratosth." S. 32 f., (outos, o andres, tous biazomenous elattonos zemias axious egesato einai e tous peithontas. ton men gar thanaton kategno, tois de diplen epoiese ten blaben, egoumenos tous men diaprattomenous bia upo ton biasthenton miseisthai, tous de peisantas outos aution tas psukhas diaphtheirein ost' oikeioteras autois poiein tas allotrias gunaikas e tois andrasi kai pasan ep' ekeinois ten oikian gegonenai kai tous paidas adelous einai opoteron tugkhanousin ontes, ton andron e ton moikhon. anth' on o ton nomon titheis thanaton autois epoiese ten zemian). Cf. *Cyrop.* III. i. 39; *Symp.* viii. 20; Plut. "Sol." xxiii., (olos de pleiston ekhein atopian oi peri

binds the woman to the husband. Since where by some untoward chance a woman suffers violation of her chastity,[1640] husbands do not the less honour them, as far as that goes, provided true affection still appear unsullied.[1641]

So sovereign a good do I, for my part, esteem it to be loved, that I do verily believe spontaneous blessings are outpoured from gods and men on one so favoured.

This is that choice possession which, beyond all others, the monarch is deprived of.

But if you require further evidence that what I say is true, look at the matter thus: No friendship, I presume, is sounder than that which binds parents to their children and children to their parents, brothers and sisters to each other,[1642] wives to husbands, comrade to comrade.

If, then, you will but thoughtfully consider it, you will discover it is the ordinary person who is chiefly blest in these relations.[1643] While of tyrants, many have been murderers of their own children, many by their children murdered. Many brothers have been murderers of one another in contest for the crown;[1644] many a monarch has been done to death by the wife of his bosom,[1645] or even by his own familiar friend, by him of whose affection he was proudest.[1646]

How can you suppose, then, that being so hated by those whom nature predisposes and law compels to love him, the tyrant should be loved by any living soul beside?

---

ton gunaikon nomoi to Soloni dokousi. moikhon men gar anelein tio labonti dedoken, ean d' arpase tis eleutheran gunaika kai biasetai zemian ekaton drakhmas etaxe' kan proagogeue drakhmas aikosi, plen osai pephasmenos polountai, legon de tas etairas. autai gar emphanos phoitosi pros tous didontas), "Solon's laws in general about women are his strangest, for he permitted any one to kill an adulterer that found him in the act; but if any one forced a free woman, a hundred drachmas was the fine; if he enticed her, twenty;— except those that sell themselves openly, that is, harlots, who go openly to those that hire them" (Clough, i. p. 190).

[1640] Or, "fall a victim to passion through some calamity," "commit a breach of chastity." Cf. Aristot. *H. A.* VII. i. 9.

[1641] Or, "if true affection still retain its virgin purity." As to this extraordinary passage, see Hartman, *op. cit.* p. 242 foll.

[1642] Or, "brothers to brothers."

[1643] Or, "that these more obvious affections are the sanctities of private life."

[1644] Or, "have caught at the throats of brothers"; lit. "been slain with mutually-murderous hand." Cf. Pind. Fr. 137; Aesch. *Sept. c. Theb.* 931; *Ag.* 1575, concerning Eteocles and Polynices.

[1645] See Grote, *H. G.* xi. 288, xii. 6; *Hell.* VI. iv. 36; Isocr. *On the Peace*, 182; Plut. *Dem. Pol.* iii. (Clough, v. p. 98); Tac. *Hist.* v. 8, about the family feuds of the kings of Judaea.

[1646] "It was his own familiar friend who dealt the blow, the nearest and dearest to his heart."

IV

Again, without some moiety of faith and trust,[1647] how can a man not feel to be defrauded of a mighty blessing? One may well ask: What fellowship, what converse, what society would be agreeable without confidence? What intercourse between man and wife be sweet apart from trustfulness? How should the "faithful esquire" whose faith is mistrusted still be lief and dear?[1648]

Well, then, of this frank confidence in others the tyrant has the scantiest share.[1649] Seeing his life is such, he cannot even trust his meats and drinks, but he must bid his serving-men before the feast begins, or ever the libation to the gods is poured,[1650] to taste the viands, out of sheer mistrust there may be mischief lurking in the cup or platter.[1651]

Once more, the rest of mankind find in their fatherland a treasure worth all else beside. The citizens form their own body-guard[1652] without pay or service-money against slaves and against evil-doers. It is theirs to see that none of themselves, no citizen, shall perish by a violent death. And they have advanced so far along the path of guardianship[1653] that in many cases they have framed a law to the effect that "not the associate even of one who is blood-guilty shall be accounted pure." So that, by reason of their fatherland,[1654] each several citizen can live at quiet and secure.

But for the tyrant it is again exactly the reverse.[1655] Instead of aiding or avenging their despotic lord, cities bestow large honours on the slayer of a tyrant; ay, and in lieu of excommunicating the tyrannicide from sacred shrines,[1656] as is the case with murderers of

---

[1647] "How can he, whose faith's discredited, the moral bankrupt..."

[1648] Or, "the trusty knight and serving-man." Cf. *Morte d'Arthur*, xxi. 5, King Arthur and Sir Bedivere.

[1649] Or, "from this... is almost absolutely debarred."

[1650] "Or ever grace is said."

[1651] Cf. *Cyrop.* I. iii. 4.

[1652] "Are their own 'satellites,' spear-bearers." Cf. Thuc. i. 130; Herod. ii. 168; vii. 127.

[1653] "Pushed so far the principle of mutual self-aid."

[1654] "Thanks to the blessing of a fatherland each citizen may spend his days in peace and safety."

[1655] "Matters are once more reversed precisely," "it is all 'topsy-turvy.'"

[1656] "And sacrifices." Cf. Dem. *c. Lept.* 137, (en toinun tois peri touton nomois o Drakon... katharon diorisen einai). "Now in the laws upon this subject, Draco, although he strove to make it fearful and dreadful for a man to slay another, and ordained that the homicide should be excluded from lustrations, cups, and drink-offerings, from the temples and the market-place, specifying everything by which he thought most effectually to restrain people from such a practice, still did not abolish the rule of justice, but laid down the cases in which it should be lawful to kill, and declared that the killer under such circumstances should be deemed pure" (C. R. Kennedy).

private citizens, they set up statues of the doers of such deeds[1657] in temples.

But if you imagine that the tyrant, because he has more possessions than the private person, does for that reason derive greater pleasure from them, this is not so either, Simonides, but it is with tyrants as with athletes. Just as the athlete feels no glow of satisfaction in asserting his superiority over amateurs, [1658] but annoyance rather when he sustains defeat at the hands of any real antagonist; so, too, the tyrant finds little consolation in the fact[1659] that he is evidently richer than the private citizen. What he feels is pain, when he reflects that he has less himself than other monarchs. These he holds to be his true antagonists; these are his rivals in the race for wealth.

Nor does the tyrant attain the object of his heart's desire more quickly than do humbler mortals theirs. For consider, what are their objects of ambition? The private citizen has set his heart, it may be, on a house, a farm, a servant. The tyrant hankers after cities, or wide territory, or harbours, or formidable citadels, things far more troublesome and more perilous to achieve than are the pettier ambitions of lesser men.

And hence it is, moreover, that you will find but few[1660] private persons paupers by comparison with the large number of tyrants who deserve the title;[1661] since the criterion of enough, or too much, is not fixed by mere arithmetic, but relatively to the needs of the individual.[1662] In other words, whatever exceeds sufficiency is much, and what falls short of that is little.[1663]

And on this principle the tyrant, with his multiplicity of goods, is less well provided to meet necessary expenses than the private person; since the latter can always cut down his expenditure to suit his daily

---

[1657] *e.g.* Harmodius and Aristogeiton. See Dem. *loc. cit.* 138: "The same rewards that you gave to Harmodius and Aristogiton," concerning whom Simonides himself wrote a votive couplet:

('E meg' 'Athenaioisi phoos geneth' enik' 'Aristogeiton 'Ipparkhon kteine kai 'Armodios.)

[1658] Or, "It gives no pleasure to the athlete to win victories over amateurs." See *Mem.* III. viii. 7.

[1659] Or, "each time it is brought home to him that," etc.

[1660] Reading as vulg. (alla mentoi kai penetas opsei oukh outos oligous ton idioton os pollous ton turannon). Lit. "however that may be, you will see not so few private persons in a state of penury as many despots." Breitenbach del. (oukh), and transl., "Daher weist du auch in dem Masse wenige Arme unter den Privat-leuten finden, als viele unter den Tyrannen." Stob., (penetas opsei oligous ton idioton, pollous de ton turannon). Stob. MS. Par., (alla mentoi kai plousious opsei oukh outos oligous ton idioton os penetas pollous ton turannon). See Holden *ad loc.* and crit. n.

[1661] Cf. *Mem.* IV. ii. 37.

[1662] Or, "not by the number of things we have, but in reference to the use we make of them." Cf. *Anab.* VII. vii. 36.

[1663] Dr. Holden aptly cf. Addison, *The Spectator*, No. 574, on the text "Non possidentem multa vocaveris recte beatum..."

needs in any way he chooses; but the tyrant cannot do so, seeing that the largest expenses of a monarch are also the most necessary, being devoted to various methods of safeguarding his life, and to cut down any of them would be little less than suicidal.[1664]

Or, to put it differently, why should any one expend compassion on a man, as if he were a beggar, who has it in his power to satisfy by just and honest means his every need?[1665] Surely it would be more appropriate to call that man a wretched starveling beggar rather, who through lack of means is driven to live by ugly shifts and base contrivances.

Now it is your tyrant who is perpetually driven to iniquitous spoilation of temples and human beings, through chronic need of money wherewith to meet inevitable expenses, since he is forced to feed and support an army (even in times of peace) no less than if there were actual war, or else he signs his own death-warrant.[1666]

V

But there is yet another sore affliction to which the tyrant is liable, Sinmonides, which I will name to you. It is this. Tyrants no less than ordinary mortals can distinguish merit. The orderly,[1667] the wise, the just and upright, they freely recognise; but instead of admiring them, they are afraid of them—the courageous, lest they should venture something for the sake of freedom; the wise, lest they invent some subtle mischief;[1668] the just and upright, lest the multitude should take a fancy to be led by them.

And when he has secretly and silently made away with all such people through terror, whom has he to fall back upon to be of use to him, save only the unjust, the incontinent, and the slavish-natured?[1669] Of these, the unjust can be trusted as sharing the tyrant's terror lest the

---

[1664] Or, "and to curtail these would seem to be self-slaughter."

[1665] *i.e.* "to expend compassion on a man who, etc., were surely a pathetic fallacy." *Al.* "Is not the man who has it in his power, etc., far above being pitied?"

[1666] "A daily, hourly constraint is laid upon him to support an army as in war time, or—write his epitaph!"

[1667] The same epithets occur in Aristoph. *Plut.* 89:

(ego gar on meirakion epeiles' oti
os tous dikaious kai sophous kai kosmious
monous badioimen.)
Stob. gives for (kasmious) (alkimous).

[1668] Or, "for fear of machinations." But the word is suggestive of mechanical inventions also, like those of Archimedes in connection with a later Hiero (see Plut. *Marcel.* xv. foll.); or of Lionardo, or of Michael Angelo (Symonds, *Renaissance in Italy*, "The Fine Arts," pp. 315, 393).

[1669] Or, "the dishonest, the lascivious, and the servile."

cities should some day win their freedom and lay strong hands upon them; the incontinent, as satisfied with momentary license; and the slavish-natured, for the simple reason that they have not themselves the slightest aspiration after freedom.[1670]

This, then, I say, appears to me a sore affliction, that we should look upon the one set as good men, and yet be forced to lean upon the other.

And further, even a tyrant cannot but be something of a patriot—a lover of that state, without which he can neither hope for safety nor prosperity. On the other hand, his tyrrany, the exigencies of despotic rule, compel him to incriminate his fatherland.[1671] To train his citizens to soldiery, to render them brave warriors, and well armed, confers no pleasure on him; rather he will take delight to make his foreigners more formidable than those to whom the state belongs, and these foreigners he will depend on as his body-guard.

Nay more, not even in the years of plenty,[1672] when abundance of all blessings reigns, not even then may the tyrant's heart rejoice amid the general joy, for the greater the indigence of the community the humbler he will find them: that is his theory.

VI

He continued: I desire to make known to you, Simonides,[1673] those divers pleasures which were mine whilst I was still a private citizen, but of which to-day, nay, from the moment I became a tyrant, I find myself deprived. In those days I consorted with my friends and fellows, to our mutual delectation;[1674] or, if I craved for quietude,[1675] I chose myself for my companion. Gaily the hours flitted at our drinking-parties, ofttimes till we had drowned such cares and troubles as are common to the life of man in Lethe's bowl;[1676] or ofttimes till we had steeped our souls in song and dance[1677] and revelry; ofttimes till the flame of

---

[1670] "They have no aspiration even to be free," "they are content to wallow in the slough of despond." The (adikoi) (unjust) correspond to the (dikaioi) (just), (akrateis) (incontinent) to the (sophoi) (wise) (Breit. cf. *Mem.* III. ix. 4, (sophian de kai sophrosunen ou diorizen)), (andrapododeis) (servile) to the (kasmioi), (andreioi) (orderly, courageous).

[1671] Or, "depreciate the land which gave him birth." Holden cf. *Cyrop.* VII. ii. 22. See Sturz, *s.v.*

[1672] "In good seasons," "seasons of prosperity." Cf. Aristot. *Pol.* v. 6. 17.

[1673] Or, "I wish I could disclose to you (he added) those heart-easing joys." For (euphrosunas) cf. *Od.* vi. 156; Aesch. *P. V.* 540; Eur. *Bacch.* 376. A favourite word with our author; see "Ages." ix. 4; *Cyrop.* passim; *Mem.* III. viii. 10; *Econ.* ix. 12.

[1674] Lit. "delighting I in them and they in me."

[1675] Or, "when I sought tranquility I was my own companion."

[1676] Or, "in sheer forgetfulness."

[1677] Or, "absorbed our souls in song and festal cheer and dance." Cf. *Od.* viii. 248, 249, (aiei d' emin dais te phile kitharis te khoroi te) | (eimata t' exemoiba loetra te therma

passion kindled in the breasts of my companions and my own.[1678] But now, welladay, I am deprived of those who took delight in me, because I have slaves instead of friends as my companions; I am robbed of my once delightful intercourse with them, because I discern no vestige of goodwill towards me in their looks. And as to the wine-cup and slumber—these I guard against, even as a man might guard against an ambuscade. Think only! to dread a crowd, to dread solitude, to dread the absence of a guard, to dread the very guards that guard, to shrink from having those about one's self unarmed, and yet to hate the sight of armed attendants. Can you conceive a more troublesome circumstance?[1679] But that is not all. To place more confidence in foreigners than in your fellow-citizens, nay, in barbarians than in Hellenes, to be consumed with a desire to keep freemen slaves and yet to be driven, will he nill he, to make slaves free, are not all these the symptoms of a mind distracted and amazed with terror?

For terror, you know, not only is a source of pain indwelling in the breast itself, but, ever in close attendance, shadowing the path,[1680] becomes the destroyer of all sweet joys.

And if you know anything of war, Simonides, and war's alarms; if it was your fortune ever to be posted close to the enemy's lines,[1681] try to recall to mind what sort of meals you made at those times, with what sort of slumber you courted rest. Be assured, there are no pains you then experienced, no horrors to compare with those that crowd upon the despot, who sees or seems to see fierce eyes of enemies glare at him, not face to face alone, but from every side.

He had spoken so far, when Simonides took up the thread of the discourse, replying: Excellently put. A part I must admit, of what you say; since war is terrible. Yet, Hiero, you forget. When we, at any rate, are out campaigning, we have a custom; we place sentinels at the outposts, and when the watch is set, we take our suppers and turn in undauntedly.

And Hiero answered: Yes, I can well believe you, for the laws are the true outposts,[1682] who guard the sentinels, keeping their fears alive

---

kau eunai), "and dear to us ever is the banquet and the harp and the dance, and changes of raiment, and the warm bath, and love and sleep" (Butcher and Lang).

[1678] Reading as vulg. (epithumias). Breit. cf. *Mem.* III. ix. 7; Plat. *Phaed.* 116 E, "he has eaten and drunk and enjoyed the society of his beloved" (Jowett). See *Symp.* the *finale*; or if, after Weiske and Cobet, (euthumias), transl. "to the general hilarity of myself and the whole company" (cf. *Cyrop.* I. iii. 12, IV. v. 7), but this is surely a bathos rhetorically.

[1679] Or, "a worse perplexity." See *Hell.* VII. iii. 8.

[1680] Reading (sumparakolouthon lumeon). Stob. gives (sumparomarton lumanter). For the sentiment cf. *Cyrop.* III. i. 25.

[1681] Or, "in the van of battle, opposite the hostile lines."

[1682] Or, "beyond the sentinels themselves is set the outpost of the laws, who watch the watch."

both for themselves and in behalf of you. Whereas the tyrant hires his guards for pay like harvest labourers.[1683] Now of all functions, all abilities, none, I presume, is more required of a guard than that of faithfulness; and yet one faithful man is a commodity more hard to find than scores of workmen for any sort of work you like to name;[1684] and the more so, when the guards in question are not forthcoming except for money's sake;[1685] and when they have it in their power to get far more in far less time by murdering the despot than they can hope to earn by lengthened service in protecting him.

And as to that which roused your envy—our ability, as you call it, to benefit our friends most largely, and beyond all else, to triumph over our foes—here, again, matters are not as you suppose.

How, for instance, can you hope to benefit your friends, when you may rest assured the very friend whom you have made most your debtor will be the happiest to quit your sight as fast as may be? since nobody believes that anything a tyrant gives him is indeed his own, until he is well beyond the donor's jurisdiction.

So much for friends, and as to enemies conversely. How can you say "most power of triumphing over our enemies," when every tyrant knows full well they are all his enemies, every man of them, who are despotically ruled by him? And to put the whole of them to death or to imprison them is hardly possible; or who will be his subjects presently? Not so, but knowing they are his enemies, he must perform this dexterous feat:[1686] he must keep them at arm's length, and yet be compelled to lean upon them.

But be assured, Simonides, that when a tyrant fears any of his citizens, he is in a strait; it is ill work to see them living and ill work to put them to the death. Just as might happen with a horse; a noble beast, but there is that in him makes one fear he will do some mischief presently past curing.[1687] His very virtue makes it hard to kill the creature, and yet to turn him to account alive is also hard; so careful must one be, he does not choose the thick of danger to work irreparable harm. And this, further, doubtless holds of all goods and chattels, which are at once a trouble and a benefit. If painful to their owners to possess, they are none the less a source of pain to part with.

[1683] Or, "ten-day labourers in harvest-time."

[1684] Or, "but to discover one single faithful man is far more difficult than scores of labourers in any field of work you please."

[1685] Or, "are merely hirelings for filthy lucre's sake."

[1686] Lit. "he must at one and the same moment guard against them, and yet be driven also to depend upon them."

[1687] Lit. "good but fearful (*i.e.* he makes one fear), he will some day do some desperate mischief."

VII

Now when he had heard these reasonings, Simonides replied: O Hiero, there is a potent force, it would appear, the name of which is honour, so attractive that human beings strain to grasp it,[1688] and in the effort they will undergo all pains, endure all perils. It would further seem that even you, you tyrants, in spite of all that sea of trouble which a tyranny involves, rush headlong in pursuit of it. You must be honoured. All the world shall be your ministers; they shall carry out your every injunction with unhesitating zeal.[1689] You shall be the cynosure of neighbouring eyes; men shall rise from their seats at your approach; they shall step aside to yield you passage in the streets.[1690] All present shall at all times magnify you,[1691] and shall pay homage to you both with words and deeds. Those, I take it, are ever the kind of things which subjects do to please the monarch,[1692] and thus they treat each hero of the moment, whom they strive to honour.[1693]

Yes, Hiero, and herein precisely lies the difference between a man and other animals, in this outstretching after honour.[1694] Since, it would seem, all living creatures alike take pleasure in meats and drinks, in sleep and sexual joys. Only the love of honour is implanted neither in unreasoning brutes[1695] nor universally in man. But they in whose hearts the passion for honour and fair fame has fallen like a seed, these unmistakably[1696] are separated most widely from the brutes. These may claim to be called men,[1697] not human beings merely. So that, in my

---

[1688] Lit. "that human beings will abide all risks and undergo all pains to clutch the bait."

[1689] Cf. *Cyrop.* II. iii. 8; VIII. i. 29.

[1690] Cf. *Mem.* II. iii. 16; *Cyrop.* VII. v. 20.

[1691] (gerairosi), poetic. Cf. *Cyrop.* VIII. i. 39; *Hell.* I. vii. 33; *Econ.* iv. 8; *Herod.* v. 67; Pind. *O.* iii. 3, v. 11; "N." v. 15; *Od.* xiv. 437, 441; *Il.* vii. 321; Plat. *Rep.* 468 D, quoting *Il.* vii. 321.

[1692] Reading (tois turannois), or if (tous turannous), after Cobet, "That is how they treat crowned heads."

[1693] Cf. Tennyson, *Ode on the Death of the Duke of Wellington*:

With honour, honour, honour to him,
Eternal honour to his name.

[1694] Or, "in this strong aspiration after honour." Holden aptly cf. *Spectator*, No. 467: "The love of praise is a passion deeply fixed in the mind of every extraordinary person; and those who are most affected with it seem most to partake of that particle of the divinity which distinguishes mankind from the inferior creation."

[1695] (alogous), *i.e.* "without speech and reason"; cf. modern Greek (o alogos) = the horse (sc. the animal *par excellence*). See *Horsemanship*, viii. 14.

[1696] (ede), *ipso facto*.

[1697] See *Anab.* I. vii. 4; Frotscher ap. Breit. cf. Cic. *ad Fam.* v. 17. 5, "ut et hominem te et virum esse meminisses."

poor judgment, it is but reasonable you should submit to bear the pains and penalties of royalty, since you are honoured far beyond all other mortal men. And indeed no pleasure known to man would seem to be nearer that of gods than the delight[1698] which centres in proud attributes.

To these arguments Hiero replied: Nay, but, Simonides, the honours and proud attributes bestowed on tyrants have much in common with their love-makings, as I described them. Like honours like loves, the pair are of a piece.

For just as the ministrations won from loveless hearts[1699] are felt to be devoid of grace, and embraces forcibly procured are sweet no longer, so the obsequious cringings of alarm are hardly honours. Since how shall we assert that people who are forced to rise from their seats do really rise to honour those whom they regard as malefactors? or that these others who step aside to let their betters pass them in the street, desire thus to show respect to miscreants?[1700] And as to gifts, it is notorious, people commonly bestow them largely upon those they hate, and that too when their fears are gravest, hoping to avert impending evil. Nay, these are nothing more nor less than acts of slavery, and they may fairly be set down as such.

But honours have a very different origin,[1701] as different to my mind as are the sentiments to which they give expression. See how, for instance, men of common mould will single out a man, who is a man,[1702] they feel, and competent to be their benefactor; one from whom they hope to reap rich blessings. His name lives upon their lips in praise. As they gaze at him, each one among them sees in him a private treasure. Spontaneously they yield him passage in the streets. They rise from their seats to do him honour, out of love not fear; they crown him for his public[1703] virtue's sake and benefactions. They shower gifts upon him of their own free choice. These same are they who, if my definition holds, may well be said to render honour to their hero by such service, whilst he that is held worthy of these services is truly honoured. And for my part I can but offer my congratulations to him. "God bless him," say I, perceiving that so far from being the butt of foul conspiracy, he is an object of anxiety to all, lest evil should betide him; and so he pursues the even tenour of his days in happiness

---

[1698] Or, "joyance."

[1699] Or, "the compliance of cold lips where love is not reciprocated is..."

[1700] Or, "to rank injustice."

[1701] Lit. "Honours would seem to be the outcome and expression of conditions utterly remote from these, in fact their very opposites."

[1702] Cf. Napoleon's accost of Goethe, "Vous etes un homme," and "as Goethe left the room, Napoleon repeated to Berthier and Daru, '*Voilà un homme!*'" (*The Life of Goethe*, Lewes, p. 500).

[1703] Reading (koines), which ought to mean "common to them and him"; if with Cobet (koine), "in public crown him for his virtue's sake, a benefactor."

exempt from fears and jealousy[1704] and risk. But the current of the tyrant's life runs differently. Day and night, I do assure you, Simonides, he lives like one condemned by the general verdict of mankind to die for his iniquity.

Now when Simonides had listened to these reasonings to the end,[1705] he answered: How is it, Hiero, if to play the tyrant is a thing so villainous,[1706] and that is your final judgment, how comes it you are not quit of so monstrous an evil? Neither you, nor, for that matter, any monarch else I ever heard of, having once possessed the power, did ever of his own free will divest himself of sovereignty. How is that, Hiero?

For one simple reason (the tyrant answered), and herein lies the supreme misery of despotic power; it is not possible even to be quit of it.[1707] How could the life of any single tyrant suffice to square the account? How should he pay in full to the last farthing all the moneys of all whom he has robbed? with what chains laid upon him make requital to all those he has thrust into felons' quarters?[1708] how proffer lives enough to die in compensation of the dead men he has slain? how die a thousand deaths?

Ah, no! Simonides (he added), if to hang one's self outright be ever gainful to pour mortal soul, then, take my word for it, that is the tyrant's remedy: there's none better suited[1709] to his case, since he alone of all men is in this dilemma, that neither to keep nor lay aside his troubles profits him.

VIII

Here Simonides took up the thread of the discourse[1710] as follows: That for the moment, Hiero, you should be out of heart regarding tyranny[1711] I do not wonder, since you have a strong desire to be loved by human beings, and you are persuaded that it is your office which balks the realisation of your dream.

Now, however, I am no less certain I can prove to you that

[1704] Or, "without reproach."

[1705] Cf. *Econ.* xi. 1.

[1706] Or, "if to monarchise and play the despot."

[1707] Holden aptly cf. Plut. *Sol.* 14, (kalon men einai ten torannida khorion, ouk ekhein de apobasin), "it was true a tyrrany was a very fair spot, but it had no way down from it" (Clough, i. p. 181).

[1708] Or, "how undergo in his own person the imprisonments he has inflicted?" Reading (antipaskhoi), or if (antiparaskhoi), transl. "how could he replace in his own person the exact number of imprisonments which he has inflicted on others?"

[1709] Or, "nought more profitable to meet the case." The author plays on (lusitelei) according to his wont.

[1710] *Al.* "took up the speaker thus."

[1711] "In reference to despotic rule."

government[1712] implies no obstacle to being loved, but rather holds the advantage over private life so far. And whilst investigating if this be really so, let us not embarrass the inquiry by asking whether in proportion to his greater power the ruler is able to do kindness on a grander scale. But put it thus: Two human beings, the one in humble circumstances,[1713] the other a despotic ruler, perform a common act; which of these twain will, under like conditions,[1714] win the larger thanks? I will begin with the most trifling[1715] examples; and first a simple friendly salutation, "Good day," "Good evening," dropped at sight of some one from the lips of here a ruler, there a private citizen. In such a case, whose salutation will sound the pleasanter to him accosted?

Or again,[1716] let us suppose that both should have occasion to pronounce a panegyric. Whose compliments will carry farther, in the way of delectation, think you? Or on occasion of a solemn sacrifice, suppose they do a friend the honour of an invitation.[1717] In either case it is an honour, but which will be regarded with the greater gratitude, the monarch's or the lesser man's?

Or let a sick man be attended with a like solicitude by both. It is plain, the kind attentions of the mighty potentate[1718] arouse in the patient's heart immense delight.[1719]

Or say, they are the givers of two gifts which shall be like in all respects. It is plain enough in this case also that "the gracious favour" of his royal highness, even if halved, would more than counterbalance

---

[1712] (to arkhein). Cf. *Cyrop.* passim.

[1713] "A private person."

[1714] Lit. "by like expenditure of power."

[1715] (arkhomai soi). Lit. "I'll begin you with quite commonplace examples." Holden cf. Shakesp. *Merry Wives*, i. 4. 97, "I'll do you your master what good I can"; *Much Ado*, ii. 3. 115, "She will sit you." For the distinction between (paradeigmaton) = examples and (upodeigmata) = *suggestions* see *Horsem.* ii. 2.

[1716] "Come now."

[1717] Cf. *Mem.* II. iii. 11 as to "sacrifices as a means of social enjoyment." Dr. Holden cf. Aristot. *Nic. Eth.* VIII. ix. 160, "And hence it is that these clan communities and hundreds solemnise sacrifices, in connection with which they hold large gatherings, and thereby not only pay honour to the gods, but also provide for themselves holiday and amusement" (R. Williams). Thuc. ii. 38, "And we have not forgotten to provide for our weary spirits many relaxations from toil; we have regular games and sacrifices throughout the year" (Jowett). Plut. *Them.* v., (kai gar philothuten onta kai lampron en tais peri tous xenous dapanais...) "For loving to sacrifice often, and to be splendid in his entertainment of strangers, he required a plentiful revenue" (Clough, i. 236). To which add Theophr. *Char.* xv. 2, *The Shameless Man*: (eita thusas tois theois autos men deipnein par' etero, ta de krea apotithenai alsi pasas, k.t.l.), "then when he has been sacrificing to the gods, he will put away the salted remains, and will himself dine out" (Jebb).

[1718] "Their mightinesses," or as we might say, "their serene highnesses." Cf. Thuc. ii. 65.

[1719] "The greatest jubilance."

the whole value of the commoner's "donation."[1720]

Nay, as it seems to me, an honour from the gods, a grace divine, is shed about the path of him the hero-ruler.[1721] Not only does command itself ennoble manhood, but we gaze on him with other eyes and find the fair within him yet more fair who is to-day a prince and was but yesterday a private citizen.[1722] Again, it is a prouder satisfaction doubtless to hold debate with those who are preferred to us in honour than with people on an equal footing with ourselves.

Why, the minion (with regard to whom you had the gravest fault to find with tyranny), the favourite of a ruler, is least apt to quarrel[1723] with gray hairs: the very blemishes of one who is a prince soon cease to be discounted in their intercourse.[1724]

The fact is, to have reached the zenith of distinction in itself lends ornament,[1725] nay, a lustre effacing what is harsh and featureless and rude, and making true beauty yet more splendid.

Since then, by aid of equal ministrations, you are privileged to win not equal but far deeper gratitude: it would seem to follow, considering the vastly wider sphere of helpfulness which lies before you as administrators, and the far grander scale of your largesses, I say it naturally pertains to you to find yourselves much more beloved than ordinary mortals; or if not, why not?

Hiero took up the challenge and without demur made answer: For this good reason, best of poets, necessity constrains us, far more than ordinary people, to be busybodies. We are forced to meddle with concerns which are the very fount and springhead of half the hatreds of mankind.

We have moneys to exact if we would meet our necessary expenses. Guards must be impressed and sentinels posted wherever there is need of watch and ward. We have to chastise evil-doers; we must put a stop to those who would wax insolent.[1726] And when the season for swift action comes, and it is imperative to expedite a force by land or sea, at such a crisis it will not do for us to entrust the affair to

---

[1720] Or, "half the great man's 'bounty' more than outweighs the small man's present." For (dorema) cf. Aristot. *N. E.* I. ix. 2, "happiness... a free gift of God to men."

[1721] Lit. "attends the footsteps of the princely ruler." Cf. *Cyrop.* II. i. 23, Plat. *Laws*, 667 B, for a similar metaphorical use of the word.

[1722] (to arkhein), "his princely power makes him more noble as a man, and we behold him fairer exercising rule than when he functioned as a common citizen." Reading (kallio), or if (edion), transl. "we feast our eyes more greedily upon him."

[1723] Lit. "feels least disgust at age"; *i.e.* his patron's years and wrinkles.

[1724] Cf. Plat. *Phaedr.* 231 B.

[1725] Or, "The mere prestige of highest worship helps to adorn." See Aristot. *N. E.* xi. 17. As to (auto to tetimesthai m. s.) I think it is the (arkhon) who is honoured by the rest of men, which (time) helps to adorn him. Others seem to think it is the (paidika) who is honoured by the (arkhon). If so, transl.: "The mere distinction, the privilege alone of being highly honoured, lends embellishment," etc.

[1726] Or, "curb the over-proud in sap and blood."

easy-goers.

Further than that, the man who is a tyrant must have mercenaries, and of all the burdens which the citizens are called upon to bear there is none more onerous than this, since nothing will induce them to believe these people are supported by the tyrant to add to his and their prestige,[1727] but rather for the sake of his own selfishness and greed.

IX

To these arguments Simonides in turn made answer: Nay, Hiero, I am far from stating that you have not all these divers matters to attend to. They are serious duties,[1728] I admit. But still, what strikes me is, if half these grave responsibilities do lend themselves undoubtedly to hatred,[1729] the remaining half are altogether gratifying. Thus, to teach others[1730] arts of highest virtue, and to praise and honour each most fair performance of the same, that is a type of duty not to be discharged save graciously. Whilst, on the other hand, to scold at people guilty of remissness, to drive and fine and chasten, these are proceedings doubtless which go hand in hand with hate and bitterness.

What I would say then to the hero-ruler is: Wherever force is needed, the duty of inflicting chastisement should be assigned to others, but the distribution of rewards and prizes must be kept in his own hands.[1731]

Common experience attests the excellence of such a system.[1732] Thus when we[1733] wish to set on foot a competition between choruses,[1734] it is the function of the *archon*[1735] to offer prizes, whilst to the *choregoi*[1736] is assigned the duty of assembling the members of the band;[1737] and to others[1738] that of teaching and applying force to those who come behindhand in their duties. There, then, you have the principle at once: The gracious and agreeable devolves on him who

---

[1727] Reading with Breit. (eis timas), or if the vulg. (isotimous), transl. "as equal merely to themselves in privilege"; or if with Schenkl (and Holden, ed. 3) (isotimias), transl. "their firm persuasion is these hirelings are not supported by the tyrant in the interests of equality but of undue influence."

[1728] Cf. *Econ.* vii. 41.

[1729] Or, "tend indisputably to enmity."

[1730] Or, "people," "the learner."

[1731] Cf. *Cyrop.* VIII. ii. 27; *ib.* i. 18; *Hipparch*, i. 26.

[1732] Or, "current incidents bear witness to the beauty of the principle."

[1733] (emin). The author makes Simonides talk as an Athenian.

[1734] Lit. "when we wish our sacred choirs to compete."

[1735] Or, "magistrate"; at Athens the *Archon Eponymos*. See Boeckh, *P. E. A.* p. 454 foll. *Al.* the (athlethetai). See Pollux, viii. 93; cf. Aeschin. *c. Ctes.* 13.

[1736] Or more correctly at Athens the *choragoi* = leaders of the chorus.

[1737] *i.e.* the *choreutai.*

[1738] Sc. the *choro-didaskaloi,* or *chorus-masters.*

rules, the archon; the repellent counterpart[1739] on others. What is there to prevent the application of the principle to matters politic in general?[1740]

All states as units are divided into tribes (thulas), or regiments (moras), or companies (lokhous), and there are officers (arkhontes) appointed in command of each division.[1741]

Well then, suppose that some one were to offer prizes[1742] to these political departments on the pattern of the choric prizes just described; prizes for excellence of arms, or skill in tactics, or for discipline and so forth, or for skill in horsemanship; prizes for prowess[1743] in the field of battle, bravery in war; prizes for uprightness[1744] in fulfilment of engagements, contracts, covenants. If so, I say it is to be expected that these several matters, thanks to emulous ambition, will one and all be vigorously cultivated. Vigorously! why, yes, upon my soul, and what a rush there would be! How in the pursuit of honour they would tear along where duty called: with what promptitude pour in their money contributions[1745] at a time of crisis.

And that which of all arts is the most remunerative, albeit the least accustomed hitherto to be conducted on the principle of competition[1746]—I mean agriculture—itself would make enormous strides, if some one were to offer prizes in the same way, "by farms and villages," to those who should perform the works of tillage in the fairest fashion. Whilst to those members of the state who should devote themselves with might and main to this pursuit, a thousand blessings would be the result. The revenues would be increased; and self-restraint be found far more than now, in close attendance on industrious habits.[1747] Nay further, crimes and villainies take root and spring less freely among busy workers.

Once more, if commerce[1748] is of any value to the state, then let the

---

[1739] (ta antitupa), "the repellent obverse," "the seamy side." Cf. Theogn. 1244, (ethos ekhon solion pistios antitupon). *Hell.* VI. iii. 11.

[1740] Or, "Well then, what reason is there why other matters of political concern—all other branches of our civic life, in fact—should not be carried out on this same principle?"

[1741] e.g. Attica into ten *phylae*, Lacedaemon into six *morae*, Thebes and Argos into *lochi*. See Aristot. *Pol.* v. 8 (Jowett, i. 166); *Hell.* VI. iv. 13; VII. ii. 4.

[1742] See *Revenues*, iii. 3; A. Zurborg, *de. Xen. Lib. qui* (Poroi) inscribitur, p. 42.

[1743] Cf. *Hell.* III. iv. 16; IV. ii. 5 foll.

[1744] "In reward for justice in, etc." See *Revenues*, l.c.; and for the evil in question, Thuc. i. 77; Plat. *Rep.* 556.

[1745] (eispheroien), techn. of the war-tax at Athens. See *Revenues*, iii. 7 foll.; iv. 34 foll.; Thuc. iii. 19; Boeckh, *P. E. A.* pp. 470, 539. Cf. Aristot. *Pol.* v. 11. 10, in illustration of the tyrant's usual method of raising money.

[1746] *Al.* "and what will be the most repaying... being a department of things least wont," etc.

[1747] Or, "soundness of soul much more be found allied with occupation."

[1748] Cf. *Revenues*, l.c.

merchant who devotes himself to commerce on the grandest scale receive some high distinction, and his honours will draw on other traders in his wake.

Or were it made apparent that the genius who discovers a new source of revenue, which will not be vexatious, will be honoured, by the state, a field of exploration will at once be opened, which will not long continue unproductive.[1749]

And to speak compendiously, if it were obvious in each department that the introducer of any salutary measure whatsoever will not remain unhonoured, that in itself will stimulate a host of people who will make it their business to discover some good thing or other for the state. Wherever matters of advantage to the state excite deep interest, of necessity discoveries are made more freely and more promptly perfected. But if you are afraid, O mighty prince, that through the multitude of prizes offered[1750] under many heads, expenses also must be much increased, consider that no articles of commerce can be got more cheaply than those which people purchase in exchange for prizes. Note in the public contests (choral, equestrian, or gymnastic)[1751] how small the prizes are and yet what vast expenditure of wealth and toil, and painful supervision these elicit.[1752]

X

And Hiero replied: Thus far you reason prettily, methinks, Simonides; but about these mercenary troops have you aught to say? Can you suggest a means to avoid the hatred of which they are the cause? Or will you tell me that a ruler who has won the affection of his subjects has no need for body-guards?

Nay, in good sooth (replied Simonides), distinctly he will need them none the less. I know it is with certain human beings as with horses, some trick of the blood they have, some inborn tendency; the more their wants are satisfied, the more their wantonness will out. Well then, to sober and chastise wild spirits, there is nothing like the terror of your men-at-arms.[1753] And as to gentler natures,[1754] I do not know by what means you could bestow so many benefits upon them as by means of mercenaries.

Let me explain: You keep them, I presume, in the first instance, for

---

[1749] Lit. "that too is an inquiry which will not long lie fallow."

[1750] Reading (protithemenon) with Cobet.

[1751] Lit. "hippic, gymnic, and choregic contests."

[1752] *e.g.* "in the choral dances (1) *money* on the part of the choragoi; (2) pains on the part of the choreutai; (3) supervising care on the part of the choro-didaskoi, and so *mutatis mutandis* of the hippic and gymnic."

[1753] Lit. "spear-bearers"; the title given to the body-guard of kings and tyrants.

[1754] Lit. "the beautiful and good," the (kalois kagathois). See *Econ.* vi. 11 foll.

Xenophon

yourself, as guards of your own person. But for masters, owners of estates and others, to be done to death with violence by their own slaves is no unheard-of thing. Supposing, then, the first and foremost duty laid on mercenary troops were this: they are the body-guards of the whole public, and bound as such to come to the assistance of all members of the state alike, in case they shall detect some mischief brewing[1755] (and miscreants do spring up in the hearts of states, as we all know); I say then, if these mercenary troops were under orders to act as guardians of the citizens,[1756] the latter would recognise to whom they were indebted.

But in addition to these functions, such a body might with reason be expected to create a sense of courage and security, by which the country labourers with their flocks and herds would greatly benefit, a benefit not limited to your demesne, but shared by every farm throughout the rural district.

Again, these mercenaries, if set to guard strategic points,[1757] would leave the citizens full leisure to attend to matters of more private interest.

And again, a further function: Can you conceive a service better qualified to gain intelligence beforehand and to hinder the secret sudden onslaughts of a hostile force, than a set of troopers always under arms and fully organised?[1758]

Moreover, on an actual campaign, where will you find an arm of greater service to the citizens than these wage-earning troops?[1759] than whom, it is likely, there will none be found more resolute to take the lion's share of toil or peril, or do outpost duty, keeping watch and ward while others sleep, brave mercenaries.

And what will be the effect on the neighbour states conterminous with yours?[1760] Will not this standing army lead them to desire peace beyond all other things? In fact, a compact force like this, so organised, will prove most potent to preserve the interests of their friends and to damage those of their opponents.

And when, finally, the citizens discover it is not the habit of these mercenaries to injure those who do no wrong, but their vocation rather

---

[1755] "If they become aware of anything of that sort." Is not this modelled on the (krupteia)? See Pater, *Plato and Platonism*, ch. viii. "Lacedaemon," p. 186.

[1756] Or, "as their police." (toutous), sc. "the citizens"; al. "the evil-doers." If so, transl. "to keep watch and ward on evil-doers; the citizens would soon recognise the benefit they owe them for that service."

[1757] Or, "as garrisons of critical positions," like Phyle or Decelia near Athens.

[1758] Or, "trained to act as one man." See Sturz, s.v.

[1759] The author is perhaps thinking of some personal experiences. He works out his theory of a wage-earning militia for the protection of the state in the *Cyropaedia*. See esp. VII. v. 69 foll.

[1760] Or, "that lie upon your borders," as Thebes and Megara were "nigh-bordering" to Athens. Cf. Eur. *Rhes.* 426; Soph. *Fr.* 349.

is to hinder all attempts at evil-doing; whereby they exercise a kindly providence and bear the brunt of danger on behalf of the community, I say it must needs be, the citizens will rejoice to pay the expenses which the force entails. At any rate, it is for objects of far less importance that at present guards[1761] are kept in private life.

XI

But, Hiero, you must not grudge to spend a portion of your private substance for the common weal. For myself, I hold to the opinion that the sums expended by the monarch on the state form items of disbursement more legitimate[1762] than those expended on his personal account. But let us look into the question point by point.

First, the palace: do you imagine that a building, beautified in every way at an enormous cost, will afford you greater pride and ornament than a whole city ringed with walls and battlements, whose furniture consists of temples and pillared porticoes,[1763] harbours, market-places?

Next, as to armaments: Will you present a greater terror to the foe if you appear furnished yourself from head to foot with bright emlazonrie and horrent arms;[1764] or rather by reason of the warlike aspect of a whole city perfectly equipped?

And now for ways and means: On which principle do you expect your revenues to flow more copiously—by keeping your own private capital[1765] employed, or by means devised to make the resources of the entire state[1766] productive?

And next to speak of that which people hold to be the flower of institutions, a pursuit both noble in itself and best befitting a great

---

[1761] "Police or other."

[1762] (eis to deon). Holden cf. *Anab.* I. iii. 8. Aristoph. *Clouds,* 859, (osper Periklees eis to deon apolesa): "Like Pericles, *for a necessary purpose,* I have lost them."

[1763] Reading (parastasi), properly "pilasters" (Poll. i. 76. 10. 25) = "antae," hence "templum in antis" (see Vitruv. iii. 2. 2); or more widely *the entrance* of a temple or other building. (Possibly the author is thinking of "the Propylea").Cf. Eur. *Phoen.* 415; "I. T." 1159. = (stathmoi), Herod. i. 179; Hom. *Il.* xiv. 167; *Od.* vii. 89, (stathmoi d' argureoi en khalkeo estasan oudio).

> The brazen thresholds both sides did enfold
> Silver pilasters, hung with gates of gold (Chapman).

Al. (pastasi), = colonnades.
[1764] Or, "with armour curiously wrought a wonder and a dread." (oplois tois ekpaglotatois), *most magnificent, awe-inspiring,* a poetical word which appears only in this passage in prose (Holden). L. & S. cf. Hom. *Il.* i. 146, xxi. 589, of persons; *Od.* xiv. 552, of things. Pind. *Pyth.* iv. 140; *Isth.* 7 [6], 30.

[1765] Reading (idia), al. (idia), = "your capital privately employed."

[1766] Lit. "of all citizens alike," "every single member of the state."

Xenophon 303

man—I mean the art of breeding chariot-horses[1767]—which would reflect the greater lustre on you, that you personally[1768] should train and send to the great festal gatherings[1769] more chariots than any Hellene else? or rather that your state should boast more racehorse-breeders than the rest of states, that from Syracuse the largest number should enter to contest the prize?

Which would you deem the nobler conquest—to win a victory by virtue of a chariot, or to achieve a people's happiness, that state of which you are the head and chief? And for my part, I hold it ill becomes a tyrant to enter the lists with private citizens. For take the case he wins, he will not be admired, but be envied rather, when it is thought how many private fortunes go to swell the stream of his expenditure; while if he loses, he will become a laughing-stock to all mankind.[1770]

No, no! I tell you, Hiero, your battlefield, your true arena is with the champion presidents of rival states, above whose lesser heads be it your destiny to raise this state, of which you are the patron and supreme head, to some unprecedented height of fortune, which if you shall achieve, be certain you will be approved victorious in a contest the noblest and the most stupendous in the world.

Since what follows? In the first place, you will by one swift stroke have brought about the very thing you have set your heart on, you will have won the affection of your subjects. Secondly, you will need no herald to proclaim your victory; not one man only, but all mankind, shall hymn your virtue.

Wherever you set foot you shall be gazed upon, and not by individual citizens alone, but by a hundred states be warmly welcomed. You shall be a marvel, not in the private circle only, but in public in the sight of all.

It shall be open to you, so far as safety is concerned, to take your journey where you will to see the games or other spectacles; or it shall be open to you to bide at home, and still attain your object.

Before you shall be gathered daily an assembly, a great company of people willing to display whatever each may happen to possess of wisdom, worth, or beauty;[1771] and another throng of persons eager to do you service. Present, regard them each and all as sworn allies; or absent, know that each and all have one desire, to set eyes on you.

[1767] Cf. Plat. *Laws*, 834 B.

[1768] Breit. cf. Pind. *Ol.* i. 82; *Pyth.* i. 173; ii. 101; iii. 96.

[1769] "Our solemn festivals," *e.g.* those held at Olympia, Delphi, the Isthmus, Nemea.

[1770] Or, "you will be mocked and jeered at past all precedence," as historically was the fate of Dionysus, 388 or 384 B.C. (?); and for the possible connection between that incident and this treatise see Lys. *Olymp.*; and Prof. Jebb's remarks on the fragment, "Att. Or." i. p. 203 foll. Grote, *H. G.* xi. 40 foll.; *Plato*, iii. 577.

[1771] Or, "to display their wares of wisdom, beauty, excellence."

The end will be, you shall not be loved alone, but passionately adored, by human beings. You will not need to woo the fair but to endure the enforcement of their loving suit.

You shall not know what fear is for yourself; you shall transfer it to the hearts of others, fearing lest some evil overtake you. You will have about you faithful lieges, willing subjects, nimble servitors. You shall behold how, as a matter of free choice, they will display a providential care for you. And if danger threatens, you will find in them not simply fellow-warriors, but champions eager to defend you with their lives.[1772]

Worthy of many gifts you shall be deemed, and yet be never at a loss for some well-wisher with whom to share them. You shall command a world-wide loyalty; a whole people shall rejoice with you at your good fortunes, a whole people battle for your interests, as if in very deed and truth their own. Your treasure-houses shall be coextensive with the garnered riches of your friends and lovers.

Therefore be of good cheer, Hiero; enrich your friends, and you will thereby heap riches on yourself. Build up and aggrandise your city, for in so doing you will gird on power like a garment, and win allies for her.[1773]

Esteem your fatherland as your estate, the citizens as comrades, your friends as your own children, and your sons even as your own soul. And study to excel them one and all in well-doing; for if you overcome your friends by kindness, your enemies shall nevermore prevail against you.

Do all these things, and, you may rest assured, it will be yours to own the fairest and most blessed possession known to mortal man. You shall be fortunate and none shall envy you.[1774]

THE END

[1772] Not (summakhoi), but (promakhoi).

[1773] Some commentators suspect a lacuna at this point.

[1774] *Al.* "It shall be yours to be happy and yet to escape envy." The concluding sentence is gnomic in character and metrical in form. See *Pol. Lac.* xv. 9.

www.ingramcontent.com/pod-product-compliance
Lightning Source LLC
LaVergne TN
LVHW040115080426
835507LV00039B/174